The Operation of Internal Labor Markets

Staffing Practices and Vacancy Chains

PLENUM STUDIES IN WORK AND INDUSTRY

Series Editors:
Ivar Berg, *University of Pennsylvania, Philadelphia, Pennsylvania*
and Arne L. Kalleberg, *University of North Carolina, Chapel Hill, North Carolina*

WORK AND INDUSTRY
Structures, Markets, and Processes
Arne L. Kalleberg and Ivar Berg

Current Volumes in the Series:

THE BUREAUCRATIC LABOR MARKET
The Case of the Federal Civil Service
Thomas A. DiPrete

THE EMPLOYMENT RELATIONSHIP
Causes and Consequences of Modern Personnel Administration
William P. Bridges and Wayne J. Villemez

ENRICHING BUSINESS ETHICS
Edited by Clarence C. Walton

LABOR AND POLITICS IN THE U.S. POSTAL SERVICE
Vern K. Baxter

LIFE AND DEATH AT WORK
Industrial Accidents as a Case of Socially Produced Error
Tom Dwyer

NEGRO BUSINESS AND BUSINESS EDUCATION
Their Present and Prospective Development
Joseph A. Pierce
Introduction by John Sibley Butler

THE OPERATION OF INTERNAL LABOR MARKETS
Staffing Practices and Vacancy Chains
Lawrence T. Pinfield

SEGMENTED LABOR, FRACTURED POLITICS
Labor Politics in American Life
William Form

THE STATE AND THE LABOR MARKET
Edited by Samuel Rosenberg

WHEN STRIKES MAKE SENSE—AND WHY
Lessons from Third Republic French Coal Miners
Samuel Cohn

A Chronological Listing of Volumes in this series appears at the back of this volume.

A Continuation Order Plan is available for this series. A continuation order will bring delivery of each new volume immediately upon publication. Volumes are billed only upon actual shipment. For further information please contact the publisher.

The Operation of Internal Labor Markets

Staffing Practices and Vacancy Chains

Lawrence T. Pinfield

Simon Fraser University
Burnaby, British Columbia, Canada

Plenum Press • New York and London

Library of Congress Cataloging-in-Publication Data

On file

ISBN 0-306-45046-1

©1995 Plenum Press, New York
A Division of Plenum Publishing Corporation
233 Spring Street, New York, N.Y. 10013

10 9 8 7 6 5 4 3 2 1

Printed in the United States of America

Preface

Employment systems consist of complex arrays of formal and informal rules that structure the relationships between employees and employers. There are many different types of employment systems. Some are specified in considerable detail in collectively bargained quasilegal employment contracts, while others are left to discretion. This book describes the latter type of employment system—one in which there is an active market for knowledge and skills. This is the salaried employment system of ForestCo—a large multiplant manufacturing company in the forest products industry. Here, supervisors and managers actively adjust the jobs and persons under their authority to meet the market, social, and institutional forces that influence the activities and performance of their departments.

The study of employment systems is a relatively recent phenomenon, and few prior studies or theories were found to guide this investigation. Neither the scope nor the components of employment system studies are yet established. The field is confused and contested. Nevertheless, there is related literature which can be used to focus attention on different features of employment systems. One emerging body of work that holds the most promise for the study of employment systems is internal labor market (ILM) theory. Derived from earlier work by Kerr (1954) and Doeringer and Piore (1971), these theories have attempted to identify the separate but interdependent components that both comprise and permit discrimination among various employment systems. A second body of work that has been most influential in shaping the actual operation of many employment systems is that associated with industrial/organizational psychology and human resource management. To date, there have been few attempts to integrate these two relatively separate disciplines.

Even though these two related bodies of work have potential to make sense of employment systems, there are substantial biases and limitations associated with each one. The early and continuing focus of ILM theory has been limited by the employment conditions that existed at the time of its development in the post-World War II period. The development of ILM theory has been strongly influenced by a preoccupation with unionized, blue-collar employment contracts. Since then, employment conditions have changed substantially and ILM theory has neither been influenced by, nor developed to account for, the nature of salaried employment systems. Consequently, the relevance of ILM theory to salaried employment systems in the current economic and social environment is problematic. Similarly, other perspectives on employment systems have not been well served by research and writing in the area of human resource management (HRM). Examination of this literature reveals a highly specialized and fragmented field of study. Topics of organizational and task design, job analysis, compensation, recruitment, selection, and training and development have been mostly considered specialty subtopics. Yet the supervisors and managers who engage in these personnel activities do not experience them as separate phenomena. Personnel management and organizational staffing are largely integrative activities, the determination and execution of which is largely contingent on diagnoses of local circumstances. How such integration is accomplished in practice is still an unexplored topic. A second feature of HRM literature is its dominant but often implicit assumption that employment systems occur mostly in stable, traditional bureaucratic organizations. Few contemporary organizations experience the stable circumstances that permit the development of the full-blown bureaucratic form of organization. The manner in which HRM practices should unfold when organizations face substantial technological, product–market, and environmental change remains an open question. A third feature of HRM literature is its strong normative and prescriptive stance. There are few, if any, descriptions of what managers actually do. Nevertheless, there is a tendency in this literature to ascribe gaps between normative theory and actual practice to either illegitimate personal motives or to limitations associated with the application of organizational rationality. Finally, as one might surmise from this summary of prior theorizing, there have been few attempts to integrate these two literatures. Neither has been used to develop appreciations of the other.

In this book, an attempt is made to integrate these two primary perspectives on employment systems through their application to the diverse phenomena found in the salaried employment system of ForestCo. The primary focus of this study is the organizational activity generally described as staffing. As illustrated here, staffing consists of often reflective, occasionally reflexive managerial decisions and actions shaped by multiple, contingent appreciations of organizational situations. Attention is focused primarily on the sense and decision-making behaviors of ForestCo's supervisors and managers. Although two partially overlapping conceptual theoretical schemas have been used to frame how we think about employment systems, the key questions being addressed here are very practical in terms of staffing: What do managers do? Why do they do what they do?

This examination of what managers do, and why they do what they do when actively involved in staffing, provides a preliminary integration of the two previously described approaches to employment systems—ILM theory and HRM prescriptions. In attempting this, other related issues have necessarily been drawn into these sense-making activities.

First, the implicit background model of organizational bureaucracy is shown not to be a fully accurate representation of ForestCo's salaried employment system. In classic bureaucracy, jobs dominate over persons. The tasks, duties, and responsibilities required for the accomplishment of organizational objectives precede the selection of persons to accomplish those tasks conceptually, temporally, and independently. In many local situations in the ForestCo organization, this was not strictly so. Jobs and combinations of different interdependent jobs in organizational units were frequently defined and designed with the capacities of particular persons in mind. In fact, jobs were often regarded as having greater flexibility than the capacities of available persons. Jobs were created, modified, and destroyed to accommodate constant pressures for organizational and technological change at a rate insignificantly less than the rate at which persons changed jobs. Jobs evolved to meet developing capacities of persons assigned to them, to accommodate different combinations of skills available in other interdependent jobs, and to meet shifting competitive product and market conditions. Sequences of jobs considered to comprise job or career ladders were also often customized to meet individual requirements for training and development. The relatively static assumptions of both bureaucratic theory and historical models of ILMs rarely applied to the shifting, dynamic arrangements of persons and positions found in this contemporary organization.

Second, the separate specialist functions such as selection, training, and compensation staked out by HRM theorists do not conform to the requirements of managerial staffing practice. Job design was found to be interdependent with employee selection as the availability of persons often influenced the design and configuration of jobs. Compensation guidelines were interdependent with assignments, as persons occupying the "same" job were often not paid similarly. The linkage between job assignments and compensation was remarkably flexible as the same pay rate could be assigned to persons occupying jobs assigned to several adjacent salary grades of the organization's hierarchy. Training and development and associated career development were interdependent with the internal selection of candidates to various assignments. Training was viewed as a significant by-product, if not the determining factor to select candidates for positions. Managerial attention was rarely focused only on the immediate performance outcomes of an upcoming assignment. Most often, candidates were selected for their potential to advance two or three positions beyond the one for which they were immediately being considered. This perspective on staffing activities requires those of us working in the HRM area to rethink both the background assumption of stable bureaucracy as well as the utility of the separate, specialist nature the field has taken in the past several decades.

Third, the nature of much contemporary writing in HRM has been conditioned by the political objectives of employment equity. Much HRM writing has been presented against an implicitly normative model of a bureaucratic organization. Omniscient notions of societal rationality have led to an emphasis on prescription rather than description. Consequently, work on social cognition, which explores the manner in which judgments are made about others, has not yet been integrated into mainstream HRM literature on personnel selection. For example, if people "naturally" exhibit certain biases in person perception because of the relatively hard-wired features of social cognition, what might this imply for the implementation of behavioral and procedural prescriptions designed to overcome such biases? Such issues are not fully explored here, but are illustrative of the types of questions that occur when incomplete and overlapping theories are used to account for what managers actually do, and why they behave as they do.

Both employers and employees occupy critical economic and social roles in contemporary society. Employment systems that help define those roles are a significant feature of the context in which organizational behavior occurs. Moreover, employment systems are significant elements of organizational theories. To the extent we ignore the nature of employment systems, illustrated here as the internal labor market of ForestCo's salaried workforce, we ignore the different contexts available for the development of theories of organizational behavior. The reader is invited to explore this study of ForestCo's ILM and to reflect on what this can imply for both past and future research on employment systems, internal labor markets, and human resource management.

Acknowledgments

Several persons and institutions have contributed to the completion of this book, and I wish to thank each of them for their most valuable assistance. First, I am most grateful for the financial support provided by the Social Sciences and Humanities Research Council of Canada. Of course, the views expressed in this book are my own and in no way reflect official views of the SSHRC.

I was stimulated to begin this project by my conversations with two overseas colleagues, Wendy Hirsh and John Atkinson, when I spent a brief sojourn at the Institute of Employment Studies at the University of Sussex. They showed me how employment theory and theoretical notions of internal labor markets (ILMs) had practical, managerial consequences for the way human resources were managed. Back in Canada, Moto Morishima was a staunch colleague in the early stages of this project and contributed much to its original design and execution. Vera Bushe was my primary liaison to the ongoing stream of personnel records at ForestCo and tracked many vacancy chains as they unfolded. Vera also did much of the fieldwork and developed a great rapport with the supervisors and managers we interviewed. David Reeves struggled with a very large data set obtained from three generations of computer systems and managed to bring coherence and consistency to a muddled set of 16 end-of-year employment records. Much of his work does not appear directly in this book, but my understanding of ForestCo's anatomy has been strengthened substantially by his extensive statistical reports. Graeme Coetzer and Tara Fedorak helped with the coding and entry of interview data. Other statistical analyses were done by Alan Monk and Leslie Baldwin.

I am particularly appreciative of the research assistance provided by Michelle Berner for the duration of the project. She diligently scoured the library for background information and educated me on what others had written. Michelle also served as my initial audience as I attempted to articulate my own understanding of the nexus between ILM theory and practice. Our initial collaboration led to the development of the model of ILM elements and outcomes presented in Chapter 1. A preliminary derivation and application of this model was also presented in Pinfield and Berner (1994). Related analyses of ForestCo's public image were also presented in Pinfield and Berner (1992).

The final version of this book is immeasurably better for comments provided by outside readers and several of my current colleagues. I particularly appreciated the comments of Bob Althauser, Ivan Chase, Carolyn Egri, Steve Havlovic, Fiona McQuarrie, Bob Rogow, Jerry Ross, Ken Strand, and Mark Wexler. I have not always followed their advice, but their fingerprints can be found on more than a few pages. Bob Althauser's critical but supportive review of the penultimate draft gave me the confidence to undertake a substantial rewrite. My colleague Mark Wexler has been a constant source of support and encouragement for this project. He has read every version of each chapter and given me critical commentary throughout the development, execution, and completion of this book. To Mark and others who have contributed: "Thank you!"

None of the previous assistance would have made sense without the primary data generously provided by the supervisors and managers at ForestCo. They freely gave their time and energy to talk about what they did and why they acted as they did. They shared their dilemmas, frustrations, and occasional victories in making sense of the shifting, evolving world they actively constructed and also experienced. They are the dominant actors on the stage described here. I am particularly appreciative of the quiet and constant support of Lorne Armstrong, who provided me access to this fascinating world. To Lorne and all the other ForestCo managers, a second but no less heartfelt "Thank you, too!"

Contents

PART II.   VACANCY CHAIN PERSPECTIVES
ON INTERNAL LABOR MARKETS

Chapter 3

Vacancy Chains as Bundles of Staffing Actions **61**

Chapter 4

Minimal Vacancy Chains **79**

PART III.   STAFFING ACTION PERSPECTIVES ON INTERNAL LABOR MARKETS

Chapter 10

Criteria Used to Evaluate Different Candidates   251

Chapter 11

Postselection Considerations of Staffing   279

PART IV.   SUMMARY AND REVIEW

Chapter 12

The Operation of Internal Labor Markets: Summary and Review 313

I

An Introduction to Internal Labor Markets and ForestCo

1

The Operation of Internal Labor Markets

Staffing Practices and Vacancy Chains

INTRODUCTION

The topics of interest in this book are the processes through which people join organizations, move from one job or status to another in those organizations, and leave the organizations. Flows of individuals into, through, and out of a single large organization, even in a limited time period, occur as a consequence of two related processes that underlie organizational staffing. In one process, decisions are made as to which jobs should be created, changed, and eliminated. Intertwined with these decisions are judgments and actions regarding who should be hired, promoted to positions of increased status and financial reward, and encouraged to leave the organization. Of equal importance in any analysis of staffing are the consequences of these processes for those who are not considered for various jobs and who are therefore overlooked, ignored, or demoted. Collectively, these staffing decisions and the organizational processes that shape and condition staffing patterns constitute the internal labor market (ILM) of the organization.

The concept of an ILM is a relatively recent construction that was developed to describe the observed phenomenon that competition for jobs and wages inside organizations is dominated both by administrative rules and regulations and by market principles. Many contemporary writers on ILMs (Baron, Davis-Blake, & Bielby, 1986; Bills, 1987; Kleiner, McLean, & Dreher, 1988; Pfeffer & Cohen, 1984) refer to the benchmark definition originally provided by Doeringer and Piore (1971, p. 2):

> The internal labor market, governed by administrative rules, is to be distinguished from the external labor market of conventional economic theory where pricing, allocating, and training decisions are controlled directly by economic variables. These two markets are interconnected, however, and movement between them occurs at certain job classifications which constitute ports of entry and exit to and from the internal labor market. The remainder of jobs within the internal market are filled by the promotion or transfer of workers who have already gained entry. Consequently, these jobs are shielded from the direct influence of competitive forces in the external market.

Although this feature of our organizational society (Presthus, 1962; Scott, 1992) is widely recognized, relatively little is known at present about how ILMs actually work

(Althauser, 1989). There are few studies of the administrative rules in use in ILMs and little appreciation of how these rules lead ILMs to operate differently from external labor markets (ELMs). We know relatively little about the manner and extent to which administrative rules shape staffing decisions and how staffing decisions influence the consequences of ILM operation. Thus, one purpose of this book is to describe the ILM of a representative modern corporation in greater detail than that in which it has been described before.

Description is not independent of prior conceptualizations and conjectures regarding the origins, purposes, processes, and outcomes of the phenomena to be described. Therefore, ILMs will be reviewed from several different perspectives in order to assemble the interdependent frames through which the employment system of the target corporation will be examined. These different frames provide both competing and complementary perspectives on ILMs and collectively represent a complex and at times confusing array of opportunities for making sense of how ILMs operate. The following discussion develops the primary conceptual frame used to make sense of ILM operation, using three nested levels of analysis chosen to examine the employment system to be studied.

Two contrasting perspectives on organizational employment systems may be identified. First, the term ILM may be used to denote a bounded set of employment relations in which administrative rules, which may or may not reflect economic choices, influence which persons attain different organizational roles and economic status. This perspective looks primarily at system-level phenomena; that is, the employment relations inside organizations are contrasted to those that exist outside the organizational boundary. For example, the internal administrative rules, such as seniority, that are used to price, allocate, and train employees are judged to produce patterns of employee mobility different from those in ELM competitions. At the system level of analysis, comparisons of ILM and ELM processes can be made in terms of their outcomes.

However, system-level phenomena may also be viewed as a consequence of micro-level processes. That is, the system-level characteristics of ILMs, as indicated by employment system boundaries and subsystem patterns of employee mobility and status, are engendered by an aggregation of local staffing decisions. Thus, it is possible to examine "macro"-ILM outcomes as a consequence of "micro"-level processes. Staffing practices— for example, the manifest preference for candidates from either inside or outside the ILM—influence overall system-level patterns of employment. In addition, it should be noted that the context within which staffing occurs, that is, either an ILM or an ELM situation, also conditions the evaluation and selection of staffing choices. System-level attributes—such as the overall job structure or the demography of the organization—can influence managerial evaluations of the relative suitability and availability of candidates from either inside or outside the ILM. Thus, the behaviors conceptualized at each level of abstraction are interdependent. An appreciation of how ILMs operate will be more complete when derived from both macro- and microperspectives.

Complicating and enriching this line of reasoning is the possibility of a level of analysis intermediate between system-level concepts of ILMs and microprocesses of staffing. The initial work of Doeringer and Piore (1971) and, more recently, work on the relationships between ILM processes and career structures (Stewman, 1986) have begun to develop an intermediate level of analysis of ILMs. For example, Doeringer and Piore argued that employee flows into, through, and out of ILMs are not random, but are patterned into "mobility clusters." They noted that flows of particularly skilled employees follow more or less regular sequences within a cluster of jobs in which employees are customarily hired, upgraded, downgraded, transferred, and laid off. In related theoretical and empirical work, White (1970) and Stewman (1986) examined the implications of different forms of employment systems for system-level demographics and individual career mobility by exploring vacancy chain structures and processes. In this perspective, a vacancy chain occurs when an initial organizational vacancy is created, either by an employee vacating an existing position or by the creation of a new position. If the initial vacancy is optionally filled with someone already employed within the organization, a second vacancy, and thus the beginning of a vacancy chain, is created. Mobility clusters and vacancy chains can therefore be seen as intermediate or "mesoscopic" (Cappelli & Sherer, 1991) constructs lying between the macrolevel concepts of ILM theory and the microlevel concepts of staffing actions and decisions. Mobility clusters and vacancy chains are component processes of ILMs, but are themselves composed of sequences of related staffing actions. Vacancy chains also constitute part of the immediate organizational context within which staffing actions occur.

The study of the corporate ILM reported in this book is presented from three interdependent, nested perspectives as represented in Figure 1.1: (1) from the perspective of the employment system or ILM as a whole; (2) from the perspective of mobility clusters or vacancy chains; and (3) from the perspective of staffing decisions and actions.

A brief description of each perspective or level of analysis is presented in the following sections.

Views of Internal Labor Markets at the Employment-System Level

The primary empirical descriptions of employment systems derive from the distributions of different types of jobs, occupations, and employees (i.e., stocks) and the movements (i.e., flows) of those employees into, through, and out of the ILM (Bennison & Casson, 1984; Mahoney, Milkovich, & Weiner, 1977; Martin & Strauss, 1959). Previous studies of ILMs indicate that their structures can also be influenced by occupational requirements (Robson, Wholey, & Barefield, 1992; Wholey, 1985), managerial choice (Osterman, 1987), and the type and level of technology employed in the organization (Elbaum, 1984; Kanter, 1984).

A number of authors have noted the interdependence of stocks and flows and the

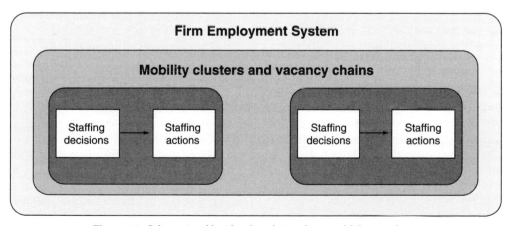

Figure 1.1. Schematic of levels of analysis of internal labor markets.

interdependence of employment flows in ILMs and employment systems (Beer, Spector, Lawrence, Mills, & Walton, 1985). For example, human resource planners have developed quite sophisticated models of employee stocks, flows, demography, and career progression (Bennison & Casson, 1984; Keenay, Morgan, & Ray, 1977; Stewman & Konda, 1983), and organizational sociologists have noted the interdependence of employee flows in different organizational strata (Barnett & Miner, 1992; Stewman, 1981). The often strict requirement for a "balance" between the requirements for a desired organizational demography and certain levels of organizational entry and internal job mobility place substantial restrictions on the different types of stock–flow structures that may be used. Nevertheless, at this macro-, system level of analysis, descriptions of ILMs typically include the size of the ILM, as indicated by the total number of employees, and the employment statuses of those employees, such as hourly or salaried, permanent or temporary, full-time or part-time. Other descriptors of employment systems include the distribution of employees by department or hierarchical grade or both; any one or some combination of organizational, departmental, and job tenure; and individual attributes such as age and gender. These "outcome" attributes of ILMs are occasioned by the application of administrative rules manifest in the personnel procedures that produce employee flows, such as hires, promotions, lateral transfers, and retirements, layoffs, and other exits from the employment system.

The structure and processes of employment systems are not independent of the context in which they exist. Outside the perspective on ILMs presented in Fig. 1.1 is the general environment of the ELM. The ELM may be viewed as the primary context in which different ILMs exist. As such, the ELM can be viewed as a set of antecedent conditions that influence the manner in which ILMs adjust to changes in the larger employment context (Bills, 1987; Pfeffer & Cohen, 1984). Alternatively, it can be viewed as the partial consequence of the aggregation of ILMs that exist within some circumscribed labor market—though this point of view is at present an underexplored feature of labor markets.

Mobility Clusters and Vacancy Chain Perspectives

The first *component* level of analysis of ILMs noted in Fig. 1.1 comprises the mobility clusters and vacancy chains found within each ILM. In a recent review, Chase (1991) has argued that vacancy chain processes are generic and remarkably stable processes of social mobility. The properties of vacancy chains, such as the distributions of origins, lengths, and terminations, affect career and demographic distributions as well as the staffing action multiplier of initiating vacancies. The most direct applications of vacancy chain theory are those that explicate the structural dynamics of career progression in organizational hierarchies (Stewman, 1986; White, 1970). Each move of a vacancy "down" a vacancy chain represents a career move for the particular employee involved in that segment of the staffing sequence. Collectively, each vacancy chain represents a potential career trajectory for the employees who are in the mobility cluster that contains related vacancy chains. One feature of the Stewman (1986) analysis of vacancy chains and career processes in organizations was his demonstration that it is possible to have only a relatively small number of tube forms (associated with the "shape" of the organizational hierarchy) that narrow or widen and that accelerate or decelerate career progression. The strong interdependence between age-based flow rates into, through, and out of the employment system, and the ensuing distributions of employees by hierarchical grade and by organizational, departmental, and job tenure, severely constrain the number and range of stock–flow interdependencies that are realistically possible in practice.

Vacancy chain processes were originally viewed as illustrating the stable job structures or systems of career ladders that shaped the mobility of employees through an employment system. However, because there is often a substantial amount of concurrent job creation and dissolution, vacancy chain processes occur against a changing background of jobs and positions. Many opportunities for the redistribution of positions are often initiated by the occurrence of vacancies, as managers use vacancies as opportunities to change job duties and responsibilities without encountering the resistance of long-term job holders. Thus, vacancy chain processes can be viewed as both the processes that give persons mobility and, concurrently and interdependently, as the processes through which jobs are created, modified, and dissolved. Through these mechanisms, vacancy chain processes also have the potential to illustrate the manner in which employment systems both maintain themselves and adapt to changing circumstances.

Such component processes of ILM adjustment are analogous to system-level processes of organizational adaptation and change. The administrative restructuring of departments often occurs as a response to changing production technologies or changing market demands. Examinations of vacancy chain processes partially illuminate how such adaptation takes place. For example, the selection of employees with nontraditional backgrounds and capacities for certain key jobs can signal both substantive and symbolic responses to changing environmental forces. Actions such as these produce different types of career "switches" and changes in career structures in the organization. Such changes can have far-reaching implications for the expectations of career payoff of prior investments in the development of occupational experiences and skills. Thus, vacancy chain processes offer a potentially rich perspective from which to view both the stable and the adaptive features of ILMs.

Staffing Decision and Action Perspectives

The second component level of analysis of ILMs shown in Fig. 1.1 is that of staffing decisions and actions. Although it is possible to examine staffing as a generic organizational activity, almost all staffing actions occur within the context of specific vacancy chains. The vacancy chain perspective encourages the organizational observer to consider both the situation-specific antecedent conditions for each staffing decision and the consequent outcomes produced by each staffing action. These outcomes, in turn, influence the antecedent and causally prior conditions for the next staffing action in the vacancy chain. For example, local staffing decisions and actions have the potential to switch vacancy chain processes to other organizational departments and locations. The choice of one candidate rather than another produces different vacancies at other locations in the organization. Thus, staffing is path dependent. First, the opportunity to engage in staffing is largely dependent on the prior staffing choices that produced a local vacancy. Second, the selection processes that result in the choice of a particular candidate also modify the local conditions and expectations associated with the manner in which subsequent vacancies should be filled. Thus, a study of ILM operation through an examination of staffing decisions and actions complements the employment system and vacancy chain perspectives already discussed.

Thus far, staffing has been presented as a compound function of both decision and action. Viewing staffing solely as actions allows the organizational observer to track vacancy chains and ILM processes through the archival records of staffing choices. Viewing staffing solely as actions, however, limits the opportunity of organizational observers to understand why managers choose as they do. The reasons for managers' choices are an important aspect of staffing. For example, a manager can respond in any of several different ways to a vacancy in his organizational subunit. He may choose to absorb the duties and responsibilities associated with the vacated job—which he may or may not do by reorganizing the jobs in the subunit. He may delay in filling the job, or assign a person to that job temporarily rather than permanently. If an employee is assigned permanently to that position, several search procedures may be used. A person may be appointed from inside the subunit, or someone may be selected from elsewhere in the organization on the basis of the manager's existing knowledge of available candidates and without posting taking place. The position could be posted and qualified candidates invited to apply and then one selected. Or a new employee from the ELM could be hired for the vacant position. The large potential variability in staffing actions, together with the contingency of outcome on process, strongly suggests that any study of ILM processes examine the reasoning that guides managerial actions along the different paths taken through sequences of staffing actions.

A READER'S GUIDE

The three interdependent perspectives on ILMs presented in Fig. 1.1 are used here to examine the employment system of a single relatively large manufacturing firm in the forest products industry. The decision to focus on a single firm arose from the appreciation that only a comprehensive study could capture the relationships among interdependent levels of analysis, as well as the multiple factors that apparently influence staffing decisions and hence the manner in which a firm's ILM operates. The choice of "ForestCo" as the firm to be studied was opportunistic and pragmatic.* Senior managers of a local firm were willing to have an academic researcher interested in ILMs examine their staffing and employment practices. ForestCo is both a convenient sample, believed to be representative of other large manufacturing firms, and an interesting firm in its own right. This book, then, is both a case study of a single firm and a focused investigation of the employment practices in that organization.

In the study reported in this book, attention is focused on the mobility patterns of the salaried workforce of ForestCo. This salaried ILM is regarded as generally illustrative of all ILMs and more illustrative of the subset of salaried ILMs. It is an illustration of employment systems used by many large, bureaucratic organizations to manage the administration of most white-collar supervisory and managerial personnel. This descriptive study of ForestCo's salaried ILM is of particular interest because it illustrates the manner in which salaried ILMs work to produce various outcomes in terms of individual careers, organizational performance, and the distribution of opportunity in society. There are many specific features of the firm and its employment system, however, that should not be considered generalizable to all other employing organizations. For example, effects of the particular economic context on this particular firm are clearly not generalizable to all other firms. However, a more generalized conceptualization of the manner in which

---

*The identity of ForestCo is not secret. However, as I wish to develop a generalized view of staffing and ILM operation, I refrain from specifically identifying ForestCo and naming the persons in its cast of characters. Nevertheless, ForestCo had a unique history, and I am indebted to Donald MacKay, who chronicled the origins and development of this fascinating company. In this chapter, I quote extensively from his major reference on ForestCo. I recommend that readers who wish to study additional particulars of ForestCo refer to his book, *Empire of Wood* (MacKay, 1982).

external economic circumstances affect the operation of this local employment system should be of interest to students of other firms.

Although a primary purpose of this book is to describe the manner in which a corporation's ILM operates, the description necessarily has a strong analytical character. Interdependencies among the perspectives invite speculation and investigation of possible relationships among phenomena conceptualized at each level of analysis. Thus, the presentation proceeds from a general description of the target corporation and its employment system, to an analysis of the patterns and features of vacancy chains found therein, and finally to an extensive consideration of staffing decisions and actions.

A second important point regarding the material presented in this book is that macro- and microperspectives are used differently by ILM theorists and practicing managers. Macroperspectives on employment systems have been developed primarily by ILM theorists, whereas microperspectives have been the primary focus of industrial psychologists, human resource specialists, and practitioners. ILM theorists (Althauser, 1989; Althauser & Kalleberg, 1981; Doeringer & Piore, 1971; Osterman, 1984b, 1987) have been concerned with the origins and definitions of ILMs, whereas industrial psychologists and human resource specialists (Gatewood and Feild, 1994; Heneman & Heneman, 1994; Schein, 1978; Schneider & Schmitt, 1986) have largely taken ILM structures for granted. Indeed, the focus of this latter group has been the development and elaboration of the administrative mechanisms through which ILMs can be maintained and expanded. There has been relatively little conceptual or empirical integration of these two perspectives and the interdependent phenomena they consider. Because of their preoccupation with immediate and local staffing needs, practicing managers are often unaware of how their individual and collective actions maintain and change the employment system to which they belong.

Thus, the stimulation and motivation to conduct this study also arose from an appreciation that a large gap existed between existing formulations of ILMs and our knowledge of the way in which practicing managers view their role in maintaining the human resource systems of their firms. Indeed, much of the existing literature on ILMs is silent on exactly how ILMs work or operate—ignoring the managerial actions and decisions that produce ILM outcomes. There has been a strong tendency on the part of both economists and sociologists to treat ILMs as "black boxes" in which undescribed organizational processes are used to hire new employees from the ELM, to arrange for the movement of the more able employees to positions of increased rank and reward, and to ease the flow out of the organization of those whose employment no longer fits either organizational or personal requirements. A related purpose of this study, therefore, was to confront ILM theory with empirical data on the manner in which ILMs actually operate. As a corollary, it was also hoped that this study would provide conceptual and theoretical interpretations that would be of practical interest to human resource specialists and managers.

The primary focus of an ILM perspective based on an examination of staffing decisions and actions is the local logic of each individual manager. In ForestCo, staffing is not a formulaic machine dominated by uniform administrative rules. Given delegated responsibility for staffing, individual managers made selection and assignment decisions that were full of dilemmas, trade-offs, nuances, and situational uniqueness. ForestCo's managers repeatedly struggled with the task of making sense of their local responsibilities in the face of considerable uncertainty. In doing this, they created and sustained their own systems of belief, thought, and action that helped them make sense of the requirements of organizational staffing. The presentation in Part III of the implicit scripts used by ForestCo's managers to explain their staffing actions is strongly ethnomethodological. The focus of this perspective on ILMs is ForestCo's managers' own commonsense understanding of the organizational context to which they related their staffing actions. Because the appreciations and understandings of staffing were often related to a wide array of other organizational issues, this ethnomethodological study of staffing necessarily expanded to cover many other aspects of ForestCo's functioning.

With the presentation of this third perspective on ForestCo's ILM, two additional audiences for this book can be identified: First are those students of organizations who believe that ethnomethodological accounts constitute superior methods of learning about organizational functioning (Czarniawska-Joerges, 1992). Second are those persons who are interested in reading a detailed account of a particular organization at a particular point in its history. For the purposes of a study of firm employment systems, or an investigation of how ILMs work, ForestCo is merely a convenient sample. As a forest products company, however, ForestCo represents an industry that is severely challenged by the burgeoning environmentalist movements of the late 1980s and early 1990s. The detailed reporting of managers' scripts in Part III should also be of interest to persons interested in learning about managerial life inside a "politically incorrect" firm.

Altogether, this book presents both a description and a grounded theory of ILM operation. The remainder of this introductory chapter elaborates the conceptual and theoretical antecedents of the three perspectives on ILMs just described. In addition, the sections that follow attempt to bring into focus the questions and issues that may be addressed by a detailed examination of ForestCo's ILM.

INTERNAL LABOR MARKETS

A Model of Internal Labor Market Elements and Consequences

Although employment structures dominated by bureaucratic control have gradually emerged since the late 19th century, formal recognition of the rules developed and used by organizations to administer the employment relationships of their employees is relatively recent. Kerr (1954) initially distinguished between unstructured (i.e., open to competition) and structured (i.e., closed to competition) labor markets and characterized most labor markets as being both structured and "balkanized." That is, there are multiple, separate labor markets that have come about because of natural, organizational, and institutional barriers. These barriers limit overall labor mobility and increase employment security for those now employed. There is very little competition between those inside the ILM and those outside the ILM.

Much of this early theorizing regarding employment systems was strongly influenced by the growth and development of labor unions and their perceived negative influence on the economic efficiency of institutionalized labor markets. Early conceptualizations of ILMs assumed rigidities in the quasi-legal contracts between employers and their unionized employees that are not necessarily generalizable to the same degree to all ILMs. Nevertheless, these early conceptualizations of ILMs provided the dominant frame within which almost all subsequent perspectives have been developed. Within stereotypical ILMs, therefore, there is limited competition between workers for jobs, as access to jobs that are "better" or higher-paying or both is through occupancy of a progression of higher-paying jobs. In unionized settings, employee organizations push for seniority to dominate the determination of who should be selected for better jobs. Today, however, most organizations use both seniority and ability criteria, with seniority rules being stronger in unionized settings and combinations of ability and seniority criteria often dominating in nonunion settings. In most organizations today, rules in use often qualify seniority provisions by advancing "the most senior of all those deemed to meet minimum standards." Similar provisions, but obviously in reverse application, also govern the sequence of layoffs when employee cutbacks are required.

Kerr also described characteristic ILMs that differ significantly from each other. Craft ILMs are those in which the union controls entry of individuals into the craft and also controls or at least strongly influences the assignments of workers to jobs. These ILMs typically occur among longshoremen, construction, and marine workers—craftspersons who typically work for a variety of employers as a function of short-term, temporary projects. In contrast, industrial ILMs are those in which the personnel office of the employing organization controls entry to beginning jobs. Industrial ILMs are usually further divided into unionized blue-collar ILMs and salaried, managerial ILMs. As already noted, however, much of the original conceptual work on ILMs has been strongly influenced by the employment practices used for unionized blue-collar workers rather than those currently in use for most professional and managerial salaried employees.

Doeringer and Piore (1971) elaborated the earlier Kerr formulation and established a benchmark definition and description of ILMs to which much subsequent work refers. An important feature of Doeringer and Piore's ILM conceptualization is that arrangements of job ladders, together with rules for which employees may be considered for vacant jobs, produce patterns of internal mobility that are critical for the accomplishment of on-the-job training. Seniority provisions, with regard to layoffs and advancement to higher-paying jobs, are functional in that they provide an incentive for employees to learn and develop new skills. Moreover, as seniority provides a relatively high degree of job security, there are few barriers to employees' being motivated to develop higher-level skills and to train other employees with lesser skill to take their "old" jobs when they are promoted or advanced.

A by-product of the application of a seniority system is that a majority of the employees of firms with ILMs often have long service records. Given general usage of seniority systems across different organizations, employees who quit one firm or ILM would face, other factors being equal, an increased risk of layoff in the new firm. Employees are therefore motivated to remain with their employer to retain their job security. Firms also benefit from having many long-service employees. These employees learn most if not all of the skills tacitly required for superior individual and group performance. Moreover, few skilled employees will quit and apply their talents at competitive firms unless there is some appreciable premium to compensate them for their loss of job security. Thus, seniority provisions help firms develop a stable source of supply of skills. Finally, because employees have well-established working relationships with managers and co-workers, social means of control such as organizational commitment and corporate culture become possible.

Within this brief review of ILMs, it is possible to define a skeletal model of ILM elements and outcomes. ILMs consist of *clusters of jobs* related by the skills and capacities required for their successful performance. Usually, the sets of skills required within one job cluster are similar, but different from those required in other job clusters. Within any one job cluster, it is possible to identify *a hierarchy of skills and capacities* such that the demands for application of skills on certain jobs facilitate the development of further skills required for other jobs. Thus, it is possible to consider jobs within a cluster as being arranged in a hierarchy—with *lower-level jobs requiring skills usually available in the ELM* and *higher-level jobs requiring capacities developed from the performance of lower-level jobs.*

Different jobs receive different levels of compensation as determined by a *compensation system*; higher-level jobs are associated with higher levels of compensation. *Selection and assignment* of persons to higher-level jobs occurs *according to rules* that describe the criteria to be used in these decisions. These rules may be quite specific or vague, and objective or subjective. The extent to which individual mobility within and between job clusters is completely determined by these rules depends on the extent to which the rules themselves are precise and unambiguous and *the extent to which managers use discretion* in their application of these rules.

With these elements of ILMs in place, there ensue a number of outcomes—each of which is likely to be evaluated differently by different actors operating within the ILM. With organizational performance relying increasingly on the application of skills and knowledge, there needs to be *an incentive system that motivates employees to invest in the acquisition and development of new skills* and *protects both the employees' and the firm's investments in employee training.* While there are differences between hourly and salaried employees, both groups of employees look for *increased pay and employment security as a function of increased organizational tenure.* Salaried employees who "buy into" the dominant belief system that there are few artificial barriers to individual success, and that economic returns will accrue from hard work, find in organizational career ladders a functional way of meeting their aspirations. Similarly, managers of organizational career systems find job ladders with limited ports of entry a not unreasonable mechanism for ensuring a stable source of known skills and capacities. As jobs within clusters are ranked according to their "worth," usually measured by the required skills and responsibilities, *patterns of vertical mobility* are typically within clusters of related jobs. Movement from one cluster to another may occur for similar clusters or from the top of one "line" to other "lines" having higher ceilings (Baron et al., 1986).

Figure 1.2 presents a schematic of a system of five structural elements and four outcomes judged to represent core components of ILM operation. The five elements are regarded as antecedent conditions that can be used instrumentally to produce the four consequent outcomes. All components are regarded as critically interdependent. For example, within the group of five antecedent conditions, the nature of job ladders cannot

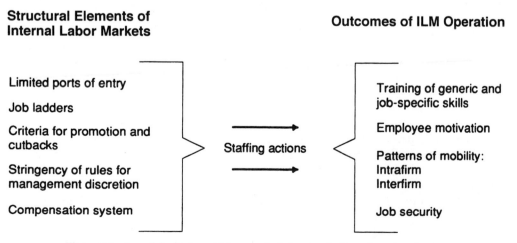

Structural Elements of Internal Labor Markets

Limited ports of entry

Job ladders

Criteria for promotion and cutbacks

Stringency of rules for management discretion

Compensation system

Staffing actions

Outcomes of ILM Operation

Training of generic and job-specific skills

Employee motivation

Patterns of mobility:
Intrafirm
Interfirm

Job security

Figure 1.2. A model of internal labor market structural elements and outcomes.

be considered independently of the location on these ladders of ports of entry for entrants from the ELM. Similarly, the determination of who moves along a job ladder, or from one job ladder to another, is influenced by the criteria used for promotions and cutbacks. Further, criteria used for promotions are likely to be dependent on the restrictions of the compensation system that assigns different rewards to different jobs. The four outcome components of the ILM model are also considered to be interdependent, as are relationships between antecedent structural elements and ILM outcomes.

Together, these structural elements and their consequent outcomes constitute a system in which the relationships among these interdependent parts change as a function of external circumstances. Thus, if circumstances are such that application of normative rules would result in less desirable outcomes, attempts would be made to increase managerial discretion regarding the interpretation and application of these rules so as to produce more acceptable results. We recognize, however, that this exercise of discretion may be contested by individual employees who would be disadvantaged by deviations from the strict application of promotion and cutback criteria. In general, interests and interpretations, both individual and collective, together with the exigencies of particular situations, shape the overall configuration of each ILM.

The model of ILM structural elements and outcomes described in Fig. 1.2 summarizes the primary theoretical components of ILM operation. Identification of these elements and outcomes helps studies such as this focus attention on core attributes of ILM operation. There are also, however, other perspectives and interpretations of ILM operation. They frame several further problematic issues that are associated with the manner in which ILMs operate and that are explored in the following sections.

Origins and Functions of Internal Labor Markets

For Doeringer and Piore (1971, p. 13), ILMs emerged because of three reasons "not envisaged in conventional economic theory: (1) skill specificity, (2) on-the-job training, and (3) customary law." The first two reasons have been viewed as consequences of the economics of transactions (Williamson, Wachter, & Harris, 1975). Administrative rules and arrangements may be viewed as pragmatic replacements for awkward and imperfect formal contracts between employers and employees characterized by firm-specific skills and asymmetrical distributions of information (Wachter & Wright, 1990). Long-term employment smooths fluctuations in output of job performance and reduces the risk that either employers or employees will behave strategically in the short term to increase their returns from the employment relationship. Moreover, because the societal and economic benefits of organizations have been viewed more and more as the application of knowledge rather than of energy, organizational arrangements for collaborative effort will be increasingly preferred (Stinchcombe, 1965, 1990). Particularly in growing industries, production varies more with the amount of knowledge and intelligence present than with the amount of energy applied. More generally, performance is derived primarily from the application of skills learned over extended periods of time. Modern terms and conditions of employment, as embodied in the customs and administrative rules of ILMs, have evolved to meet the exigencies of this secular trend. Most notably, continued learning over progressions of jobs held over periods of many years is structured most appropriately through work roles as careers and rewarded through salary progression. Career management and the administration of salaried ILMs are characteristic of almost all large organizations today.

The putative economics of transaction costs notwithstanding, a significant tension between market and administered processes can be found in the operations of ILMs. First, it is generally assumed by economists that because traditionally defined ILMs exclude the operation of competitive market forces, these ILMs are relatively inflexible and economically inefficient. That is, substantive outcomes of ILM operation such as the compensation and assignment of employees to particular jobs are judged to be different when administrative rules rather than market forces are used for such purposes.

In addition, there is little complementarity between sociological and economic frames of reference used to explain ILM phenomena (Bridges & Villemez, 1991; Granovetter, 1986). In particular, there has been a traditional distrust exhibited by many economists for non-market-driven allocative mechanisms (Lazear, 1991, p. 89):

> The economic approach is more rigorous, more rational and probably better for prediction than that of the industrial psychologist. It is based on optimizing behavior in an environment where constraints are well defined.

Similar prejudices have been ascribed to the field by the most respected representatives of that profession (Stiglitz, 1991, p. 15):

> Somewhat surprisingly, most economists have traditionally relegated the study of organization to business schools, or worse still, to sociologists. The general attitude seemed to be that while it might be important for managers, or the firm's personnel officers, to know something about organizations, the subject was not worthy of Economic Science.

The mutual antagonism between the two philosophies is not assumed only by economists. Citing the propensity for "most Americans to spend the majority of their working years in the employ of a single enterprise," Osterman (1984b, p. 1) has also argued that "we pass only briefly through the market and instead spend most of our lives inside the firm." In terms of substantive outcomes, as well as philosophy and approach, ILMs represent spheres of activity in which there is tension between administrative rules and market competition. Though these concepts are distinct, there are few studies of ILMs that examine the empirical separation of these factors in personnel practices. Three specific issues worthy of further examination, therefore, are:

1. To what extent are ILMs distinct and separate from ELMs? That is, are ILMs and ELMs connected only at ports of entry?
2. To what extent are economic considerations reflected in the administrative rules used for pricing, allocating, and training decisions?
3. Are assignments of employees to most jobs in ILMs shielded from the direct influence of competitive forces?

Within the pragmatics of transaction economics, both management and labor benefit (and bear costs) of the various ILM arrangements that characterize the terms and conditions of employment. This being the case, ILMs may be regarded as arenas in which workers exchange their labor in return for wages, status, and other job rewards (Kalleberg & Sorenson, 1979). As conditions change, the parties involved in bargaining over the terms and conditions of employment may find their potential influence being either enhanced or constrained by changes in the context of the ILM. These changes may be short-term, as for example when the local labor supply increases or becomes tight. Longer-term changes can occur because of technological change or because of the investment strategies of the firm, which favor plant locations where labor supply is plentiful and cheap (Kochan, Katz, & McKersie, 1986).

In the short term, it can be argued that flexibility in labor market arrangements occurs when management has considerable discretion in its application of the rules used to assign employees to different jobs. In most collective agreements, these rules are both extensive and explicit, leaving little room for managerial discretion. In contrast to unionized settings, salaried ILMs often permit considerable managerial discretion, which permits much flexibility in the structuring of employment relationships (Osterman, 1987). In salaried ILMs, employment relationships between employees and their employer are often implicit and rarely circumscribed by a formally negotiated contract. Although managers have much greater degrees of discretion than in unionized or contract-bound settings, they also face a complex array of implicit obligations if they are to maintain legitimacy in the social environment within which work is carried out.

Doeringer and Piore's original presentation of ILM theory also incorporated a total of 11 mechanisms through which firms could adjust to labor market imbalances. Four of these mechanisms (compensation, job structures, allocative structures, and managerial procedures) were judged to be more difficult to implement because of rigidities associated with the ILM model they outlined. The remaining seven mechanisms (subcontracting, overtime, open vacancies, adjustment of recruitment procedures, adjustment of hiring and of screening procedures, and training) were judged to be less difficult to implement. However, these seven mechanisms may be regarded as being substantially less central to a firm's operations than the core issues of job structure (how should the firm be organized?), distribution and allocation (who should do what?), and compensation (how much should employees be paid?). It remains an open question as to which ILM mechanisms are used by firms in general, and by ForestCo in particular, to adjust to labor market imbalances and technological change.

Doeringer and Piore's focus on adjustment mechanisms was necessary, for their presentation of ILMs indicated that what went on inside organizations had considerable consequence for the way in which resources in modern societies were allocated. Economic theories of markets in general provide strong, elegant, and logical models of adjustment processes. Therefore, if an organizational/institutional model of labor allocation was to challenge the dominant alternative model, it should be capable of explaining adjustment processes also. A second potential reason for giving adjustment processes significant attention in their study at that time was that notions of "free" or "closed" markets had become potent political symbols and slogans for both global and national conflicts. Bureaucracy and its associated ideology of administration by rule were the primary administrative mechanisms through which Communist and Socialist states were maintained. More recently, free market mechanisms have been advocated by the political right within the mixed economies of the United States, Canada, and Western Europe, whereas labor organizations, particularly those associated with state administrations, have advocated increased bureaucratic and procedural controls over managerial discretion. A further significant issue to be examined by this investigation of ForestCo's ILM therefore concerns the manner in which this firm uses ILM processes to adjust to technical, market, product, and environmental change. More specifically:

1. How are system-level concerns for organizational change and adaptation communicated and implemented operationally in ILM processes?
2. How do component features of ILMs such as staffing practices and vacancy chain processes facilitate incremental organizational change and adaptation?

A second set of reasons for the origination, establishment, and elaboration of ILMs originate in analyses of the role of government in the historical development of bureaucratic control. The origins of ILMs were not the same everywhere, but arose from "several regimes ... which became increasingly interconnected over time and helped form separate strands of modern bureaucratic control" (Baron, Jennings, & Dobbin, 1988, p. 509). For example, governmental intervention in labor markets during World War II "wrought fundamental changes in contemporary human resource management" (Baron, Dobbin, & Jennings, 1986, p.378). In particular, government intervention and guidance of employment practices accelerated and further legitimated the use of modern personnel practices that in turn reinforced the ideology of bureaucratic rationality as a means of managing employment relations.

Other theorists speculating about the origins of ILMs have argued that they emerged because of their effectiveness as mechanisms through which interclass conflict between management and labor can be limited and controlled (Burawoy, 1979; Edwards, 1979). As a class, workers are weakened by internal competition for small increases in status and rewards. ILM mechanisms manufacture the consent of the governed as interclass conflict between capital and labor is channeled into intraclass conflict among workers. In this radical interpretation, the primary function of ILMs is ideological, as widespread dissemination and acceptance of the premises of ILM operation mask and secure the extraction of surplus value from employees.

Related to the argument of social control and exploitation of employees is the argument that asserts that the rationalization of the rules used to allocate workers to various statuses and rewards legitimates the enterprise's power by making its application more predictable and stable. Bureaucratic control evokes stable and predictable behavior from employees, thus simplifying and legitimating managerial control. Exercise of staffing discretion by managers within the bureaucratic procedures of ILM operation obscures the exercise of managerial power. Allocations of worker assignments that result from the exercise of managerial discretion and power are legitimated by employees' accepting the normative assumptions of managerial staffing authority. This study of ForestCo's ILM therefore also presents an opportunity to examine the functions of ideology and legitimation in contemporary staffing practices.

The three separate but related reasons cited for the development of ILMs—economic rationality embedded in transaction costs, government legislation as the institutionalization of beliefs, and rational ideology as a means of managerial control—have all been judged to have contributed in various ways at various times to the development of modern ILM systems. It remains to be seen whether these three interdependent strands of ILM origins continue to surface as reasons for the continued maintenance and actual operation of a contemporary ILM system.

Methodological Implications

A recent review of theoretical and empirical studies of ILMs has documented several of the difficulties encountered in conducting studies on ILMs (Althauser, 1989). For example, there is an "absence of consensus about the characteristics defining the ILM concept" as researchers have struggled with where and how boundaries should be drawn around the phenomena that characterize "the market" for labor. ILMs have been conceptualized as: (1) all the jobs within a firm—in which the boundary of the organization constitutes the boundary between ILM and ELM; (2) discrete clusters of jobs within firms—in which unit, departmental, divisional, or notions of related skill constitute the intrafirm boundaries within which an ILM operates; and (3) clusters of occupationally related jobs that exist within and across firms—in which occupational skills or certifications or both are used as the primary system for the clustering of related jobs.

As used here, the concept of a boundary between the ILM and the ELM, or between related ILMs within a single firm, is a convenient relational construct. Boundaries between the ELM and the ILM are in fact permeable, as people move from the ELM to the ILM as hires and from the ILM to the ELM as quits, retirements, or layoffs. The extent to which an ILM can be distinguished from its more general labor market context depends on its degree of openness, which is inferred from a comparison of patterns of employee mobility within an ILM with those between the ILM and its ELM. ILMs are not static phenomena— they are constituted as relatively stable patterns in a dynamic system of personnel stocks and flows.

Thus, the boundary conditions that are assumed or inferred from patterns in the flows of people into, through, and out of one or several organizations are problematic. One reason Althauser (1989) characterized the literature on ILMs as a "conceptual pot-pourri" is that many of the initial conceptual models, especially those resembling "ideal-type" ILMs, were assumed to be context-free. Little attention was paid to the empirical difficulty of identifying the boundaries that shape and define different types of ILMs.

Previous work on ILMs indicates that ILMs emerge, and the boundaries that partially separate different clusters of jobs vary, as a function of the history and situation within which employment relationships develop (Bills, 1987; Pfeffer & Cohen, 1984). Craft ILMs occur where job clusters are skill-dominated and employers can offer few establishment- or firm-based rewards. Industrial ILMs occur where the incentives for firm-based attachments secure both industry- and firm-specific skills. Occupational ILMs are likely to occur within multiplant firms in which horizontal moves contribute to skill development. Finally, within any one firm, there may be several types of ILMs in use—with stereotypical industrial ILMs being used for unionized hourly employees and less deterministic ILMs characterizing the employment of salaried employees.

Given the prior review of the bureaucratization of personnel practices, one would expect the primary empirical system-level attribute of an ILM to consist of various descriptions of its job structure. However, because the status of an employee in bureaucratic theory is defined as the status of the job to which that employee is assigned, the most readily measurable attributes of an ILM are the distributions of employee status and the patterns of employee mobility into, through, and out of the employment system that contains those jobs. At the system level of analysis, then, ILMs can be described initially through a preliminary definition of system attributes (e.g., all full-time employees of a particular firm, all salaried employees of a particular division, or all persons of a particular occupational category employed in a geographic area).

Additional characteristics of the ILM can be found in descriptors of the stocks and flows of employees that comprise the dynamic system just defined. Descriptions of these mobility patterns require some judgment regarding the boundaries between different employment statuses. Certainly, the boundaries that distinguish the ILM from its contextual ELM have to be defined, as do the characteristics of groups of employees considered to have "different" employment statuses within the ILM. For example, it is possible to describe the members of the ILM system in terms of their organizational status such as hierarchical level, organizational tenure, and departmental affiliation, as well as in terms of their occupation and of their demographic attributes such as age and gender. In addition to these "stock" characteristics, there are those of the employee flows that maintain this employment system. For example, many organizations monitor the exit rates from the ILM to the ELM, especially voluntary quit rates, at different parts of the employment system. If the employment system of an organization is to maintain its size, the overall quit rate needs to be balanced by an equivalent aggregate rate of hire. But exit rates and hire rates will rarely be equally balanced at the same levels of an organization's hierarchy. In the salaried employment systems of large organizations, most employees experience some degree of internal progression and career advancement. Thus, entry rates are likely to be higher than exit rates at lower levels of an organization's hierarchy. Similarly, exit rates are likely to be higher than entry rates at more senior levels of an organization's hierarchy. In stereotypical ILMs, we would expect significantly positive associations between hierarchical level and exit rates and significantly negative associations between hierarchical level and hire rates.

While relatively stable, but not static, attributes of an organization's ILM can be described and measured, ILMs also maintain a dynamic interdependence with the larger labor market and economic context in which they are situated. A demand for different skills, perhaps because of new products, markets, or technologies, can result in both temporary and long-term changes in the compositional balance of employee flows into and through an organization. Similarly, an economic recession, or the maturation of a product-market cycle, can increase the flow rates out of an organization's ILM, thus changing the pattern of flows from one that maintains that system to one that alters the dynamics of the system. As ILMs are dynamic systems, changes in the composition of these systems—namely, the nature of the stocks of employees that comprise those systems—occur because of changes in the flows that maintain organizational ILMs. Similarly, as stocks and flows in ILMs are highly interdependent, changes in flows also lead to changes in secondary and related attributes of stocks. For example, if an organization wishes to reduce its size by increasing outflows and decreasing inflows, there will be short-term consequences for the resulting demography of the organization. Typically, the distribution of the length of service of the organization's employees will shift to the "right" (i.e., to an older population), and promotion prospects will be changed.

Mobility patterns of employees will have both stable and dynamic properties. Stable patterns in the composition of stocks of an ILM will be maintained by regularities in the flows of employees into, through, and out of the ILM. Static stability will never be obtained. To be noticeable, changes in flow patterns of employees into, through, and out of an employment system must occur over one or more periods of time. When such changes do occur, irregularities in the ensuing demographic distribution invariably take much longer periods of time to dissipate. For example, in firms that respond to opportunities for growth in employment over the business cycle by hiring additional employees with a focused set of demographic characteristics such as age, these demographic "lumps" will persist over many subsequent years. Preliminary system-level descriptions of an organization's ILM therefore also often contain information that permits inferences regarding the system's response given certain combinations of managerial initiatives in response to changing environmental conditions (Bennison & Casson, 1984).

In summary, ILMs can be viewed from perspectives at the employment-system level in terms of the criteria used to identify the boundary defining the phenomena of interest, details of the stocks and flows that comprise that system, and the general nature of the interdependencies between the ILM and its context.

MOBILITY CLUSTERS AND VACANCY CHAINS

In the model of ILM structural elements and outcomes presented in Fig. 1.2, two important component elements of ILMs are identified as job ladders and ports of entry. These two elements of ILMs are the immediate antecedents of the mobility patterns identified as ILM outcomes. Employees enter ILMs at ports of entry and advance through a progression of increasingly demanding and rewarding jobs until they exit the ILM. In stereotypical unionized, blue-collar ILMs, there are limited ports of entry into the ILM. Once hired, employees are assigned to a progression of jobs, typically requiring a progression of skills and responsibilities, as vacancies occur. As noted in the previous discussion of ILM theory, such accounts of ILM operations give prominence to jobs and job structures as the dominant feature of ILMs. Individual talents and capacities are considered only at ports of entry, where there is presumed to be substantial competition for entry into the ILM. Once employed, employees are largely protected from competition from persons who are not yet members of the ILM.

In stereotypical ILMs, competition from other employees is also largely absent. Rules for advancement are presumed to be based on unambiguous criteria, such as seniority, that may or may not be strongly related to job performance. The conditions that allow employees to acquire increased skills and capacities related to job performance, such as learning from on-the-job experience and employment security in the form of job protection from less-skilled employees, are present. However, there are few positive incentives for employees to continuously seek improvements in performance. Implicitly, the organizational system is that of a very stable, large bureaucracy in which there is a close association between clear organizational objectives and the resulting job structure. Individual capacities, especially individual capacities both to learn from experience and to apply the results of that learning in future situations, are not problematic.

In models of ILMs such as this, mobility is triggered by the occurrence of a vacancy. That is, a stable job structure represents the frame over which employees move. When an employee vacates a position in this job structure, mobility processes are initiated to fill that vacancy. Such processes have been termed "pull" processes, as typically an employee from a lesser position (or possibly a lateral position) is "pulled" upward (or sideways) into the vacant position. This system of mobility contrasts with "push" models of mobility, in which the attributes of the individual employee have a strong effect on both the timing and the direction of subsequent mobility (Forbes, 1987; Stewman, 1975).

When lines of progression are fully specified, as in union contracts, identification of job ladders is relatively simple. However, when lines of progression are not specified, as in many salaried ILMs, they can only be inferred from patterns in the frequency of "promotion moves" of different employees from one job classification to another (Baron et al., 1986). A related way of identifying lines of progression is to follow sequences of related staffing actions initiated because a vacant position occurred in the ILM. Because all but entry-level positions are stereotypically filled with persons already employed at similar or lower levels of skill, responsibility, and compensation, such internal staffing often creates a cascade of subsequent vacancies and staffing actions. Thus, it is possible to identify sequences of related staffing actions that constitute a vacancy chain. Combinations of related and similarly located vacancy chains produce mobility clusters.

In stereotypical models of ILMs, vacancy chains and mobility clusters would be identical with the patterning of job ladders in overall job structures. However, vacancy chains only approximate job ladders, and mobility clusters only approximate overall job structures because: (1) organizational systems are rarely stable and closed; (2) job performance is not independent of the persons assigned to jobs; and (3) job performances are not independent of the ways in which other jobs are performed. Arrangements of positions and jobs are not static, but change in reaction to and anticipation of internal and environmental exigencies. Because ILMs are continually adjusting to various features of their contexts, it is not necessary that vacancy chains terminate only with the hire of someone from the ELM. Vacancy chains can also terminate with reorganizations and realignments of persons and positions in which vacancies become absorbed. Indeed, the presence of a vacancy often provides increased opportunity for managers to reorganize their departments by realigning portions of the overall job structure to better fit their local task environments.

Vacancy chains also deviate from formal, previously established job ladders because employees often demonstrate differential capacities to learn and perform. When managers have discretion, they take cognizance of these capacities to select employees for organizational positions. Thus, recurrent vacancies in a particular position are not necessarily filled by the occupants of a single other position. Depending on the characteristics of employees who are available for consideration as candidates for the vacant position, over time several different vacancy chains may be triggered by the same recurring vacancy. Even though probabilistic, the stability assumed by Markov models of employee moves from one job status to another is unlikely to be realized in practice (Stewman, 1975), particularly as employee moves are path-dependent. That is, the favorableness of candidates for a vacant position will depend not only on their current status but also on the nature of previous positions they may have held. Perceptions of employee inertia and likely career progression will also influence the choice of candidate to fill any particular vacancy.

The third primary reason that vacancy chains are not identical to job ladders is that the performance of many jobs is dependent on the performance of other, interdependent jobs. In bureaucratic models of organizational functioning, job performance is not considered problematic once an employee has been assigned to a particular job or position. However, there is often considerable variation in job performance as a function of an employee's experience or tenure in that job. Typically, a learning curve is manifested as experience is gained and job performance improves. Moreover, because the outcomes of job performance are often interdependent with those of other jobs, the skills and attributes of some employees may complement or inhibit the skills and capacities of others. Jobs are more than job titles. They consist of complex arrangements of skills, capacities, duties, and responsibilities in a complex matrix of social processes. In their fine detail, job requirements are not static but evolve as a function of those employees who perform other interdependent jobs.

While vacancy chains and mobility clusters inferred from employee moves are not perfect indicators of job ladders and job structures, they are nonetheless often the only empirical indicator of ILM operation. Moreover, vacancy chains reflect actual rather than ideal mobility patterns, as they include the many local adjustments made to implement organizational change, subtle individual differences that are judged to lead to substantial differences in job performance, and the real complexities of job interdependencies.

Empirically, the primary feature of a vacancy chain as a component attribute of an ILM is the number of staffing actions in that vacancy chain. Because stereotypical vacancy chains terminate only when there is an entry from the ELM, the "length" of the vacancy chain is the primary indicator of the preference for internal rather than external candidates for vacant positions. In general, *ceteris paribus*, the longer the set of vacancy chains found in an ILM, the greater the protection of internal candidates from the competition of the ELM. Even so, vacancy chains of equal length, or numbers of related staffing actions, can still operate quite differently. For example, a vacancy chain can consist of several horizontal moves but relatively few vertical moves. In vacancy chains of this type, mobility across departmental or occupational boundaries, but at the same level of the organizational hierarchy, would typically produce horizontal patterns of on-the-job training and cross-functional career development. Alternatively, vacancy chains can consist of few horizontal moves but relatively many vertical moves. Such a chain can either occur within a single department or follow narrow lines of occupational specialization. In either case, the chain would emphasize depth of experience and vertical mobility. Thus, two further attributes of a vacancy chain are those of its horizontal and vertical span. A related attribute of any vacancy chain is the derived measure of the average number of vertical steps associated with each move. Many small incremental steps indicate a career and development system in which rewards are spread relatively evenly. In contrast, an ILM system characterized by a few large steps suggests higher levels of individual competition for larger organizational "prizes" (Lazear, 1992).

Standard models of human resource planning (Bennison & Casson, 1984) assume that vacancies originate either because an employee exits from an existing organizational position or because a new organizational position is created. For the manager responsible for internal staffing, these two antecedents represent quite different circumstances. In the former, particularly if the exit is in the form of an unanticipated voluntary quit, managerial action is likely to be reactive. In the latter circumstance, however, considerable thought and prior authorization often precede the consequent staffing action. Under these circumstances, staffing is more likely to be proactive. Thus, the origin of a vacancy chain is likely to condition the manner in which the vacancy chain subsequently unfolds.

Similarly, the conditions under which vacancy chains terminate could also have a potential impact on vacancy chain length. In stereotypical models of ILMs, strong preferences for internal candidates lead vacancy chains to continue to move toward jobs identified as ports of entry into the ILM. Vacancy chains originating from vacancies that occur in the upper levels of organizational hierarchies would be expected to be quite long, due to the hierarchical location of ports of entry. However, if job structures are in a modest state of flux, and vacancies are used as opportunities to reorganize, vacancy chains will exhibit predominantly short lengths. Such distributions of vacancy chain lengths would be consistent with open-system models of organizational functioning in which ILMs are responsive and adaptive to environmental change.

In summary, ILMs viewed from a vacancy chain perspective can be considered to be partially revealed by the distribution of the lengths of vacancy chains in relation to the levels at which originating vacancies occur. A secondary characteristic of vacancy chain length is the horizontal and vertical scope of the positions related in that chain. In addition to these attributes, the degree of uncertainty associated with the origination of each vacancy chain is likely to provide some indication of the factors that influence both the length and scope of the subsequent chain. Finally, the reasons identified for the termination of each vacancy chain should provide information on the relationships between persons and positions in the ILM under study.

STAFFING PRACTICES

An as-yet-undefined attribute of the components of the core model of ILM operation presented in Fig. 1.2 is that of the staffing mechanisms and processes that underlie the implicit causal arrows linking "elements" to "outcomes." Previous work on ILM theory has generally assumed these staffing processes to be a black box. There is very little if any previous work that demonstrates (1) how staffing actions are shaped by antecedent ILM elements to produce ILM outcomes and (2) how supervisors and managers intendedly consider potential ILM outcomes to define jobs and job clusters and "select" employees to be "appointed" to those jobs. In particular, we know very little regarding the exercise of managerial discretion and judgment in salaried ILMs. In these settings, the decision premises of managers who have been delegated the authority to staff the jobs and positions for which they are responsible, as well as their actual decisions, produce the consequences of ILM operation. Thus, we argue that staffing practices constitute a critical linkage between ILM elements and their outcomes for the operation of salaried ILMs.

The view of ILM operation presented here is that sequences of staffing actions linked through vacancy chains are the primary mechanisms through which ILMs operate. These processes, often labeled "internal staffing" by personnel specialists, involve the manner in which employees are selected and assigned to different jobs (Conner & Fjerstad, 1979). Many prescriptive personnel procedures such as lines of progression, human resource information systems, posting systems, and succession plans have been developed to manage the staffing of organizational positions. However, there are relatively few field studies of actual staffing practice that describe in detail the manner in which and the extent to which these procedures are actually used (Eder, 1989; Schneider & Schmitt, 1986).

Most contemporary textbook treatments of staffing typically consider the separate personnel functions of employee planning, recruitment, selection, orientation, socialization, training, deployment, and evaluation (Milkovich, Glueck, Barth, & McShane, 1988). There exists a large literature regarding theory and normative practice for each component, but there are very few descriptive accounts of how managers in real life juggle the interdependencies among these practices and other organizational considerations. Indeed, the *ASPA Handbook of Personnel and Industrial Relations* notes that "staffing is an integrated system for moving people into, through, and eventually, out of an organization" (Albright, 1979). A similar point is made by Schneider and Schmitt (1986) in their identification of four reciprocally interdependent staffing components: (1) attributes of individuals in the organization, (2) characteristics of jobs in the organization, (3) organizational practices and procedures, and (4) the aspects of the larger environment in which the organization is located.

Concomitant with the elaboration of ILM theory over the past 20 years has been the continuing development, formalization, and normalization of personnel practices— including those that shape staffing. These practices manifest the rationalization of administrative rules through which job structures are established; employees are selected for entry, advancement, and possible layoff; and compensation systems are designed and implemented. Not surprisingly, these practices reflect the normative assumptions of bureaucratic theory, even though the appropriateness of the administrative forms and practices associated with the operation of bureaucracies has been increasingly challenged and modified in recent years (Kanter, 1989).

Before and since World War II, a significant preoccupation of personnel specialists and academic researchers in the human resource management field has been the development and application of scientific principles to personnel management (Jacoby, 1985). While there has been more success in the development rather than the application of such personnel practices, development of more sophisticated procedures has progressed most readily under assumptions closely associated with rational, bureaucratic forms of organization (Scott, 1992). A rational model of organizations assumes that the activities and behaviors of organizational participants (employees in the case of business firms) are coordinated to achieve explicit, clearly defined goals. Concurrent with the articulation of explicit goals are formal rules that define roles and role relationships among occupants of individual positions so as to accomplish those goals. Personal attributes of employees and other social relationships that might emerge between employees are considered to be illegitimate and irrational within this model of organizational functioning. Thus, explicit goals "provide unambiguous criteria for selecting among alternative activities" (Scott, 1992, p. 23), including the decision to hire or promote one person rather than another.

Closed-system, rational models of organizations provide one conceptual context for appreciations of staffing. However, at least two alternative perspectives—natural-system models and open-system models—can also be used to make sense of staffing activities (Scott, 1992). Natural-system models focus attention on the maintenance and survival of the social-system aspects of organizations. Open-system models consider organizations in relation to their environments and focus attention on processes of adaptation and change. The relevance of all three types of system models for managerial staffing decisions and actions is explored fully in Part III. It need only be noted here that the preferred normative context for both the development and application of personnel practices is that of closed-system organizational models.

In these contexts, the primary purpose of personnel practice is to improve organizational performance, such as the productivity of organizational members, through procedures tested and validated through increasingly sophisticated scientific methods. For example, Gatewood and Feild (1994, p. 1) note that "selection in job performance ... is the basis for the development of other programs devoted to maintaining or increasing the productivity of employees." Reinforcing the linkage to closed-system models are arguments similar to those that claim that "the best staffing systems are those that are designed around a careful specification of organizational goals ... the chore for the staffing specialist becomes one of finding people able to meet the goals of specific jobs" (Schneider & Schmitt, 1986, p. 4). In bureaucratic theory, jobs rationally link organizational activities to organizational goals. In personnel practice and its associated theory, jobs are the logical linkage of employees to organizational activities.

Governmental legislation designed to limit systematic discrimination in employment has also reinforced the emphasis on jobs in personnel practice. For example, Gatewood and Feild (1994, p. 25) argue that

> every selection program should have the following major objectives: (a) to maximize the probability of making accurate selection decisions about applicants, and (b) to ensure that these selection decisions are carried out in such a manner as to minimize the chance of a judgment of discrimination being made against the organization.

In seeking personnel procedures that would protect organizations from charges of discrimination, personnel practitioners have sought refuge in an emphasis on job requirements as the legitimate basis for selection. Thus, Schneider and Schmitt (1986, p. 14) note that

> the most important outcome of numerous court cases and tremendous effort on the part of personnel researchers has been a focus on job relevance in the design of measures used as a basis for making selection decisions.

Although personnel selection necessarily includes consideration of the knowledge, skills, abilities, and other attributes (KSAOs) of employees, these KSAOs are formulated and evaluated primarily in terms of jobs needing to be performed. Indeed, most formal and normative treatments of personnel selection invariably follow a logical sequence from (1) job analysis and identification of the dimensions of job performance through (2) the specification of KSAOs and the development and validation of assessment devices to measure KSAOs to (3) the use of those assessment devices to evaluate and select candidates. Concurrent with the emphasis on jobs has been an accentuation of scientism in validating personnel practices (Gatewood & Feild, 1994, p. 19):

The development of a selection program requires the measurement of characteristics of jobs, individuals, and, work performance. By measurement we mean quantitative description, that is, the use of numbers. ... Numbers are necessary because they facilitate comparison of people; they transmit information more succinctly than words; and they permit statistical manipulation which provides even more information about the selection program.

The implicit assumptions of personnel management embedded in these prescriptive perspectives are those of large, rule-bound forms of bureaucratic administration. Orderly scientific administration in stable, known contexts replaces the disorder and transactional inefficiency of market mechanisms. Goals are taken as given, and the translation of organizational objectives into job structures is not problematic. Both job structures and the sets of candidates available for assignment to positions are viewed from a perspective of stability. There is an assumption of a surplus of candidates for positions, with little overt consideration given to the manner in which employees develop the performance skills that match job structures. In this view of organizational functioning, training is not problematic, as it is disassociated from on-the-job development, which requires appreciations of the learning consequences of successive moves from one job to another. The extent to which these assumptions reflect actual staffing practices can also be investigated by our study of ForestCo's ILM. Moreover, if these assumptions are not borne out in practice, it should be possible to discover and identify the mechanisms through which staffing occurs when goals are not known and organizational operations are not stable.

Whether one takes an integrated or a component view of organizational staffing, it is clear that the bureaucratization of personnel practices noted earlier is the predominant context within which the topic is evidenced. Jobs, presumably derived from clear, specific, stable organizational objectives, are the rational, logical precursors to other personnel practices such as job analysis and evaluation, compensation policies, recruitment, selection, and training. Normatively, at least, these specialist activities have been developed with a strong technical and scientific basis. For example, job evaluation has been characterized "as an eminently 'rational' process, with rational people setting rational standards and ending up with rational outcomes..." (Quaid, 1993, p. 223). In fact, as Quaid (1993, p. 234) illustrates, this emphasis on rationality serves as an institutional, rationalized myth that maintains the social order and "legitimates such social arrangements ... as status hierarchies."

Whether one accepts the surface positivism of personnel researchers or alternative interpretations of social constructivism, there is little question that concepts of bureaucratic rationality undergird the normative academic elaborations of personnel practices. Jobs are the primary focus of organizational activities, and employees are evaluated solely in terms of their contribution to job performance. Staffing can be reduced to considerations of employee selection, and an ample supply of candidates can be assumed to be available for any position that becomes vacant. Organizational considerations are limited to the pursuit of specific, known objectives, and these objectives dominate over concerns for individual welfare, motivation, and career development. While training is not necessarily regarded as problematic in formal models of bureaucracy, contemporary treatments of training nevertheless manifest the scientific rationalism noted earlier (Goldstein, 1986). Views of selection are consistent with stereotypical models of ILMs and vacancy chains. Vacant jobs are regarded as the initiating mechanism for selection activities, and individual jobs frame both recruitment procedures and selection criteria. Also, issues of maintenance and preservation of the social system are downplayed. Little attention is given to questions of positive motivation required for continued motivation, commitment, and job performance. Similarly, little attention is given to the possibility of disillusionment for candidates who are considered but not selected for advancement.

A distinctive feature of most contemporary treatments of staffing is that the cognitive complexities of the decision process are rarely discussed. For example, in a typical staffing process, a manager may suddenly find that one of his employees has quit—either to accept a job with another firm or to take a position that has recently become vacant elsewhere in the organization. In deciding how to respond to this vacancy, the manager must consider multiple factors over an evolving, multistage action plan. Initially, and concurrently through the set of subsequent actions, the manager needs to take account of the immediate and broader context within which this vacancy occurs. For example, what are generally held values regarding vacancies? Do senior managers in general, and the current manager's immediate supervisor in particular, believe that vacant positions should be absorbed into existing assignments and responsibilities? Does the manager have some discretion regarding the replenishment of his or her unit's complement of personnel? Is the vacancy occurring at a time when the manager is considering potential realignments of jobs in the unit? Contextual factors such as these influence how the manager decides to proceed with subsequent staffing actions.

In considering subsequent staffing actions, the manager is likely to evaluate whether or not there is an immediate solution available that fits the problem of the vacant position (Mintzberg, Raisinghani, & Theoret, 1976). There may be an established pattern of job moves in the unit that provides a precedent for the vacancy-filling move, but there may or may not be a well-qualified candidate available. If these potentially immediate reviews do not produce a vacancy-filling action, the manager is likely to initiate various standard administrative procedures for staffing. These procedures may vary from division to division as a function of other pressures. For example, one unit may wish to develop candidates with strong intradivisional knowledge, whereas another unit may wish to open its vacant positions to candidates who can bring in different skills from other work areas. These considerations, in turn, are likely to be conditioned by problematic features of the temporal and environmental context in which a particular organizational unit is located.

Staffing may or may not involve the internal posting of the vacancy. Posting is the organizational procedure in which details of a job vacancy, together with candidate requirements, are advertised in various parts of the employing organization. This practice often requires some prior consideration of the nature of the job vacancy to be filled and the desired qualifications of potential candidates. Staffing may or may not involve others in the actual selection process. For example, the screening of applicants' resumes and participation in the selection interview itself may involve local personnel specialists, the manager's supervisor, and possibly one or more coworkers. If all these people have a stake in the selection process, the determination of the job requirements may not be a straightforward process. In addition, if a vacant job is to be posted, the extent to which advertisements are distributed throughout various parts of the organization also has to be decided upon and arranged. Thus, the procedures that are used to identify candidates for positions also have the capacity to influence the eventual choice of candidate for appointment to a vacant position. Collectively, these procedures have the potential to influence the patterns of flows of employees into, through, and out of the organization.

Once some relatively specific staffing plan has been established, the person(s) involved in the selection process typically review the resumes of candidates and reduce the total applicant pool to some shortlist of candidates. This review may include background checks with the candidates' current supervisor(s) and coworkers. Candidates short-listed would then be interviewed. The overall criteria used in the initial screening of all applicants, as well as the specific criteria used in the selection interviews, together with the interview procedures that assess the degree to which each candidate meets these criteria, are typically open to some degree of interpretation by the interviewers.

Once the "best" candidate has been decided upon by the person(s) involved, the position is typically offered to that candidate. Depending on the evolving appreciation of available candidates, however, the overall requirements and expectations demanded of the best candidate may not be exactly the same as those for others considered for the vacant position. Often, there is considerable flexibility in arranging the jobs within a unit, and the evolution of a job often depends on the evolving mix of skills and capacities of employees in the work unit. Thus, the appointment of a new person to an organizational unit could lead to minor or substantial changes in the current assignment of duties and responsibilities within that unit.

For many managers, the staffing process rarely concludes at this point. The initial assignment of an employee to a nominal position in a work unit often carries with it an ongoing responsibility for training and developing that employee. Also, the manager may believe that coworker acceptance could limit the effectiveness of a recent staffing decision and therefore institute actions that would lessen risks to his reputation as a "good" manager of human resources. Another possibility is that the manager's experience of the immediately past staffing process may have sharpened his or her appreciation of potential reorganizations that may be possible in the medium-term future. Finally, learning from this experience can influence subsequent staffing actions, as the manager may have become aware of other candidates who would be suitable for anticipated vacancies.

As illustrated here, staffing is not at all a simple process. Execution of its various processes entails much uncertainty. Moreover, staffing actions are not confined to the simple mechanics and outcomes of the selection interview, but rather consist of a temporal sequence of linked considerations and actions that occur (1) prior to the selection decision, (2) immediately before and concurrent with the selection decision, and (3) following the selection decision itself. Shaping this temporal sequence of considerations and actions are (1) contextual factors that frame selection processes in this organization; (2) actions, events, and histories that have an indirect impact on this particular selection decision; and (3) the specific actions, procedures, and considerations that influence how this job vacancy, these candidates, and the fit between them are viewed. This 3×3 conceptual frame was used in this study of ForestCo's ILM to collate the information on actual managerial staffing practices that was obtained.

PLAN OF THIS BOOK

As indicated previously, this book both describes and analyzes the operation of the employment system of a single firm from three perspectives: a system-level point of view that encompasses the ILM of the firm as a whole; the patterns of vacancy chains that include clusters of related staffing actions; and finally the decision frames of managers responsible for these staffing actions. Each of these perspectives is discussed in three primary parts. In each part, prior theoretical perspectives are used to frame what was found—to confront theory with practice and to search for theoretical insights that could guide future practice.

Part I comprises this introductory chapter to the theoretical background and concepts of ILMs, vacancy chains, and staffing and Chapter 2, which describes the history and current situation of ForestCo, the firm used as the base for this investigation. This history and present organizational structure provide the context within which ForestCo's current employment system operates. Overall features of this employment system are described by taking a macroperspective on ForestCo's salaried ILM as a whole. Policies and procedures, together with details of stocks and flows of employees through different levels of ForestCo's hierarchy, are described and evaluated in terms of their fit with more stereotypical models of ILM operation.

Chapter 2 also presents a wider perspective on the operation of ForestCo's ILM by examining various contextual and historical influences on its staffing processes. Historical norms and the effect of ForestCo's organizational culture on the values invoked in staffing are presented. For example, because ForestCo experienced a traumatic decline in profits in the worldwide recession of 1981–1982, it had to implement new and different personnel policies in response to that threat. The organizational structures and policies implemented at that time continued to operate during the late 1980s when this study was undertaken. The consequences of these "old" policies can be found in the staffing actions of ForestCo's managers some seven and eight years later. Finally, the psychological effects of this "survival" experience on managerial orientations to staffing are presented along with the consequences of these experiences tracked to various staffing decision dilemmas faced by managers in the postrecession years of the late 1980s.

Part II describes the results of this study of ForestCo in terms of two samples of vacancy chains found there. One sample consisted of 71 vacancy chains containing approximately 300 staffing actions. In this sample, the managers directly responsible for these actions and decisions were subsequently interviewed regarding the reasons for the nature of the staffing action taken. A second sample of 110 vacancy chains was obtained from an inspection of archival records, but no managers responsible for these staffing decisions were interviewed. While these two samples can be considered to be representative of the vacancy chains in the organization, the amount and type of information obtained from each was different. In the first and primary sample, knowledge about each vacancy chain was built up from detailed information obtained from interviews with the managers responsible for each staffing action. For the second sample, information about the nature of each vacancy chain was inferred from comments made on the formal notices used to record changes in the status of each employee. In the first sample, expanded appreciations of staffing actions such as "lateral promotions" or "transfers" could be investigated with the managers who were responsible for those actions. In the second sample, a record of an employee's being "promoted" or "transferred" to a position with the same title and numerical identifier as one recently vacated by someone else was regarded as prima facie evidence of a link in a vacancy chain.

Because greater levels of descriptive detail are available from the perspective of vacancy chains than from that of the overall ILM, the vacancy chain analysis of ForestCo's ILM presented in Part II comprises the four component Chapters 3 through 6. The primary means of organizing this material is in terms of the length of the underlying vacancy chains. Chapter 3 presents a statistical review of objective features of ForestCo's vacancy chains. Chapter 4 describes "short" vacancy chains in which an initial triggering vacancy leads to only a small number of, specifically, one or two subsequent "moves" or staffing actions. Chapter 5 describes "medium-length" vacancy chains that consist of either three, four, or five moves. Chapter 6 describes the longest of the vacancy chains found to operate in the firm under study and considers those vacancy chains with six or more moves. Part II concludes with a brief review of the implications of this vacancy chain analysis for ILM theory.

Part III consists of five subperspectives on staffing in ForestCo. Following a brief discussion of staffing theory, and the rationale for the identification and grouping of these five subissues, Chapter 7 describes the effects of the ForestCo's policies and its economic context on staffing decisions. This chapter focuses on antecedent and contextual conditions that influenced the manner in which staffing took place and, at times, influenced the choice of person to fill a position. For example, the general features of the personnel system at ForestCo and the formal procedures prescribed for the staffing of vacant positions are described. In this decentralized organization, local managers had considerable discretion as to how they actually staffed positions. Staffing practices could vary from managerially controlled, administered staffing actions to ones that were more competitive and market-based as managers relied on the posting system to identify candidates seeking jobs. The factors that managers considered in their choice of staffing procedures are reviewed in light of a substantial number of individual accounts of the antecedent and contextual conditions identified as factors that led managers to chose specific staffing actions.

Chapters 8 and 9 describe the issues associated with viewing staffing as either an administered process or a more competitive process administered through a posting system. In these two chapters, detailed appreciations of two primary but contrasting approaches to staffing and selection decisions are presented. Chapter 8 presents a detailed discussion of staffing as an administered process and the considerations that led managers to use this method of staffing. Chapter 9 presents a detailed discussion of staffing as a competitive, market-based process as embodied in ForestCo's system of posting vacant positions. Both chapters present further details of the issues identified by ForestCo's managers as being pertinent to each staffing system.

Whether staffing was accomplished through the use of administrative means or through the posting system, in each case a significant issue concerned the criteria used to match candidates and job requirements. Chapter 10 presents a detailed discussion of the criteria managers used to match candidates with jobs or vice versa. Finally, Chapter 11 reviews postselection considerations of staffing. In this chapter, managers' appreciations of the consequences of staffing procedures and outcomes are presented together with discussions of how these postselection considerations influenced both managers' choices of staffing processes and their postselection behaviors.

Part III concludes with a review of these staffing action perspectives on internal labor markets.

In Part IV, Chapter 12 confronts various elements of ideal-type conceptualizations of ILMs and the opposing facts of their operation in this firm. It reviews what has been learned from this examination of ForestCo's employment system from three interrelated and interdependent perspectives. It examines the detailed model of ILM operation developed and outlined in Chapter 1 and compares the assumptions underlying that model with actual practice. It summarizes and reviews how staffing actions both influence and are influenced by the vacancy chain of which they are a component, and also how staffing practices are interdependent with the ILM context in which staffing occurs. This chapter concludes with speculations regarding lessons learned from this detailed examination of ForestCo's ILM. It identifies directions for future research and presents features of ForestCo's ILM that can be used to implement high-performance human resource systems in other organizations.

2

ForestCo

Frame for an Internal Labor Market

INTRODUCTION

An "internal labor market" (ILM) is an abstraction that can cover a wide variety of different employment conditions. Different types of ILM develop as a function of the external labor markets (ELMs) in which the particular ILMs are embedded and as a function of the specific administrative arrangements that are characteristic of particular organizations (Bills, 1987). The extent to which an "establishment" or separate production unit of an organization exhibits characteristic attributes of an ILM has been also been shown to depend on the size of the establishment within which the ILM operates, the type of technology employed, whether the establishment is linked to other establishments through a branch network, and the extent of firm-specific training (Baron et al., 1986). In addition, local factors such as the proportions of professional and managerial jobs, the extent of establishment-specific training, the type and degree of unionization, and sexual stereotyping of jobs also influence the final form of the ILM.

The staffing of organizational positions is also dependent on the context within which staffing occurs. For example, Schneider and Schmitt (1986, p. 3) view staffing as a process implicated in the practices and procedures of the organization itself, the organization in turn being embedded in a larger economic and institutional environment. If detailed descriptions of vacancy chains and staffing actions are to be used to better understand how ILMs operate, the general and the more immediate organizational attributes that frame the organization's ILM need to be specified. Thus, in the sections that follow, there is an initial description of the broad outlines of ForestCo, followed by an examination of further levels of detail of the internal procedures that, prima facie, appear to influence the operation of its ILM.

AN OVERVIEW OF FORESTCO TODAY*

The following succinct description of ForestCo is excerpted from the annual report issued while this study of its employment system was taking place:

> ForestCo is one of North America's largest forest products companies, with integrated operations in Canada and the United States as well as major investments in Canada, the United Kingdom and Continental Europe.
>
> ForestCo manages 1.5 million hectares [approximately 5,800 square miles] of productive timberlands which supply most of its fibre requirements. Of these timberlands, one million hectares are in British Columbia where approximately two-thirds of ForestCo's property, plant and equipment, and the company's head office are located.
>
> The products of ForestCo and its affiliated companies which are marketed throughout the world include lumber, panelboards, kraft pulp, newsprint, groundwood printing papers, fine papers, containerboard and corrugated containers.

In 1990, ForestCo's sales were in excess of $3 billion Canadian. Adjusting for differences in Canadian and United States dollars, ForestCo would rank in the top 200 of North America's largest firms. Because of its size, ForestCo is required to adhere to the rules, regulations, and norms that apply to all large business organizations that do business in North America, Europe, and Asia. Its stock is traded publicly, and it raises capital from stock offerings and from debt with international banks. It competes in a global marketplace and is required to develop cooperative relationships with its suppliers and customers. It has thousands of employees—many of whom have moved from, or will move to, other firms. These are some of the reasons that an examination of the ILM processes at ForestCo is likely to reveal attributes similar to those to be found in many other large corporations.

While we believe that our findings regarding the nature of vacancy chains and the operation of ForestCo's ILM may be generalized to those that are likely to exist in other large business firms, there are limits to the generalizations that may be made. The more specific and detailed our descriptions of why specific staffing decisions were made, the less likely it is that those same conditions would apply to other organizations. Investigators of the microprocesses of ILM processes are caught in the reality of social science research. The more details examined in an attempt to find "truth," the less apparent will be the generalizability of the results obtained to other organizations. Nevertheless, at the risk of prejudicing the generalizability of the results found in this investigation, the investigative strategy used here is to provide as much detail as possible regarding the operations and rationale of staffing in ForestCo.

For these reasons, the following sections present a relatively detailed examination of ForestCo's history together with descriptions of more recent events that have shaped ForestCo's current operating philosophies.

Origins and Traditions

The man who founded ForestCo was appointed as the first Chief Forester of British Columbia in 1912. Having acquired detailed knowledge of the resource base of softwood

---

*The identity of ForestCo is not secret. However, as I wish to develop a generalized view of staffing and ILM operation, I refrain from specifically identifying ForestCo and naming the persons in its cast of characters. Nevertheless, ForestCo had a unique history, and I am indebted to Donald MacKay, who chronicled the origins and development of this fascinating company. In this chapter, I quote extensively from his major reference on ForestCo. I recommend that readers who wish to study additional particulars of ForestCo refer to his book, *Empire of Wood* (MacKay, 1982).

lumber in British Columbia, the ForestCo founder left government service in 1916 to gain lumber production experience with a firm that was then one of the province's largest lumber producers. After three years of hard but frustrating work as a manager with insufficient authority, the founder formed his own company in 1919, and this company eventually grew to become ForestCo.

Initially based on the production and export of lumber through the 1920s and 1930s, ForestCo prospered and grew in sales, profits, and dominance of the British Columbia forestry industry. It bought out other lumber mills, built its own pulp mill in 1947, merged with the second-largest firm in the industry in 1951, and in 1960 merged with another firm that was then the province's foremost papermaker. The resulting corporate entity, though now much expanded, is the clear progenitor of the modern corporation that is ForestCo today.

While ForestCo today has all the trappings of a modern corporation, it is still firmly rooted in the strong, tough requirements of harvesting trees from the forest. The men who excelled at taking 200-foot trees and "bucking" them into 2-ton, 40-foot lengths for transportation and processing at the mill had to be physically and mentally tough. While these tasks are much easier now that fallers use high-powered saws, and the "highballing" of logs to a landing at 600 feet a minute is no longer practiced, strength, agility, and skill remain part of the pride in the craft of the woodlands crews. No doubt tough conditions required tough workers who in turn required tough bosses (MacKay, 1982, p. 199):

> In the old days the fallers were pretty tough people, so their "bull bucker" boss had to be even tougher, like the camp push, or foreman. Quite often the only way you ruled the camp was with your fists.

Tough bosses in the woods and tough bosses in the mills need tough bosses in the offices that sell the products of their endeavors. ForestCo is no exception, as its "buccaneer" founder was a match for anyone who worked in his company's operations.

The Imprint of the Founder

A description of ForestCo's history would be incomplete without consideration of the personality and role of its founder—associated for more than 50 years with the company that continues to bear his name. His personality and management style were so strong that echoes of his influence can still be traced to values and styles in today's organization—most notably in the patterns and styles of executive succession. In this, ForestCo is considered to be little different from other organizations that have grown under the aegis of a strong founder (Levinson & Rosenthal, 1984). Through their reactions to critical incidents and organizational crises, founders and subsequent organizational leaders model what they believe is important for organizational survival and success (Schein, 1990). Operationally, the things founders and leaders pay attention to, measure, and control, including the means used to accomplish goals, such as reward systems, organizational structure, and methods of staffing, reflect the cultural paradigm presumed to diffuse through the corporation from its initial formation in the founder's head (Schein, 1993). Founders and CEOs are the primary repositories of corporate cultures, the beliefs and values that guide managerial actions—especially those related to the development of senior managers and the management of executive succession (Gitlow, 1992). For these reasons, the role of ForestCo's founder is presented in some detail.

Insight into the founder's values can be found in an 11-page memorandum he wrote in the late 1950s in which he reflected on his experiences with ForestCo. In these personal observations, he summarized what he thought he had learned after more than 50 years in the industry and having built one of the largest forestry firms in North America:

Some lessons learned
1) Could be summarized: analyze/organize/deputize/supervise/energize and, if necessary, *excise*
2) Failure in any one of these steps weakens or ruins the enterprise.
   a) If anyone fails in these essential practices, correct quickly with best possible judgment.
   b) ForestCo is a living entity—protect it from infection by those ills that weaken so many businesses, [which] were liquidated by creditors or estates sold to newcomers or to stronger competitors.
   The universal reason for end of the original corporate life [of ForestCo's potential competitors] was failure to select, train and test succession in management.

In later sections of this memorandum, the founder elaborates further on the principles, "the fruit of hindsight and experiences in various organizations" that guided his management philosophy. Surprisingly, given his reputation as a "timber baron," these 15 principles spell out prescriptions for human resource practices in considerable detail. These principles appear in the Appendix at the end of this chapter.

The strongest impressions of the founder in action come from others who worked in his shadow. For example, the first person, other than the founder, to be President of ForestCo commented wistfully some years later (MacKay, 1982, p. 179):

When I was President, in point of fact I was really only executive vice-president and [the founder] was still really the President. When I became Chairman of the Board, well, I was Chairman in name. [The founder] wanted to know everything that went on.

When this President, an ex-army major general, attempted to assert his authority, he trod on the toes of a man accustomed to doing what he wanted. As President of ForestCo, the heir apparent requested members of the finance and policy committee of the board to "refrain from visiting company operations without informing managers they were coming." This request did not sit well with the founder, as he had "been fond of arriving unannounced at some mill or logging operation, and thought nothing of it. It was after all *his* company, and he was angry at the suggestion that he should change his old habits" (MacKay, 1982, p. 180). Not surprisingly, while the founder was still a member of the finance and policy committee, the heir apparent was asked to resign shortly thereafter when profits showed a significant decline.

With no internal candidate capable of standing up to the founder, a new Chairman and CEO was handpicked by the founder and brought in from outside. This man, an ex-justice of the British Columbia Supreme Court, remained as CEO of ForestCo for the next 15 years. A story reported in *Macleans* magazine shortly after the new CEO was appointed captures the flavor of his boardroom style (MacKay, 1982, p. 265):

The $300,000-plus men who help him run the country's biggest forest products firm always arrive a few minutes early for Friday's meetings. They sit around the long boardroom table, lounging or chatting or shuffling papers like lawyers getting ready for a long day in court. Then, at precisely 10:30, the master of ForestCo, strides into the boardroom. No one calls, "Order in the court!" and there is no magisterial swirl of black robes as he takes his place at the head of the long table, but the whiff of authority is unmistakable. Suddenly, everyone sits a little straighter. The conversations fade and there is no more shuffling as the CEO settles his large frame, gazes at his assembled vice-presidents and department heads, gives a prim smile, and asks, "Gentlemen, shall we begin?" They do begin, instantly, and some of the things they talk about could affect the pocket books of several hundred thousand people…a flap in the provincial cabinet, or a bellicose roar from 100 union halls.

One also wonders whether the founder's style has influenced present methods of performance evaluation—perhaps as a reaction to, rather than a continuation of, that past style. If the founder was daunting to executives, he was often larger than life to other employees. One manager reported (MacKay, 1982, p. 161):

> I think [the founder] frightened most people when they met him, particularly if they were working for him, because he was such a strong character, and this was obvious from his speech, his manner and his piercing expression.

Another executive recalled the founder (MacKay, 1982, p. 150):

> He was very warm-hearted, but he covered it. He was sometimes very ruthless, very hard. He would call some of his people in and give them a dressing down which they would never forget, but it didn't last long.

Even when he no longer had a formal role in the operations of the company, the founder would grill employees he encountered in the elevator. If he was dissatisfied with an employee's answers, he would then urge that that employee be dismissed.

Consistent with his relationships with ForestCo employees, the founder operated a functional organizational structure that relied on centralized command. This organizational form continued for many years under the direction of his handpicked successor. As ForestCo developed multiple product lines, however, there was insufficient coordination among various interdependent departments. A review by the consulting firm of McKinsey and Company in 1962 found 57 separate units reporting to the CEO. These units were subsequently rationalized into four production groups: wood products, including lumber, shingle, and plywood mills; pulp and paper mills; logging; and the converting group that produced containerboard and packaging. However, the customs and habits learned over a generation of centralized management could not be changed merely by a change in structure. Five years later, a further survey by McKinsey "revealed a lack of understanding of company objectives among middle management, superintendents and foremen. Even top-level executives felt it necessary to check daily on what was being done in the mills" (MacKay, 1982, p. 71).

The centralized management also meant that mergers did not always proceed smoothly. The 1960 merger between ForestCo and the largest paper manufacturing firm in the province became a case in point. The contrast in management styles between the two firms is partially captured by the following quotation from the staff lawyer for the paper firm (MacKay, 1982, p. 232):

> [The president of the paper firm] ran a happy ship. He did it on personal charm. His family would know the name of every employee, the name of his wife and children and how they were. It was a warm, friendly relationship. [The founder's] style was the exact opposite. He was for terseness of language almost to the point of obscurity. His style was to put a good man in the job and ride the hell out of him.

The paper company had "a decentralized, easy-going business approach" that was no match for ForestCo's "tough, highly centralized machine," and as a consequence the merger was "painful, frustrating and disillusioning." The initial board of directors following the merger comprised of 32 representatives—16 from each company. Within two years, however, all but one of the representatives of the paper firm were gone, with bitter recriminations being expressed by the losing side. In a public letter to ForestCo's CEO, the past president of the paper firm announced his resignation from ForestCo's board and complained (MacKay, 1982, p. 237):

> Your prejudiced attitude and actions since the amalgamation, contrary to all our under-
> standings, leave me no alternative but to conclude that I can be of no further use to ForestCo
> while you remain as chairman of its board of directors.

The founder's personality and style were appropriate for the growth of a major forest products firm in the first two thirds of this century. While his imprint remains in the traditions, values, and culture of today's modern corporation, many past practices and operating assumptions are being challenged by current conditions. ForestCo therefore represents a contemporary site in which staffing actions are framed by both traditional values and the demands of modern society.

Evolution of a Modern Corporation

The decade of the 1970s was a time of transition as ForestCo attempted to develop a less centralized organization and also experimented unsuccessfully with diversification away from its traditional base in the forest products industry. Executive succession contin- ued to be problematic for ForestCo, as the founder's successor postponed his retirement, and senior executives who had been brought in from other corporations were often frustrated in their expectations for executive authority. In the middle of the decade, attempts to reduce the dependence of the company on the cyclical nature of the forest products industry led it into various programs of diversification. These experiments were not successful, however, and ForestCo's financial performance took a severe downturn. In April 1976, the President and CEO, as well as the Chairman and CFO, who together had been primarily responsible for these ventures, were asked to resign in what the *Financial Times* (April 5, 1976) called "the greatest bloodletting in Vancouver's corporate history."

Executive succession at the senior levels of ForestCo was finally resolved later that year when a new President and CEO was appointed from outside the corporation. This appointment of an experienced forestry executive reflected a return to the traditions and roots of ForestCo—namely, the production and marketing of forest products. However, the new CEO also brought a different perspective to ForestCo. His management style was characterized as being that of a "team man" whose strengths lay in finance, international operations, and the American market. Both symbolically and in actual practice, the new CEO brought more "modern" and sophisticated management practices to ForestCo. These practices, especially the use of planning and management teams to coordinate and inte- grate operations, began to modify the traditions and historical perspectives of the require- ments for executive success. Most notably, the next two CEOs to be appointed were men who had developed their careers within ForestCo rather than being appointees from outside the corporation.

One of the new CEO's first actions was to counteract the old centralist tendencies he found in the past management system (MacKay, 1982, p. 318):

> I found a basically capable management group who had no leader and who did not
> communicate well with each other because they never had. The management style had been
> for the chief executive officer to communicate separately with each of the people reporting to
> him. Each had run his own sector subject to the CEO, who was at the hub of the wheel. The
> spokes went out in different directions, and as a result not one of the those persons really had
> much knowledge of what the others were doing.
>   One of the most important things I did was to develop a management team. I established
> an operating committee as well as a senior management committee. The senior management
> committee consisted of myself and senior operating and administrative managers, seven of
> us. It was set up to deal with questions of major policy and direction…in meetings, for two or
> three days twice a year…where we would review sales forecasts, capital budgeting forecasts,

the wood fibre balance for British Columbia, and so forth. That way all senior managers had a perspective of the total business and we got a chance to see opportunities for trade-offs among the groups to improve the bottom line. Prior to that everyone was operating in a separate compartment.

In many respects, the attempts at increased integration were successful. ForestCo was able to gradually improve its economic performance so that in 1979 it reported record sales and profits.

Discontinuity, Catastrophe, and Trauma

In 1980, extraordinarily high interest rates in the United States had begun to depress housing starts and demand for ForestCo's lumber. Because ForestCo was able to maintain sales of pulp, paper, and packaging, the company still recorded its second-best year ever despite a 27% decline in annual earnings. However, before the full effect of the large world recession was fully registered, ForestCo's identity as British Columbia's premier business corporation was to be radically changed.

While ForestCo's founder was still alive, it was clear who owned and controlled the company. But after the founder's withdrawal from active participation in the management of his company in the mid-1960s, control became diffused through various trusts, public share ownerships, and stock swaps undertaken for increased access to timberlands. For example, four representatives of a large Canadian conglomerate sat on ForestCo's board as a consequence of the conglomerate's purchase of ForestCo shares in exchange for cutting rights on old railroad grant lands. When ForestCo attempted to buy another forestry firm in 1978, and was resisted by a reverse takeover, the conglomerate got into the game and attempted to gain control of ForestCo. Ownership and control remained with ForestCo, however, when this proposed takeover was publicly resisted by the provincial premier with the headlined declaration that "BC is not for sale." The implication of the premier's assertion was that the conglomerate ran the risk of losing ForestCo's major asset—access to the prime timber resources available on publicly owned lands.

Seemingly secure in early 1981, ForestCo's management was unprepared for a second, and much larger and complex, financial battle for control of the company. This time, the provincial premier declined to protect the company from potential takeovers and ForestCo's management was able to do little to prevent a large Toronto-based Canadian conglomerate, with businesses in forestry products, mining, metallurgy, and natural gas, from buying a controlling interest in ForestCo's shares. Moreover, as a result of accommodations worked out when the Canadian conglomerate itself was the target of a takeover bid later that year, financial control was diffused even further. A financial holding company based in Montreal obtained a major, if not controlling, interest in the Toronto-based conglomerate, which now controlled ForestCo. ForestCo was no longer an independent and autonomous British Columbia corporation. Its character was still rooted in its heritage of the forests of British Columbia—but its strategic decisions from now on were more in line with the impersonal economics of the international marketplace.

Perhaps because the attention of ForestCo's management was focused on these issues of ownership and financial control, the worsening national and international economic situation was not fully acknowledged until later that year. In 1980 and early 1981, the extent of the looming world recession was not readily visible. By mid-1981, however, there were indications that the recession in the industry was the worst since the depression of the 1930s. In the face of plummeting prices, as well as a six-week strike, ForestCo's building materials group, together with its supporting raw materials group, posted an operating loss of $82 million. Profits from pulp and paper and a one-time cash infusion from the sale of one of its mills enabled ForestCo to break even with a nominal profit of $3.3 million for the year. However, clear disaster loomed ahead for 1982, and ForestCo scrambled to develop a "managing for survival" policy. Specific actions included multiple mill closings, layoffs of 8000 hourly employees, large reductions in administrative and managerial staff, salary and dividend cuts, and drastic reductions in capital expenditures. At the same time, major efforts were made to increase overall productivity through changes in machines, processes, and work practices.

Concurrent with these short-term reactions were longer-term changes in policy. As the CEO commented in late 1981 (MacKay, 1982, p. 343):

> The dramatic changes in the economic environment have forced ForestCo management to view the company from a very different perspective. Aided by the major economic shifts of the past year or so we are now able to see clearly that the ForestCo of the last decade— however appropriate the structure, policies and decisions for that period—must be re-formed, with contemporary directions and policies. That is essential if we are to flourish in the changed conditions we see evolving in the western world.

What is not evident from a clinical assessment of ForestCo's short-term survival tactics is the confusion, guilt, and trauma experienced by the managers who survived the "holocaust" of 1981–1982. ForestCo was not, and is not at present, an impersonal corporation. Personal relationships typified relations among managers and between supervisors and subordinates. While hard times had been experienced in the past, no previous downturn had ever been as deep or as lengthy as the one experienced in the recession of 1981–1982 and the recovery to 1986. Moreover, in the previous 50 years, ForestCo and its organizational ancestors had built mills and plants close to its supply of timber. The communities that developed to support these mills and to house and support these mill workers, supervisors, and managers were single-industry towns that were completely dependent on the economics of the forest products industry. Within these communities, it was not uncommon for whole families to be employed at the local mill. Community involvement was a natural extension of ForestCo's paternalistic style. In 1978, when one of ForestCo's pioneers died, the sentiment expressed was that ForestCo had an "obligation as a corporate citizen [to] play a significant part in the economic and social affairs of the communities where it operates" (MacKay, 1982, p. 324). As the industry rapidly declined in 1981 and 1982, however, managers were required to fire close colleagues, friends, and neighbors with the clear appreciation that if these skilled employees who had been fired remained in their communities, there would be no employment possibilities for them. Complicating all this as the recession deepened and showed no signs of upturn was the often realistic fear of the managers doing the firing that they themselves could soon be fired as well.

While ForestCo had experienced a previous financial crisis, namely, a reported loss of $18.9 million in 1975, the experience of 1981–1982 was far more catastrophic. First, the level of financial loss was much greater, as ForestCo reported a loss of $57.3 million in 1982. Second, the experience of the recession was far more widespread and far more devastating for individual incomes, employees' careers, family viability, and community health. Many fired employees found that they could not readily leave their community because housing prices plummeted and they were therefore left with no way to raise capital to support a move elsewhere. Moreover, most employees had industry-specific skills at a time when the whole industry was downsizing. Although managers attempted to rationalize their actions to help ForestCo survive, they knew they were participating in decisions and actions that would violate almost every principle they had understood to represent the core values of their corporation. Obligations to subordinates, to fellow managers, to friends, to neighbors, and to their own sense of worth were broken. For many managers, personal reactions to these situations were traumatic and visceral. Even eight years later, when managers were interviewed about the contextual factors they considered in making a staffing decision, recollections of the recession in 1981–1982 remained vivid in their memories and made their actions cautious. Collectively, they had no wish to re-create the organizational conditions that could cause them to relive those experiences.

At the time of the 1981–1982 crisis, a major policy change was undertaken to restructure ForestCo from a production orientation into a more integrated form. This new integrated structure has remained in effect through the remainder of the decade—including the period during which this investigation of ForestCo's ILM was undertaken. The primary change was the establishment of three large regional units that were to operate as vertically integrated production units, each "responsible for harvesting its own timber and for converting that timber into end products in its own mills" (MacKay, 1982, p. 343). In addition to these units, ForestCo retained a large marketing division that also had specialty manufacturing operations; a fifth operating unit, that of the Containerboard and Packaging Group, which had its headquarters in the southern United States; various smaller specialty divisions; and a corporate office. Ancillary to these primary units, several smaller units provided operational support through groups such as Research and Development, Corporate Forestry, and Raw Materials Services. This overall structure influenced both the orientations and the interaction patterns among employees of different divisions. In doing so, it structured and differentiated the employment system that constituted ForestCo's ILM.

Specialty skills associated with different technologies also influenced the form of ForestCo's ILM. The three regional divisions had as their primary orientation the harvesting and processing of timber into various products, and each contained manufacturing plants that used both similar and different technologies. For example, all three regions had plants that produced market pulp and plants that produced lumber products. Two regions also had plants that produced paper products and a different two regions had plants that produced specialty products. The technology of pulp and paper manufacturing is a continuous-process technology, requiring skills different from those used in the large-batch or mass-production technology of a lumber mill. However, different orientations and skills could also be required by nominally similar plants. A paper mill that produces newsprint requires different skills and orientations than does a paper mill that produces fine paper. A sawmill that produces a standard timber commodity requires different skills and orientations than does a sawmill that produces high value-added, specialty lumber. Although there were some differences in the skills required by different regional divisions, there is little evidence of an external technological imperative to suggest that skills developed in one region would not be applicable in other regions. For example, from an occupational perspective, all three regional divisions employed plant supervisors and managers, engineers, accountants, and other professionals.

Recovery and Renewal

Almost unnoticed in the still-dismal economic news of 1983 were two items concerning executive succession. The CEO of the past eight years formally passed the baton of corporate direction to a younger man, a ForestCo manager of long standing. The founder's ghost no doubt still occupied the thoughts of ForestCo executives—but his dominant presence had been diminished by the financial takeover and the fight for economic survival of the past two years. In contrast to the autocracy of the founder and his handpicked successor, the third CEO's capacity for teamwork and his introduction of a more professional management system finally produced an in-house executive capable of directing this large corporation.

Recovery from the 1981–1982 recession was difficult and long. Low levels of profit were reported in each of the next three years, but amounts were still well below those reported in the period 1978–1980. However, ForestCo finally reported record profits in the three years immediately prior to the conduct of this study. As interviews were conducted over a two-year period, from late 1988 to 1990, ForestCo's profits declined modestly in 1989 from the records established in 1988 and fell markedly in 1990. Thus, at the time of our investigations, the economic context of ForestCo's ILM was that of a firm in a cyclical industry moving past a peak of profitability.

Both before, and most certainly after, the 1981–1982 recession, there had been a long-term trend for ForestCo to increase the efficiency of its operations. This trend resulted in increases in output being obtained with significant reductions in both direct and indirect costs. Ignoring the large "temporary" reductions in employment over the 1981–1982 recession, there has been a significant and long-term reduction in ForestCo's workforce. The total number of hourly workers employed by ForestCo was reduced from approximately 18,000 in 1975 to about 12,000 in 1990. Similarly, the number of salaried employees was reduced from approximately 5000 in 1975 to fewer than 3500 in 1990. Thus, although total output and its associated dollar value have increased, there has been a consistent pressure to reduce the numbers of both hourly workers and salaried administrative, professional, and managerial employees in the corporation.

At present, ForestCo can be characterized appropriately as a traditional firm in a mature industry. There have been relatively few technological advances in the production of lumber products and the manufacturing of paper in the past 50 years. The supply of trees has become marginally less accessible, but systems of transportation from logging operations to mills have become marginally more efficient. The only new advance of potential but still largely unrealized importance is the development of technologically advanced materials in which wood fibers are reconstituted into high-quality lumber products. For the most part, change has come about because of overall economic conditions—not because radically different ways of doing business have been required.

A significant threat to the traditional ways of the forest industry has recently emerged through public concerns for the environment. Because almost all of ForestCo's fiber supply comes from timber growing on public land, environmentalists have increasingly challenged ForestCo's land use policies. Substantial stands of old-growth timber have been removed from ForestCo's control. ForestCo's access to other stands of timber in ecologically sensitive areas has also come under challenge, and there is a long-term threat of a significant reduction in ForestCo's source of wood fiber.

THE ADMINISTRATIVE FRAME FOR FORESTCO'S INTERNAL LABOR MARKET

One way of thinking about corporate ILMs is to use the metaphor of a climbing frame (what is called a "jungle gym" in the United States). In this perspective, "organizational career logics can be thought of as the shape of the climbing frame over which managers make their careers" (Gunz, 1989, p. 44). The climbing frame can be thought of as the basic shape(s) of the firm's ILM and the ways in which various parts relate to each other. A significant component of such a climbing frame is the structure of the organization that comprises the ILM. Typically, organizations group together administrative units that share either expertise or products and markets, and within each unit there are further groupings of employees whose performances are interdependent. These interdependencies shape the knowledge and skills required in organizational positions. Employees in positions proximate to one that becomes vacant, especially those in positions that are immediately subordinate to the vacated position, often have both the detailed knowledge of the job requirements and the skills required for assignment to that position. In addition, the personal capacities of these employees under a variety of organizational conditions are usually well known to those seeking to staff the vacant position. Thus, "local" employees are often advantaged as candidates for positions that become vacant. For these reasons, it is anticipated that subcomponents of ForestCo's ILM are likely to be influenced by the overall groupings of administrative units.

Administrative Structures

As described previously, the primary structural form of ForestCo consists of three vertically integrated regional units: a marketing and distribution division, a container-board and packaging division, and a corporate unit to provide overall direction and coordination. Within each of these major divisions, several subdivisions also influence how activities are organized and grouped. In the case of regional units, these subdivisions correspond to specific plants and mills. For the units attached to corporate headquarters and the marketing group, subdivisions correspond to functional specialties and to geo-graphic units, respectively. For salaried employees, these subdivisional forms are impor-tant, as they often define a small administrative, supervisory, and managerial ILM through which midtier supervisors and managers can advance before reaching senior manage-ment or executive status.

At the time managers were interviewed regarding how they staffed vacant positions, there were 68 divisional subunits spread across the larger structural groupings described previously. Table 2.1 shows the distribution of *salaried* employees by the numbers assigned to these subunits at the end of 1989. As the table shows, 3 divisional subunits had more than 300 salaried employees, and 11 subunits had more than 100 salaried employees.

Table 2.1. Distribution of
Salaried Employees by Divisional
Subunit in 1989

Number of salaried employees in the subunit	Number of subunits
0–9	10
10–19	9
20–34	21
35–49	10
50–99	7
100–299	8
≥300	3

Further, 50 subunits had fewer than 50 salaried employees, with almost half these 50 subunits having 20 or more but fewer than 35 similarly compensated employees.

One consequence of this distribution was that most of ForestCo's salaried employees worked in relatively autonomous ILM subunits. Considerations of staffing effectiveness and efficiency suggest that divisional subunits with more than 50 employees, and certainly those with 100 or more, should be able to find a minimal number of qualified internal candidates for most of the non-entry-level positions likely to become vacant. These candidates should be familiar with the responsibilities of the vacant position and possess the knowledge and skills required for acceptable levels of job performance. Consequently, candidate searches outside each of the larger divisional subunits, unless local considerations indicate otherwise, are unlikely to yield candidates significantly better than those already available inside that division. Moreover, as searches outside a divisional subunit are likely to cost more in time and effort, and also are unlikely to uncover candidates about whom as much is known, or is known with the same degree of confidence, as is known about internal candidates, ForestCo's overall ILM is likely to show moderately strong patterns of job mobility within each medium-to-large-size division.

Geographical Separation

A second feature of ForestCo's divisional structure that is likely to have an impact on the operation of its overall ILM is that of the geographic location of its various divisions and plants. Mobility from one job to another will be facilitated or hindered by the degree of geographic dispersion among similar jobs (Gunz, 1989). All three regional headquarters are moderately close to each other. Two regional organizations have their head offices in towns on Vancouver Island located about 50 miles apart. The third region has its headquarters located in a coastal town approximately 150 miles north of Vancouver. All three regional divisions, together with several service units, as well as the Marketing Division and Corporate Management, are located in a geographic area that stretches approximately 250 miles to the west and northwest of the city of Vancouver. Although these are relatively short distances, the rugged nature of the west coast of British Columbia means that many of these operations are psychologically removed from the influence of headquarters. Certainly, transportation involving seaplanes or ferries is far more difficult here than would be the case for a typical United States corporation with headquarters in New York City and branch plants in New Jersey. If travel were not by private aircraft, the driving and ferry travel time between Headquarters and Regional Offices would be at least four or five hours.

It is anticipated that the moderate geographic separation of ForestCo's divisions is likely to reinforce the local focus within each of the three regional units. First, some employees develop strong attachments to the communities they live in. They express preferences for either urban or rural locations and the lifestyles associated with these communities. Second, the differences in living costs, especially the high cost of housing in city and urban locations compared to that in small towns, restrict the inflow of skilled and experienced employees from rural areas. However, not every employee necessarily wants to stay in one location all his or her working life. Family considerations, especially those associated with suitable educational opportunities for children about to enter high school, often lead employees to request transfers to work sites compatible with family demands. Thus, while personal and organizational considerations appear to be mutually reinforcing with respect to the development of localized patterns in the selection and assignment of most salaried personnel, idiosyncratic preferences are also likely to be accommodated in this mildly paternalistic employment system.

Personnel and Salary Administration

Although each primary operating unit within ForestCo is relatively autonomous, the units are not independent. They share and potentially compete for financial resources, they exchange products and services, and— most important for the purposes of this analysis—their salaried employees are jointly administered through a corporate personnel system. Although ForestCo's employees may develop skills and knowledge that reinforce attachments to particular operating units or geographic areas, collectively they are not considered to belong solely to each separate unit. Instead, their primary employee identity derives from their employment by the corporation as a whole.

One of the primary mechanisms through which employees are attached to ForestCo, rather than to a specific division, is through a corporate-wide system of staffing and salary administration. ForestCo operates a traditional system of salary administration—keeping hourly payrolls separate from those of salaried employees. Salaried employees work at jobs that are assigned to "grades," with the lowest being salary grade "2" and the highest in the high 20s. These grades can be considered to fall into four general occupational groups: Secretarial and Clerical for grades 2–5; Administrative and Technical for grades 6–10; Professional and Managerial for grades 11–15; and Senior Management and Executive for grades 16 and above. These titles are used as convenient labels for the purposes of this study, as there were few obvious employment conditions requisite to an employee's membership in any of these large occupational groups.

As with most salary systems, a salary range was associated with each salary grade and there was substantial overlap of these ranges for adjacent salary grades. Thus, the same salary could be paid to several different employees who held different salary grades. For example, in the lowest of these overlapping salary grades, the employee receiving a particular salary could be at the upper end of the range associated with that salary grade. In the highest of these overlapping salary grades, the employee receiving a particular salary could be at the lower end of the range associated with that salary grade. Thus, two employees could receive the same salary even though one could be as many as four or five salary grades higher than the other. Similarly, different employees working at jobs with identical salary grades could receive different salaries as a function of their positions in the salary range for that salary grade. Thus, the job classification, that is, the salary grade, of a particular position or job was not rigidly linked to the immediate salary level associated with that job.

One consequence of this system of salary grades was that ForestCo's managers had considerable flexibility in managing the assignment of different employees to different jobs and arranging the salary rewards associated with those assignments. While formal job evaluation procedures provided general guidelines as to which grade a job should be assigned, the actual evaluation of a job was often dependent on the manner in which that job was collectively defined and individually performed. Thus, the assignment of an employee to a particular job or position was usually accompanied by an assignment of both a monthly salary and a salary grade. Determination of a salary grade also established the top of the salary range for that job as long as that job continued to be assessed at that salary grade. Thus, fine control of rewards and incentives was obtained by setting substantive rewards such as monthly salary, with incentives for further performance coming from increases in salary while in the same position. Symbolic rewards could also be derived from the salary grade of the position, and the possibility of even more incentives and rewards could be obtained from either subsequent promotions to positions associated with higher salary grades or promotions occurring because the current position was regraded. This flexibility often meant that normally unambiguous employment concepts such as the notion of a "promotion" could occasionally become problematic. For example, a move of an employee from one position to another could be associated with either an increase or a decrease in salary grade with no change in monthly salary. Under this system, it was also possible for an employee to receive an increase in salary and a decrease in salary grade or, even more problematically, a decrease in salary and an increase in salary grade.

While managers actively used this local flexibility to direct the human resources under their control, they nevertheless worked within the structure of the larger distribution of jobs by salary grade that existed for the whole corporation. Thus, a further critical feature of the ForestCo ILM associated with the administration of its staffing and salary system concerns the distribution of jobs by level. Figure 2.1 shows the distribution of salaried employees at ForestCo by their salary grades. As can be seen, the bulk of ForestCo's salaried employees have middle-level salary grades, with 80% of these employees assigned to salary grades 6–15, that is, to the two middle occupational groups: Administrative and Technical, salary grades 6–10, and Managerial and Professional, salary grades 11–15. Approximately 10% of salaried employees are assigned to each of the two groups that occupy the lower (Secretarial and Clerical, salary grades 2–5) and the higher (Senior Management and Executive, salary grades ≥ 16) occupational groups of the organizational hierarchy. A more detailed inspection of the distribution of employees by salary grade also shows that grades 10–14 are the most-used salary grades, with 46% of all salaried employees being assigned to these grades.

The distribution of employees by salary grade has a strong influence over patterns of career mobility in organizations (Stewman & Konda, 1983). Because of the interdepen-

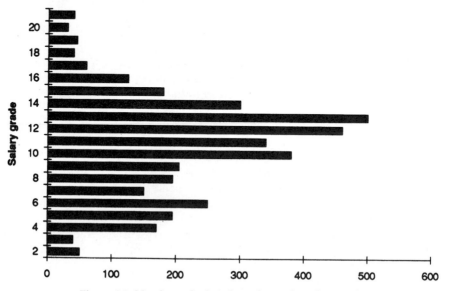

Figure 2.1. Numbers of salaried employees by salary grade.

dency of stocks and flows, stable distributions of employees by age (and hence experience) and grade can be obtained only by a limited range of flows of employees into, through, and out of the employment system. In particular, if lower grades are regarded as a primary source for vacancies in higher grades, and vacancies occur in approximate proportion to the numbers of persons in each grade, then the grade ratio (i.e., the number of employees in each higher grade over the number in each lower grade) represents a partial indicator of relative mobility in organizational hierarchies. Thus, if ForestCo were considered as a single ILM rather than many sub-ILMs partially bounded by operating unit and occupational considerations, movement up the salary system to grade 13, the most frequent grade, would be associated with grade ratios greater than 1. Movement beyond grade 13 would be associated with grade ratios less than 1. Up to grade 13, there are generally more jobs at each higher grade than at the one immediately below. Thus, if all but lower-level positions were to be filled from lower grades, career progression up to grade 13 would be substantially enhanced. On the other hand, the reverse of this effect operates for grades above grade 13. Here, there are fewer jobs at each higher grade, causing a smaller vacancy rate and hence less opportunity for persons in lower grades to be promoted to higher grades.

However, the validity of any inferences about relative promotion prospects drawn from these observations about different grade ratios at different levels of the organizational hierarchy depends on the critical assumption of a uniform ILM within ForestCo's employment system. Because of the divisionalized structure previously described, there is unlikely to be such a uniform ILM. Moreover, the consequences of grade ratios for career progression also depend on the rates at which positions are filled by candidates who enter from the ELM. Even though features of the grade system, such as the grade ratios greater than 1 up to salary grade 13, indicate enhanced promotion prospects for employees below grade 13, this consequence holds only if vacancies are not filled from the ELM to a larger offsetting extent. Thus, although grade ratios are suggestive, their net effects cannot be determined until other characteristics of ForestCo's ILM have been examined.

ForestCo's Policies and Procedures

As a starting point for a discussion of staffing practices at ForestCo, the formal corporate policies that guide the recruitment, retention, and promotion of salaried personnel are presented in Table 2.2.

The policies that nominally governed staffing practices during 1988–1990, the period during which managers and supervisors were interviewed, were originally issued in 1962.

Table 2.2. ForestCo's Policy Statement on Staffing

The Company recognizes the need to develop its employees and to make known the opportunities for advancement within the Company so that each employee has an opportunity to seek out and realize individual career goals.

The Company will fill position vacancies by promoting individuals from within the Company whenever qualified candidates are available.

External candidates will not be considered unless:

a) the position has been circulated internally and no suitable candidate has been identified, or
b) Personnel Planning & Development has knowledge of the vacancy and knows there to be no suitable candidates and therefore approves external consideration.

These general corporate policies provide the background and framework within which specific interpretations and emphases were added as circumstances warranted. As presented in Table 2.2, ForestCo's overall policy regarding the staffing of salaried positions clearly appears to approximate classic ILM requirements. Position vacancies are to be filled "by promoting individuals from within the Company. ..." There also appears to be strong support given to posting as the preferred process for filling vacancies, as the policy emphasizes the need "to make known the opportunities for advancement" and that external candidates not be considered unless notice of vacant positions "has been circulated internally." Although any specific policy needs to be interpreted in light of other management policies and its execution assessed in terms of managerial actions, an examination of this policy statement by itself reveals no direct concern for corporate objectives other than those implied by the use of the terms "qualified candidates" and "suitable candidate." Indeed, as with any general policy statement, one might wonder whether this policy statement has any material effect on staffing actions, as the terms "qualified" and "suitable" have no independent, operational definition. Nevertheless, the overt intent of ForestCo's policy on staffing is clearly consistent with the stereotypical models of ILM operation described in Chapter 1.

Implementation of ForestCo's overall policy on staffing was accomplished through various procedures—especially those dealing with promotion and transfer as presented in Table 2.3. Several features of this procedure are of potential interest. First, ForestCo makes a relatively clear distinction between positions that are subject to the posting "requirements" and those that are not. In particular, assignments to senior-level positions were viewed as being under greater managerial control than those below. Vacant positions in the general occupational groupings of Secretarial and Clerical (salary grades 2–5), Administrative and Technical (salary grades 6–10), and most of those in Professional and Managerial (salary grades 11–15), subject to various qualifications, are expected to be posted. Only positions at the highest grade of Professional and Managerial (salary grade 15) and those in Senior Management and Executive ranks (salary grades 16 and above) were normally not required to be posted.

Second, despite the aforestated policy, positions were not expected to be posted in those areas of the company in which a subsequent relocation of an employee would be too costly. Implicitly, this qualification regarding the application of general corporate procedures acknowledges other costs that might be associated with a wide search for the "best" candidate.

Table 2.3. ForestCo's Policy Statement on Promotions and Transfers

PROCEDURE: Promotion and Transfer within the Company

Supervisors will ensure that all position vacancies to the level of Salary Group 14 are circulated. Reasonable judgment should be used in circumstances where circulation beyond the immediate geographical area may not be appropriate considering the overall costs involved in relocating employees. Where a fully qualified successor has been clearly identified in Region, Group, or Departmental succession plans, the Employee Relations Manager or Personnel Planning and Development may approve filling positions without posting. Supervisors are strongly encouraged to circulate position vacancies above Salary Group 14 where no obvious successor has been identified. Entry level positions will not require a circular.

Notification of salaried position vacancies to Personnel Planning and Development should include a position description and a list of minimum and preferred qualifications.

Third, these procedures describe more explicitly the conditions under which posting may not be required—for example, in those situations in which "a fully qualified successor has been clearly identified."

Finally, when posting is undertaken, the posting process requires "a position description and a list of minimum and preferred qualifications."

While ForestCo's general policies appear to be consistent with stereotypical models of ILM operation, a more detailed inspection of the firm's procedural guidelines for staffing provides information on practices that stereotypical models ignore. For example, within the general preference for internal candidates typically associated with ILMs, ForestCo's recommended procedures give increased emphasis to market-based practices in which candidates are aware of and compete for vacancies at middle and lower levels of the corporate hierarchy. However, senior-level vacancies are filled through less open procedures in which managerial and administrative judgments are exercised more strongly. Thus, at least two structural partitions can be identified in ForestCo's overall ILM. First, there is a substantial distinction between the terms and conditions in the employment systems for hourly wage earners and salaried personnel. Second, within the salaried employment system, there is an attempt to distinguish between those persons and positions that are subject to competitive, market-based processes and those that are driven by administrative judgments.

Adjustments of Policies to Suit Circumstances

While the policies and procedures presented in Tables 2.2 and 2.3 can be considered to provide the overall policy framework for staffing, particular circumstances could lead ForestCo's management to modify or emphasize different features of these policies as a function of its environmental situation. Thus, the extraordinary recession experienced in the early 1980s led ForestCo to implement changes in the manner in which it staffed positions. Some indication of these changes can be seen in the excerpts from internal memoranda distributed at the time and presented in Table 2.4.

As can be seen, the new policies demanded that managers reduce the numbers of employees in their units by eliminating nonessential work, by consolidating functions, and by keeping only employees whose performance was regarded as satisfactory. Moreover, as employees were retired or "let go," replacements were not to be hired from the ELM, but existing employees were to be retrained and reassigned to crucial vacant positions. Overall, the consequence of these policies was to reduce hirings to a minimum, to significantly increase outflows of employees from the corporation, and to place increased emphasis on internal reassignments.

These policies were followed closely during the hard economic times of the early 1980s, but were relaxed somewhat at the time of this study in the late 1980s. Nevertheless, as documented in later chapters, vestiges of these modifications of general personnel policies were still influential when ForestCo's managers were interviewed about how they staffed positions and why they staffed them the way they did. In fact, as elaborated in Section III, ForestCo's overall policies were interpreted loosely. While these policies provided an overall framework for appreciating the overall staffing system in this firm, managers had much discretion in their specific application.

As the administrative rules that guide staffing at ForestCo are guidelines subject to interpretation by the CEO, they were also modifiable as a function of the circumstances facing each manager. Thus, although there is a general rule that all jobs below salary grade 15 should be posted, posting was not always done for vacant jobs in these lower salary

Table 2.4. Evidence of Shift in Corporate H.R. Practices

---

a) *Memo from President to V.P. Human Resources Oct. 1981 re Key Issues in Head Office Staff Reductions*:

"... must consider some releases of employees whose performance is generally recognized as marginal or worse. ..."

"... when a vacancy occurs ... be absolutely certain a replacement is essential and justified ..."

"... must continue to reach in and ferret out low-activity areas which have not yet been pared down or considered ..."

"... must be willing to undertake some training to make senior employees with good performance acceptable in new positions ..."

"... must consider internal placement priorities to go to employees who have long service and good performance ..."

b) *Memo from President to all Head Office Managers Feb. 1982*:

"... requests for additional staff or replacement staff must be examined more critically ..."

"... need a critical review to reduce or eliminate work which is not essential, or which can be combined with other duties, reduced in scope, simplified, done less often, or temporarily suspended ..."

"... position vacancies which are filled must go to current employees and we must adopt an even stricter promote-from-within policy than has been our practice. ..."

---

grades. Some divisions had clear ideas regarding how their prospective managers should be developed and had well-established lines of progression along which they advanced candidates. In other settings, posting was done reluctantly, as an employee relations manager might "push" the posting rule even though a local line manager might have already identified his preferred candidate. For the most part, staffing was guided by pragmatic considerations, as managers juggled demands for the accomplishment of work, cost reduction, reorganizations, and development and advancement of subordinates, and their appreciation of a need to keep the human resource system moving. The exercise of managerial discretion was facilitated by there being relatively few penalties for line managers' not following regulations. In addition, employee relations representatives were often not directly involved in day-to-day departmental activities, but invariably were aware of the need to balance system-wide concerns for more open staffing with the interests of local managers. Implicit negotiation and bargaining between potentially opposing interests over staffing procedures favored local rather than system-wide concerns. Immediate work performance was regarded as a strong imperative, whereas the integrity of the staffing system was a more amorphous objective.

DATA COLLECTION

The original purpose of this study was to describe the manner in which employees moved into, through, and out of a large business organization. In particular, a deliberate attempt was made to obtain empirical data on staffing actions and vacancy chains as manifestations of ILM processes. This focus on ForestCo was both pragmatic and opportunistic, as ForestCo was a large, local corporation the senior personnel of which were willing to facilitate an examination of their staffing processes by an outside academic.

Three primary data bases were used in this study. First, historical data on the stocks and flows of all salaried employees were compiled from computerized payroll records. Comparisons of consecutive end-of-year records permitted inferences of employee "flows" in the intervening year. For example, if an employee was shown as being employed in the first end-of-year record, but not employed in the second end-of-year record, that employee was assigned a status as an "exit" during the year covered by the two end-of-year records. Similar logical inferences were used to designate "hires" and "promotions." As these records also contained basic demographic information such as gender, date of birth, and original date of hire, as well as divisional assignment and salary grade, these data on employee flows permitted an extensive analysis of aggregate employee stocks and flows both historically and during the time period when interview data were also obtained. These data provide the statistical basis for the system-level analysis of ForestCo's ILM presented later in this chapter.

The second primary form of data acquisition entailed more than 100 interviews with supervisors and managers who had made the staffing decisions that, when linked as antecedent and consequent staffing actions, produced data on attributes of the vacancy chains described in Section II. This data set was analyzed at two levels. As just noted, specific managers were targeted for interview as a means of finding out about specific staffing actions that constituted vacancy chains. In addition, more general assessments of issues and considerations in staffing were compiled. Descriptions and analyses of staffing as a component of ILM operation obtained from these interviews constitute the primary data source of material presented in Section III. A third data set on vacancy chains was also obtained from an examination of archival and ongoing records of changes in employee status. Once the general staffing patterns became familiar to the field researchers, it was possible to identify a substantial number of vacancy chains from archival records alone without corroborating evidence from interviews with the responsible managers. Thus, two sets of vacancy chains were studied: (1) those in which the manager responsible for each staffing actions was interviewed and (2) those vacancy chains identified solely from personnel records.

The procedure used to obtain data on the first set of vacancy chains was identical to that used to obtain information on the details of each staffing action. Over a two-year period, all notices of new appointments made in this corporation were reviewed to identify sets of staffing actions that could be considered to represent vacancy chains. The first few staffing actions identified for further study were chosen at random. From these actions, linkages to other staffing actions were traced both backward and forward to identify vacancies that had either led to or followed from the initial vacancies selected at random. For each staffing action, the manager responsible for the selection decision was identified, and an interview was requested. Initially, an interview protocol was designed to elicit information about a recent staffing action from a pilot sample of those managers who had been responsible for a recent appointment. Approximately a dozen managers who had recently completed a staffing action were interviewed. Information from these interviews was used to develop an understanding of these experiences to learn more about ForestCo's operations and to refine the interview protocol. Once this preliminary work was done, the interview study began with an initial sample of approximately 50 interviews. When these interview were completed, additional appointments and vacancy chains that would provide a representative cross-selection of regions, departments, occupations, and salary grades were sought. A conscious effort was made to sample a wide range of appointment processes in all major divisions and a wide range of mills and plants. In terms of formal sampling theory, the representativeness of this sample for all staffing actions and vacancy chains is unknown. Care was taken, however, to avoid any systematic biases in the selection of staffing actions and vacancy chains that were investigated further through interviews.

Once some initial idea of how a set of appointments constituting a vacancy chain had been obtained, an attempt was made, usually by telephone, to identify the initiating event that had triggered the vacancy chain under study. Often this event would be a higher-level retirement or quit, or occasionally a reorganization or start-up of a new operation. With this information, arrangements were made to interview the manager responsible for the staffing action that led to the first appointment on the subsequent vacancy chain. Almost all managers and supervisors were willing to be interviewed about staffing practices in general and the specific considerations they had taken into account in making the recent, targeted appointment. Interviews generally lasted from 1–2 hours—with many managers being very willing to discuss the staffing dilemmas they faced in managing the units for which they were responsible.

It was not always easy, however, to arrange interviews to find out about how all the staffing actions associated with a particular vacancy chain were readily obtained. Often, it took more than a year to trace long vacancy chains, or even short vacancy chains that were held up or delayed, from initiating to concluding event. At times, a vacancy chain would be traced "backward" to the initiating events that had perhaps occurred more than 12 months previously. At other times, the consequences of an initiating event could be traced to the point at which it was currently being processed, but then the follow-up could wait for several months until these processes yielded a conclusive appointment.

Shortly after the conclusion of each interview, extensive notes taken during the interview were amplified into a taped report that was subsequently transcribed and filed with other supporting information and documentation (e.g., copies of organization charts, copies of job descriptions, copies of posting notices, lists of selection criteria) often provided by the interviewee. After the taped notes from almost all interviews had been transcribed, each interview was coded using the classification scheme described in Chapter 1 (p. 26). The statements classified by this coding process provided the substance of the illustrations of the general concepts on the staffing process presented in Chapters 6 through 10, which document the detailed results from this study of staffing in ForestCo.

A STATISTICAL PORTRAIT OF FORESTCO'S INTERNAL LABOR MARKET

Employee Stocks and Flows

In Chapter 1, it was argued that the primary means of demonstrating an empirically based description of a firm's ILM was in terms of employee stocks and flows. Data from the computerized payroll records described previously were used to track the employee flows that maintained or modified the distribution of salaried employees presented in Figure 2.1.

Stocks of employees in a firm's employment system are maintained and modified by three different employee flows: those into the ILM, those within the ILM, and those out of the ILM. In typical stock–flow models of employment systems, vacancies are considered to originate primarily from "exits," namely, those from the focal ILM to either the ELM, or a different ILM such as the hourly workforce. These vacancies are in turn filled by combinations of "promotions," namely, movements from one salary grade to another within the salaried ILM, and "hires," namely, movements from the ELM or the hourly ILM to full membership in the salaried workforce. Other types of employee mobility are those in which an employee moves from one position to another but within the same salary grade. In this study, because employee mobility was inferred from comparisons of end-of-year data, such lateral moves were not discernible in this system-level analysis. In addition, "demotions" in which employees moved to lower salary grades were not included in this analysis.

Within these constraints, a snapshot of these flows by salary grade for the calendar year 1990 is presented in Table 2.5. In this table, the reference point for each group of salaried employee is their salary grade at the beginning of the year. The number of "Exits" is the number who were no longer employed by year-end. The number of "Hires" is the number who were not working as salaried employees at the beginning of the year but had the designated salary grade status by year-end. The "Outflows" column under "Promotions" lists the number of employees in each salary grade status at the beginning of the year who had a higher salary grade status at year-end. Similarly, the "Inflows" column lists the number of employees who had moved from a lower salary grade status at the beginning of the year to the designated higher salary grade status by year-end.

Table 2.5. 1990 Snapshot of Stocks and Flows
of ForestCo Salaried Employees

Salary grade	Beginning stock	Exits	Hires	Promotions[a]	
				Outflows	Inflows
2	51	8	41	3	0
3	42	13	13	12	0
4	163	25	32	22	3
5	194	35	35	33	23
6	246	37	46	24	28
7	144	17	18	30	27
8	191	29	40	18	28
9	206	22	18	22	19
10	379	40	37	52	27
11	339	23	32	23	43
12	444	36	33	37	27
13	502	36	22	22	41
14	303	14	15	23	23
15	171	16	8	9	22
16	115	11	4	4	15
17	60	7	4	2	5
18	46	3	1	2	3
19	50	3	1	3	4
20	23	0	0	0	2
21	10	0	0	0	1
22	6	0	0	0	0
23	3	1	1	0	0
24	7	0	0	0	0
≥25	13	1	0	2	2
ALL GRADES:	3708	377	401	343	343

[a]Employee flows due to demotions are not included.

Several features of this distribution of employee flows are worthy of comment. First, it can be seen that for almost the entire salaried workforce, there were movements both from and to the ELM for almost all salary grades. Entries into the firm from the ELM occurred for all but the highest salary grades. Clearly, at the employment-system level of analysis, there is no simple "model" of few grade-specific ports of entry underlying the operation of this firm's ILM. The evidence presented here could be consistent with a model of grade-specific ports of entry only if ForestCo's salaried employment system consisted of a wide variety of subsystem ILMs, each having a different port of entry. This is certainly a distinct possibility, as there are many specialist occupations employed in a large corporation such as ForestCo. Moreover, as these specialist skills are often obtained from experience outside ForestCo's salaried ILM, the salary for specialist occupations would reflect labor market prices for those skills. For example, engineers, foresters, accountants, purchasing agents, and persons in other specialist occupations obtain their basic knowledge and skills from combinations of postsecondary and graduate education and on-the-job experience. Similarly, first- and second-line supervisors in production and maintenance develop the knowledge and capacity to manage groups of hourly employees as a result of their direct experience as hourly employees in plants and mills. Whether all hires represent moves into a relatively small number of ports of entry for each occupational ILM remains to be determined, but without a deeper investigation of actual staffing "rules," this possibility cannot be excluded. Nevertheless, given the extensive range of salary grades at which hires occur, the likelihood that this is a valid characterization of ForestCo's ILM appears to be remote.

A second aspect of this distribution of employee flows into and out of the salaried employment system is that entry flows (hires) are generally higher than exit flows (predominantly voluntary quits and retirements) for the two lowest occupational groups, Clerical and Secretarial (salary grades 2–5) and Administrative and Technical (6–10), but the reverse is true for the two higher groups, Managerial and Professional (11–15) and Senior Management and Executive (16 and higher). These patterns are consistent with an ILM model in which there is, on average, modest progression from the entry salary grade to that obtained before exiting from the organization. However, these overall patterns do not appear so clearly when entry and exit flows are compared for each salary grade. For the Clerical and Secretarial group, exits were numerically identical to entries for two of the four salary grades. For the Administrative and Technical group, two of the five salary grades had higher exits than entries. Similar variations within each occupational group also existed for the two highest occupational groups. Thus, there appears to be a moderate amount of "noise" surrounding the exercise of a simple model of ILM operation in which there is relatively uniform progression from lower to higher salary grades.

Part of the imbalance between exits and hires is attributable to a net increase of 24 in the number of employees in all salary grades, as indicated by the following relationships:

$$\text{Ending stock} = \text{Beginning stock} - \text{Exits} + \text{Hires} - \text{Outflows} + \text{Inflows}$$
$$3732 \quad = \quad 3708 \quad - \ 377 + 401 - \quad 343 \quad + \quad 343$$

However, this overall increase was distributed unevenly across different levels of the grade hierarchy. Salary grades 2–5 decreased by 4 employees, salary grades 6–10 decreased by 3 employees, salary grades 11–15 increased by 27 employees, salary grades 16–20 increased by 4 employees, and finally salary grades greater than 20 remained at the same level. Even larger relative differences occurred within some individual salary grades. For example, salary grade 2 increased by 30 employees as a consequence of a large number of hires, whereas salary grade 3 decreased by 12 employees, with hires balancing exits but 12 employees being promoted to a higher salary grade.

The third aspect of overall employee flows noted here concerns the losses and gains in each salary grade over the year attributable to promotions into and out of each salary grade. As presented in Table 2.2, lower salary grades were generally the sources, and higher grades the destinations, of internal promotion flows. Altogether, between 9% and 10% of ForestCo's salaried workforce experienced a formal promotion, as indicated by increases in their salary grades, in the calendar year 1990. For these employees, the average increase was approximately 1½ salary grades. Not reported in Table 2.2 are data on 64 employees, or 1.7% of ForestCo's salaried employees, who experienced decreases in their salary grades in calendar year 1990. For these employees, the average decrease was slightly less than the average 1½-step salary grade increase for those who were promoted.

Relative Rates of Employee Flows

While primary measures of ILM activity are the absolute levels of employee flows into, through, and out of an employment system, these levels are clearly not independent of the size or the distribution by grade of the workforce complement. One way of comparing ILMs of different sizes, or the relative effect of different employee flows by grade within an ILM, is to examine flow rates—that is, the proportions of a particular workforce complement that experience a move either into, through, or out of the ILM under consideration. A summary snapshot of employee flow rates for calendar year 1990 is presented in Table 2.6. In this table, as in Table 2.2, the primary referent for calculations of flow rates is the group of salaried employees occupying a particular salary grade at the beginning of the year.

As illustrated in Table 2.6, an overall exit rate of 10.2% was recorded for all of ForestCo's salaried employees. These exits came from voluntary quits, retirements, and a small number of layoffs and moves to the hourly payroll. One implication of this exit rate is that if ForestCo wishes to maintain its overall levels of staffing, accessions from the ELM or other moves into the salaried employment system need to be at least as large as this amount. In actual fact, the salaried workforce complement actually grew by 24 persons in this illustrative year, and consequently the hire rate of 10.8% was slightly larger than the exit rate. Thus, even assuming a stable size for ForestCo's salaried employment system, there is still a substantial annual need for the organization to search for new employees to offset the moderate, and not untypical, exit rate. An alternative way of viewing this dynamism is to consider the overall "newness" of all salaried employees by year-end. Of a total stock of 3732 employees actively employed at year-end, 401 (10.7%) were hired within the last 12 months, and 343 (9.2%) received a promotion. Even ignoring lateral transfers and substantial job changes in job content without changes in job title or number, more than one fifth of ForestCo's salaried employees experienced a job change in the previous year.

A second feature of the dynamics of ForestCo's employment system concerns the distribution of exit and hire rates by groups of salary grade. For Clerical and Secretarial occupations (salary grades 2–5), exit rates were relatively high (18.0%), but entry rates were substantially higher (26.9%). These numbers indicate a high rate of job accession, particularly when viewed in conjunction with internal promotion rates. The extent of the dynamism at these lower levels of the organization can be appreciated from the experiences of the 450 employees considered to be in this broad occupational group at the

Table 2.6. 1990 Snapshot of ForestCo Employee Flow Rates

Salary grade	Beginning stock	Exit rate	Hire rate	Promotions[a] Outrate	Promotions[a] Inrate	"Make" % vacancies
2	51	15.7%	80.4%	5.9%	0	0
3	42	30.9%	30.9%	28.5%	0	0
4	163	15.3%	19.6%	13.5%	1.8%	8.6%
5	194	18.0%	18.0%	17.0%	11.9%	39.7%
6	246	15.0%	18.7%	9.8%	11.4%	37.8%
7	114	11.8%	12.5%	20.8%	18.8%	60.0%
8	191	15.2%	20.9%	9.4%	14.7%	41.2%
9	206	10.7%	8.7%	10.7%	9.2%	51.4%
10	379	10.6%	9.8%	13.7%	7.1%	42.2%
11	339	6.8%	9.4%	6.8%	12.7%	57.3%
12	444	8.1%	7.4%	8.3%	6.1%	45.0%
13	502	7.2%	4.4%	4.4%	8.2%	65.1%
14	303	4.6%	5.0%	7.6%	7.6%	60.5%
15	171	9.4%	4.7%	5.3%	12.9%	73.3%
16	115	9.6%	3.5%	3.5%	13.0%	78.9%
17	60	11.7%	6.7%	3.3%	8.3%	55.6%
18	46	6.5%	2.2%	4.4%	6.5%	75.0%
19	50	6.0%	2.0%	6.0%	8.0%	80.0%
20	23	0	0	0	8.7%	100.0%
≥21	39	5.1%	2.6%	5.1%	7.7%	75.0%
ALL GRADES	3708	10.2%	10.8%	9.2%	9.2%	46.2%

[a]Employee flows due to demotions are not included.

beginning of the year. More than one third of these employees had a different employment status 1 year later. In all, 18% exited (it is speculated that these were mostly voluntary quits) and more than 16% were promoted to positions having higher salary grades. As this analysis did not permit consideration of both employee transfers at the same grade level (which cannot be discerned from comparisons of end-of-year payroll data) and changes in jobs that did not change their salary grade level, this proportion is likely an underestimate of the extent to which employees were in jobs that were different from those they held at the beginning of the year. This analysis also underestimates the extent to which managers were required to match people and jobs as an ongoing function of maintaining ForestCo's salaried employment system.

An alternative way of viewing this dynamism is to again consider the newness or extent of person–job changes in the year. By year-end, just from hires (27.1%) and promotions (5.8%) alone, approximately one third of all Clerical and Secretarial employees were new to their jobs. This proportion remains substantial but decreases as a function of level in the salary grade hierarchy. For Administrative and Technical occupations (salary grades 6–10), the hire rate decreased to 13.6%, but the promotion rate into and within this broad occupational group increased to 11.1%, producing a new job–person match rate of 24.7%. Stability, as indexed by lower rates of new job–person matches, increases as a function of level in the grade hierarchy, with the greatest levels of stability (a relatively low new job–person match rate of 10.3%) being experienced in the executive salary grades greater than 20. While these general patterns held in groups of salary grades, there was substantial variance within each group. For example, the hire rate within the Secretarial and Clerical occupational group (salary grades 2–5) varied from 80.4% for salary grade 2 to 18.0% for salary grade 5. This latter hire rate was less than those recorded for two salary grades in the Administrative and Technical occupational group (salary grade 6 had a hire rate of 18.7%, and salary grade 8 had a hire rate of 20.9%). Thus, while there some general relationships between salary grades and patterns of employee flows, salary grade was not definitively associated with staffing modes.

A third aspect of flow rates within ForestCo's ILM concerns the relative contribution of either internal promotions or external hires as the means used to replenish stocks lost either as exits to the ELM or as promotions to higher grades. This managerial selection preference has been labeled "make vs. buy." Staffing actions that manifest a "make" policy seek candidates from within the ILM, whereas those that are oriented to "buy" policies seek candidates from the ELM. In Table 2.6, this measure is defined as the percentage of vacant positions filled by internal rather than external sources of supply. Over all grades, there was an approximate balance between make and buy policies, as just under half the flows (directly inferable from the comparisons of end-of-year records) into all vacant salary grades during the year were already employed within ForestCo's salaried ILM. For example, in calendar year 1990, there were 343 promotions and 401 hires. Excluding an unknown number of lateral transfers and other changes not discernible from archival records, 46.2% of vacancies were filled by promotions that reflect make policies and 53.8% by hires reflecting buy policies. Although there is substantial variation in the "make vs. buy" ratio for adjacent salary grades, there is again a general pattern in which lower salary grades are more likely to be filled by hires from the ELM and higher grades are more likely to be filled by promotions from within. For example, in the Secretarial and Clerical occupation group (salary grades 2–5), more than 82% of new positional assignments in place by year-end were obtained by hires from the ELM, but fewer than 18% were obtained through make policies. The proportion of new positional assignments filled through make policies increased as a function of increasing level in the salary grade hierarchy. For Administrative and Technical occupational groups (salary grades 6–10), the make proportion was 44.8%; for Managerial and Professional occupational grades (11–15), it was 58.6%; and for Senior Managers and Executives (salary grades $\geq$ 16), it was 74.4%.

Inferences Regarding Vacancy Chains

Aggregate data on stocks and flows of employees in ForestCo's employment system can also be used, under various assumptions, to infer the relative distribution of vacancy chains as a function of their origin in the organizational hierarchy. Before proceeding to derive indicators of vacancy chain length, however, we stress that the relationships assumed to hold in this derivation represent a very simplified model of ILM operation. This analysis assumes no lateral transfers, no demotions, and no consolidation of jobs associated with changed job structures in departments. Nevertheless, this analysis is presented as a partial linkage between analyses of ILMs at employment system levels and those undertaken in terms of vacancy chains to be presented in Part II.

When viewed as a self-contained system, the following equality between stocks and flows holds:

$$S_{t+1} = S_t - E_t + H_t$$

where S_t is the Stock at beginning of time period t, S_{t+1} is Stock at the beginning of time period $t + 1$, E_t is the Exits during time period t, and H_t is the Hires during time period t.

Assuming that originating vacancies occur *only* because of the creation of new positions and the exit of employees from existing positions:

$$\text{Originating vacancies} = (S_{t+1} - S_t) + E_t \text{ and}$$
$$\text{Vacancies filled} = P_t + H_t$$

where P_t is the Promotions during time period t.

Therefore, Average "nominal" vacancy chain length (defined as the average number of staffing actions produced for each originating vacancy)

$$= \frac{P_t + H_t}{(S_{t+1} - S_t + E_t)}$$

This derived measure is an approximate indicator of the ratio of the number of originating vacancies and the number of vacancies filled. For reasons noted above—namely, that this formulation ignores the possibility of lateral transfers—this is not a fully developed measure of vacancy chain length. It is therefore expected that this ratio underestimates the "true" average vacancy chain length that would be obtained from a detailed inspection of actual staffing patterns. Nevertheless, if one can examine an ILM only from an aggregate perspective, such approximate measures may provide insight into the potential distribution of vacancy chain lengths as a function of level in the organization's hierarchy. A sample distribution for the calendar year 1990 is presented in Table 2.7.

Even though there are several restrictive assumptions (such as no lateral transfers or demotions) limiting a full derivation of vacancy chain length from aggregate data, the general patterns shown in Table 2.7 are nevertheless consistent with prior speculations. There is a general tendency for nominal vacancy chain length to increase with hierarchical grade. The average nominal vacancy chain length for salary grades 2–5 was 1.29, increasing to 2.11 for salary grades 6–10, increasing again to 2.89 for salary grades 11–15, and reaching 4.19 for salary grades 16–19. Nominal vacancy chain lengths could not be calculated for salary grades 20 and higher, as there was insufficient mobility to permit a reliable estimate to be obtained.

Further analyses of the internal variations of a firm's ILM from the perspective of the overall employment system can be undertaken in terms of the underlying demography of the organization. It is possible to examine the composition of an organization's workforce

Table 2.7. Distribution of Nominal Vacancy
Chain Lengths by Hierarchical Level in 1990

Salary grade	Nominal vacancy chain length	Salary grade	Nominal vacancy chain length
		11	2.56
2	1.05	12	1.91
3	1.08	13	3.23
4	1.25	14	2.87
5	1.77	15	3.88
6	1.67	16	5.25
7	2.83	17	2.50
8	1.73	18	4.00
9	2.33	19	5.00
10	1.97	20	NA

by both individual and organizational attributes. In terms of individual attributes, an organization's workforce can be analyzed in terms of each employee's gender, age, marital status, educational background, and other attributes. Similar analyses can also be made of organizationally based characteristics of employees such as organizational tenure, job tenure, rank tenure, divisional affiliation, and occupational specialization. Baseline measures, together with changes in these attributes over time, can be used to infer the processes of change from aspects of the dynamic relationships among these characteristics. While much more detailed descriptions of ForestCo's employment system could be obtained from further analyses of archival data, such presentations would not necessarily add further insight. For that, the reader is encouraged to look to the vacancy chain and staffing perspectives presented in Parts II and III.

FORESTCO'S INTERNAL LABOR MARKET FROM THE PERSPECTIVE OF AN EMPLOYMENT-SYSTEM LEVEL

Developing an appreciation of ForestCo's salaried ILM solely from an employment-system level of analysis reveals multiple rather than unitary perspectives. The origins and traditions of the corporation, together with recent history, have strongly shaped various features of the organization and the patterns of employee stocks and flows. The corporate strategies associated with ForestCo's industry as well as its particular location in that industry provide the operational groupings of economic activities: fiber supplies; production of lumber, pulp or paper, packaging, and so on; distribution and marketing of products; and general Head Office support in the form of specialist functions such as research, legal services, and corporate governance. More recently, the experience of the deep recession that began in 1980–1982 and continued through to 1985 modified the interpretation and application of corporate policies that guide the manner in which ForestCo's ILM is manifested in staffing procedures. The processes through which ForestCo's ILM is maintained or modified are constrained by structural features such as the size and distribution of divisional groupings, the geographic separation of the work locations of these divisions, the similarity of occupational skills across different plants, and the size and distribution of jobs and employees within a hierarchy of salary grades.

While specific features of these general attributes are undoubtedly unique to ForestCo, the general attributes just described would also shape the ensuing structures and processes of other corporate ILMs. Compared to other business organizations, ForestCo is a relatively stable, medium-size firm. It is not regarded as an exemplar organization but the operation of its ILM is likely representative of that of many other similar-size, stable firms.

A more detailed examination of ForestCo's ILM from an employment system perspective focuses attention on the manner in which this dynamic system is maintained and changed. The structural attributes that shape distributions of employees by division, by grade, and by other individual and organizational features occur as a consequence of the flows of employees into, through, and out of ForestCo's employment system. Approximately 10% of all salaried employees leave this organization in any one year, and if there is no net growth or decline in the salaried workforce complement, they are replaced by comparable numbers of new hires. A further 10% of the total salaried workforce also move internally from one salary grade to another in any one year. Thus, approximately one fifth of all employees in ForestCo's employment system experience some degree of mobility in any one year. Although some employees may stay in the same positions for several years, possibly even as long as a decade, many other employees will experience some form of mobility each year, or even more frequently. Nevertheless, on average, the total workforce complement is likely to roll over (i.e., experience some mobility) once every four or five years.

Within ForestCo's ILM, different rates and forms of mobility are emphasized in different segments of the organization's hierarchy. Mobility rates are highest in lower salary grades. Of employees in salary grades 2–5, one third are likely to experience some mobility in any one year. In the next higher set of salary grades (6–10), one quarter are likely to experience some form of mobility. The proportion who experience some form of mobility decreases gradually as salary grades increase and approaches a level of approximately 10% in the executive ranks of the corporation. The composition of these mobility rates also varies as a function of hierarchical grade. Employees in lower salary grades are more likely to experience mobility *into* ForestCo ILM, whereas employees in higher salary grades are more likely to experience mobility in the form of promotions.

Although it is possible to examine multiple further perspectives at the employment-system level of analysis, further understanding of the processes through which ForestCo's ILM is maintained and modified is more likely to emerge from component-level analyses. For these perspectives, the reader is encouraged to consider the analyses of vacancy chains presented in Part II and the analyses of staffing presented in Part III.

APPENDIX: THE FOUNDER'S HUMAN RELATIONS MANAGEMENT PRESCRIPTIONS FOR BUSINESS SUCCESS

Staff is the brain, heart, circulatory, and nervous system of a business with so many functions as ForestCo. Seems appropriate to restate a few principles—the fruit of hindsight and experiences in various organizations:

a) select beginner and other new employees carefully by—selecting from the ranks, or, bringing in new and appropriately qualified persons. (Suggest constitutions important as well as other qualities),

b) occasionally, when opportunity offers, bringing in experienced persons from other organizations—cross fertilize the homegrown,

c) maintaining healthy competition for promotions—seniority to be disregarded except when candidates equal—otherwise frustration set up against brightest of the younger and staff average age rises too fast. (A clear road ahead for open competition for top jobs in [the forerunners to ForestCo] was made by owners agreeing their sons and sons-in-law would not be taken into the Company).

This was to–avoid nepotism,
       –encourage competition amongst rising professional management,
       –encourage selection of, and rewards for, those selected as the best qualified.

d) avoiding appointments in apparent permanence to important positions before appointee has proved himself. If appointee unsuitable, correct quickly,

e) promoting or moving sideways or otherwise without fear, affection or favour. The Company or function should not be weakened and only rarely bent to fit the man,

f) moving the most promising looking occasionally from function to function so as to broaden their experience and to cross-check on qualities,

g) Deputizing a duty does not bury it, or put it out of sight. It is necessary to learn how the deputy is performing, and, if needed, direct and help him. Otherwise, too much policy will by default come from the bottom instead of the top. In other words, the Company sometimes will be run "from the bottom up."

The higher executive still carries his responsibility and authority to be exercised to maintain standards. Study Monty of Alamein [British Field Marshall Bernard Law Montgomery]: he was a successful leader and manager. After he analyzed—organized—deputized, he supervised to the end that *his* standards prevailed.

h) Beware of nepotism, "apple polishers," office politicians and pets. (I have run into many and know when I did wrong and when I did right; I did right when I got rid of them).

i) Some companies are handicapped by having field jobs to fill—forest services, forest industries—bush jobs where wives complain. If a wife complains, never yield. If the family can't "stick it out" where the job is, let the man quit. If he succeeds in "politicking" to get moved to HO, or to a good town before he has normally earned the promotion by good performance, as his contemporaries must do, "the fat is in the fire"—the disease will spread.

j) Only the very best men should be selected and retained in managerial positions anywhere, and emphatically so at HO. The prominence of strikingly competent persons in these positions radiates immense leadership and influence. (There is no equal way to build up morale).

k) Supervision and contact must be continuous, top to bottom, to produce reliable, productive, brainy performance, good habits and quick communication of news, threats, market trends and action accordingly. Otherwise, insufficient authority will be exercised at some levels and too much at others.

The tendency to sit back in HO., or other offices, and await reports from subordinates, should be supervised out of existence in all companies, particularly in a company where labour is so high a percentage of sale price, where the radius of operations is so short in miles, and where the road system is so good as in ForestCo.

The top men, including the Chairman, the President, as well as responsible VP's., should show up around the operations without laying on a "do," and without any of the "drill" as in a super-organized institution like an army. The local top man is sufficient to meet and go around with.

Otherwise, our "tops" will have only hearsay, will be slow in sizing up "comers," and practices, will come to rely too much on the typed word. So the organization will slow down and stiffen. A few years can easily see walls built around jobs, defensive thinking, which I have observed more than once in other companies—a detriment to growth.

Emergencies sometimes demand that any level in an organization, from the top down, an executive, without violating protocol, has to have the road open for quickly getting ideas and facts and bringing about action, thus strengthening rather than weakening the fabric.

This is the art of supervision—perhaps a difficult but also an essential art. It should be impossible for an executive to be doing wrong for weeks or months without his superior failing to sense it before the "blow-off."

l) Let weak persons go—no discrimination or pride involved—protect ForestCo, is good for the other staff, who see the poor performance before the boss does.

m) Guard against Parkinson's Law—"empire building"—production, piling, filing and circulating of records and papers not worth what they cost—some even arising from obsolete instructions and habits.

n) As functions shrink, conditions change, reduce overhead accordingly.

o) Face up to trouble to do, and correct things habitually; otherwise troubles will multiply.

II

Vacancy Chain Perspectives on Internal Labor Markets

3

Vacancy Chains as Bundles of Staffing Actions

INTRODUCTION

This chapter, the first of four that comprise Part II, introduces a vacancy chain perspective on ILMs that is elaborated in Chapters 4 through 6. This introduction to Part II extends the stereotypical model of internal labor market (ILM) elements and outcomes presented in Chapter 1 and develops a model of an ideal-type vacancy chain. The representativeness of such ideal-type models is evaluated through a statistical analysis of objective, quantitative attributes of two samples of vacancy chains found in ForestCo's organization. In this and subsequent chapters, it is argued that the primary defining attribute of a vacancy chain as a component of an ILM is its length, measured as the number of sequentially related employee moves. Relationships between this defining attribute and other characteristics of vacancy chains are also investigated. The three subsequent chapters dealing with vacancy chains report on more complex interpretations of ForestCo's vacancy chains. These descriptions and analyses are based on the descriptions, comments, and interpretations provided by the managers who made the staffing decisions that comprise each vacancy chain. Thus, the nonstatistical analyses presented in Chapters 4 through 6 focus on the substantive content of staffing decisions and provide information on the micro-processes that accumulate to produce mobility patterns and vacancy chains.

Most formalized organizations can be characterized by a strong vacancy assumption reflecting the primacy of jobs over persons. That is, "collections of tasks for each job exist prior to and independent of the traits of specific individual incumbents" (Miner, 1987, p. 327). In Miner's study of a large decentralized research university, strong vacancy chain assumptions appropriately characterized approximately 90% of all job transitions, as only a small proportion of new jobs, between 7% and 12%, were judged to *not* "precede logically and temporally their incumbents." The importance and pervasiveness of the vacancy chain assumption can be seen in the extent to which it underlies several substantive topics in organizational theory: (1) job design; (2) job search and selection; (3) employee selection; (4) bureaucracy, organizational structure, and formalization; (5) organizational design; and (6) intraorganizational mobility. All six of these topics are closely associated with the operation of ILMs. Practices of organizational design generally establish the degree to which organizations possess formalized bureaucratic structures, which in turn are interdependent with the processes of job design. The nature of jobs available is, in turn, generally viewed as influencing the job search and selection activities of potential employees and the employee selection practices of organizations. Collectively, the activities subsumed under these topics strongly influence observed patterns of intraorganizational mobility. Vacancy models and perspectives undergird multiple appreciations of contemporary organizational theory.

In employment systems, a vacancy chain is an artifact of a general process that begins when a vacant position is filled by the appointment of a person already employed elsewhere in the firm. The movement of that person to the vacant position creates a second vacancy, in the position just left. Thus, as a consequence of person-moves, the initial vacancy may be thought of as having moved from one position to another. Subsequent internal moves may be considered to extend the initial link in the vacancy process to create a vacancy chain. This process continues until the most recently created vacancy is either left vacant, absorbed, or filled by a hire from the external labor market (ELM). Most often, but not always, vacancies move downward, from higher-level position to lower-level ones. Correspondingly, employee moves are mostly upward in the form of promotions or sideways in the form of lateral transfers. Characteristics of vacancy chains found in employment systems have been shown to be related to the distribution of opportunity for members of the employment system (White, 1970; Stewman 1986, Stewman & Konda, 1983). In addition, when mobility or vacancy-filling rules are closely associated with candidates' age or length of time in rank, vacancy chain processes also change, and in the long run determine, the demographic attributes of the organization (Stewman, 1981, 1988). Vacancy chain perspectives on ILMs complement the macrolens of employment-system perspectives presented in Chapter 2.

Vacancy chains are also strongly interdependent with staffing actions. Specific components of each vacancy chain comprise part of the causally antecedent contexts within which staffing decisions are made. In turn, each staffing decision has the consequence of either extending or terminating the vacancy chain of which it is a part. In addition, for situations in which a staffing decision extends the vacancy chain to which it "belongs," the staffing decision has the potential to "switch" the vacancy chain process from one organizational location to another as a function of which internal candidate is chosen to fill the vacant position. Thus, vacancy chains and vacancy chain processes establish the context for a microperspective on ILMs focused on staffing actions. Vacancy chain perspectives therefore represent an intermediate linkage between macro- and microperspectives on ILM operation.

This chapter analyzes ForestCo's ILM in terms of the objective, quantitative attributes of the vacancy chains found there. As a means of focusing and organizing this material, a model of an ideal-type vacancy chain is presented first to provide conceptual support for the subsequent classifications of observed phenomena.

AN IDEAL-TYPE VACANCY CHAIN

A model of an ideal-type vacancy chain is presented in Figure 3.1. Several features of this ideal-type vacancy chain are noteworthy for subsequent comparisons to actual vacancy chains. First, the vacancy chain is presented as a series of staffing actions, or people "moves," against an implicit background of relatively fixed organizational positions. This view is similar to the strong vacancy chain assumption of Miner (1987) noted above and the climbing frame or jungle gym metaphor of Gunz (1989) discussed in Chapter 2. Second, the vacancy chain is presented as a cascade of staffing actions from a higher level

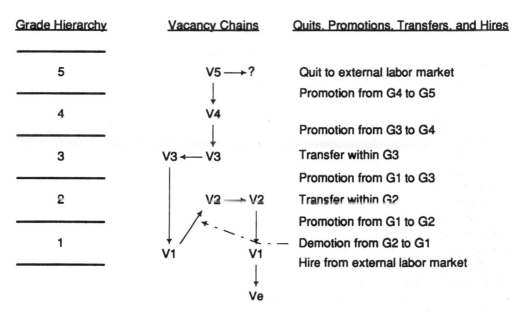

Figure 3.1. Ideal-type vacancy chain and staffing actions.

of the organizational hierarchy to its bottom, so the vacancy chain terminates with the entry of a hire from the ELM. Third, between the originating and terminating actions in this vacancy chain, there is a sequence of staffing actions—mostly promotions, but also lateral transfers and demotions—that constitute the linkages between the beginning and the end of the vacancy chain. Fourth, this vacancy chain diagram shows the consequences of what was decided in terms of generic moves, but provides no information on potential staffing actions or moves that were considered but rejected. Fifth, each staffing decision is presented as a consequence of unidentified factors. No information is provided on the situational conditions at each staffing decision node that determined why those particular decisions were made. Most important, each staffing consideration could have resulted in a decision to fill the vacancy from the ELM. Had that choice been made, then the vacancy chain would have terminated at that point.

The first three features of this ideal-type vacancy chain—namely, an emphasis on jobs rather than persons, a cascade of vacancies from the top to the bottom of the hierarchy, and a sequence of staffing actions between origination and termination of the vacancy chain—provide an initial base for speculations regarding the patterns of vacancy chains likely to be found at ForestCo. The emphasis on jobs is consistent with the job ladder element of the ILM model noted in Figure 1.2. In that model, groupings of jobs (or job ladders) were viewed as independent and antecedent conditions that contributed to relatively stable patterns of intraorganizational mobility. Because organizational structures and associated jobs are viewed as relatively stable properties of most large, formalized organizations, intraorganizational mobility associated with vacancy chain activity would be initiated primarily by the exit of existing employees rather than by the creation of new positions. Patterns of mobility would occur predominantly inside the employment system, with vacancy chains typically terminating with the hire of new employees from the ELM into the lowest levels of the organizational hierarchy. On the relatively rare occasions when new jobs were created, the design and definition of those jobs would occur independently of any persons who might be considered for those jobs.

These considerations suggest that only those vacancy chains that originate close to ports of entry (stereotypically lower levels of the organizational hierarchy) would consist of relatively few moves. Under strong vacancy chain assumptions, most vacancy chains would contain larger numbers of moves. In addition, the number of moves in a vacancy chain would be positively associated with the hierarchical level of the originating vacancy. A large majority of vacancy chains would be expected to originate with the exit of employees from existing positions. Continuation of vacancy chains would be expected to occur through processes that replaced the previous occupants of vacant positions. Although most discussions of vacancy chain processes are silent with respect to the manner in which replacement employees are to be selected, two quite different orientations can be identified. In unionized blue-collar or contract-based ILMs, public, or quasi-contractual, administrative rules determine the selection of the replacement. In the more theoretical psychological and personnel literature on employee selection, competition based on likely job performance is emphasized.

Whatever method is used to select the next occupant of a recently vacated position, further consideration of vacancy chain processes indicates that patterns of vacancy chains are unlikely to provide a complete representation of job ladders. Opportunities to exercise a staffing choice at any point subsequent to the initiating vacancy are critically dependent on all previous staffing choices. This dependence has at least three features. First, the existence of all subsequent vacancies depends on the filling of all previous vacancies in the vacancy chain by internal appointments. Any staffing decision to opt for a "buy" from the ELM rather than a "make" from the ILM would terminate the vacancy chain and obviate the need for all subsequent staffing actions in the chain.

Second, the location and characteristics of all vacancies being considered for potential staffing actions (with the exception of the originating vacancy) are critically dependent on all previous staffing actions in the chain. For example, a decision to promote along the line of progression within a department would produce another vacancy within that department, whereas a decision to institute an interdepartmental search that resulted in a departmental transfer would switch the vacancy chain to other parts of the organization. Each staffing decision, then, has the potential to either terminate related staffing actions or initiate staffing activity in one of several alternative organizational locations in which successful candidates for that particular vacancy might be found.

Third, each previous staffing action has a relatively strong proximate effect on the general issues considered in each focal staffing decision. For example, previous staffing actions that followed a line of progression could have a marginal impact on the perceived need for new blood or the quality of new recruits that should be brought into entry-level positions. Similarly, vacancies arising from interdepartmental transfers, especially those that leave a department's resources thin on experience, could influence future staffing decisions in that department to favor loyalty and to avoid fast-trackers who leave shortly after being trained. Thus, considerable "noise," or situationally relevant variation in patterns of vacancy chains, is also expected.

The ideal-type vacancy chain depicted in Figure 3.1 is provided as a heuristic derived from considerations of the stereotypical model of ILM operation presented in Figure 1.2. Actual vacancy chains may vary from this representation, as it exemplifies a simplification of what is often a more complex and robust reality. In the section that follows, various statistical attributes of the samples of vacancy chains observed at ForestCo are described, together with the methods used to obtain them.

A STATISTICAL ANALYSIS OF FORESTCO'S VACANCY CHAINS

This statistical analysis is limited to the primary, quantitative attributes of ForestCo's vacancy chains. Because two samples of vacancy chains were investigated, and one was examined in greater depth than the other, the analysis considers only the types of data that were readily available for both samples. For each sample, primary attributes of the constituent vacancy chains (i.e., vacancy chain length, hierarchical grade of the origin and termination of each chain, reason for origination or termination) were evaluated to assess the extent to which the different methodologies associated with data collection produced systemic bias in the samples obtained. Finding none, or at least none with statistical significance, permitted the samples to be combined for further analyses. For example, attributes of these vacancy chains were assessed to investigate the extent to which the length of each vacancy chain could be associated with the hierarchical levels of its origination or its termination or both. Other potential correlates of vacancy chain length such as the hierarchical span between origination and termination and the average number of grades per move were also investigated. The final section of this chapter reviews both the data obtained and the empirical validity of ideal-type representations of vacancy chains derived from stereotypical models of ILM operation.

Descriptions of Two Sampling Procedures

The two procedures described in Chapter 2 were used to obtain statistical information on the incidence and attributes of vacancy chains in ForestCo's ILM. These procedures are similar to those described by Chase (1991). The first involved an active, real-time tracking of staffing actions from a series of linked interviews conducted near the time the staffing action actually occurred. The second involved the tracking of vacancy chains, reconstructed and inferred, from organizational records of staffing actions. These two methods produced two different samples of vacancy chains, with overlapping but not identical sets of information about each chain.

The first data-collection procedure yielded a sample of 71 vacancy chains containing more than 300 staffing actions. For each staffing action, the person who was either directly responsible for or directly involved in the selection decision was interviewed about the issues associated with that staffing action. Approximately 100 different managers and supervisors were interviewed as part of this investigation.

The second sample of vacancy chains was reconstructed from organizational records of staffing actions. At the conclusion of any staffing action, a form noting the details of the new assignment was forwarded to the corporate office for entry into a computerized personnel records system. Once data from this form had been recorded, the form was returned to the "home" department or division to be filed in the employee's permanent personnel record. Only by intercepting these records, and inspecting them for the brief window of time they were in the corporate office, could data on current staffing actions be obtained. Like many other firms, ForestCo had excellent data on employee stocks. However, their internal procedures were not designed to capture real-time information on the detailed nature of staffing actions that resulted in changes in employee status.

The reconstruction of linkages between staffing actions to infer attributes of vacancy chains was done by outside researchers. The reliability and validity of this process depended to a large extent on the thoroughness with which staffing forms were completed. In this decentralized organization, perhaps 50 or more different persons could be involved in completing the staffing documents for a given vacancy chain. Although each of these documents was countersigned by two or three superior supervisors, consistency in form completion was not a salient performance issue for senior persons in this hands-on organization. An added difficulty was that for this sample, no managers who had made these staffing decisions were interviewed. Little or no information, other than that recorded on the formal staffing notice, was obtained about the manner in which staffing occurred or the reasons behind a particular selection decision. However, when a particular vacancy chain did get lost in the paperwork, a telephone call to the last node in the vacancy chain often indicated where and when to look for the next staffing action in the sequence. Despite these qualifications regarding their accuracy, archivally deduced vacancy chains were regarded as a useful supplement to the original interview-based study because they permitted a larger sample of vacancy chains to be identified without correspondingly large time investments.

The sample of vacancy chains reconstructed from organizational records was selected by a different method than those identified directly from interviews. In terms of developing a preliminary statistical profile of ForestCo's vacancy chains, it is therefore an open question whether these two samples lead to similar or different inferences regarding the nature of the total population of vacancy chains in ForestCo's organization. One way to investigate this question is to assess the extent to which each sample presents similar or different measures of vacancy chain attributes.

Vacancy Chain Length as Number of Employee Moves

Vacancy chains are here considered as linked sequences of related staffing actions. As such, vacancy chains are complex phenomena having multiple attributes. For example, a vacancy chain can be measured in terms of relatively objective, archivally recorded characteristics such as the number of staffing actions contained in the vacancy chain, the hierarchical location of its originating vacancy, the hierarchical location of its terminating vacancy, and the average size of each move as indicated by the average number of grades per move. Vacancy chains can also be assessed in terms of other characteristics that can be learned from interviews, such as the nature of the originating vacancy, the nature of the terminating vacancy, and so on. However, the examination presented here focuses on objective data that could be obtained for both samples.

It is argued here that the *primary* attribute of a vacancy chain, considered as a characteristic of an ILM, is its length as indicated by number of person-moves between originating and terminating vacancies. This length directly indicates the extent to which a sequence of staffing actions consistently chooses candidates who are already employed in the ILM. The length of a vacancy chain is an indicator of the repeated preference for internal rather than external candidates. In terms of ideal-type vacancy chains, the length of each vacancy chain would be strongly correlated with the hierarchical level of the originating vacancy. However, the strength of this association would depend on the extent to which actual vacancy chains were similar to ideal-type models. For example, organizations that had little or no separation from the ELM would, *ceteris paribus*, chose external candidates with approximately the same frequency as internal candidates. Therefore, the greater the number of moves in each vacancy chain, the stronger the propensity for selection decisions to favor workers who have already gained entry to the ILM (Doeringer & Piore, 1971).

In this study of ForestCo, the first sample contained extensive information on 71 vacancy chains. The second sample contained information on 109 vacancy chains. The number of related staffing actions comprising the vacancy chains in these two samples varied from one to nine moves, as presented in Table 3.1.

While there are some differences between these two samples of vacancy chains, these differences appear to be small and attributable to the different methods used to obtain the two samples. For example, the vacancy chains included in the second sample were reconstructed from organizational records. The search among the large monthly flow of reports was done with the assumption that a vacancy chain existed when there was direct evidence of a link between two or more staffing actions. With one exception, this assumption directed attention away from apparently isolated staffing actions. Thus, this method of identifying vacancy chains deliberately excluded single staffing actions. However, the method used for the first sample, which began with a random sample of staffing actions, and then searched for other related staffing actions, had the potential to include independent staffing actions. The methods used to obtain the two samples therefore contain a bias for the second sample to exclude single staffing actions. The two samples did indeed manifest this bias: Approximately 10% of the first sample, but less than 1% of the second sample, consisted of single staffing actions.

One can speculate regarding other biases that may be reflected in these data. As will become more apparent in subsequent chapters dealing with staffing actions, vacancies were occasionally used as opportunities for reorganizations. In some of these circumstances, a previously identified vacancy chain of strongly linked successions can apparently terminate, but begin again elsewhere with the creation of a new position. Unless the documentation of this linkage is especially thorough, such connections between apparently unconnected staffing actions would not normally be recognized by the archival reconstructions associated with the development of the second sample. Thus, there could be bias in the second sample toward "normal" successions. In contrast, the active pursuit of reasons for staffing associated with the development of the first sample would more readily uncover organizational adjustments such as the reorganizations just described.

At the other end of the distribution of vacancy chain length, the two samples were more similar. The longest vacancy chain in the first sample consisted of nine moves,

Table 3.1. Distribution of
Vacancy Chains by Number
of Staffing Moves

	Chains			
	Sample 1		Sample 2	
Number of moves	N	%	N	%
1	7	9.9	1	0.9
2	20	28.2	48	44.0
3	20	28.2	28	25.7
4	8	11.3	20	18.3
5	5	7.0	5	4.6
6	7	9.9	3	2.8
7	1	1.4	2	1.8
8	1	1.4	2	1.8
9	2	2.8	0	0.0
TOTALS:	71		109	

whereas the longest chain in the second sample was eight moves. In addition, the average vacancy chain length of the first sample was 3.37 moves, whereas the average length for the second sample was 3.06 moves. These differences are not statistically significant ($t = 1.18$, $p < 0.24$). Although there appear to be minor differences between these two samples, arising primarily from the methods used to obtain information on vacancy chains, they appear to be remarkably similar in terms of their primary characteristic. With this caveat, much of the following statistical description of ForestCo's vacancy chains will be presented as though the two samples are more similar than different. Whenever appropriate, statistical information will be presented on the total sample of 180 vacancy chains.

For the two samples combined, the average vacancy chain length was slightly larger than 3 moves. This empirical evidence fails to support the forecasts of a preponderance of "long" vacancy chains derived from the stereotypical models of ILM operation presented earlier. Nevertheless, there is some support for a modest but statistically significant association between length of vacancy chain and hierarchical level of the initiating vacancy ($r = 0.31$; $p < 0.01$). However, the hierarchical level of the initiating vacancy has little explanatory power, as less than 10% of the variance in vacancy chain length can be explained by this factor. These data on ForestCo's vacancy chains also indicate that the ideal-type vacancy chain illustrated in Fig. 3.1 is representative of only a very small proportion of vacancy chains that typically occur in this organization. Almost 70% of all the vacancy chains revealed by our sampling of ForestCo's personnel files contained three or fewer moves or staffing actions. The ideal-type illustration with which we began our speculations about the nature of vacancy chains contains eight moves, which would place it in the 95th percentile of the sample distribution! A more representative illustration of a vacancy chain would be one containing either two or three staffing actions, as nearly two thirds of all the vacancy chains discovered fell into these two categories.

In fact, the average length of ForestCo's vacancy chains is very similar to average lengths reported elsewhere. For example, Chase (1991, p. 141) reports that "usually average chains have a length around 3.0.... Chains with lengths in these ranges have been reported for mobility systems as ostensibly diverse as those for people obtaining jobs in bureaucracies (Stewman, 1975, 1985; White, 1970), hermit crabs acquiring snail shells (Weissburg, Roseman, & Chase, 1991), and people buying houses (Lansing, Clifton, & Morgan, 1969; Marullo, 1985) and cars (Smith, 1941)". The sources of this stable phenomenon as manifest in employment systems are investigated further in the sections that follow. In particular, the preponderance of short vacancy chains may be attributable to the location of either their origin or their termination in the organizational hierarchy. As there have been very few previous empirical studies of vacancy chains, the following sections may also be regarded as preliminary investigations of the covariance of objective attributes of vacancy chains.

Hierarchical Origin

A second attribute of vacancy chains analyzed here is that of the location of their origin. In the ideal-type chain illustrated of Fig. 3.1, the origin of that vacancy chain was presented as the highest "grade" in the hierarchy. In fact, originating vacancies can occur anywhere in the organization's hierarchy, though the actual distribution will also be influenced by the distribution of positions by grade as well as by the demographic characteristics of persons in those positions. The distribution of originating vacancies will be influenced by the proportion of jobs in each grade considered to be end-of-career grades for employees already at those ranks. For employees in those jobs, future chances of upward mobility will approach zero as a function of increasing length of service at that grade level. Appreciations of the relative merits of staying or leaving will influence propensities for voluntary turnover. In addition, actual distributions of employees by age relative to statutory and early retirement requirements will influence levels of involuntary turnover. Actual distributions of jobs will be the primary correlate of locations of originating vacancies, though the effects of this base distribution could be altered by attributes of the underlying processes through which employees stay and advance through the hierarchy.

In stereotypical models of ILMs, vacancy chains are expected to originate primarily from the higher levels of job ladders or grade hierarchies. Some degree of labor turnover or exit from the ILM is anticipated from levels below these grades because of terminations associated with poor health or disability of employees, poor job performance, or lack of work. Vacancies originating from the latter sources, however, would be expected to be fewer than the "normal" retirements from senior-level positions.

Actual distributions of origins of ForestCo's vacancy chains are presented in Table 3.2. Again, the distributions of this feature for the two samples of vacancy chains appear to be

Table 3.2. Distribution of Vacancy Chains
Salary Grade of Origin

	Distribution					
	Sample 1		Sample 2		Total	
Initiating grade	N	%	N[a]	%	N	%
5	1	1.4	3	2.8	4	2.2
6	2	2.8	0	0.0	2	1.1
7	0	0.0	2	1.8	2	1.1
8	0	0.0	1	1.9	1	0.6
9	2	2.8	5	4.6	7	3.9
10	1	1.4	5	4.6	6	3.4
11	13	18.3	10	9.2	23	12.9
12	4	5.6	19	17.4	23	12.9
13	16	22.5	24	22.0	40	22.5
14	11	15.5	13	11.9	24	13.5
15	6	8.5	9	8.3	15	8.4
16	4	5.6	3	2.8	7	3.9
17	2	2.8	3	2.8	5	2.8
18	3	4.2	4	3.7	7	3.9
19	1	1.4	1	0.9	2	1.1
20	1	1.4	2	1.8	3	1.7
21	0	0.0	0	0.0	0	0.0
22	0	0.0	2	1.8	2	1.1
23	2	2.8	0	0.0	2	1.1
24	1	1.4	1	0.9	2	1.1
25	0	0.0	0	0.0	0	0.0
26	0	0.0	0	0.0	0	0.0
27	0	0.0	0	0.0	0	0.0
28	1	1.4	0	0.0	1	0.6
TOTALS:	71		107		178	

[a]There are two chains missing.

quite similar. The mean salary grade of origin for sample 1 is 13.76; for sample 2, it is 13.06 ($t = 1.28$, $p < 0.2$). Moreover, the modes of each distribution are identical at 13.

Inspection of the overall distribution of the origins of ForestCo's vacancy chains shows no originating vacancies at salary grades 4, 3, or 2, indicating that jobs at these grades may be considered to be ports of entry for certain occupations in ForestCo's ILM. At the upper end of the grade hierarchy, it is noted that slightly more than 17% of ForestCo's vacancy chains originated in the Senior Management and Executive levels of salary grade 16 and above. The largest proportion of ForestCo's vacancy chains were concentrated in the Managerial and Professional occupational groups associated with salary grades 11–15. More than 70% of ForestCo's vacancy chains originated in these five salary grades.

The concentration of vacancy chain origins in the Managerial and Professional salary grade range is partially attributable to the relatively large numbers of jobs at these levels of the hierarchy. In addition, because of the modest but positive association between vacancy chain origins and hierarchical grade, the relatively high location of Managerial and Professional occupations in the total hierarchy also generates more vacancies than occupations at lower levels. This distribution is illustrated in Table 3.3.

As illustrated in Table 3.3, there is a tendency for higher grades to be filled through a cascade of staffing actions downward through the hierarchy. Such processes skew the distribution of vacancy chain origins upward from the base distribution of employees by current grade. Salary grades 16 and above, associated with Senior Management and Executive occupations, represent 9% of all salaried positions, but over 17% of vacancy chain origins. Similarly, salary grades 11–15, associated with Managerial and Professional occupations, represent 47.4% of all salaried positions, but more than 70% of vacancy chain origins. Together, these two senior occupational groupings represent a majority 56.4% of all salaried positions, but 87.6% of all vacancy chain origins. In distinction to the upper end of the grade hierarchy, the lower salary grades 2–10 represent 43.5% of all salaried positions, but only 12.3% of vacancy chain origins.

One possible interpretation of these findings is that many of the Managerial and Professional jobs located in salary grades 11–15 are career termini for employees in these occupations. In addition, however, this segment of the hierarchy is where most competition among candidates for appointment to higher salary grades occurs. As noted in Chapter 2, these grades are the ones with relatively small salary grade multipliers. That is, there are fewer positions at the immediately higher grade than at any immediately lower grade. Thus, there are relatively more internal candidates for any vacant position here than

Table 3.3. Distribution of Employee Stocks
and Vacancy Chain Origins

Salary grades	By grade range		Cumulative	
	Employee stocks	Vacancy chain origins	Employee stocks	Vacancy chain origins
30–21	1.1%	3.9%	1.1%	3.9%
20–16	7.9%	13.5%	9.0%	17.4%
15–11	47.4%	70.2%	56.4%	87.6%
10–6	31.5%	10.1%	87.9%	97.7%
5–2	12.0%	2.2%	99.9%	99.9%

elsewhere in the corporation. The lower levels of these occupations (i.e., grades 11 and 12) are where supervisory skills are developed, and the upper levels of these grades (i.e., grades 13–15) are where managerial and professional skills are matured and tested more thoroughly. A combination of a concentration of a large number of positions together with the squeezing of the organizational hierarchy produces a critical, competitive passage in this employment system. Once through this competitive passage to Senior Management positions located above salary grade 16, nominal competition apparently decreases as grade ratios increase. If this interpretation is correct, employee mobility into, through, and out of salary grades 11–15 is quite competitive as employees strive for the assignments and rewards associated with appointments to senior positions. However, as only 9% of all positions may be labeled Senior Management or Executive, whereas almost half of positions are "immediately" below those ranks, a large number of managerial and professional employees also top out in their organizational careers at these grade levels. These career terminations contribute to the relatively large number of vacancy chain origins found in the Managerial and Professional salary grades.

Terminating Salary Grades

Complementary to the question of the origin of each vacancy chain is the question of its termination. That is, what is the distribution of the salary grades at which vacancy chains terminate? In stereotypical models of ILMs, most vacancy chains would terminate at those salary grades identified as port of entry to the ILM. In the case of ForestCo's ILM, we previously noted that no vacancy chains originated at the lowest three salary grades, indicating that these grades might be potential ports of entry—at least for Secretarial and Clerical occupations. However, there is reason not to believe this simple representation of the mechanisms that underlie the actual distribution of vacancy chain terminations. Vacancy chains originate predominantly in salary grades 11–15, and most vacancy chains are short, consisting of relatively few employee moves. Thus, predictions based on stereotypical ILM models regarding the distribution of vacancy chain terminations are already suspect.

The actual distribution of the terminating grades for each of the two samples of vacancy chains obtained at ForestCo is presented in Table 3.4. However, before these data are discussed in greater detail, some cautions and qualifications are in order. Not infrequently, vacancy chains in ForestCo's salaried ILM terminated with the "promotion" of a person from the ranks of hourly employees. Within ForestCo's record-keeping system, there was no readily available way of assigning an equivalent salary grade level to the hourly position such a person vacated. As the hourly and salaried employment systems were quite distinct, and there were no corresponding equivalent salary grades for hourly employees, the terminating grade was assumed to be the salary grade position assumed when this new appointment was confirmed. This practice probably introduces an upward bias in the distribution of terminating salary grades and in any distribution derived from data on hierarchical location of terminating move (see the subsection entitled "Vacancy Chain Length as Number of Employee Moves" above and that entitled "Average Size of Each Move" below).

With this caveat concerning probable bias, the two samples again appear to be quite similar. The average terminating grade was almost identical for each sample (11.97 for sample 1 and 11.93 for sample 2), even though the mode terminating salary grade of 12 for sample 1 was slightly lower than the mode terminating salary grade of 13 obtained for sample 2. Nevertheless, these data continue to support the judgment that the two samples

Table 3.4. Distribution of Vacancy Chains
by Salary Grade of Termination

Terminating grade	Distribution					
	Sample 1		Sample 2		Total	
	N	%	N[a]	%	N	%
4	3	4.2	1	0.9	4	2.2
5	1	1.4	2	1.8	3	1.7
6	1	1.4	2	1.8	3	1.7
7	1	1.4	2	1.8	3	1.7
8	2	2.8	4	3.7	6	3.4
9	3	4.2	5	4.6	8	4.5
10	5	7.0	8	7.3	13	7.3
11	14	19.7	16	14.7	30	16.9
12	10	14.1	22	20.2	32	18.0
13	12	16.9	24	22.0	36	20.2
14	6	8.5	11	10.1	17	9.6
15	6	8.5	3	2.8	9	5.1
16	2	2.8	1	0.9	3	1.7
17	1	1.4	2	1.8	3	1.7
18	2	2.8	0	0.0	2	1.1
19	2	2.8	2	1.8	4	2.2
20	0	0.0	1	0.9	1	0.6
21	0	0.0	1	0.9	1	0.6
TOTALS	71		107		178	

[a]There are 2 chains missing.

are similar, as no statistically significant differences between them were found ($t = 0.08$, $p < 0.9$).

As suspected, these data fail to confirm predictions based on stereotypical models of ILM operation. Despite there being approximately 44% of all salaried positions located below salary grade 11 (see Fig. 2.1), fewer than 23% of all vacancy chains terminated at these lower grade levels. In addition, about 8% of vacancy chains terminated in the Senior Management and Executive ranks at salary grade 16 and above. Most surprising, approximately 70% of all vacancy chain terminations occurred between salary grades 11 and 15. These data reinforce the earlier observation that most staffing activity, and hence most vacancy chain phenomena, occur in the upper-middle range of the salary grade hierarchy.

Hierarchical Span between Origin and Termination

Vacancy chains in employment systems can serve the purposes of managerial succession directly by manifesting a series of vertical career moves up the organizational hierarchy. Vacancy chains can also serve the purposes of training and career development by manifesting a series of horizontal moves in which employees move from one organizational function or sphere of activity to another. It is anticipated that most vacancy chains will embody employee moves for both purposes. The breadth of experience obtained from horizontal mobility is often a precursor for future vertical mobility. Similarly, rewards such as promotions or increases in organizational status are often used as incentives to motivate employees to accept new assignments that require them to adapt to new challenges and to learn new skills.

So far, attributes of vacancy chains have been considered in terms of the number of employee moves in each sequence of related staffing actions and of the span of salary grades between the originating and the terminating vacancies in the chain. In stereotypical models of ILMs, such spans would be nominally indexed by the hierarchical span of each job ladder. If ForestCo's employment system were a unitary ILM, such job ladders would cover several salary grades at least. However, given the previous presentations on the distributions of origins and terminations of ForestCo's vacancy chains showing concentrations of staffing activity in salary grades 11–15, it is anticipated that the average hierarchical span will be relatively small. The actual distribution of these hierarchical spans is presented in Table 3.5.

The most striking feature of the distribution of the hierarchical spans of ForestCo's vacancy chains is that more than 70% span two salary grades or fewer. Indeed, more than a third of all these vacancy chains were ones in which the salary grade at which the vacancy chain originated was the same as that at which it terminated. Vacancy chains that covered larger ranges of salary grades were relatively rare. Fewer than 9% of these vacancy chains terminated more than three salary grades below their origin. Also surprising in light of the ideal-type model of vacancy chains presented in Figure 3.1 is the finding that 14, or approximately 8% of these vacancy chains terminated at salary grades that were *higher*

Table 3.5. Distribution of Vacancy Chains
by Hierarchical Span

	Distribution					
	Sample 1		Sample 2		Total	
Hierarchical span	N	%	N[a]	%	N	%
13	0	0.0	1	0.9	1	0.6
12	2	2.8	0	0.0	2	1.1
11	0	0.0	1	0.9	1	0.6
10	0	0.0	0	0.0	0	0.0
9	1	1.4	0	0.0	1	0.6
8	0	0.0	0	0.0	0	0.0
7	2	2.8	0	0.0	2	1.1
6	1	1.4	2	1.9	3	1.7
5	2	2.8	4	3.7	6	3.4
4	6	8.4	4	3.7	10	5.6
3	6	8.4	3	2.8	9	5.1
2	10	14.1	9	8.4	19	10.7
1	12	16.9	33	30.8	45	25.3
0	23	32.4	42	39.3	65	36.5
−1	3	4.2	5	4.7	8	4.5
−2	2	2.8	2	1.9	4	2.2
−3	1	1.4	1	0.9	2	1.1
TOTALS	71		107		178	

[a]There are 2 chains missing.

than their origin! These latter vacancy chains are clearly anomalous with conventional assumptions of vacancy chain operation.

Average Size of Each Move

The final attribute of ForestCo's vacancy chains to be described here is that of the average size of each move. This attribute is derived from two previously described attributes of vacancy chains: the number of person moves associated with each vacancy chain and the salary grade span between the origination and termination of each vacancy chain. The average size of each move associated with a vacancy chain is the ratio of the salary grade range and the number of moves. Higher numbers indicate that on average each move in a vacancy chain covers several salary grades, suggesting higher degrees of vertical mobility. Lower numbers indicate lower degrees of vertical mobility.

There is little prior theory directly related to the operation of vacancy chains to guide the development of hypotheses regarding the average size of moves in these component processes of ILMs. In somewhat related work, Jacobs (1981) has argued that the slope of the pay vs. individual performance relationship will vary as a function of the relationship between individual performance and its consequences for organizational performance. If individual performance has a strong positive impact on organizational performance, then attention directed to employee selection should be substantial and individual pay incentives for performance should be quite high. However, if individual performance has only a marginal impact on organizational performance, then individual pay incentives will be relatively low. In contrast to these two situations are those in which positive increments in individual performance have little impact on overall performance, but negative individual performance can have a devastating impact on organizational performance. For example, when an organization's reputation is based on collective trust, as for example in a police department, a single illegal act can weaken the performance of the whole organization.

In the case of business organizations such as ForestCo, compensation systems are often similar across comparable organizations because firms mimic each other and share the normative designs of national and international consulting firms. Generic compensation systems are adapted to local circumstances by the assignment of particularly important jobs to higher salary grades, the use of supplementary rewards such as end-of-year managerial bonuses for upper-middle jobs, and stock options for selected executive positions. Orderly career progressions as depicted in stereotypical models of ILMs suggest that the average number of salary grade increases per move would be strongly distributed around 1. Moreover, given that levels of executive compensation are often rationalized in terms of the relative contribution executive performance makes to overall organizational performance, it is anticipated that the size of the average move would be positively correlated with the hierarchical level of the originating vacancy. Data on the average size of each move are shown in Table 3.6.

Consistent with other features of ForestCo's vacancy chains, data on the average size of each move fail to confirm a stereotypical model of this firm's ILM. More than one third of the vacancy chains showed no net gain or loss in hierarchical level between originating and terminating salary grades, and hence the average size of each move for these vacancy chains was 0. Altogether, most vacancy chains originated at higher levels of the salary grade hierarchy than those at which they terminated. While positive career progression was associated with a majority of vacancy chains, almost 45% of all vacancy chains had either zero or negative overall career progression. Nevertheless, overall career progression was discernible in the patterns of vacancy chains analyzed here, as the

Table 3.6. Distribution of Vacancy Chains
by Size of Average Move

Average size each move	Sample 1		Sample 2		Total	
	N	%	N[a]	%	N	%
2.50 to 2.99	0	0.0	2	1.9	2	1.1
2.00 to 2.49	0	0.0	0	0.0	0	0.0
1.50 to 1.99	3	4.2	6	5.6	9	5.1
1.00 to 1.49	13	18.3	5	4.7	18	10.1
0.50 to 0.99	16	22.5	15	14.0	31	17.4
0.01 to 0.49	10	14.1	29	27.1	39	21.9
0	23	32.4	42	39.3	65	36.5
−0.49 to −0.01	3	4.2	3	2.8	6	3.4
−0.99 to −0.50	2	2.8	4	3.7	6	3.4
−1.49 to −1.00	1	1.4	0	0.0	1	0.6
−1.99 to −1.50	0	0.0	1	0.9	1	0.6
TOTALS	71		107		178	

[a]There are 2 chains missing.

average move per chain was slightly less than 0.4 salary grade. This mobility was associated with downward movements for vacancies and upward movements for career progression. Moreover, as predicted, there was a positive and statistically significant association ($r = 0.41$, $p < 0.01$) of the size of the average (career progression) move in each vacancy chain with the hierarchical level of the originating vacancy.

SUMMARY OF THE STATISTICAL ANALYSIS OF FORESTCO'S VACANCY CHAINS

The reader is reminded that these vacancy chains represent sequences of linked staffing activities in the *salaried* workforce in this relatively large forestry firm. These data do not represent all vacancy chains occurring at ForestCo, as the firm employs far fewer salaried than hourly personnel. It has approximately 3500 salaried employees, but more than 15,000 hourly employees. Within the salaried workforce, however, the distribution of jobs had almost 80% of all positions located in the middle range of the salary grade hierarchy. Over 30% of all positions were in salary grades 6–10 (generally Administrative and Technical positions), and just under 50% were in salary grades 11–16 (generally Management and Professional positions).

Within this overall distribution of salaried jobs, observed patterns of vacancy chains were not consistent with characterizations of ForestCo's employment system as a stereotypical model of an ILM. First, the distributions of both the origins and the terminations of the vacancy chains sampled were heavily concentrated in the salary grade range 11–15. Approximately 70% of all vacancy chains either originated or terminated or both in this segment of the organizational hierarchy. As might be expected, the distribution of origins of vacancy chains was displaced a little higher than terminations in the organizational hierarchy. Of origins, 17% were above salary grade 15 and 12% at salary grade 10 or below. In comparison, only 8% of terminations were above salary grade 15, but 22% were at grade

10 or below. Neither the hierarchical origin nor the hierarchical termination of vacancy chains was revealed as a factor that either determined or strongly influenced vacancy chain length.

Second, average vacancy chain length, as indicated by the number of staffing moves in each vacancy chain, was short. Approximately 69% of all observed vacancy chains consisted of three or fewer moves. This proportion is likely an underestimate because of the methodological procedures used to collect data on the second sample of vacancy chains. There were very few vacancy chains that covered a large range of salary grades. Most vacancy chains consisted of relatively small sequences of staffing actions that terminated relatively close to the hierarchical level of the originating vacancy.

Third, further evidence of the local rather than system-wide nature of vacancy chains can be found in the data on the average size of each move in each chain. While the overall pattern indicates that ForestCo's vacancy chains are associated with positive career progression, such career progression appears to occur in very short, limited bursts. Even when single move staffing actions are excluded from the analysis, one third of "true" vacancy chains (i.e., ones associated with two or more moves) are ones in which there was no net career progression. Altogether, the average career progression associated with ForestCo's vacancy chains was less than ½ salary grade per move.

A preliminary interpretation of these data is that the patterns of vacancy chains associated with sequences of related staffing actions are associated only partially with underlying job and career ladders in ForestCo's organization. Although job ladders are essential elements of a core model of ILM operation, the hierarchical lengths of job ladders may not be inferred directly from patterns of vacancy chains. Vacancy chains are sequences of related staffing actions, each of which typically involves a different employee. Because the total number of career moves made by any one employee may occur over one, two, or three decades, each career move would be part of a different vacancy chain process. Substantial career progression is possible within the patterns of vacancy chain spans such as those revealed here if there are multiple career pathways through the employment system. Small sequences of moves typically associated with any one vacancy chain would indicate only part of the web of career pathways in the overall employment system.

For reasons as yet undetermined, most vacancy chains terminate shortly after they have been initiated. Moreover, most vacancy chains in this corporation are concentrated in the heavily populated but relatively narrow range of the salary grade hierarchy associated with Managerial and Professional occupations. The segments of salary grades covered by these jobs are the average working levels of these occupations. Perhaps significantly, the upper range of the hierarchy associated with these and even higher salary grades has a restricted grade ratio. That is, for any particular salary grade, there are generally fewer positions at the next higher grade than at the focal grade. For example, there are more positions at grade 12 than at grade 11. Similarly, there are more positions at grade 13 than at grade 12. However, there are significantly *fewer* positions at grade 14 than at grade 13, and even fewer at grades 15, 16, 17, and 18 than at each next lower grade. The stereotypical pyramid shape of the hierarchy manifests itself primarily between grades 13 and 18. Distributions of grades and associated grade ratios such as these suggest a relatively intense competitive sorting-out of candidates for senior management positions. A predominance of short vacancy chains in this region of the organization's hierarchy facilitates a competitive, adaptive process through which upper-middle Managers and Professionals are assessed, developed, and assessed again as to their suitability for senior-level Management and Executive positions.

Although further speculations about the general nature of ForestCo's ILM are possible from this preliminary statistical portrait of vacancy chains, further evidence is available from more detailed investigations of the vacancy chains studied through interviews. It is to this perspective on vacancy chains that we now move. In fact, the primary and extended discussion of ForestCo's vacancy chains presented in the next three chapters is based on interview data. This qualitative approach was considered essential for understanding *why* certain vacancy chains emerged as they did.

4

Minimal Vacancy Chains

INTRODUCTION

This second chapter of Part II elaborates a vacancy chain perspective on ForestCo's internal labor market (ILM). It is also the first of three chapters to examine vacancy chain processes from a more detailed and interpretive perspective than the more objective, quantitative, statistical analysis presented in Chapter 3. Further details and interpretations of the contextual and situational reasons for each vacancy chain evolving as it did are based on information obtained from interviews with persons responsible for the decisions at the staffing nodes in each vacancy chain. Although based on interviews concerning staffing decisions, the information obtained is presented from a vacancy chain perspective. The interpretive focus comes from attempts to make sense, not of each staffing decision and action, but of the overall set of issues associated with each vacancy chain.

Making sense of interview data on vacancy chains in this manner is not straightforward. The sheer volume of information on the more than 300 staffing decisions and actions comprising the 71 vacancy chains (the ones for which interview data were obtained) cannot be digested without some means of focusing attention on selected subgroups of the sample. Even when such focus has been accomplished, individual vacancy chains can be revealed as quite complicated social phenomena. An underlying methodological concern, therefore, is with the means used to identify the component attributes of the vacancy chains studied. In the discussions that follow, attention is focused on different groupings of the first sample of 71 vacancy chains organized by the number of moves in each chain. The reason for proceeding this way is similar to the argument presented in Chapter 3, where it was noted that vacancy chain length, as measured by the number of sequenced staffing actions, was the primary indicator of ILM processes. That is, longer vacancy chains exhibited a sustained preference for internal candidates over those from the external labor market (ELM). De facto, longer vacancy chains are more characteristic of ILM processes than are short ones.

In this chapter, the primary focus is on individual staffing actions and minimal vacancy chains composed of two sequentially related staffing actions. If long vacancy chains constitute the primary evidence for existence of an ILM, then single staffing actions and minimal vacancy chains can be considered as evidence antithetical to ILM phenomena. This chapter therefore focuses on the equivalent of a null hypothesis regarding the stereotypical operation of ILMs. Subsequent chapters examine longer vacancy chains that may be considered to be more representative of ILM processes. Chapter 5 presents information on medium-length vacancy chains of three, four, or five moves. Chapter 6 presents information on the longest vacancy chains encountered: those of six or more moves.

The examination of single staffing actions and of two-move vacancy chains is presented in two separate sections. In each section, objective features of minimal vacancy chains, such as their frequency of occurrence, hierarchical location, and general occupational attributes, are first considered. More complex qualitative and interpretive descriptions of each set of minimal vacancy chains follow. For the set of single staffing actions, these descriptions are presented in an approximate sequence that reflects the extent to which competitive market processes appear to be present. For the set of two-move vacancy chains, "reasons" for their origination and termination are examined. Following these preliminary assessments of each set of minimal vacancy chains, a retrospective and collective appreciation of these phenomena for the operation of ILMs is presented.

SINGLE STAFFING ACTIONS

The topic of single staffing actions initially appears to be an incongruous introduction to a discussion of vacancy chains. The incongruity arises because single staffing actions are the antithesis of vacancy chains. By definition, a vacancy chain embodies at least one choice, if not several, of a preference for candidates already employed within the firm. Single staffing actions exhibit no such preference. A comparison of single staffing actions with sequences of staffing actions (linked into vacancy chains) could potentially reveal insight into the characteristics of vacancy chains considered as a collective phenomenon. A focus on vacancy chains alone (e.g., short vs. long) has the potential to reveal differences among the attributes of vacancy chains, but not the capacity to identify characteristics that are either always or never present in all vacancy chains. Thus, this examination of single staffing actions could reveal why these staffing actions stand alone and indicate why none either preceded or was followed by sequences of related staffing actions.

In a stereotypical model of ILM operation, single staffing actions can be expected to occur when jobs normally considered to be located at a port of entry become vacant. While such jobs are considered to be part of the ILM, they are also very proximate to the ELM. Applicants from the ELM may be considered to be competitive with candidates from the ILM, as performance of these jobs may be considered to require little firm-specific knowledge. Still other single staffing actions may occur when positions require skills that are not normally developed within a firm's ILM. Finally, other diverse and idiosyncratic reasons for the existence of single staffing actions may be embedded in the local context of each staffing opportunity. Because there is little prior theory to explain these relatively anomalous staffing actions, this chapter is presented initially as a detailed description of these single staffing actions, from which more general properties of ILM operation may be inferred.

Objective Descriptions of Single Staffing Actions

Seven single staffing actions, that is, ones apparently unrelated to other staffing actions, were uncovered as part of the interview-based survey of all salaried staffing actions reported to the central personnel section of ForestCo. Table 4.1 presents summary information on these staffing actions.

Although relatively small, this sample of single staffing actions does not appear to be

Table 4.1. Summary of Single Staffing Actions

Staffing action number	Salary grade	Occupation or function	Initiation of vacancy	Staffing action
22	13	Maintenance	New position	Promote from hourly ranks.
24	14	Research	New position	Hire from ELM with headhunter.
32	9–11	Computers	Personal qualifications	Promote within position.
42	17	Marketing	New product	Opportunistic hire.
43	13	Training	Reorganization	External search, internal appointment.
57	11	Stores	New position	Promote from hourly ranks.
59	11	Relief foreman	Fill long-term vacancy	Promote from hourly ranks.

anomalous when compared to various features of the distribution observed in the total sample of vacancy chains. Six of the seven staffing actions occurred at salary grades in the range 11–15, which is where most vacancy chains and staffing actions take place. Thus, apparently, these single staffing actions are not occurring because of vacancies in positions normally considered to be ports of entry. This judgment could be premature, however, as three of these single staffing actions occurred for positions that were proximate to the "boundary" between this salaried ILM and that of the senior members of the hourly workforce. As these three positions were strongly related to production (No. 22, Maintenance Supervisor; No. 57, Project Receiver; and No. 59, Relief Shift Foreman), experienced hourly employees who were familiar with both production technologies and the work cultures of different mills were prime candidates for these new positions. Appointment of an hourly employee to a salaried position could trigger a subsequent sequence of staffing actions within the hourly ILM, but such consequences could not be discerned from the salaried side of the relatively opaque boundary maintained between the hourly and salaried employment systems of this single organization. Therefore, these staffing actions are not necessarily single staffing actions, but are so labeled because of this boundary.

A second speculation regarding the incidence of single staffing actions, rather than sequences of staffing actions linked to produce a vacancy chain, was that ILM processes were least appropriate when the distributions of required skills favored ELMs rather than ILMs. Modest support for this interpretation could be found in this relatively small sample of single staffing actions. With the exception of single staffing action No. 32, the six other appointments involved situations in which candidates were being sought for new positions. While novelty of skill requirements is not a sufficient condition for hiring personnel from the ELM, certainly there is less tradition and precedent for staffing new positions internally than there is for positions located in previously established job ladders. Staffing actions 22, 43, 57, and 59 were to fill new positions associated with new plants or new methods of production or both. Staffing action 24 was to fill a "new" position designed to meet increased demand in a project-based work-assignment system. Finally, staffing action 42 was an opportunistic matching of a potentially available employee with a new position that had not yet been fully defined.

Market versus Administered Aspects of Single Staffing Actions

Because there is no established order or hierarchy of attributes of vacancy chains, the seven single staffing actions reflect the tension between competitive "market" mechanisms for the pricing and distribution of labor and the administrative rules used as substitutes for such mechanisms. The sample of seven single staffing actions presented in Table 4.1 illustrates a variety of organizational staffing actions. Some of these actions exemplify neoclassical and competitive economic views of labor markets; others illustrate administrative shortcuts. Each of these single staffing actions will be discussed in an approximate sequence from those that appear to closely emulate competitive market precepts to those that appear to be more dominated by either expediency or administrative rules.

Staffing action 24, which involved the identification of a need for a Senior Research Chemist, appeared to match the market model most closely. Changes in the external environment had been recorded and responded to through new products and processes inside the organization. In particular, the competition for markets for fine paper required ForestCo to undertake basic and applied research on image analysis for paper and print quality assessment. As the knowledge, skills, and competencies required for these specialized tasks would not normally be available inside the organization, they had to be sought in the ELM.

There were two distinctive features of this hire. First, because of the highly specialized and technical demands that would be made of the new hire, the search for suitable candidates was itself highly focused and specialized. There was only a relatively small number of potential candidates, perhaps fewer than 30 in all of North America, with the requisite expertise and experience considered appropriate for the new job. Hence, the search method used was highly focused on targeted persons. Second, because this recruitment task was outside the "normal" expertise of research scientists already employed at ForestCo, and because the technical requirements of the proposed new hire could be specified with considerable precision, the initial task of searching this specialized niche of the total labor market could be contracted out to a specialist. Consequently, the Department Head hired a headhunter (executive search firm) to identify suitable candidates. A total of ten candidates were evaluated, and four were interviewed by the Department Head. The preliminary choice of the "best" candidate was subsequently reviewed by several other senior members of the research group, as well as by senior people in the Production and Marketing Departments who would be working with this person.

The procedures used in this hiring process appear to be consistent with the normative requirements of the neoclassical model of labor markets. First, the job requirements were known and could be specified. Second, the costs of searching the appropriate ELM were reduced by identifying the small market niche in which candidates were likely to be found and contracting the task to a specialized agency. Third, a "reasonable" number of potential candidates were reviewed, and a more detailed examination was made of those on the shortlist. This selection procedure follows an effectiveness–efficiency paradigm of increased focus on a reduced set of possible solutions. Finally, the preliminary selection of the preferred candidate was assessed against nontechnical job criteria, through interviews with senior managers in Production and Marketing.

Although the economically rational requirements of a neoclassical model of labor markets appear to have been met in hiring this Senior Research Chemist, the continuing employment of this person and other research scientists fits less well. First, there is an established line of progression within the technical specialty of Chemistry with occupational level indicated by the titles: Chemist, Research Chemist, Senior Research Chemist, Research Associate, and Senior Research Associate. These positions, their relative ranks, and the compensation associated with their relative ranks are based primarily on the seniority, experience, and performance of these scientists. Mobility up this implicit hierarchy from one position to the next is heavily dependent on experience, as indexed by the employees' age and seniority. There is no fixed "job" for these employees, as they apply their talents from project to project. The economic return resulting from an application of their skills is most difficult to measure. Consequently, appropriate rates of compensation are determined more by administrative rules and social comparisons than by an application of the neoclassical model of labor markets. Thus, entry into this occupational hierarchy in ForestCo's ILM is dominated by neoclassical considerations, whereas mobility within the ILM departs significantly from this model.

Staffing action 43, though a more traditional appointment, also manifested a rational, adaptive response to environmental change by the organization. This appointment was that of a new position in a newly organized, rebuilt mill. At this new mill, local management was attempting to instill new ways of operating into a workforce that was still dependent on very experienced craft employees. Complicating this task was the recognition that many of these senior employees would qualify for retirement in the next five years. A significant task associated with the rebuilding of the new mill, then, was to elicit and codify much of the craft wisdom currently held by the most senior employees and to ensure that this knowledge was passed on to their replacements. The formal role developed to accomplish this task was that of a Training and Development Coordinator.

Because the mill rebuilding was a significant and high-priority investment that had been in progress for two years, several recent internal postings had left the local managers with a good knowledge of all potential internal candidates. They judged that the qualities they required were not available internally and consequently decided to search the ELM. Again, executive search firms were used, and approximately a dozen candidates brought forward for further review. A shortlist of three candidates was obtained following group telephone interviews between each candidate and three members of an interview panel. Each shortlisted candidate was brought to town and interviewed personally by local managers. In addition, all three candidates were assessed by a firm of consulting psychologists.

These recruitment and selection procedures are extraordinarily thorough. Indeed, they are among the most thorough of any found in this organization. This thoroughness derived from two principal characteristics of the local situation. First, the training function was judged to be a critical component in realizing the benefits from a $50 million investment in a mill upgrade. Local managers clearly viewed the mill operation as a sociotechnical system. While engineers and mill designers could build a very modern processing plant, the ways in which plant employees thought about and used this new capital equipment was a necessary component of plant efficiency and productivity. Instrumentally, a most thorough selection method could be justified in terms of the performance payoffs associated with the assignment of the best available candidate.

Second, this selection was a high-profile appointment. The reputation of the candidate selected, and the reputation of those who chose him, rested on his capacity to work closely and effectively with the most skilled and experienced craft workers in the mill. Many of these men had worked in the industry for more than 30 years, and their cooperation depended to a large extent on their accepting the genuine capacity of the Training Coordinator. The political reputation of those in the Employee Relations function depended on their being able to select a candidate who could work with this critical group of experienced employees.

A third factor that may also have influenced the intensity of the search for a suitable candidate was that the new hire would belong to the Personnel or Employee Relations occupational group. Selection of this appointee was therefore being done by employees whose professional expertise was supposed to cover the tasks of employee selection! In this mill at least, the credibility of employee relations was manifestly on the line in the quality of the candidate they affirmed for this new position. Not surprisingly, the selection procedures were most thorough.

Staffing action 59 also occurred as a consequence of a reorganization. In fact, the local manager noted that "we're in a constant reorganization because the woodroom is being remanned and restructured." Again, this was a large, high-profile capital investment in a "new" mill involving a complement of more than 60 salaried employees ranging from the Mill Manager through various Department Heads to First-Line Supervisors, Secretaries, and Clerks. Methods of work and the nature of supervision were considered critical requirements of this new mill, as noted previously in the discussion of staffing action 43. Two new positions were confirmed as being required and needing to be filled. One of these was that of a Relief Shift Foreman for the planer mill.

In the search for a suitable appointee, the requirements for the position were posted and qualified candidates were invited to apply. Approximately 35 candidates from both this division and other divisions were considered as part of a large-scale review and survey of hourly employees. In addition, a roundtable discussion was organized with several senior supervisors who had experience with most of these men on their crews to review the abilities, capacities, and attitudes of future hourly employees. This initial screening process turned up no immediately suitable candidates for the Relief Shift Foreman's job. Nevertheless, a shortlist of potential candidates was prepared, and each of these candidates was invited to attend a panel interview. Following the initial interviews, some candidates were brought back for second interviews, and a few were referred to a firm of consulting psychologists for assessment. Even after this large investment in searching for a suitable candidate, this first survey failed to identify anyone who the selection panel believed had the desired capacities for the vacant job.

Consequently, the positions were advertised in the local newspapers. Some 30–40 applications were received, candidate qualifications were reviewed, and those of applicants initially shortlisted were checked through reference calls to current and prior employers. Six shortlisted candidates were interviewed by the same selection panel that had not found a suitable candidate from within the hourly ranks of the division. A suitable candidate was finally identified and appointed. Interestingly, this person was already a ForestCo employee working in an hourly position in a Region different from that in which the current job was available and one in which the original internal posting had *not* been made.

A complicating feature of this "hire" was the tension between the implicit requirements of the position and the expectations of most of the hourly workers who applied for the position, but who were judged to be unsuitable. Clearly, there was a substantial mismatch between the expectations of the 35 hourly employees who either applied for consideration or allowed their candidacy to go forward and those of the supervisors responsible for selecting the chosen candidate. In microcosm, this selection process encapsulated a significant feature of organizational staffing, namely, what factors influence the choice of make or buy? How are expectations of future performance established independently of those manifested in a large sample of nominally qualified candidates? Even when there are many internal candidates available, what factors lead a selection process to reject candidates from the ILM and search the ELM, as happened here?

In this particular instance, the search of the ELM was initiated for two reasons. First, the selected candidate was to be a member of a management team committed to a "new way" of producing lumber. Attachments to tradition, old customs, and previous ways of doing things were regarded as an impediment to the desired innovation. Potential appointees from the ILM, even those from a different sector such as the hourly employees of the same firm, were examined carefully to see whether they exhibited initiative with respect to new ideas and thoughts. Second, the selection panel was searching for someone who had the capacity, interest, and desire for advancement beyond this initial position. They were not looking for "good workers" or wishing to "reward loyalty." They looked for initiative, education, and potential for succession. However, by "going outside," they placed pressure on both the management team, which rejected many internal candidates, and the person finally appointed to the new position. According to the Regional Employee Relations Manager, local management was

> ... chastised for not hiring "one of the guys." Even the local foreman was upset. The selection caused disenchantment because in the past we almost always brought people in on the basis of them being likable and knowing how to do the job. This appointment became a sensitive political issue, and there was both overt and covert backlash.

Nevertheless, the appointment served as a highly visible, symbolic signal that management was doing something differently than they had in the past. By sticking to a hiring policy that selected people primarily to suit the position, they "shook up the built-in culture" of the plant. In both substance and style, this appointment was an integral component of the evolutionary change in production operations required by the competitive marketplace. In this instance, the pressure for change was in conflict with the traditions of a craft-based workforce. This appointment also provides insight into a potential limitation of ILM operation: Internal staffing is more likely to sustain past practices. Internal rules and established procedures for staffing can limit the responsiveness of the organization to pressures for change. When substantial change is required, wider and external search will be a more suitable process.

Single staffing actions 22 and 57 also involved "hires" from the ranks of hourly workers, and both were associated with local aspects of organizational change. Staffing action 57 was a new job that emerged from new capital investments—in this case, an upgrade of a lumber mill: A new position of Project Receiver was created for someone to manage the receipt, inventory, and replacement of materials used in the mill rebuilding. Once the rebuilding had been completed, this employee would manage the same function for the regular maintenance of the mill. Because the mill had been shut down and the new mill had not yet begun production, there was no pool of known candidates readily available locally from the hourly workforce. Therefore, the vacant position was posted within the Region, and a small number of candidates applied. Three of these candidates were interviewed by a panel of three local managers, and the final candidate was selected.

Although standard operating procedures were followed in the selection of this candidate, the intensity of the scrutiny by the selection panel was less than that noted in the other hires described so far. For example, the manager responsible for this appointment had no rigorous selection criteria and anticipated little regret if the appointment failed to work as anticipated:

> Promotability wasn't as important as competence to support the stores function—at most it would be good if the person hired was able to provide relief supervision if required.
> If he's ineffective, his selection could cost quite a few dollars in over-investment in parts or the lack of needed parts.

Although the performance of the Project Receiver was considered to be relatively important, his performance was not critical to the success of the whole capital investment.

In addition, a poor selection did not necessarily reflect badly on the professional competence of the members of the selection panel.

In the case of staffing action 22, there was a major reorganization of the Maintenance/Engineering/Training operations at a large paper mill. This reorganization was occasioned by a significant level of technical upgrading of the mill. The new position was that of a permanent Maintenance Supervisor as the project crew responsible for installing the new paper machine turned it over to regular operations. In this instance, a "young" hourly employee who had "good millwright experience on paper machines" and who had recently been used as a Relief Supervisor from time to time was considered to be an "up-and-coming" candidate for a Supervisor's position. On the basis of his previous job performance, he was considered to be "enthusiastic, smart, and fast-learning," and the Maintenance/Engineering manager reported that "we wanted him before someone else got him." In addition, the local mill "needed someone fast," as the maintenance job was clearly and rapidly getting beyond the capacities of the skeleton staff currently assigned to these functions and tasks. A quick fit was seen between the problem situation and a possible solution, and the decision to appoint the new supervisor was readily made with little additional search and analysis. Expediency and opportunity shaped this assignment process. While some search among competing candidates may have been done implicitly, there was no overt, public, competitive process.

The two remaining single staffing actions are more idiosyncratic in their form. In the case of staffing action 42, a Vice-President who managed operations that generated sales in excess of $500 million was searching for someone to manage the introduction of new products. While his group was already testing a generic product for the marketplace, the final form of the new product had not yet been determined. Moreover, the management group for this Division had not yet established the qualifications and requirements for the person they wished to have manage the marketing process for the new product. A general appreciation of this whole process had been developing for some time when the Vice-President received a call from a past subordinate. This person had previously worked for ForestCo in a position similar to the one the management team was currently trying to fill. Moreover, this person had recently been laid off from another firm in the industry because that firm was dropping a particular product line that was similar to the one being introduced at ForestCo. A potential match was immediately seen. A senior manager was looking to fill a position that was not yet completely defined. A candidate, with appropriate qualifications, called to find out about potential openings. An opportunistic hire was quickly arranged.

In contrast to several of the other single staffing actions discussed, this hire was regarded as a temporary, provisional arrangement. If the new product went bust, the Vice-President had little obligation to find an alternative position for the new hire elsewhere in ForestCo. Advancement and succession potential were not considerations because of the appointee's age (late 50s). In addition, the rank, authority, and discretion of the Vice-President allowed him to make this staffing action without being questioned publicly by his immediate supervisor. Many of the constraints operating on lower-level managers, such as a requirement to find very high-quality candidates and to do so through a process that legitimized the choice, were not operating here. Consequently, it was relatively easy for the Vice-President to take advantage of this serendipitous opportunity.

The final single staffing action to be reviewed (32) involves the promotion, within his current position, of an Intermediate Computer Technician to Senior Computer Technician. This action involved a "promotion" to a position two salary grades above his previous level. As with research scientists, the work of computer technicians is project-oriented. It is difficult to assign a pay-for-job compensation package, as projects, trivial and critical, come and go. In situations such as this, advancement is not a pull-flow—that is, driven by a position vacancy—but a push-flow—that is, it is driven by the candidate's accumulation of experience and qualifications. Triggers for advancement emerge from considerations of the timing of professional development, indicators of performance, and appreciation of the rewards required to motivate both current performance and potential learning and development required for future performance. The supervisor's rationale for the appointment reflected his appreciation of these factors:

> He was doing the work of two people, and was doing more complex tasks. He's put no end of effort into his work, he's self-driven, flexible and now very well-rounded. We felt this man shouldn't be exploited but should be paid what was fair. After seven years service he should be rewarded.

There was no overt competition for this promotion and no explicit comparison of this candidate's performance against the likely work performances of other potential candidates. In the absence of market comparisons, application of administrative rules can lead to employee assignments that differ from those that market mechanisms would have produced. However, these deviations from market could favor equally either the employee or the organization. In this situation, the social norms and implicit comparisons brought into the organization led to notions of a normative relationship between pay level and performance. These mechanisms then substituted for pricing and allocation solutions normally obtained through market actions.

This more detailed summary of single staffing actions reveals a wide array of search practices. Search practices were largely shaped by the practical exigencies encountered in each staffing situation. Public, competitive searches were used to serve instrumental, political, and symbolic purposes. When there were likely large payoffs in organizational performance, and consequently large payoffs from wider, more competitive searches for suitable candidates, more candidates were considered and each was investigated more thoroughly. When the self-interests and reputations of those performing the search for candidates depended on meeting others' interests, searches were also more extensive. Finally, the manner in which some searches were conducted also fulfilled symbolic functions. Extensive but inconclusive searches of an ILM and the consequent selection and appointment from outside signaled discontinuity and change in established traditions.

Even within this small sample of single staffing actions presented in Table 4.1 and described above, different search practices were associated with the extent to which strong vacancy assumptions applied. If a search for suitable candidates was to be extensive, the attributes and requirements of the job to be filled preceded the search and selection of candidates. Thus, the more extensive searches for a Research Chemist (24), a Training Coordinator (43), the Relief Foreman (59), and the Project Receiver (57) were ones in which job requirements were well defined. In the case of the first two staffing actions (24 and 43), such definition permitted the delegation of the search to parties external to the firm. In the three instances in which a search was either not required, or opportunistic, or expedient, the qualities of the persons chosen were at least as important as, if not more important than, job requirements. The promotion of the Computer Technician (32) was based on only a general assessment of his work performance compared to social norms. The selection and appointment of the New Products Manager (42) and that of the Maintenance Supervisor (22) were strongly influenced by the qualities of the persons themselves. The jobs that each would be expected to perform would depend more on their personal talents and capacities than on some previous, nonpersonal assessment of job requirements.

Organizational Change

A retrospective review of this sample of single staffing actions in ForestCo's organization reveals the extent and importance of organizational change found in that company. It was not uncommon for there to be concurrently areas that were expanding in their organizational complement and other areas that were cutting back on their staffing levels. Because similar or related skill sets were often required in different plants and divisions, including both those that were expanding and those that were cutting back, a number of moves occurred because a cutback in one area could be matched with an expansion elsewhere. There were many instances, however, in which these expansions and contractions did not match—either because of skill incompatibility or because the timing of layoffs in one place could not be synchronized with the hiring and utilization of new employees elsewhere.

A second aspect of organizational change at ForestCo was that general assignments of groups of individuals to large, functional tasks could vary greatly in the detailed assignment of employees to particular jobs. For example, two similar departments could have the same total workforce complements, and have identical annual budgets, but still arrive at quite different organizational arrangements for accomplishing departmental objectives. This freedom and flexibility (or lack of determinism) permitted considerable experimentation on the part of local managers and allowed much local fine-tuning of organizational adaptation. Although the pace of organizational change varied from section to section, from division to division, and from one time period to another as a function of changes in the larger economic environment, few organizational arrangements were regarded as fixed. There was astonishing dynamism in the assignment of individual employees to particular jobs. The climbing frame (jungle gym) of organizational positions over which employees moved was a skeletal framework that altered its overall shape very slowly. However, the local details of particular job arrangements changed frequently. Thus, many "new" jobs could be created consequent to a reorganization of preexisting jobs—with no change in the overall complement of employees assigned to a particular section or division. At other times, additional jobs would be created when the existing complement or the existing skill set was regarded as insufficient for the emerging demands on a particular organizational unit.

From time to time, managers in this organization would behave opportunistically and experiment with temporary arrangements until they had a better appreciation of the overall changes that might be affecting their unit. Thus, it was not uncommon for a preexisting position to be left vacant once its previous occupant had moved elsewhere. However, if implementation of the temporary arrangement proved to be not worthwhile on a more permanent basis, then actions would eventually be initiated to fill the long-standing vacant position. Thus, a "new" position or a net increase in a temporary complement could occur even though there was no change in the long-term complement of the organizational unit. Not surprisingly under these circumstances, there was little relationship between the immediate staffing actions and the historical events that had originally produced this "vacant" position.

There is also preliminary evidence that single staffing actions are likely to occur in contexts associated with technological and organizational change. Several of the single staffing actions were associated with technical specialists and their jobs. Given technological change, new positions and functions provide organizations with opportunities to break with custom and tradition. Merely switching a previously established line of progression from an old job to a new one runs the risk that change will not occur. Inertial tendencies associated with previous customs and socializations could nullify the effort and intent expended to create the new position. However, many new jobs also require the extension of past knowledge and experience. Hence, selection for new positions requires a delicate balance between extensions of past skills and experiences and the development of new, different applications of those skills.

Summary of Single Staffing Actions

Initial counts of the incidence of single staffing actions appear to be overstated. Four of the seven staffing actions initially labeled as single were so classified because of the administrative separation of salaried and hourly employment systems. For these "single" staffing actions, initial vacancies in ForestCo's ILM produced no further evidence of subsequent related staffing actions because, if such actions occurred, they did so in the hourly employment system, and pursuit of administrative paper trails across this boundary was not feasible in this study.

Whether these four staffing actions are included in the total sample of single staffing actions or not, there is little evidence to indicate that single staffing actions are initiated only when vacancies occur at positions deemed to be ports of entry. In fact, the distribution by salary grade of all single staffing actions was consistent with the overall distribution of vacancy chains. Furthermore, most of these single staffing actions were initiated by the creation of new positions as part of a pervasive phenomenon of technological and organizational change. Traditional job ladders are not necessarily relevant for the staffing of new positions. Only two staffing actions (57 and 59) more or less followed established lines of progression.

More detailed examination of single staffing actions also reveals the limitations of ILM processes. In the case of the highly specialized professional Research Chemist position (staffing action 24), the skills required for the new line of business could not be developed or made within ForestCo's ILM. Consequently, there was little potential payoff in searching inside, and a formal search of the ELM was immediately undertaken.

Wide competitive searches for suitable candidates served instrumental, political, and symbolic functions. When individual performance could be viewed as having a material impact on overall departmental or organizational performance, investments in competitive search procedures were substantial. Competitive searches for candidates were also initiated when the reputation and self-interest of those responsible for candidate choice were potentially at risk. The investments of time and energy in the search process helped legitimate staffing outcomes and lessened the political risks to those held responsible for staffing outcomes. Competitive searches were also pursued when the senior managers responsible for the selection of candidates for a vacant position wished to signal a change in traditional practices. This phenomenon was a distinct feature of staffing action 59, in which an external candidate was chosen after an extensive and rigorous search within ForestCo's ILM. In this instance, normal ILM practices were regarded as dysfunctional, and a change from established norms and traditions was sought.

When a search was extensive, job definitions and requirements preceded individual attributes, both conceptually and temporally. However, when the persons looking to fill vacant positions were influenced by experiences of expediency and urgency, strong vacancy assumptions were less evident. Certainly, the Vice-President's expedient choice of a past subordinate as a New Product Manager was strongly influenced by the immediacy of a potential match between a specific person and rather vague appreciation of the new job to be performed. In addition, the need to recognize the talents of the up-and-coming young hourly worker before he was enticed elsewhere was as much a factor in his appointment (22) as the precise fit between his skills and the requirements of the Mainte-nance Supervisor job. Finally, the lack of job definition typically associated with computer-related project work (32) also limited the application of the strong vacancy assumption. Here, the promotion was driven by the employee's attributes and comparisons of his work performance with implicit norms.

This interpretive evaluation of single staffing actions based on information obtained from interviews has elaborated a number of further issues associated with the operation of vacancy chains. Single staffing actions, however, are but one set of minimal vacancy chains considered in this chapter. In the section that follows, a larger sample of two-move vacancy chains is similarly examined.

SINGLE-LINK STAFFING ACTIONS: TWO-MOVE VACANCY CHAINS

Single-link staffing actions are those that involve two persons, in which the move of the first person produces the antecedent conditions leading to the move of the second person. Conceptually, these two-move bundles of staffing actions are also representative of minimal vacancy chains, as there is a single linkage between an antecedent move and a consequent staffing action.

While these two-move vacancy chains may be considered to consist of an antecedent and a consequent staffing action, the antecedent "move" may not necessarily be an organizationally motivated staffing action. For example, an individual employee could voluntarily quit, independent of any plans or intentions on the part of organizational representatives. Vacancy chains can also be initiated by factors that reflect neither organi-zational nor individual interests. For example, staffing actions can be initiated by an involuntary action on the part of an employee, such as being required to take long-term disability. In other instances, involuntary employee actions such as early or regular retirement may be anticipated, even if not controlled, by organizational planners. In these circumstances, organizational interests may or may not be served by the lack of control over the initiation of the vacancy chain. However, some proportion of single-link staffing actions do occur as a consequence of conscious, voluntary acts on the part of an agent representing the organization. For example, a manager may promote an existing em-ployee to a new position and then hire a replacement for the vacated position from the ELM. Alternatively, managers may reorganize their departments and reassign their sub-ordinates to a mixture of new and old positions. Nevertheless, whatever the specific antecedent conditions, the next group of minimal vacancy chains to be examined here are associated with changes in two job–person matches in the organization.

Table 4.2 presents a summary of the 20 two-move vacancy chains found at ForestCo, in which a change in the organizational status of one person could be attributed directly to a prior change in the status of another. This subsample represents 28% of the sample of 71 vacancy chains analyzed by means of interviews with the managers responsible for each staffing action.

The classification scheme presented in Table 4.2 should be regarded as approximate for several reasons. As with single staffing actions, the classification of two-move vacancy chains is partially compromised by the artificial separation of the salaried and hourly wage employment systems. Three of the sets of two related staffing actions identified as two-move vacancy chains involved "hires" from the hourly wage employment system to salaried positions. Whether these moves were associated with subsequent moves within

Table 4.2. Summary of Two-Move Vacancy Chains

Vacancy chain No.	Salary grades[a]	Occupation or function[b]	Initiation of vacancy[c]	Staffing actions[d]
6	5–5	Clerical	New project	Transfer from temporary postion.
7	10–10	Accounting	Reorganization	Transfer plus hire from ELM.
10	12–12	Engineering	Implicit transfer	Hire from ELM.
11	12–12	Engineering	Resignation	Opportunistic hire from ELM.
15	19–19	Management	Development	Switch of two managers.
18	HH–15	Supervisory	Resignation	Promote from hourly ranks.
21	12–14	Supervisory	Long-term disability plus Development	Promote to new position.
26	6–6	Clerical	Discharge	Hire from ELM.
30	11–14	Computers	Progression	New position plus internal replacement
31	11–12	Computers	New position	Promotion plus hire from ELM.
41	10–12	Purchasing	New position	Promotion plus internal replacement
49	11–12	Supervisory	Reorganization	Promotion plus internal replacement
51	12–13	Supervisory	New position	Transfer plus internal replacement
52	HH–13	Supervisory	Preretirement	Transfer plus replacement from hourly
53	11–14	Accounting	Development	Rotation
55	HH–11	Maintenance	Preretirement	Planned replacement from hourly
58	11–11	Supervisory	Reorganization	New position plus replacement from ELM.
61	13–13	Forestry	Reorganization	New position plus replacement from ELM.
63	13–15	Forestry	Reorganization	New position plus internal replacement
67	16–20	Management	Resignation	Limited succession

[a–d]Column heads: [a]salary grades of the terminating and originating vacancies (HH indicates a move from the hourly payroll); [b]occupational or functional area in which staffing occurred; [c]interpretation of antecedent cause of originating vacancy; [d]summary description of overall staffing sequence.

or into the hourly wage employment system was not discernible from available records. There are other reasons for cautious interpretations and classifications. For one, single-link staffing actions involve two related individual moves. Depending on whether emphasis is placed on the first move, the second move, or both moves, the interpretation of the primary antecedent condition that produces the sequence of staffing actions can vary. In addition, it has been argued, and found, that few staffing actions can be considered to make sense independently of their context. Staffing contexts are complex, and this complexity has the clear potential to render any interpretation problematic. This complexity is particularly true of these two-move vacancy chains, as several involved multiple issues.

Distribution of Two-Move Vacancy Chains by Hierarchical Level

Like the sample of single staffing actions described previously, this second sample of minimal vacancy chains was not concentrated in a small band of the organizational hierarchy. Two-move vacancy chains originated across a wide range of salary grades, from 5 to 20. As with the distribution of positions, however, a large proportion (65%) of the 20 staffing actions associated with two-move vacancy chains were located in the Managerial and Professional occupational group defined as salary grades 11–15. There is little evidence, therefore, to indicate that these minimal vacancy chains were initiated because the originating vacancy occurred close to traditional ports of entry. Once again, however, such interpretations should be made cautiously because three of these vacancy chains resulted in moves from the hourly wage employment system.

Other quantitative attributes of two-move vacancy chains also indicate little to distinguish them from the larger sample of vacancy chains studied. For example, the distribution of range of salary grades between initiating and terminating vacancies for this subsample was similar to that for the whole set surveyed. Three had indeterminate ranges of salary grades, as they involved moves from the hourly wage employment system. Of the remaining 17, 8 involved no net change in salary grade, 3 involved changes of only a single salary grade, 3 involved changes of two salary grades, 2 involved changes over a range of three salary grades, and 1 involved changes over a range of four salary grades. When compared to the distribution of salary grade changes for the whole sample, this subsample is weighted slightly more heavily toward no salary grade change. However, these differences are small, and the majority of these two-move vacancy chains are also associated with salary grade ranges of two or fewer.

For both types of minimal vacancy chains, namely, single staffing actions and two-move vacancy chains, no objective, quantitative attributes have been found that distinguish them from the longer vacancy chains considered to be derivative of stereotypical models of ILM operation. Minimal vacancy chains may indeed have features other than their length that distinguish them from stereotypical vacancy chains, but that are peculiar to each local situation. It is to an analysis of these contextual factors that we now turn.

Classification of Two-Move Vacancy Chains by Originating Cause

Given several caveats regarding interpretation of contextual factors, the 20 single-link staffing actions involving the moves of two persons have been classified according to their primary, originating causes as presented in Table 4.3.

A review of these vacancy chains indicates that seven (11, 18, 21, 26, 52, 55, and 67), or approximately one third, were initiated by employees exiting from an existing position. This cause is consistent with traditional interpretations of ILM operation as being stable arrangements of jobs that benchmark and frame employee mobility. Different situations, however, provided different opportunities for managerial control over the nature and timing of these exits. Three vacancy chains were initiated when incumbents resigned from established positions, providing little apparent opportunity for managers to plan for these exigencies. One vacancy chain was initiated when an incumbent experienced ill health and

Table 4.3. Summary of Causes of Origination
of Two-Move Vacancy Chains

Primary originating cause	Number	Vacancy chain numbers
Reorganization/new position	11	6, 7, 30, 31, 41, 49, 51, 53, 58, 61, 63
Resignation/long-term disability	4	11, 18, 21, 67
Retirement	2	52, 55
Discharge/fired	1	26
Confirm transfer	1	10
Development	1	15

went on long-term disability. The remaining three vacancy chains provided more opportunity for managers to anticipate and control the selection and assignment of persons to
positions, as two were associated with preretirement adjustments in anticipation of more
forthcoming exits and one was associated with the termination for cause, or discharge,
of an employee.

Anticipated and Unanticipated Vacancies

A preliminary comparison of two of the three vacancy chains initiated by resignations
(11 and 18) with two initiated by retirements (52 and 55) shows that factors in addition to
planning opportunity also affect staffing processes and outcomes. In vacancy chain 11, an
engineer with specialist technical skills resigned to take a job in a different industry.
Because these specialist skills were considered essential and were not readily available
among less talented and experienced employees, a wide search of the ELM was immediately undertaken. Also, because this vacancy reinforced the manager's appreciation that
his department had limited depth of succession, candidates with clear advancement
potential as well as specialist skills were sought. As this search was generating disappoint-
ing results, a serendipitous inquiry from a previous employee who did possess similar
skills came out of the blue. Quickly, an opportunistic match was made, and the previous
employee was hired to fill the vacant position.

In vacancy chain 18, a previous search inside ForestCo's organization had revealed an
hourly employee who had the potential to move to a supervisory position. However, the
hourly employee was judged not yet ready to take on full supervisory responsibilities.
Consequently, the manager of the department created a developmental "Project Supervisor" position for this person. When a resignation was received, this employee was
sufficiently trained and experienced to take on new responsibilities. In this case, the
manager responsible for the department had anticipated the likelihood that one of four
persons in similar positions might leave the department. Previous investments in training
and development limited the disruptions that might have accompanied this particular
unexpected resignation. Such investments could be made relatively easily, as replacements were sought for several positions, all requiring generic supervisory and paper mill
operating skills. This situation contrasts with that encountered in vacancy chain 11, in
which investments in specialist skills were more difficult to justify. There was only one
position making current use of those skills, and any employee having those skills and also
judged to be surplus to local work demands would have been poached by other firms or
another division within ForestCo.

In contrast to these relatively unexpected staffing requirements are those in vacancy
chains 52 and 55, in which well-anticipated retirements produced initiating vacancies. In
vacancy chain 52, a very experienced employee was transferred to a new, temporary
position on a construction project to ease his eventual retirement. His position was filled
through "normal" succession by the selection and promotion of an hourly employee. This
succession was handled readily by the department that experienced the vacancy, as the
department was located at a remote site and was accustomed to operating independently.
In vacancy chain 55, another anticipated vacancy was used to initiate a search for a
replacement. The position was posted in all pulp mills, and 16 applications were received.
Ten candidates were interviewed in depth by a panel of senior managers, who chose one
candidate for the position. As a further means of confirming the appropriateness of their
choice, the candidate was also interviewed by the mill manager and sent out for psychological testing and counseling.

This brief but more detailed review of two pairs of either anticipated or unanticipated two-move vacancy chains suggests that staffing actions are not influenced solely by the abruptness of their appearance. Prior planning may lessen the effects of surprise, but investments in prior planning may not always make sense. Serendipitous opportunism was encountered in reactions to both anticipated and unanticipated vacancies. One unanticipated vacancy was filled by a fortuitous application by a previous employee. One anticipated vacancy permitted an opportunistic assignment of a retiring employee to a temporary job, facilitating a regular succession from the hourly ranks. These illustrations of traditional ILM operation in which employees leave a stable arrangement of jobs indicate substantial degrees of underlying complexity and uncertainty in the staffing actions associated with each vacancy chain process.

New Positions and Organizational Change

Themes of uncertainty and situational complexity also characterize a majority of two-move vacancy chains. Most surprising, given stereotypical models of ILM operation, was that 11 (55%) of the 20 two-move vacancy chains were associated with either new positions or reorganizations. The stereotypical notion that staffing is primarily concerned with the selection of a person to fill a well-defined, long-established position is not at all representative of ForestCo's salaried ILM. Even though ForestCo may appropriately be regarded as a relatively traditional organization in which a high degree of organizational stability might be assumed, there is much job evolution and change. Within sections, departments, and divisions, the definitions and groupings of tasks and responsibilities into jobs are extraordinarily fluid. New jobs are created to meet changes in the external environment such as increased demand, new equipment and technology, and new ways of doing and thinking about the business. Other actual and anticipated changes in personnel, such as resignations and anticipated retirements, also precipitate reorganizations. Finally, some new jobs are created, and reorganizations made, to facilitate the further development of key staff. Of course, resignations, retirements, or development needs could be met, and were met, by means of staffing actions that did not involve the creation of new positions or reorganizations. However, the significance of the preliminary classification of two-move vacancy chains presented in Table 4.3 is that these issues of organizational change and adaptation were frequently associated with the creation of new positions and the selection and assignment of new and existing employees to those positions.

Staffing was not seen solely as the technical aspects of personnel selection in which candidates were assessed in terms of their capacity to perform a predetermined job. Instead, the selection and assignment of persons to jobs/positions was almost always considered to be interdependent with wider organizational issues that seeped into choice opportunities. Thus, staffing was often seen as a way of implementing a partial solution to an organizational problem or as a means of modifying a problem definition. Staffing actions were also considered to be components of larger organizational problems/issues and of potential solutions. The mix of issues considered as part of these larger problem definitions often included considerations of potential jobs to be filled. However, definitions of these jobs in turn were regarded as parts of possible "solutions" to reassignment issues, driven by the qualities and attributes of persons potentially available for such reassignments. Staffing actions therefore often resulted from decisions that considered a mélange of interactive and reflexive issues. As a way of illustrating these ideas, further details of two representative single-link staffing actions are described.

In vacancy chain 7, the Controller for a Regional Office believed it was time to reinstitute a training and development program for his staff. One such program had been in place in the late 1970s, but had been discontinued in the early 1980s when ForestCo and the whole forestry industry had experienced a long, survival-threatening recession. Discontinuation of the training program, together with concurrent and subsequent restrictions on the hiring of additional personnel, meant that seven years later, the availability of required skills was at risk. A large proportion of middle- and senior-level staff who were both professionally qualified and experienced in company operations were approaching retirement. In addition, there were few qualified employees in the pipeline available for succession.

Implementation of such a training program was not easy, however, as complement controls meant that the Controller could not add training and development positions to his existing complement. Consequently, he had to reorganize his section, in effect giving up a senior clerical position, so as to establish a new position for an Accounting Trainee who would eventually advance to one of the Divisional Accountant jobs likely to become vacant in the future. One consequence of this reorganization was that the secretarial group in his department considered themselves to be understaffed and were unhappy with what they regarded as an implicit increase in their workload.

Nevertheless, a development position was established and the vacancy was posted. Six candidates applied. One was already known to the Controller, as she had recently applied for a similar position at one of the Divisions in the Region and the Controller had been a member of the selection panel that had chosen another candidate. Nevertheless, he remembered this person as having potential. Following the interviews of four shortlisted candidates, he selected her to be appointed to the Accounting Trainee position.

In making this move to the Accounting Trainee position, the successful candidate moved across an implicit career threshold from one line of progression to another. Previously, she had been considered to be an Accounting Clerk, as she had no formal professional qualification. However, as she had been slowly completing various courses, and was now within one or two years of completing the requirements for her professional accounting designation, this appointment moved her from the top of a clerical line of progression to the bottom of a professional line of progression. The transition from one career path into its professional extension, from one role identity in the corporation to another, was not guaranteed by this appointment. The candidate still had to demonstrate competence at the new level of skill likely to be demanded of her. Even so, the appointment represented a significant change in potential stature that was not immediately visible from the simple archival record, which merely noted a transfer of a person from one position to another at the same salary grade level.

This appointment was not without risk to the Controller who initiated the creation of the new position. Members of his secretarial staff were less than happy with the reconfiguration of responsibilities that lessened their numbers. In fact, the female Accounting Trainee, together with the Controller, had to remove a typewriter from her desk, which had previously been the workstation of a secretary. Until this was done, other secretarial staff refused to do typing for her that they did for other Accountants. In addition, there were other personality conflicts associated with the new appointment. The largest risk to the Controller if this appointment did not work out was that he would lose support for the idea of cross-training in his Region. He firmly believed in the value of this training for subsequent organizational performance, but recognized that not every manager in the Region supported his point of view. While he felt that he would still be regarded well by his colleagues if the appointment "failed," he also believed that his overall reputation and credibility would be damaged if his first cross-training appointment did not work out well.

The appointment of the Accounting Trainee left an Assistant Cost Accountant vacancy in another Region. As it happened, another Assistant Cost Accountant had also recently transferred from this Region to another as a result of a competitive posting. Thus, the source group was under some pressure to obtain replacements quickly, as they had recently lost two similarly skilled members of their staff. Both positions were posted inside the corporation, but no candidates applied. The supervisor of the group with the two vacant positions attributed this lack of response to the relatively low salary associated with each position and the general unattractiveness of the plant's location "at the end of the road." In addition, he noted that ForestCo had made large investments in new plant and equipment over the previous three years and that currently there was a good supply of interesting "project" jobs for Assistant Cost Accountants available elsewhere.

When no internal candidates applied, the job vacancies were advertised in the local newspapers. More than 60 applications were received. These applicants were reviewed and screened down to a shortlist of ten candidates. A panel of two managers traveled to the metropolitan area where most of the shortlisted candidates lived and spent two days interviewing the candidates. The two candidates tentatively recommended for the vacant positions were invited to the area in which the Regional office was located, and each spent a day talking with other managers with whom they would work. Finally, their appointments were confirmed, and they took up the duties and responsibilities of their new positions.

Vacancy chain 51 follows a related pattern. This two-person staffing action is set in a rebuilt sawmill in which older production lines were being shut down and replaced with newer equipment and production methods. The whole mill had been experiencing a transition mode for approximately a year—with some supervisors being assigned to various aspects of the rebuilding project and others retained on existing production lines. The vacancy occurred in the context of the large-scale organizational change associated with the technical upgrading of the mill. Within the mill, departmental superintendents collectively engaged in a process referred to as "the draft" in which 12 supervisors were assigned to old and new departments and production functions—including three new, but not additional, positions. Out of this process, a Department Foreman for an existing production function was promoted to one of these new positions. While the total complement of supervisory positions remained constant, three "old" positions were abolished and three new ones created. The replacement for the Department Foreman assigned to one of the new positions was another supervisor whose department was being phased out with the mill upgrade.

Although this process appears to be relatively simple on the surface, the assignment of supervisors to an evolving set of active departments, functions, and crews was a messy one at best. The whole decision process had multiple components, multiple phases over an extended time period, and high degrees of interdependence between initial assignments and those occurring later. In this process, overtly rational processes of decision making were impossible to implement. Local managers did what they could to approximate rationality by incrementally muddling through. Nevertheless, toward the end of the whole process, several superintendents were unconvinced that they had achieved the best solution possible to the dilemmas of staffing the supervisory positions of this large mill.

Organizational change and the creation of new positions were significant features of the sample of two-move vacancy chains. Because sets of overlapping issues often characterized organizational change, only occasionally did job definitions precede both conceptually and temporally the selection and assignment of employees to positions. Instead, job definitions and the potential assignment of persons to positions qualified and modified job definitions. Thus, again there is substantial evidence indicating only modest application of the strong vacancy assumption presumed to underlie ILM processes.

Classification of Two-Move Vacancy Chains by Terminating Cause

As minimal vacancy chains can be categorized on the basis of the initiating move or reason, so too can they be classified on the basis of their "final" move. In theory, at least, a vacancy chain can continue almost indefinitely, as multiple transfers could be made both within and between departments as a consequence of any initiating event. Two-move vacancy chains are distinctive in that the "terminating cause" is usually closely associated in time and context with the causal forces that initiated that vacancy chain.

A preliminary insight into the causes of vacancy chains' termination can be found by examining the 20 simple, two-move vacancy chains initially summarized in Table 4.4. With the same caveats as used previously, Table 4.4 presents a preliminary classification of the reasons that emerged to account for the termination of these two-move vacancy chains. As can be seen in the table, eight, or 40%, of these single-link staffing actions were concluded by hires from the external labor market. However, only one (vacancy chain 31) resulted in a net addition to the workforce complement. All others were associated with the replacement of other employees who either had left or intended to leave the organization.

Vacancy chain 58 was one of those initiated by a reorganization of a sawmill associated with larger aspects of organizational change. An experienced foreman was moved to a position the duties and responsibilities of which were modified as a function of a reorganization associated with the impending retirement of the plant Superintendent. An intensive search was undertaken to identify his successor, and approximately 30 hourly employees were considered for possible appointment to the foreman's position. Because of technological change, candidates were required to have at least a grade 12 education, be familiar with computer technology, and have well-developed interpersonal skills. In addition, candidates were required to demonstrate that they possessed "succession potential." Several candidates were interviewed twice, and a few were sent for further psychological testing by an outside consulting firm. However, none was judged to be suitable for the "new" requirements of the vacant position. Consequently, the vacancy was advertised in the local newspapers, and candidates from the ELM were invited to apply. After a further intensive selection process, an experienced person was hired.

Vacancy chain 61, which also resulted in a hire from the ELM, was initiated by a sequence of staffing actions that were tightly interwoven with a planned evolution of a departmental culture. Because of intense critical examinations of forestry practices, the Forestry function was reorganized and a new Divisional Forester position that had non-

Table 4.4. Summary of Causes of Termination
of Two-Move Vacancy Chains

Terminating cause	Number	Vacancy chain numbers
Hire from ELM	8	6, 7, 10, 11, 26, 31, 58, 61
Transfer from hourly	3	18, 52, 55
Transfer production trainee	1	49
Job absorbed	7	21, 30, 41, 51, 53,[a] 63, 67
Job switch	2	15, 53[a]

[a]Vacancy chain 53 falls equally into both categories.

traditional duties and responsibilities was created. After an internal search, an experienced and traditional forester was appointed to the new position. Because there were several new additional forester jobs being created around that time, the second vacancy was posted internally and also advertised in various newspapers. A few internal candidates applied, but were rejected because they had little capacity for the new requirements of teamwork and public relations skills, even though they met all the technical requirements of the job. Evaluation of candidates from the ELM who applied revealed a superior candidate who was looking to transfer to ForestCo from one of its competitors. Interestingly, this candidate had been on a fast-track development program and was looking to broaden his experience by an interfirm move.

When other reasons for the termination of these minimal vacancy chains are examined, it can be seen that very few two-move vacancy chains resulted in net additions to ForestCo's workforce. For example, seven chains could be traced directly to situations in which the chain terminated because the duties and responsibilities were absorbed by others in the work unit. Two chains involved a switch in which two employees changed jobs, and one chain resulted in the assignment of a Production Trainee to a specific position. This latter move has some technical interest, as the group of Production Trainees, like several temporary employees, were considered to be part of a pool of potential employees who had not yet been assigned to a particular position. Both statuses permitted the organization a greater degree of flexibility than was normally available when it was required that all employees be assigned to specific positions.

One such instance of an absorbed vacancy was encountered in vacancy chain 41. In this case, a purchasing department attempted to maintain quality service even though its manager regarded the department as being understaffed, especially as this department had reduced its complement from 39 to 17 in the "purge" associated with the 1981–1982 recession. However, increased demands because of various construction projects in one region led to the authorization of a new temporary position. An experienced purchaser was reassigned to the region for the duration of the projects, and a replacement was sought for the vacated position. The position was posted, and about ten candidates from other departments applied. The highest-ranked candidate was offered the job, but when he informed his home department of his intent to move elsewhere in the ForestCo organization, his home department improved his situation and talked him out of making the move. The successful second-ranked candidate applied because she currently occupied a job in a division that was being phased out. Thus, the vacancy chain terminated with an implicit absorption of the last position vacancy in the chain.

When vacant positions were not absorbed, candidates were often sought from the ELM because internal searches failed to produce acceptable candidates. External searches were viewed as potentially more risky for the manager responsible for the search procedure and the selection of the chosen candidate. There was often a generally held assumption, manifested most strongly by internal candidates, that they should be preferred over those from the ELM. These assumptions are consistent with stereotypical models of ILMs, but were found to have only limited applicability in a majority of the two-move vacancy chain situations encountered in ForestCo.

Classification of Two-Move Vacancy Chains by Originating and Terminating Causes

As part of the effort to discern possible relationships among various attributes of vacancy chains, this section presents, in Table 4.5, a cross-classification of two-move

Table 4.5. Classification of Two-Move Vacancy Chains
by Causes of Origination and Termination

Cause of origination	Cause of termination				
	Hire from ELM	Transfer from hourly	Transfer production trainee	Job absorbed	Job switch
Reorganization/new position	6, 7, 31, 58, 61	—	49	30, 41, 51, 53,[a] 63	53[a]
Resignation/long-term disability	11	18	—	21, 67	—
Retirement	—	52, 55	—	—	—
Discharge/fired	26	—	—	—	—
Development	—	—	—	—	15

[a]Vacancy chain 53 falls equally into both categories.

vacancy chains arranged by both originating and terminating causes. While no definitive answers are likely to be found in an analysis of only 20 two-move vacancy chains, more detailed examinations of potential associations between originating and terminating causes could provide insight into possible systematic relationships. These relationships would connect the conditions that led to the origination of a vacancy chain and its termination after but one move inside the ILM. If indeed potential relationships can be uncovered, they might account for the occurrence of minimal vacancy chains consisting of only two moves.

As a hypothetical example, consider reorganizations that result in new positions. Such reorganizations may create higher levels of uncertainty than desired. Therefore, assuming the requirements of the new positions can be met, there may be a tendency for the resulting originating vacancy to be filled by known internal candidates. However, as part of a trickle-down effect of the reorganization, the resulting vacant position may remain relatively unchanged, but an outside hire may be brought in to backstop the changes associated with the new position.

As noted in Table 4.5, five two-move vacancy chains initiated by reorganizations and the creation of new positions were terminated by hires from the ELM and five were terminated by the (third) vacated position being absorbed. Only one (vacancy chain 49) unambiguously terminated with the appointment of an existing employee. Even this relatively simple staffing sequence was complicated, however, by the "special" status of Production Trainees. In bureaucratic models of organizations, employees are assigned to individually based positions that determine the employees' status, pay level, and other terms and conditions of employment. Production Trainees, however, were assigned to a "pool," equivalent to a collective vestibule from which individual assignments could be made as circumstances allowed. Because Production Trainees were not assigned to specific positions, there was no automatic pressure to fill a vacant position when a Production Trainee was posted to a specific position. In the short run, the size of the Production Trainee pool could fluctuate and buffer pressures for immediately reactive staffing actions. In this one potential illustration of an existing employee being assigned to the second vacancy in a two-move vacancy chain, there is little direct evidence that progression along a job ladder was used when the original vacancy was triggered by the creation of a new position as part of a reorganization. Thus, there is some modest evidence in support of some potential relationships between originating and terminating causes for two-move vacancy chains.

A competing interpretation asserts no relationship between originating and terminating causes for two-move vacancy chains. Apart from the modest relationships revealed for chains initiated by reorganizations, few other connections can be discerned in Table 4.5. The small sample size and the sparse distribution of cases across different conditions limit further inductive reasoning regarding potential relationships. However, further description of one additional two-move vacancy chain is presented, as it illustrates the application of managerial motivation to develop skills—a significant feature of the stereotypical model of ILMs that underlies this analysis.

In vacancy chain 15, a switch of senior-level managers was arranged both for the development needs of each manager and for organizational requirements. From an organizational perspective, a large aging sawmill complex was to be rebuilt. This was a large capital project that represented a significant reaffirmation of ForestCo's faith in a particular plant, but with new technology, new methods of production, and a different style of administration. This highly visible flagship project needed a very competent manager— and the person selected was someone who had worked successfully on a similar but smaller project. The manager responsible for the existing, older mill that was to be rebuilt had spent much of his managerial career in this plant. His background experience was judged to be quite localized, as he had not yet worked in a plant that was dependent on export of production to overseas markets. As the vice-president responsible for several mills in this region observed:

> We decided it was time for him to get a new look on life. He needed to get some export experience he hadn't gotten so far. It was time for him to learn and to round himself out as a manager.

A switch of these two managers appeared to make sense. No formal postings were made, no doubt because appointments above salary grade 15 were almost always made through administrative means by more senior managers. Moreover, the jobs to be performed and the salary grade associated with these jobs were tied quite closely to the personal attributes and career experience of the employees appointed to those jobs. This switch was not seen as having either substantive or symbolic importance to the corporation. Each move was undertaken to facilitate the further development and deepen the experience of each manager. The moves had the potential to increase the bench strength of the pool of experienced and capable managers in the organization. For this simple two-move vacancy chain, the origin and termination were closely aligned, as a "local" adjustment was made in managerial assignments that improved the fit between managerial capacities and the requirements for the new mill. It also provided an opportunity to challenge and develop further the capacities of the manager assigned to the smaller mill.

Market versus Administered Aspects of Two-Move Vacancy Chains

A significant tension in early definitions of ILMs and implicit in the stereotypical model of ILM operation was the pull between market and administered approaches to searches and assessments of candidates. Market approaches place increased emphasis on competition, particularly competition from candidates currently in the ELM. In contrast, administrative approaches emphasize the application of explicit or implicit administrative rules. Internal candidates are often favored because of prior investments in firm- or even department-specific knowledge and skills. These contrasting philosophies were manifested in ForestCo by two different but overlapping procedures. Competitive, market-based approaches were implemented by posting notices of vacancies inside or advertising outside ForestCo's ILM. Administrative approaches were taken when managers searched inside ForestCo's ILM and chose appointees on the basis of their informal managerial assessments of potential candidates.

The pervasive effects of organizational change in ForestCo's organization have already been shown to affect the preference for existing employees in two-move vacancy chains. It is speculated that such moves, particularly those to new positions, would be handled most readily by administrative arrangements. However, subsequent moves would likely indicate a preference for "new" employees to backstop the newness, innovation, and change associated with the creation of new positions. While the qualities required to support new assignments could come from existing lines of progression, such progressions could maintain existing practices and work against the changes that led to the creation of the new position. In two-move vacancy chains, competitive searches are more likely to be favored when candidates are sought for the second and subsequent vacancies.

Data on the staffing methods used in either initial or final moves of two-move vacancy chains are presented in Table 4.6. It can be seen that in the small, local adjustments represented by two-person vacancy chains, the initial staffing manifestation of these adjustments was most frequently in the form of an administrative appointment in which a current employee was reassigned to a new position. In a much smaller number of instances, the reassignment of employees was effected through the competitive, more market-oriented mechanism of job posting. Of course, several two-person vacancy chains were initiated by the actions/behaviors of the person who made the first move—as when an employee quit, took early retirement, or went on long-term disability. However, in contrast to the administrative assignment of employees to new or recently vacated positions, posting was used most often as the method of filling the final vacancy. The change in relative emphasis from staffing procedures used to respond to initiating conditions and those used to "complete" these limited vacancy chains is quite strong ($\chi^2 = 7.8$, $p < 0.01$).

One interpretation of these results is that the total amount of uncertainty originating from the assignment of an employee to a job is related to some additive or multiplicative function of the amount of uncertainty associated with the nature of the job and the uncertainty associated with the employee assigned to that job. When both job and employee are not well known, any negative performance could be attributed to either the job or the employee. In situations such as this, incremental adjustments of either the job (through a restructuring of tasks, duties, and responsibilities) or the employee (through training or replacement with another person) are problematic. For the manager responsible for the accomplishment of performance arising from both the design of jobs and the assignment of persons to those jobs, learning from trial and error is difficult. There are two

Table 4.6. Staffing Process for Initial and Final Moves
in Two-Move Vacancy Chains

Method of employee move	Initial move	Final move
Move initiated by job incumbent	5	NA
Move by administrative assignment	13	8
Move by competitive posting	2	12

primary sources of uncertainty: the design of the job and the capacities of the person. Under these conditions, a more practical, problem-solving approach would be for managers to initially respond with the assignment of employees they know. On the other hand, when a known vacated position remains relatively unchanged, opportunities for learning and for positive additions to performance are enhanced if the manager searches widely for the "best" person for that position.

SUMMARY AND REVIEW OF MINIMAL VACANCY CHAINS

Minimal vacancy chains may be considered to represent the opposite of ILM processes. From the perspective of stereotypical models of ILMs and derived ideal-type models of vacancy chains, single staffing actions and two-move vacancy chains were considered to illustrate the proximity and dominance of the ELM rather than ForestCo's ILM. However, closer examination of the details surrounding the origin and termination of these minimal vacancy chains suggests that such simple interpretations fail to capture the underlying complexity of organizational processes. Very few if any of ForestCo's minimal vacancy chains could be attributed to originating vacancies occurring close to ports of entry. Also, only two single staffing actions resulted in searches of the ELM because specialist skills were unavailable and could not be developed within ForestCo's ILM.

The single staffing actions and two-move vacancy chains considered to represent minimal vacancy chains constituted a substantial proportion (38%) of the first sample of 71 vacancy chains found and studied at ForestCo. A strong factor associated with a majority of these minimal vacancy chains was that of organizational change and adaptation. Minimal vacancy chains were one of the mechanisms through which local adjustments were made either by one or, more frequently, by two supervisors or managers as a two-phased response to changed organizational conditions. ForestCo is an organization that has experienced and is experiencing many internal, local adjustments as a consequence of several, much larger, adaptations to changes in the firm's external environment. These adjustments often involved considerable local uncertainty: New mills were built and brought into operational status; new equipment was installed, and crews were taught new methods of production; and new ways of "thinking about the business we're in" were introduced. In this dynamic context, few jobs and organizational arrangements were stable through extended periods. Managers often responded directly to changing conditions by reorganizing the assignments of tasks, duties, and responsibilities within their units.

Managers responded to the consequent need for new employees, new energies, and new skills and also concurrently adjusted the organization of their sections in response to the aging, maturation, and loss of existing employees. Initially, an existing position would become vacant or a new position would be created as part of larger reorganizations of tasks, duties, and responsibilities. Most often, these vacancies would be filled through the administrative assignment of an existing employee. However, the replacement of that employee in the vacant position would most often be made through the more competitive, market-oriented procedure of posting.

These staffing patterns are consistent with theories of incremental decision-making under uncertainty. Managers attempted to balance innovation with some stable momentum from past practices. When external demands required reorganizations and the creation of new jobs, uncertainties were limited by assigning known persons to those new positions. In filling the subsequent vacancy, however, managers often wished to maintain the push for innovation by *not* selecting from previous lines of progression. Therefore, they favored competitive internal postings or external advertising for outside candidates as ways of maintaining and extending the organizational change that originated the sequence of staffing actions.

Minimal vacancy chains were originally expected to illustrate staffing activity close to the boundary between the ForestCo's ILM and the ELM. While there were occasional instances of minimal vacancy chains meeting these expectations, most minimal vacancy chains were the means through which larger processes of organizational adaptation and change occurred. In Chapters 5 and 6, medium-length and long vacancy chains are examined to see whether these nominally different types of vacancy chain present similar or different interpretations of ILM operations.

5

Medium-Length Vacancy Chains

INTRODUCTION

Medium-length vacancy chains are here considered to be bundles of three, four, or five related staffing actions. Vacancy chains of this number of sequentially linked person-moves represent a middle range of vacancy chain phenomena, between the minimal vacancy chains comprising one or two person-moves discussed in Chapter 4 and the much longer vacancy chains presented in Chapter 6. Staffing actions in medium-length vacancy chains exhibit a stronger preference for persons already hired than is the case for minimal vacancy chains. In medium-length vacancy chains, each initiating vacancy produced at least two, three, or four further vacancies as a consequence of subsequent staffing choices that preferred candidates from the ILM rather than the ELM. This examination of medium-length vacancy chains therefore builds upon and extends the insights developed from the preceding analysis of minimal vacancy chains. Medium-length vacancy chains are examined for attributes that characterize their role in maintaining ForestCo's ILM. In the three primary sections of this chapter, medium-length vacancy chains are described in the sequence of three-, four-, and finally five-move sequences of staffing actions.

We preface this analysis with the caution that the previous characterizations of minimal vacancy chains are likely to be less useful as descriptions of medium-length vacancy chains. In one-person, single-move vacancy chains, reasons for originating and terminating were identical. In two-person, two-move vacancy chains, reasons for the origin and termination were closely associated. As vacancy chain length increases, however, each of the staffing actions that comprise a single vacancy chain can occur in a different context. Each staffing situation is likely to present different choice opportunities, characterized by appreciations by different managers of different problems and potential solutions. As a consequence, the synthesis of multiple linked staffing decisions into a meaningful whole requires substantial interpretation. Support for the validity of these interpretations necessarily comes from detailed descriptions of these sequences of linked staffing actions, as understood by the supervisors and managers responsible for executing them. Consequently, the descriptions of three, four and five-person vacancy chains evolve from those used previously. Much greater use is made of the accounts of managers describing *what* they did and *why* they acted as they did.

THREE-MOVE VACANCY CHAINS

Three-move vacancy chains are bundles of related staffing actions in which the organizational status of three persons was changed. These moves often followed a sequence from an initiating condition or staffing action to another staffing action involving the move of another person and then finally to a staffing action involving a third person whose move terminated the vacancy chain. There were 20 three-move vacancy chains (28%) in the sample of 71 vacancy chains at ForestCo. Table 5.1 presents summaries of these vacancy chains.

The distribution of the hierarchical origins of the sample of three-move vacancy chains is similar to that of all vacancy chains. Three-move vacancy chains originated across a wide range of salary grades, from 6 to 23. As with two-move vacancy chains, a substantial proportion (80%) of three-move vacancy chains originated in the Managerial and Professional occupational group defined as salary grades 11–15. This occupational group contained a clear majority of all staffing actions associated with three-move vacancy chains, as more than 60% of all terminating moves also occurred in its associated salary grade range. As in the total sample of all vacancy chains intensively studied, the span of salary grades between origin and termination for three-move vacancy chains was predominantly small. In all, 13 three-move vacancy chains, or 65% of the 20 three-move vacancy chains, both originated and terminated with salaried appointments that spanned two or fewer salary grades. The largest span, of seven salary grades, was for vacancy chain 33, which was associated with a reorganization in the Forestry occupational group. On the

Table 5.1. Summary of Three-Move Vacancy Chains

Vacancy chain number	Salary grades[a]	Occupation or function	Initiation of vacancy	Staffing actions
2	6–11	Accounting	New position	Succession/hire from ELM
5	15–16	Finance	Development	Rotational reassignments
8	9–11	Accounting	New position	Succession/hire from ELM
12	15–20	Management	Retirement	Succession/reorganization
19	HH–12	Supervisory	Long-term disability	Succession/hire from hourly
20	HH–12	Supervisory	Resignation	Succession/hire from hourly
25	4–6	Clerical	Temporary to full-time	Succession/hire from ELM
27	11–13	Supervisory	Retirement	Succession/hire from ELM
29	12–13	Employee relations	New position	Succession/hire from ELM
33	16–23	Forestry	Retirement	Succession/reorganization
37	13–15	Production management	Retirement	Reorganization/reassignment
38	10–15	Sales	New position	Reorganization/hire from ELM
45	14–15	Employee relations	New position	Succession/hire from ELM
47	9–11	Sales–Production	Termination	Succession/development
50	12–14	Supervisory	Retirement	Succession/rotation
56	13–15	Supervisory	Termination	Reorganization/succession
60	9–13	Sales–Production	Reorganization	Development/hire from ELM
62	13–15	Engineering	Transfer out	Succession/reorganization
64	12–13	Forestry	New position	Reorganization/development
70	12–14	Supervisory	New position	Reorganization/succession

[a](HH) indicates a move from the hourly payroll.

basis of this evidence, three-move vacancy chains do not appear to be distinctively different from the overall sample of intensively studied vacancy chains in their objective characteristics such as the hierarchical grade of their origin, the hierarchical grade of their termination, and the span of salary grades between origin and termination.

In the discussion that follows, a number of features of three-move vacancy chains are described and explored. Initial descriptions of these vacancy chains are first presented in terms of "objective" data related to the origin and termination of these sequences of staffing actions. However, the functions of these longer vacancy chains are best interpreted when viewed as a whole. For this reason, a graphic method of presenting longer vacancy chains was developed. The methodology of drawing vacancy chain diagrams, which is used extensively in this chapter and the next, is illustrated through its application to describe seven illustrative chains. Each vacancy chain diagram permits the development of more detailed, contextual, and interpretive assessments based on information obtained from interviews with the managers responsible for the staffing actions that comprise each chain. Much of the following discussion highlights various features of three-move chains as discovered from managers' assessments of staffing actions they undertook and their reasons for acting as they did. Discussions with ForestCo's managers reveal an employment system in which there is flexibility and interdependence between persons and positions. This flexibility facilitates patterns of change that reflect models of punctuated equilibrium. That is, organizational change occurs both as large-scale transformations associated with strategic staffing and as incremental, local processes of adjustment to shifting conditions. Consideration of these perspectives reveals staffing as a complex process of problem formulation and solution development. Wider organizational issues filter into staffing "problems." Subsequent definitions of jobs and selections of candidates represent partial solutions and transformation of those problems.

Reasons for Originating and Terminating Three-Move Vacancy Chains

The summary of three-move vacancy chains presented in Table 5.1 should be interpreted with modest caution, as a relatively simple classification scheme was used to characterize a three-move sequence of quite complex staffing actions. Nevertheless, within these limits, Table 5.1 indicates that nine three-move vacancy chains, or nearly half the number examined, were initiated by events, such as resignations, retirements, and terminations, over which agents of the organization had relatively little discretion. The other 11 three-move vacancy chains were initiated by supervisors and managers to meet local needs such as reorganizations in response to demands for the development of new skills or requirements.

The relative frequencies of reasons for termination of these three-person vacancy chains were similar to those for the two-person vacancy chains described in Table 4.4. Eight (40%) were terminated by a hire from the ELM, and eight (again 40%) were terminated by processes of reorganization and job absorption. Two additional chains were terminated by reorganizations involving a switch of individuals between positions, and two others involved moves either from the ranks of hourly employees or from the pool of Production Trainees.

Preliminary classifications of the samples of 20 two-person and 20 three-person vacancy chains reveal few conceptual distinctions between these two groups of staffing actions. For both sets of vacancy chains, the most frequently cited or inferred reason for the initiation of a vacancy chain was the need to respond to changing organizational conditions. Ten of the 20 three-person vacancy chains studied were initiated by reorganizations or the creation of new positions. The next most frequent reason for initiation of staffing actions occurred when a position became vacant—often because the original occupant retired, resigned, or went on long-term disability. For example, seven three-person vacancy chains were identified as originating for these reasons. However, five of these seven, plus two other chains, subsequently led to either modest or substantial reorganizations. Thus, 85% of three-person vacancy chains were associated, either initially or subsequently, with some form of reorganization of positions and persons. Only three three-person vacancy chains (15%) followed a straight line of succession in which no position was changed. Of these three staffing sequences, two terminated with hires from the ELM and one with the transfer of an employee from another operation that was about to be closed down.

The separation of medium-length vacancy chains from minimal vacancy chains was done initially to provide a reasonable descriptive coverage of all vacancy chains in suffi-cient depth to be meaningful to readers not familiar with ForestCo's operations. Within the limits of characterizing increasingly complex organizational and social phenomena, how-ever, a preliminary assessment is that two-move and three-move vacancy chains are more similar than they are different. First, within the limits of our sampling procedures, these two types of vacancy chain were found equally to occur most frequently. Together, these two types of vacancy chain constituted 40 of 71, or 56%, of the total sample obtained. Attempts to find characteristics that distinguished each type from the total sample were largely unsuccessful. This result can be attributed to both compositional and similarity effects. Two-move and three-move vacancy chains each constituted a significant propor-tion of the total sample, and the two sets were remarkably similar. Distributions of their origins and terminations by hierarchical grade were similar, as were the distributions of the salary grade spans associated with each vacancy chain. Thus, the more complete descriptions of three-move vacancy chains that follow should be understood in this light.

These data on three-person vacancy chains, together with the brief review of two-person vacancy chains, reinforce the association between vacancy chains and processes and organizational adaptation and change introduced earlier. Before these issues are examined in greater detail, however, a graphic method of describing and illustrating specific but complex vacancy chains is presented.

A Method of Diagramming Vacancy Chains

Vacancy chain 33 is described initially by means of the diagram presented in Figure 5.1. Schematically, this vacancy chain is presented as a series of person-moves on a grid that locates the beginning and end of each move. The horizontal axis indicates geographic and divisional boundaries, as well as the boundary between the ILM and the ELM. The vertical axis indicates the location of moves in terms of ForestCo's salary grade structure. Horizontal mobility indicates employee moves that are either intra- or interdivisional, intra- or interregional, or between the ILM and the ELM. Vertical moves indicate either promotions or demotions.

The vacancy chain illustrated in Fig. 5.1 begins with the movement (a retirement) of employee E1 from position/function F1 (at salary grade 23) to a role outside ForestCo's ILM. This employee was replaced by employee E2, who moved (P1) from the position/function F2 (at salary grade 20) in Division B to the newly vacated position F1 (now at salary grade 22) at Corporate Headquarters. The position/function F2 vacated by em-ployee E2 was filled by the move (P2) of employee E3 from the position/function F3 that had previously been established at salary grade 16 in Corporate Headquarters. However,

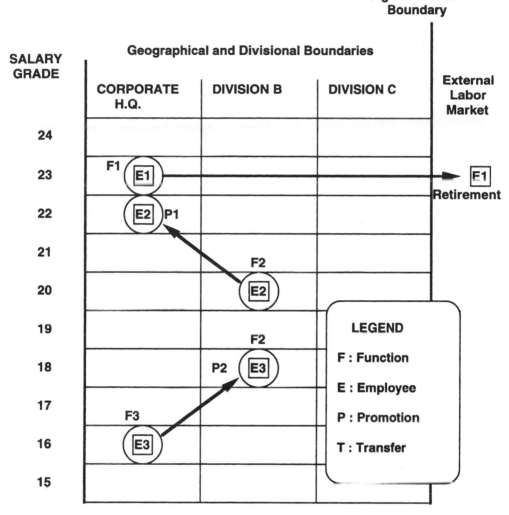

Figure 5.1. Vacancy chain 33.

the position/function F2 previously occupied by employee E2 was downgraded from salary grade 20 to salary grade 18 concurrent with the appointment of employee E3.

More complete descriptions of these vacancy chains could indicate both the names and other personal attributes of the individual employees involved in these vacancy chains as well as the detailed titles and descriptions of the jobs to which they were assigned. However, one condition stipulated by ForestCo for providing this public account of the staffing activities in the organization was that the identities of employees would remain confidential. Individual employees are therefore identified primarily by their order in a particular vacancy (e.g., employee E2 in vacancy chain 33) and positions by generic job descriptions. While these less than complete descriptions may require more effort on the reader's part to follow the specifics of each staffing sequence, they are used here to protect the anonymity of individual employees and the confidences of managers who remarked on them.

With the overall schema within which the three staffing actions of vacancy chain 33 occurred having been established, a fuller description of various issues that influenced each staffing action can be presented. Vacancy chain 33 was initiated by the retirement of a senior executive whose formal professional/official status (Chief Forester) was that of a licensed representative of the corporation in its dealings with external constituencies. The requirements of this position were critical, both for internal organizational functioning and for representation to outside agencies. Extensive knowledge of the huge tracts of land under ForestCo's management, as well as detailed knowledge of ForestCo's operations and emerging strategy, were critical requirements for satisfactory performance of this job. Much firm-specific knowledge was required, together with an integrated perspective on local, regional, national, and international aspects of forest industry dynamics. The only way a person could meet these requirements was to be groomed through a succession of positions that provided in-depth, firm-specific experience and to have this background integrated with professional knowledge and expertise. Thus, succession through a line of progression, rather than the acquisition of these skills from outside the firm, was perhaps the only logical response to meeting the requirements of these positions when they became vacant. Thus, persons were chosen from within ForestCo's ILM until position F3 became vacant and it was decided to absorb the duties and responsibilities of that job among related positions.

Flexibility and Interdependence of Persons and Positions

A further interesting feature of vacancy chain 33, as diagrammed in Fig. 5.1, is that positions vacated were not filled at the same salary grade they had before they were vacated. Thus, the first position/function F1 vacated by employee E1 was originally designated as being at salary grade 23. When new incumbent E2 was assigned to that position, however, the salary grade was adjusted to salary grade 22 to reflect the recency of the appointment and the new appointee's lower seniority. A similar practice was followed in the replacement of employee E2 in position/function F2. This position was regraded from that of salary grade 20 to salary grade 18.

Job grading is a common feature of almost all contemporary bureaucratic systems (Patton & Smith, 1949; Quaid, 1993). In formal systems of job grading, employee rank in a hierarchy reflects the attributes of the position to which a person is assigned (Dick, 1974). In particular, pay and other forms of compensation are most often based on the require- ments of the job to which the employee is assigned (Stettner, 1969). In more formal bureaucratic systems, such as government organizations, organizational and positional requirements dominate. Employees have no status or individual identity independent of their organizational assignment. That is, organizational arrangements are made "without regard to persons" (Weber, 1946, p. 215). While these general principles lay behind the development and implementation of ForestCo's system of employment and compensa- tion, the firm operated a pragmatic compromise between job- and person-based assign- ment systems. That is, ForestCo commonly practiced the grading of positions primarily as a function of the requirements of the position, but as modified by the qualities of each job's incumbent. This compromise was facilitated further by the implementation of a compen- sation system that incorporated overlapping pay ranges for jobs with proximate salary grades. Together, these two features of ForestCo's ILM permitted very flexible arrangements of job definitions, persons assigned to jobs, and rewards associated with performance of those jobs.

For example, when an employee was originally appointed to a position, the salary grade rating of the initial appointment would often be different from that previously assigned to the position and, by implication, to the person previously assigned to that job. As individual employees gained experience in their new assignments, their improved performance would often be recognized by promotion within the job. The salary grade associated with that job would increase in line with the job tenure, experience, competency, and performance of the job incumbent. This feature of ForestCo's staffing also provided supervisors and managers with subsequent opportunities to fine-tune the match between persons and jobs. Promotions within jobs were subject to less outside scrutiny than appointments involving employee assignments to new positions. Thus, managers who wished to reward individual subordinates could do so within overall complement and budgetary controls and without detailed supervisory oversight.

One consequence of this flexibility in job assignments is that comparing the salary grades of originating and terminating moves to arrive at estimates of the hierarchical length of a vacancy chain, and the derived measure of the size of the average move in a vacancy chain, may yield overestimates of these characteristics. For example, in vacancy chain 33 illustrated in Figure 5.1, the net effect of the retirement of employee E1 was that employees E2 and E3 were each promoted two salary grades, producing an average promotion move of two salary grades. However, because position/function F1 was downgraded one salary grade, and position/function F2 was downgraded two salary grades, there was a span of seven salary grades between the originating and terminating positions (i.e., salary grade 23 to salary grade 16) in this vacancy chain. The size of the average promotion move based on vacancy chain span therefore overstates the actual scale of the promotions received. Four of the seven levels of salary grade spanned were "covered" by actual promotions, while three salary grade levels were absorbed by the downgrading of positions.

The Effects of Context: Strategic Staffing

Further insight into the idiosyncratic dynamics of the staffing actions contained in vacancy chain 33 as diagrammed in Fig. 5.1 can be obtained from interviews with one of the senior executives responsible for the selection and appointment of employee E2 and with employee E2 regarding the appointment of employee E3.

The retirement of employee E1 had been imminent for some time, as employee E1 had been unwell for several months. Employee E2 had been ForestCo's de facto representative and had informally taken E1's place even though no official action had yet been taken to confirm his new status. While E2 was occupied doing much of the formal job previously performed by E1, employee E3 had his duties expanded to include many of those previously discharged by employee E2. The formal staffing actions described in Fig. 5.1 confirmed an informal arrangement that had been in place for several months.

This was not a straightforward organizational succession, however, as the whole process was strongly influenced by forces in the larger organizational context. These forces were influential at three identifiable choice opportunities: the selection of employee E2, the selection of employee E3, and the organizational absorption of the position/function previously performed by employee E3. In each instance of actual or potential staffing choice, there were several contenders for each vacant position. Choice of one person rather than any other was regarded as substantively and symbolically important. For example, different contenders would have brought different strengths and potential weaknesses to the senior position F1, which was critical for the development and execution of corporate strategy. The person eventually appointed to this position would have a large degree of influence over how ForestCo would be represented in the larger, public domain. In addition, the employee's performance in this representational role could have a substantial influence on the economic performance, and possibly survival, of the firm. Selection of the criteria used to evaluate different candidates was therefore strongly influenced by assessments of the skills required to perform vacated positions. These assessments included broad arrays of issues considered to be interdependent with the performance of each job.

Contextual issues and considerations of current and emerging corporate strategy were particularly important in the selection from among the candidates considered for appointment to position/function F1. In this staffing situation, outgoing occupant E1 was regarded as a traditionalist who focused his energies on a technical–professional interpretation of his job. While this interpretation had been functional for organization–environment relationships during the past 20 years, the effectiveness of such a focus was judged to be no longer appropriate. Increasingly, ForestCo's economic future, particularly its access to timberlands and its supply of wood fiber, were dependent on political factors. Therefore, the selection criteria used to affirm employee E2 in position/function F1 were quite different from those used to select and affirm E1 in that role several years previously.

Similar contextual influences were also present in the selection of employee E3. The role of the person assigned to position/function F2 was to complement the performance of E2. Given the quite different and increasingly political aspects of the requisite organizational role performance in F1, the criteria used to select E3 were also strongly influenced by emerging contextual forces. In particular, employee E3 was chosen to liaise between government agencies and the managers responsible for harvesting practices in the field.

A further contextual effect was manifested in the decision not to replace employee E3 in vacated position F3. This decision was made quite consciously and explicitly by the group of senior managers, including E2, who discussed and implemented the organizational changes following E2's appointment to position/function F1. In this instance, the relevant context was the corporate downsizing that had been part of ForestCo's culture for almost the entire decade of the 1980s. Whenever possible, consistent with the policy outlined in Table 2.4, internal successors would be appointed along the chain into modified positions until the remaining parts of the particular vacated job under consideration could be dissolved or delegated elsewhere. This outside pressure was manifest in the general policy orientations captured by the slogans "more workers—fewer managers" and "fewer people—increase the rewards." In this particular instance, the tasks of the position/function F3 previously performed by employee E3 were distributed among coworkers, whose salaries increased in line with their increased responsibilities. From the perspective of internal politics, this arrangement was also functional in smoothing unmet expectations, as potential candidates who were not chosen to replace E3 nevertheless received some recognition and reward.

Staffing Choice as Responses to Demands for Change

The three-person vacancy chain 33 described in Figure 5.1 presents a specific example of a more general process through which ForestCo often responded to a demand for change. In this instance, an opportunity to respond to changing environmental pressures presented itself when employee E1 became ill and had to take early retirement. In both this instance and many other instances, organizational change involving the redesign of jobs and positions faced fewer constraints and encountered less resistance when positions became vacant. With no occupant to argue for his or her vested interests in a particular job design, changes reflecting the political interests of others were agreed upon and implemented more readily. In this vacancy chain, had employee E1 remained in good health, the opportunity to respond would have arisen under different circumstances. Nevertheless, as E1 did vacate position F1, shifting performance requirements associated with evolving corporate strategies became manifested in the requirements of a reconceptualized position F1. Appreciation of these new demands led to an initial organizational response, which in turn required other organizational adjustments.

Processes of organizational change and adaptation can be viewed as processes of managerial problem solving and decision making in the context of organizational staffing. Staffing decisions, particularly those at more senior levels of the organization, represent choice opportunities in which both external and internal issues come together. Internal conditions often present both potential resources and solutions to externally defined problems. However, external conditions can also present solution possibilities and opportunities to internally generated problems. Internal and external issues become part of the larger problems and solutions considered in the choice opportunities. How these issues are manifested in staffing decisions depends on the manner in which the choice opportunity is framed by the responsible manager(s). For example, an initial problem could perhaps be met by either a direct hire, as in a single-action vacancy chain, or by a sequence of two moves, as in a two-person vacancy chain. However, when other problems become associated and intertwined with an original, relatively simple problem, such as how to replace a person in a position, the scope of problem definition increases. Increased problem scope also increases the size and complexity of the set of action–solutions required to meet this larger problem. Thus, an initial organizational problem–condition that often could be met by simple, quick, and direct actions instead provided the initial impetus for a more complicated set of actions designed to meet other emerging problem issues in the organization.

A second illustration of this general process of organizational adaptation and change accomplished through staffing can be seen in vacancy chain 62 diagrammed in Figure 5.2. In this case, the performance of a recently hired Production Supervisor (E1) was increasingly being viewed as unacceptable by the manager responsible for the unit. As part of a long-term effort to change the culture of a mill, this manager was attempting to move the dominant supervisory style in this unit away from an authoritarian and individualistic approach to one that gave significantly greater emphasis to teamwork. The relatively new Production Supervisor (E1) "wanted to run a one-man show" and had alienated several of his supervisory colleagues who managed parallel units that were interdependent with his:

> There was a lot of conflict as to how things would work around here and it was getting in the way of us getting the work done.

Nevertheless, this supervisor was still regarded as someone with potential to develop further. However, as his talents were not compatible with the emerging view of the way this unit was to be managed, he was encouraged to accept a transfer (T1) to a different and independent unit that performed contract work for ForestCo.

The departure of the Production Supervisor presented the current manager with an unusual development opportunity ideally suited for an old colleague: someone who had been employed as an engineer, but who wanted to move into management. In a prior

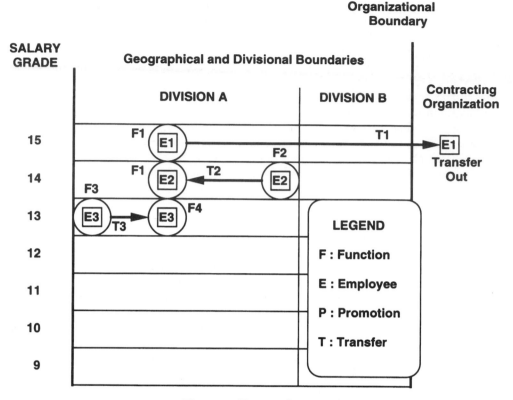

Figure 5.2. Vacancy chain 62.

move about two years before, this person had transferred from being the Divisional Engineer in another unit to the same role in this division. The local manager described this previous move as follows:

> _____ expressed a desire to work with me. He wanted to change from being an autocratic engineer because he'd previously lost a manager's job at [another unit] because he hadn't developed his people skills. He felt he couldn't change at [his previous unit] and that it would be easier for him to change if he were to come here.

Given this background, it was quite clear that personal knowledge and relationships influenced the administrative assignment (T2) of the selected individual (E2) to the vacated position (F1) of Production Supervisor. The two decisions were not independent of each other. The decision to move E1 out of the unit was facilitated by the manager's understanding that he had a replacement already in place. The proximity and availability of a solution (i.e., the availability and potential suitability of employee E2) to the issue of the performance of employee E1 in position F1 reduced the costs associated with effecting the transfer of employee E1 to an outside contractor. Employee E2's recent performance was also a significant factor in his being chosen for the newly vacated position. This performance record increased the manager's confidence that there would be little downside risk associated with this replacement:

He's done remarkably well at growing and letting go of being too controlling since coming here. He's been a success and production is up.

An additional factor that may have pushed the appointment of E2 arose from the personal obligation the manager felt to develop further the capacities of his friend and subordinate:

I chose _____ because we go back a long way. We worked in the same Region and started out together as engineers. We're close business acquaintances who've both come from traditional engineering backgrounds. _____ had been at [another unit] for the past seven years, and we'd been in close contact all of that time before he came here.

This support was not unconditional. The position F1 vacated by employee E1 was originally assessed as being at salary grade 15, whereas employee E2 was assigned to the same job but assessed at salary grade 14. Should employee E2 continue to develop as expected, it would be relatively easy for the mill manager to regrade F2 to salary grade 15 and effect a promotion of E2 within a continuing position. Thus, the staffing process in which employee E1 was transferred out and replaced by employee E2 served both the needs for organizational performance in the area of production and the individual development needs of a close colleague who had begun to bloom under the grooming provided by the local manager. These changes were accomplished incrementally, with the local manager retaining strong control over the inducements and rewards associated with continuing performance.

Although the replacement of E1 by E2 was viewed as positive by the manager, his dissatisfaction with his unit's performance was not limited solely to the performance of old and new Production Supervisors. He also questioned the distribution of functions among different jobs in his unit and decided that it was necessary to reorganize these functions. As a means of reducing the conflict between production, engineering, and forestry functions, the local manager decided to combine parts of the two latter functions, engineering and forestry, into one job (F4). Consequently, the employee (E3) who had previously been employed as Divisional Forester (F3) had his responsibilities enlarged to include some of the functions (F2) previously performed by the Engineer (E2) who moved to Production Superintendent (F1). Thus, the set of moves that comprise vacancy chain 62 can be viewed as a set of overlapping problems concerned with issues of organizational succession and performance, individual development, and a reorganization arising from the unit manager's ongoing pursuit of a team-based organization.

Ostensibly, this three-person vacancy chain may also be regarded as another illustration of supervisory downsizing. A senior supervisor was transferred out to another arm's-length unit that did contract work for ForestCo, an engineer who was being groomed for a management position was appointed to the position vacated, and a Forester had his responsibilities expanded to include those previously covered by the new supervisor. From this narrow perspective, the work previously performed by three persons was now being covered by two. From a perspective that includes the larger context, however, it can also be seen that the nature of the work itself was being redefined. The distinctions that previously permitted identification of individual job assignments were becoming blurred as the unit manager encouraged increased teamwork. In addition, other changes associated with other vacancy chains either had been implemented or were being planned. Each of these changes also had minor consequences for the work levels likely to be experienced by the two remaining supervisors, E2 and E3, left in the unit.

In both three-move vacancy chains reviewed so far, processes of organizational change have been intimately associated with the staffing process. Studies of vacancy chains show ILM processes as dynamic opportunities for organizational adaptation. Organizational performance arises through the collective efforts of employees assigned to jobs. The ways in which jobs are defined and the assignment of persons to those jobs are part of an ongoing organizational process of adaptation and change.

Vacancy Chains, Choice Opportunities, and General Management

In practice, staffing is rarely a simple matter of finding the "best" employee for a well-defined job. More frequently, the selection and assignment of employees to organizational jobs/positions occurs in close conjunction with parallel, interdependent decision processes that attempt to determine how the work of larger organizational units should be assigned to particular jobs and positions. Organizational staffing was therefore rarely seen as a separate specialist function divorced from the general management of an organizational unit. Organizational staffing was most often viewed as an integral, functional component of organizational management.

Illustrations of this compounding of staffing and management surfaced in the previous accounts of vacancy chains 33 and 62. In vacancy chain 33, staffing remained the primary focus, and other emerging organizational issues influenced the choice of candidates for vacant positions. In vacancy chain 62, issues of staffing were counterbalanced with concerns regarding the organization of work. Positions and jobs were redesigned with an appreciation of candidates available for assignment to those positions. In a third illustrative vacancy chain (29) diagrammed in Figure 5.3, staffing issues flowed directly from issues of organizational change.

A brief note on the evolving presentation and interpretation of vacancy chain diagrams is in order here. In Figure 5.3, as in the two previous diagrams, the statuses of employees E2 and E3 are shown both before and after the conclusion of the staffing actions that constitute this vacancy chain. These statuses are not shown for employee E1 in this diagram as they were in Figures 5.1 and 5.2, however, because of a convention used to construct these diagrams. In vacancy chain 29, employee E1 initially occupied position F2, which was then filled by employee E2 after E1 was appointed to position F1. The convention followed in drawing vacancy chain diagrams is to present the vacancy chain from a time perspective *after* the conclusion of all staffing activity. Thus, employee E1 is shown after his promotion to F1, employee E2 is shown after his transfer to F2, and employee E3 is shown after his hire from the ELM. Because the specific positions previously occupied by employees E2 and E3 were not subsequently filled, it is also possible to show their previous positions. However, because employee E2 was assigned to the position previously occupied by E1, representation of the staffing sequence does not show E1 in position F2 *before* his promotion to F1. Instead, E2 is shown occupying F2 *after* completion of the staffing sequence. Appreciation of this convention becomes more important when considering longer vacancy chains in which the positions vacated were identical to those filled by a subsequent staffing action.

Vacancy chain 29 was initiated as a consequence of a major mill re-building. As the construction and refitting of the mill was almost complete, the mill manager began to turn his attention to the training that would be required to get the mill's employees to work together in a manner that suited the design of the mill, but that was different from the one that had been traditionally used. The new style of management and mill operation was an integral component of the vision that accompanied the decision to make this major investment in new plant and machinery. It was believed that the technical benefits of the new mill could be realized only if new styles of mill management and operation were

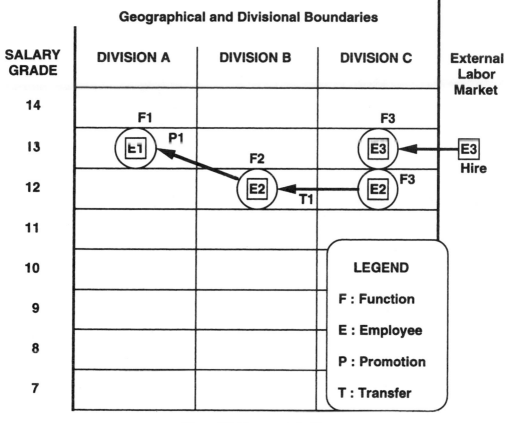

Figure 5.3. Vacancy chain 29.

implemented. Thus, training for increased usage of teamwork was an integral component of the strategy for this plant.

The training to be performed was a new function for this organization. Before this vacancy chain was initiated, training was being conducted by an outside consultant. However, mill management wanted an experienced ForestCo employee to do this work. They believed that instruction coming from an insider would have greater credibility with experienced mill workers than would instruction coming from someone who was not part of the traditional organization. Therefore, a new position description was developed through which someone, preferably an experienced ForestCo employee, could perform the training function.

With the position description established, the vacant position was posted. Approximately 15 internal candidates applied for the vacant job. Each candidate was evaluated in terms of his suitability for the position—but none was judged to meet the requirement that he have "training experience." Disappointed, but resolute, the senior managers at the mill persisted in their search by enlisting the assistance of a firm of headhunters to help find a person who did fit their requirements. The headhunters identified 45 additional potential candidates. Again, the background and record of each candidate were reviewed carefully. Two were interviewed by telephone, and two were brought into the plant for a series of interviews. Again, however, none of these additional candidates was judged suitable.

Faced with a null result from a substantial search, the local manager reexamined the files of the internal candidates he had reviewed previously and consciously rethought the requirements of the vacant position. His conclusion was that his original job definition had been incorrect and that the training job should be redefined. Once he had done this, he judged that one of the better internal candidates should be appointed to the newly defined position. This preliminary decision was discussed with two other senior managers, and the appointment was made.

While this process appears to be convoluted and inefficient, it is not necessarily the primary feature of this case. The requirements of the new training function and their translation into a job description were not a well-defined or well-understood problem. The local manager assessed a large number of possible solutions to his original definition of the "problem" and, finding no satisfactory match, redefined the problem. He did not do so solely to complete the routine associated with a staffing action. Rather, the original problem definition was recognized as a best guess in an uncertain and not well-understood situation. Under these circumstances, the manager learned about the terrain of useful problem definitions from his evaluations of many potential candidate solutions.

While the first move in vacancy chain 29 is of interest because the job definition was modified in light of an unsuccessful search for a suitable candidate, the subsequent moves also illustrate the large interdependencies between staffing and general issues of management. The selection of the training person for the mill rebuilding led to his transfer from another Division. The position he vacated there was posted, and several candidates applied. The local manager reviewed the qualifications of these candidates and interviewed those shortlisted. The person selected and appointed was regarded as being first-rate, and the local manager was quite pleased with his choice. After less than six months in the job, however, the new appointee (an Employee Relations Supervisor) left to take a much better position in another unit of the organization. This experience left the manager of the original unit with the feeling he had been burned. He had followed normative organizational prescriptions to "select the best," but believed he had received no benefit from his compliance with wider organizational norms. As a consequence, his selection criteria for the next appointee would place greater emphasis on local loyalty and less on advancement potential.

Meanwhile, the initial move of this Employee Relations Supervisor from another division left a vacant position there. In the third division associated with this three-person vacancy chain, the Divisional Manager had a clear vision of the type of organization he wanted. He believed he could transform a very traditional organization into one with fewer levels of supervision and greater autonomy and decision-making authority for employees. It was his goal to develop an organization that placed significantly greater emphasis on teamwork and individual responsibility for product quality. In this context, the Divisional Manager posted the recently vacated position. But in doing so, he emphasized qualities such as team-building, communication, and motivational skills that he believed would move his division closer to his view of what was possible. Four internal candidates applied for the vacancy, and the manager interviewed all four candidates. However, in terms of the critical requirements for his view of what the division could become, he did not believe that any of these four candidates would contribute substantially to attainment of his goal. As these staffing processes unfolded, the manager saw an opportunity to reduce the amount of supervision in his division by not automatically filling the vacancy created by the transfer of the previous Employee Relations Supervisor. Instead, he actively considered the possibility of distributing the responsibilities of this specialist function to his line managers and supervisors. But while this move may have been part of his vision, it was shared by few others. He reported that he received little support for this potential innovation, either from others in the Regional Office or from line managers in his division, who believed they would have an increased burden of responsibility without any compensating benefit.

Unsure how to resolve this dilemma, but not convinced that any of the internal candidates were suitable, the Divisional Manager advertised the vacant position in the local newspapers. More than 100 applications were received. These applications were screened, and through standard operating procedures such as shortlisting and interviews, a superior candidate was identified. However, the Divisional Manager remained ambivalent in his assessment of the need to fill the vacant position. He did not wish to appoint someone to a position that he believed was not in the long-term interests of his division. Looking for some means of resolving his dilemma, he discussed his mixed feelings with other senior employee relations representatives and arrived at a compromise. If the candidate tentatively selected for the position was agreeable, he would be appointed to that position on the understanding that one of his tasks would be to train line managers and supervisors to take on, within three years, the responsibilities of the employee relations function in their own units. In this way, the new appointee became an instrument through which the Divisional Manager could maintain progress toward his vision of long-term organizational change. Because the new appointee was charged with making his current job obsolete, the manager also gave his personal guarantee that if the appointee was successful, he would find a good position for him elsewhere in the organization.

A review of this particular vacancy chain again illustrates that fundamental issues of organizational adaptation and change are embedded within microcosms of organizational staffing. The first manager faced a new situation in which there were no clear guidelines as to how an organizational problem should be addressed. He translated his organization's needs into an organizational function that would be performed by an employee in a newly defined job. However, the requirements of the translation were uncertain, and the manager did not fully appreciate the limits to problem definition that arise from the availability of potential "solutions." A more complete understanding of how the problem could be addressed did not develop fully until he had expended considerable energy looking for a solution to what was revealed as an "unsolvable" problem. In contrast, the last manager associated with this vacancy chain had an extraordinarily clear vision of what he wished to accomplish. However, other significant constituents in the organization were not ready to accept the consequences of actions proposed to implement that vision. Political and organizational resistance to change caused him to rethink the nature of the position to be filled and to adapt both the means he used and the timeline he established to accomplish his overall objective.

The sequence of organizational contexts through which vacancy chains proceed frame the problem definitions and possible solutions considered in each staffing situation. In many situations, the framing of actions to address emerging organizational issues is triggered by the occurrence of a staffing opportunity. Vacant positions represent relatively open choice opportunities in which managers can define and focus attention on particular "problems" and emphasize particular "solutions." Job definitions, and the associated requirements for occupants, are established as standard ways in which organizational problems can be addressed by the selection and assignment of a person to a particular job.

REVIEW OF THREE-MOVE VACANCY CHAINS

Although the set of 20 three-move vacancy chains was obtained by grouping all chains of the same length, each vacancy chain appeared to be highly idiosyncratic. The problems associated with each staffing action on each vacancy chain varied considerably in terms of the various issues and attributes they presented to the responsible supervisor or manager. Different managers faced quite different organizational situations, even when they were in the same division. Also, different issues were often involved in staffing similar occupations and similar levels in the hierarchy. These idiosyncrasies occurred because different departments provided different contexts within which staffing took place. As staffing often involved the detailed consideration of complex matches of sets of jobs and personalities in jobs/positions, the necessary attention to detail limited the development of universal approaches to staffing. Solutions to staffing issues that may have been successful in one situation would not necessarily generalize to other situations. This lack of generalizability also applied to processes and procedures. The functionality of a particular procedure was largely dependent on the situation in which it might be used. Thus, while managers could learn various professional techniques and gain much experience in staffing, most staffing actions were ones in which a manager's previous knowledge and experience provided few guarantees of success.

A recurring theme in all vacancy chains reviewed so far is that organizational staffing is a significant process of organizational adaptation. As conditions facing each organizational unit change, supervisors and managers attempt to understand the implications of these changes for the collective endeavors of organizational participants. A significant proportion of all the staffing decisions associated with three-move (and two-move) vacancy chains were initiated by changes in the local context or problem environment of the organizational unit undertaking the staffing. Another two thirds of the remaining staffing actions were initiated because an existing position was vacated—because of either resignation, retirement, long-term disability, or discharge. More than half these latter vacancy chains were subsequently reframed to include issues similar to those in which organizational adaptation was required. As a result, only a small proportion of the vacancy chains reviewed so far were concerned with straight succession in which there was no change in the definitions of jobs and positions.

In general, there appears to be some balance between the procedures used to staff vacant positions. About two thirds of the time, positions were staffed primarily by means of administrative assignment. That is, the person responsible for staffing a vacant position was aware of the qualities of potential candidates and the different forms the job/position might take and decided to assign the selected candidate to a position without invoking any formal, rule-oriented selection process. In these situations, there were two major sources of uncertainty—those associated with the definition of the position to be filled and those associated with the attributes and qualities of the person chosen. These two sources of uncertainty were closely interdependent. Personal attributes and characteristics of potential candidates, especially their needs for further experience and skill development, were often instrumental in determining the characteristics of the position to be filled. In other circumstances, jobs were regarded as being relatively fixed and employees were chosen on the basis of their fit with both the job and the personalities and values of work teams. Even in these latter cases, however, supervisors and managers often believed they had sufficient knowledge of both jobs and potential candidates to permit them to make good selection and assignment decisions without relying on formal selection processes. Considerable energy was put into the pursuit of a competitive, market-driven search in only approximately one third of the staffing situations reviewed so far. Most often, these searches were undertaken in an attempt to find the best person, already employed within the firm, for the job/position that had been relatively well defined. In addition, most but not all hires from the ELM were also often subject to extensive examination as part of a competitive selection process.

There is considerable interdependence between the length of a vacancy chain and the likelihood that issues other than succession are considered in staffing vacant positions. Each staffing action presents an opportunity for issues other than succession to be considered. The longer the vacancy chain, the greater the number of choice opportunities represented by staffing actions. The larger the number of choice opportunities, the greater the chance that nonsuccession issues would be considered in at least one of the choice opportunities in the vacancy chain. When organizational problems, other than those of succession, enter the manager's appreciative frame, they broaden and complicate the set of issues/problems to be met by a staffing action. The more complex these issues, the less likely it is that they can be met by a single staffing action. Thus, complexity of issues tends to increase the length of the vacancy chain, and the longer the vacancy chain, the more likely it is that nonsuccession issues will be considered.

FOUR- AND FIVE-MOVE VACANCY CHAINS

The second set of medium-length vacancy chains reviewed in this chapter are those associated with either four or five person–moves. Table 5.2 presents summary information on these vacancy chains, indicating the salary grade range of positions or persons or both affected by each sequence of staffing actions, the primary "initiating reason," and a summary label of the concerns that led different managers to undertake the staffing actions in each vacancy chain. The caution noted previously in the discussion of three-move vacancy chains—namely, that simple labels may not adequately describe complex social phenomena—applies to an even greater degree to these longer vacancy chains.

In the sections that follow, illustrations of four- and five-person vacancy chains are described together with assessments of their shared features. As with three-person vacancy chains, the management of organizational change and adaptation again emerges as a significant theme but one intertwined with the task of finding and developing first- and second-line supervisors, reorganizing the arrangements of jobs and persons in departments, and accomplishing strategic staffing. This presentation of medium-length vacancy chains also includes a discussion of the conditions encountered in a particular division of ForestCo that encourages the use of a centralized staffing system.

Table 5.2 summarizes 13 medium-length vacancy chains. Detailed reviews of these 13 vacancy chains suggest that they can initially be considered to comprise four different groups of concerns: issues of succession associated with first- and second-line supervision (chains 16, 17, 23, and 71), administration of a sales and marketing division (36, 39, 40, 46, and 54), administration of lines of succession in the professional occupation of forestry (34 and 35), and administration of management in the context of technological and organizational change (9 and 66).

Finding and Developing First- and Second-Line Supervisors

The first group of four- and five-move vacancy chains to be considered are those concerned with the appointments of persons in lines of succession to supervisory

Table 5.2. Summary of Four- and Five-Move Vacancy Chains

Vacancy chain number	Salary grades[a]	Occupation or function	Initiation of vacancy	Staffing actions
		Four-person vacancy chains		
9	13–17	Technical Management	New position	Succession/hire from ELM
17	HH–15	Supervisory	Resignation	Succession/development
23	HH–13	Supervisory	Retirement	Succession/hire from hourly
35	10–16	Forestry	Retirement	Succession/development
39	10–15	Sales	New position	Succession/development/hire from ELM
40	9–11	Sales	New position	Succession/development/hire from hourly
54	TT–11	Clerical	New position	Succession/development/temporary → permanent
71	11–14	Supervisory	Reorganization	Succession/absorbed
		Five-person vacancy chains		
16	HH–13	Supervisory	Reorganization	Reorganization/succession/hire from hourly
34	12–14	Forestry	New position	Succession/development
36	8–12	Marketing	New position	Succession/development
46	11–14	Sales–Production	Resignation	Reorganization/succession
66	17–19	Management	Reorganization	Reorganization/succession

[a](HH) Indicates a move from the hourly payroll; (TT) indicates a move from a temporary position.

positions. These successions were targeted at first- and second-line supervisory positions, the occupants of which typically followed a line of progression from the ranks of experienced hourly employees to take on supervisory responsibilities associated with "man-management" and the hands-on production activities of various mills and logging operations. Three of these supervisory lines of progression involved four-move vacancy chains and one involved a five-move vacancy chain.

Vacancy chain 17, shown in Figure 5.4, illustrates the staffing actions associated with a relatively uncomplicated line of progression of mill supervisors. The vacancy chain was initiated when employee E1, an Area Supervisor in the mill, resigned unexpectedly. While this unexpected move created its own local uncertainty, it produced added pressure in the wider context also characterized by managerial uncertainty. The pressures associated with this resignation can be better understood in the historical context of the appointment of E1 as Area Supervisor less than six months previously. At that time, the appointment of employee E1 to the position of Area Supervisor had been hurried because of the recent departures of two other Area Supervisors. Faced with an unexpected need to appoint a person to an Area Supervisor position, local mill management found themselves with less than six months rather than a preferred development period of four to five years to prepare him for this level of responsibility.

> When [E1] was appointed to a supervisory position, we'd been intending to train him for four to five years to take the place of _____ when he retired. But everything got pushed forward when _____ [the previous Area Supervisor] decided to take early retirement. About the same time, another Area Supervisor got ill and took early retirement.

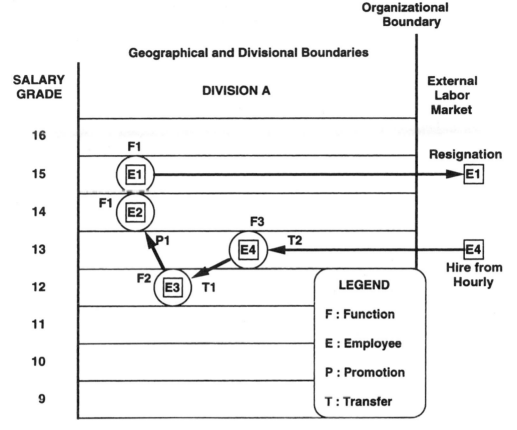

Figure 5.4. Vacancy chain 17.

> We were in a bit of a jam. We had [E1] and two others share the Acting Area Supervisor job for about four months. But the other supervisors had other job responsibilities, so we appointed [E1] to the position of Area Supervisor, which he's had for about six months.

Thus, when relatively new Area Supervisor E1 told senior management at the mill that he was leaving to go "back East," appreciation of the aggregate inexperience of mill supervisors became a repeated, significant problem.

> We weren't prepared for two unexpected departures—one went on long-term disability and one resigned. We'd been trying to prepare for the future and were planning on who should be developed over the next two to three year period. But because of those losses, potential supervisors are getting six months' training at the most, and they're being put in jobs for which they're not yet ready.

In this context, employee E2, who was the Senior Processing Engineer in the mill and who had initially been considered for assignment to the development position of Shift Supervisor, never received that assignment, but instead went more or less directly to the position of Area Supervisor. In appointing him to this position, management reduced the salary grade of position F1 from 15 to 14 in recognition of E2's relative lack of experience. As his replacement, employee E3—a Relief Supervisor "who had wanted to get into

Production five years ago, had been given the opportunity, but hadn't worked out" but who "wanted to return to being a technical process engineer"—was appointed in his place. Technically, this involved a demotion, as position F2 had a formal salary grade of 12, whereas employee E3 had previously been assigned to a position at salary grade 13. However, there was no decrease in salary associated with this assignment, as it was understood that this readjustment was in line with the capacities of employee E3 in job/position F2.

The appointments of E2 to the Area Supervisor position and that of E3 to the Senior Processing Engineer position were made through the administrative authority of the senior managers in the mill. No vacant positions were posted. In the case of the Area Supervisor appointment, another search had been undertaken less than a year previously to find a suitable candidate for a similar position. As the mill manager noted:

> I didn't post the position because I felt the same people would apply as had applied last year and I didn't want to tell them they weren't getting the job for the same reasons they didn't get it last year.

In addition, there was some urgency associated with the appointment because the ranks of the mill supervisors had been thinned by recent departures. The mill manager acknowledged that he knew the supervisors who had stayed were "getting antsy" for a break from too many long hours on shift. In the case of the previous Senior Process Engineer (E2), the appointment was made administratively, as use of this procedure did not overtly violate organizational requirements, yet also permitted him to satisfy the particular career wishes of the appointed employee. If the mill manager had posted vacant position F1, the process would not have concluded quickly, and he would have had less control over the selection and assignment of the Shift Supervisor who wanted to return to a technical job. By staffing through an administrative appointment process, the mill manager was able to address both the urgent organizational problem of finding a new Area Supervisor and the individual career development wishes of E2, the person appointed.

In contrast to these two administrative appointments, the vacant position (F3) previously occupied by the Relief Supervisor was posted. This job represents an entry-level position for career advancement from the ranks of hourly employees into first- and second-line supervision. As the terms and conditions of employment for first-line supervisors were quite different from those for hourly employees, competitive screening of candidates reduced the risk associated with unsuitable selections. However, advertising a vacant position inside the organization did not guarantee that anyone would apply, and in this instance no one did.

The move from the protected hourly employment system to that of first-line supervision offered both increased opportunity and increased risk. The mill superintendent commented on his understanding of the trade-offs associated with these moves:

> Men in the plant saw a lot of supervisors lose their jobs in the recession. If they'd stayed with their hourly job instead of going for supervision, given their seniority they'd have still had a job during the rough times. Lots of them think being in the union is more secure. Besides, they see the future of this mill as being shaky. It's old, the process is obsolete, and there aren't many guys here between the ages of 25 and 45.

Faced with the lack of response to the posting of the Relief Supervisor job vacancy, the Mill Superintendent went around the mill and spoke with a small number of senior employees he thought might do well in the job. As a result, four employees were persuaded to be considered for the vacant position. While these discussions were taking place, the mill also advertised in the local newspaper for a young engineer who might also be considered for the vacant position—but again no response was received. Consequently, the senior managers at the mill focused their attention on the four internal candidates from the ranks of hourly employees.

A team of three managers conducted panel interviews and evaluated each candidate. On the basis of their results, the panel team judged that none of the candidates was suitable. Nevertheless, they were unsure of their judgment in this matter and sent the four candidates for further assessment by a firm of consulting psychologists. Again, the assessments were not strongly supportive of any of these candidates. Shortly after these results had been obtained, however, the Mill Superintendent "had an opportunity to see one of the candidates in action." To his surprise, he observed this candidate performing well at one of the tasks for which the psychological tests had indicated he had little competence! Relying on his personal judgment, the mill supervisor proceeded to make an increasingly urgent appointment:

> I dumped the test results and approached _____ about taking the position because he had the most raw talent and I decided it was time to invest in his training. He got the job because he made the commitment to tackle his own self-development and I made the commitment to train him. Without either one, the appointment wouldn't have happened.

In making this appointment, the Mill Superintendent was keenly aware of his obligations to the chosen candidate:

> If I don't train and pay attention to _____, he'll go downhill fast. He's not a self-motivator. If I don't take care of him, we'll lose a valuable asset. The major risk of this appointment will happen if I'm not fully committed and effective in teaching him what's required.

In summary, vacancy chain 17 illustrates the real pressures often experienced by middle managers as they attempt to manage the lines of progression associated with the development of hourly workers into first- and second-line supervisors. Contextual uncertainty often upset programs of planned development. Positions became vacant before potential successors had received sufficient training. Potential successors who had experience and were trained could be poached by other departments. Moreover, appointments along lines of progression were also shaped by other contextual pressures. In production operations, work could not be delayed. Positions kept vacant for any length of time increased the administrative load on other supervisors. Urgency and quick accommodation were often concomitants of the appointments and vacancy chains associated with supervisory succession.

Because an intimate knowledge of the production process was judged to be required for superior performance of production supervisors, supervisory lines of succession eventually drew from the ranks of experienced hourly workers. Also, because the terms and conditions of the employment contract were different for salaried than for hourly positions, moves across this employment boundary could put the employment security of supervisory aspirants at risk. Moreover, norms of equality associated with unionized hourly employees limited the expression of personal ambition to eventually supervise coworkers. Not surprisingly, therefore, candidate selections were often problematic, with few, if any, hourly employees advancing their candidacy for supervisory positions.

Under these circumstances, the selection and negotiated assignment by the mill manager of an experienced hourly employee to the position of Relief Supervisor can be seen as the additional social support required to make succession happen. The resulting employment contract for the new Relief Supervisor is an impersonal one between ForestCo and the employee. But more important, it is also a personal commitment between the new Relief Supervisor and the mill manager. The mill manager implicitly contracted to protect the new Relief Supervisor by providing the training and support that would help him perform in that job. Such personal understandings were not guarantees. There was still a requirement that the Relief Supervisor expend effort and attempt to learn how to perform his job well. Moreover, the mill manager had little control over commodity prices, which, if they dropped drastically, could make the mill obsolete. Nevertheless, within these constraints, the personal commitment of the mill manager was required to sustain the ILM and effect progress along this line of progression.

Sales: Administered Lines of Progression

Within the sample of vacancy chains surveyed at ForestCo, those in the sales organization were notable because of their characteristic emphasis on administered lines of progression. Staffing decisions in the sales organization were typically far more centralized within the authority of senior line management than was the case for other occupational groups. Delegation of selection and staffing decisions to local managers, who had the immediate authority and responsibility to fill the vacant position, was observed more frequently in other divisions, regions, and occupations. While the local manager's views on the suitability of candidates were considered in the sales organization, selection decisions were usually made at least two levels, and occasionally more, above the hierarchical level of the position being filled. Associated with this increased centralization was a greater emphasis on administered appointments. Other than an occasional decision to hire from the ELM in which potential vacancies would be advertised, few vacancies above entry-level positions were posted. For these positions, candidate suitability was assessed most often by senior line managers.

The distinctiveness of the staffing processes in the sales organization can be traced to the different basis of organizing in this division in contrast to that used elsewhere in the company. Although ForestCo is a large, multidivisional company with several bases of organizing being used concurrently (e.g., by function, by geographic region, by product), most hourly employees, and the majority of salaried employees, work in production-related jobs in production-related forms of organization. The organizational logic of these production units is based on economic rationality embedded in the geographic distribution of raw materials—different segments of land and the forests that are available for harvesting. Within these production-based organizational units, different specialist occupations such as Engineering, Accounting, Forestry, First- and Second-Line Supervisors, and Maintenance were organized to serve the ends of the production function.

Jobs in production units were designed for occupational specialist functions that directly or indirectly served the dominant production function. These jobs were often closely linked to other jobs in the same geographically located unit through close task interdependencies. For example, information from Foresters about the nature of the lumber and fiber that could be harvested was critical for the design of machines to process the forest resource. Engineers who designed machines were interdependent with Maintenance Supervisors who kept these machines running. Engineers provided critical information to Foresters about different methods that could be used to produce more efficient harvesting operations, and Foresters provided information on how to meet environmental protection regulations. Accountants performed critical cost and revenue measurement functions that guided Production, Maintenance, and Supervisory functions.

Built to realize economies of scale, these production units, particularly pulp mills, were often quite large. Within any one of these organizational units, there was often a sufficient number of related jobs, arranged in a modest hierarchy, to facilitate mobility into, through, and out of these hierarchies sufficient to establish the minimal requirements of an ILM. For more senior positions in these production units, interdivisional mobility within each Region was feasible and facilitated by the posting system. In effect, the posting system permitted information about candidates and jobs to cross the implicit boundaries created by the limits to personal knowledge on the part of managers making selection decisions. Moreover, within any one Region, there were often several moderately interdependent production units. Intraregional but interdivisional posting tended to reinforce the coincidence of the ILM boundary with that of the regional organization. These arrangements—the distribution of related jobs, the system of posting and decision criteria that influenced when it would be used, and the staffing needs of the organization—helped develop opportunities for employees to actively voice their career interests within a competitive market framework.

In contrast to the multifunctional character of Production units, Sales and Marketing (which also included Distribution) operated as a separate, single functional entity to serve the three primary production-based Regions. Jobs within Sales and Marketing tended to be unifunctional but geographically diverse, whereas Production operations were concentrated in coastal British Columbia (with two separate production units in the United States). Sales and distribution functions were spread across national and international boundaries. Therefore, within customer-driven sales units, organizational structures tended to be small and flat with relatively few interdependencies between units. Also, excellent performance of a lower-level job did not necessarily translate into the likelihood of superior performance at the next higher level within the unit because different skills and competencies were required to perform jobs at different levels. Consequently, career progression within any one sales unit was very limited, and most career development for organizational needs could be arranged only by transfers between units.

Within this organizational context, posting was unlikely to meet organizational needs. Posting places the initiative and control for staffing between the local manager and the candidates in the system who choose to apply for those positions. Local managers knew local candidates and local conditions. If competitive posting procedures were initiated, the selection of local candidates would be favored. Moreover, candidates in other geographic areas were less willing to apply for positions in less desirable geographic areas even though such positions offered opportunities for further career development. Individual decisions to invest in career development were made more readily when there was some organizational obligation for these investments to be rewarded in the future. Often, this obligation required an explicit acknowledgment on the part of senior managers that if lower-level subordinates demonstrated loyalty and performance, they would be rewarded with moves "back" to favored areas and positions. Finally, within the administrative apparatus of posting, there was less opportunity for someone to represent the wider needs and interests of the sales division and its relationship to the organization as a whole. Because market-based procedures assume distributions of information and knowledge that could not be met in the sales organization, centralized staffing was a more effective response to the conditions encountered there.

Because staffing in the sales organization tended to be administratively centralized, the extensive dilemmas associated with staffing positions in other parts of the organization occurred more often within the cognitive frames of the sales managers who made those decisions. There were fewer "public" debates such as those that occasionally accompanied panel interviews. There were also fewer open discussions regarding the nature of jobs to be filled, because the performances of employees in sales jobs were less dependent on the performances of employees in other jobs.

An illustration of this independence comes from an interview held with a Regional Sales Manager (RSM) regarding his views of the staffing process. In this interview, the RSM discussed his proposed plans for a four-person vacancy chain all within his area of responsibility. These plans were implemented approximately six months later exactly as he had described previously. Figure 5.5 presents vacancy chain 39—an illustration of an administered line of progression in the sales organization. The origin of these moves was a decision to create a product specialty within the general sales function. This resulted in a new position (F1) and a modification of the position (F2) that the new appointee (E1) had occupied previously. These proposed changes had emerged in discussions between the RSM and his immediate supervisor. The establishment of the new position (F1) was facilitated by the absorption of the functions of a vacated job in a previous vacancy chain that concerned positions outside the scope of the RSM but were under the jurisdiction of his immediate superior. Interestingly, the absorbed job was that of a Warehouse Shipper at

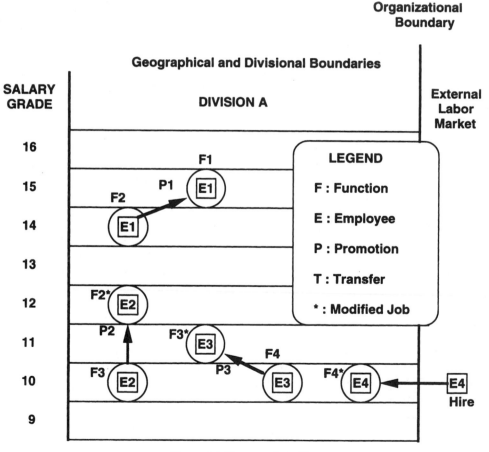

Figure 5.5. Vacancy chain 39.

salary grade 8 and was replaced by that of an RSM (Product X) at a salary grade of 15. Following discussions and development of plans with his immediate supervisor, the RSM was delegated the authority and responsibility to implement these plans. His preferred operating style was one of relatively close supervision that was consistent with centralized staffing:

> I prefer shorter lines of communication so I can deal directly with my "horses." I find this gives me more control of sales and profits in my area of responsibility.

Consequently, within the established traditions and culture of the sales organization, he assessed whom he had available and how he might arrange the various moves to bring about the desired changes. In doing this, the local manager gave the impression of moving pieces on a chessboard. Different configurations of jobs were considered in conjunction with different configurations of persons assigned to those jobs. After he and his supervisor had thought through what they believed was the best solution within the limits of what they understood to be possible, the RSM went through the actions of implementing his plan. As described in Figure 5.5, the new position entailed a promotion of employee E1. In rationalizing why he chose employee E1, the local manager provided the following succinct and focused summary:

> He's got the background experience and knowledge of the products we want him to sell. He's highly regarded by the mill managers. I can trust him to have good judgment and do a good job. He's known to sell what's produced, so mills won't end up with an inventory of rotting product. He does what we want—he sells! I didn't consider anyone else, as he's the obvious choice.

Other appointees were given similar characterizations, though the specific attributions varied from one person to another. Because this vacancy chain was also associated with organizational change, namely, the identification of a sales group focused on a new product line, several positions were modified. The generalist position vacated by E1 was regraded down two salary grades (from 14 to 12), as it was redesigned to focus on one rather than several product groups. Employee E2 was promoted to this new position because "there were no other choices" given the manager's assessment that "it's important to promote from within." This appointment also illustrated the difficulties of timing associated with the management of lines of progression, as the appointment of employee E2 was regarded as being "a bit premature—he's aggressive and has solid sales skills but he hasn't had enough grooming." The next move was one made as much for individual development (i.e., a "push" move) as one driven by the match between the job requirements of modified position F3*. Again, however, the manager making this administrative appointment "didn't consider anyone else." Finally, the "hire" of employee E4 was opportunistic, as he was well known as a representative of a small company that had just been bought by ForestCo. The assignment of employee E4 to position F4* was to produce an assignment "in line with [the employee's] qualifications and experience."

One consistent feature of the characterizations of all four employees involved in this vacancy chain was that the RSM believed that each appointee was either "the obvious" or "the only" choice available for the position to which he would be assigned. There are several potential explanations for this behavior. One possibility is that the manager wished to reduce the cognitive dissonance associated with his choice. Related to this is the possibility that he used public affirmation as a means of reducing his uncertainty regarding his choice. A third option is that this manager wished to convince organizational outsiders of the correctness of his decision. Nevertheless, there was little opportunity for anyone to challenge these decisions. In terms of several prior discussions of the extent to which organizational staffing systems represent competitive labor "markets," this vacancy chain appeared to meet the fewest market criteria of any described so far. However, much of this discrepancy can be also attributed to the fact that all the positions noted in vacancy chain 39 were under the direct authority of the RSM, and all positions were changed as a consequence of these staffing actions. There was no switching of the vacancy chain from one divisional unit to another, and the centralized control of a relatively flat and dispersed organization gave the local manager both the knowledge and the authority to make changes of people and positions as an integral whole. A combination of organizational conditions came together in this vacancy chain, and in others found in the sales organization, to produce a staffing system characterized by administered lines of progression. The posting system was rarely used, and public competition for positions of increased reward and responsibility was rarely engaged.

Strategic Staffing

A theme beginning to emerge from descriptions of the vacancy chains and staffing actions discussed so far is that of organizational adaptation. In many instances, organizational adaptation was manifest in the many small accommodations made by local managers as they adjusted the tasks, duties, and responsibilities of the various jobs under their jurisdiction in response to changing local conditions. A number of these changes represented temporary adjustments to immediate issues such as the introduction of new equipment, short-term changes in demand, and temporary imbalances between the demand for, and the supply of, skilled staff. In other instances, jobs changed as part of larger patterns of organizational change. For example, a new product line might be added to an existing line of products, or one might gradually be replaced with a substitute. Similarly, a particular processing technology might gradually be replaced by one that was regarded as superior, perhaps because it produced less toxic effluent.

In addition to these adjustments, other more significant changes in personnel would be implemented from time to time. Although there was no formal indication that these latter changes were qualitatively different from most others, they appeared to signal a significant change in the traditions and values of the organization. One area in which this type of change appeared to be taking place was in Forestry. In the more senior levels of this occupational group, several vacancy chains were encountered in which staffing issues represented the cutting edge of a change in the strategic direction of the company.

Traditionally, the practice of Forestry was primarily a technical occupation. Foresters had to understand the complex ecology associated with the plant and animal species of the temperate forests harvested by ForestCo. They had to become familiar with the interdependencies of terrain, soil composition, rainfall, growth cycles, and animal and fish habitats. They had to develop a detailed understanding of the current and potential commercial value of various tree species at various stages of their growth cycle. Associated with this knowledge, they needed to understand the sources of natural decay cycles of mature trees and to recognize the incidence of disease, rot, and insect infestations. Forester functions spanned the boundaries between the ecology of the temperate rain forests and the business founded on the commercial harvesting of trees. Foresters' technical expertise was recognized by their receiving a professional designation and, depending on their position, formally representing ForestCo in its accountability to local government for the management of public lands.

Over the past 15 years, there had been a gradual change in the social, political, and business environment faced by ForestCo. Increasingly, environmental activists have pub-

licized their view of the consequences of logging activities on the lands managed by
ForestCo. Recently, there has been exponential growth in both the number and the
proportion of all ForestCo-related news articles that deal with environmental issues
(Pinfield & Berner, 1992). These changes in ForestCo's business environment have not been
trivial. The company's primary resource, namely, access and harvesting rights to the local
forests, has become vulnerable to the technical and controversial news stories that could
lead to restrictions on its access to supplies of prime timber and wood fiber. In at least two
celebrated instances that were finally determined through legal challenges settled in court,
ForestCo's access to prime timber, previously accepted as being within its sole domain,
was withdrawn.

Foresters have become front-line troops in what some have seen as a battle for the
public mind. Company foresters have extensive knowledge of the particular lands and
timber stocks available on company-licensed land, as well as the professional expertise
needed to develop and defend land-management plans. More important, their expertise is
a critical requirement for an assessment of the validity of claims made by environmentalists. As these changes in the company's business and political environment have occurred,
Foresters have needed to develop public relations skills to maintain the social and political
legitimacy of ForestCo's current and planned activities. From a strategic perspective, a
huge threat to the security of access to raw materials needed to be addressed through the
deployment of appropriate corporate resources. Traditional "dirt" Foresters were considered unsuitable for this task, as their technical focus often hindered their appreciation of
public relations and communications subtleties. On the other hand, professional public
relations experts were considered to lack the requisite technical expertise and professional
certifications to legally represent the company in formal public hearings. One solution to
this challenge was to gradually change the skill-set of a few of ForestCo's professional
Foresters in key positions. One way to accomplish this was to use the staffing system to
choose persons who could meet the strategic demands of the organization to perform
critical boundary-spanning relations. Although the persons charged with staffing these
positions were not consciously aware of the label for their activities, they engaged in
strategic staffing.

The illustration of strategic staffing associated with the Forester occupational group
can be found in vacancy chain 35 diagrammed in Figure 5.6. Formally, this vacancy chain
was initiated by the impending early retirement of employee E1, a Regional Forester.
When it became known that this position would become vacant, the forthcoming vacant
position was posted, and seven candidates applied. Each person was interviewed by a
panel consisting of two Senior Foresters, the Regional Employee Relations Supervisor,
and a Senior Regional Manager. Formally, there was no reorganization involving a change
in job number or job title. However, there was substantial discussion within the panel of
senior managers as to the requirements of the job. This debate was manifested in the
preferences for two candidates. One was the clear candidate of choice within a traditional
definition of the job of Regional Forester. This candidate had considerable field experience
and had worked extensively on the management plan for the harvesting and development
of the forestry resource. A second candidate had little knowledge of the details of the local
forests, but was experienced in the development of overall corporate policies. Moreover,
this second candidate appeared to have superior communication skills and was judged to
be more capable of handling relationships with various local constituencies. The traditional candidate "clearly knew the job," but there was also a strong feeling that "the job
needs to be done differently."

The critical aspect of the internal debate regarding the choice between these two

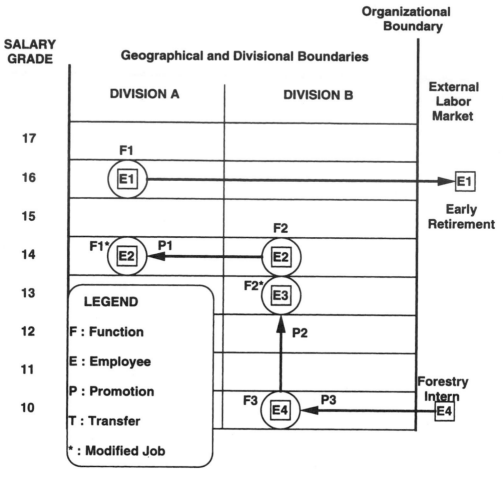

Figure 5.6. Vacancy chain 35.

candidates concerned an emerging, environmentalist "hot spot" in the region. An extraordinary and potentially unique stand of old growth timber had been found in a remote part of the public land under ForestCo's management. Environmentalists had focused much of their publicity efforts on this stand of timber, and the more radical among them argued that the whole watershed containing this stand of timber should be withdrawn from ForestCo's control. Such a move would have seriously depleted the forests available for harvesting. In addition to the necessary technical and professional competence and experience, capacity to deal with various public constituencies thus became an additional critical job requirement of this changed job. After much discussion, the second candidate was selected and appointed to a shadow position (F1*) for approximately nine months to work with the departing Regional Forester to "get close to the land and the people." Because this was a shadow appointment, with much further development of E2 planned for the succeeding year, the position was initially set at salary grade 14. As E2 developed additional experience and took on additional responsibilities, the salary grade of his position would be accordingly elevated one or two levels.

Once employee E2 was selected, his previous position F2 was posted, and ten candidates applied. Four of these candidates were subsequently interviewed by the supervisor of the position and the previous occupant E2, as he was considered to be most knowledgeable about the requirements of the position. The supervisor also telephoned other Divisional Managers to obtain additional information on the candidates who applied. Ultimately, the supervisor chose a candidate (E3) from within his own unit rather than a "dirt" Forester from one of the divisions. This candidate was better known to the supervisor of the unit than were the Divisional Forester candidates considered. In addition, this candidate was already familiar with the technical requirements of the vacant position and required no training time. As the supervisor noted, urgent demand pressures limited the opportunity to grow candidates into the requirements of the vacant position.

> _____'s departure to the Regional Forester position was unexpected. I just couldn't afford to have a trainee come into his position and spend time learning the job even if such a candidate might eventually be better than the one eventually chosen.

Once employee E3 was chosen to occupy the position previously occupied by E2 (but at a slightly lower salary grade), his position, in turn, was filled by the appointment of a Forestry intern, a young preprofessional who had recently joined the company and who was about to receive her legal designation as a professional Forester.

The interesting feature of this illustration of strategic staffing is that there was no structural change involving a reorganization of organizational positions. Instead, the external requirements for a formally designated Regional Forester were maintained, but the internal requirements of the position were changed. These internal changes reflected the importance of changes in the external environment and signaled, at least in this instance, a change in the requirements for career advancement in this professional occupation. Concerns regarding career development and advancement within this occupational specialty were reinforced by the choice of employee E3 to take the position vacated by the person designated as the new Regional Forester. Traditional career paths had emphasized fieldwork—the operational aspects of forestry associated with the management and harvesting of the forestry resource. With the high-profile appointment of E2, someone with a nontraditional background, and his replacement by someone with a similar orientation toward more abstract policy issues, several persons who thought they were in line for more senior positions began to question whether the traditional paths for professional career development and advancement had been abandoned.

The supervisor of the key unit (Division B in Figure 5.6) located in Head Office reported:

> I received some flak from the supervisors of several of the other candidates we interviewed. They thought Head Office types were getting an inside track for career advancement in forestry. Regional Foresters are concerned their jobs are becoming dead end. I talked with them and think I've allayed their concerns.

The dynamics revealed in vacancy chain 35 also reflect the tensions between corporate staff and field operations. There was little questioning of the selection of employee E2 to the Regional Forester position, as he was seen to possess the "new" requirements of an adaptive corporate system. However, Divisional Foresters who aspired to Regional Forester positions were concerned that they would never be given the opportunity to develop the technical skills learned in F2. Moreover, they believed that the selection of employee E3 to occupy the vacated position F2 both affirmed and institutionalized the requirements of those technical skills. This denied them further career opportunities and apparently blocked their access to Regional Forester positions. As these selection decisions were taken largely under the personal authority of the supervisor of the corporate staff group, other supervisors questioned both the process (a biased and unrepresentative selection panel) and the outcomes of these staffing actions.

Reorganizing Managerial Persons and Positions

In contrast to the three vacancy chains just described, the series of related staffing actions associated with medium-length vacancy chains 9 and 66 have little to do with managerial succession along lines of progression. Instead, they are an integral component of a reorganization of the duties and responsibilities of the senior jobs in large subunits of ForestCo's organization. Vacancy chain 66 was part of a reorganization of a large pulp–paper mill complex. The reorganization was triggered by the appointment of a new general manager, who quickly realized that he had to delegate the operational management of the mill complex to experienced line managers. He also realized that several of the senior managers who were now his subordinates had also considered themselves to be suitable candidates for the position he now occupied. Therefore, he and the senior manager he replaced discussed at length the emerging priorities for the mill and the strengths of the existing management team. Then, the two senior managers also met with each senior manager in the mill and

> talked with them about how each saw their area being covered, how they saw themselves in their jobs, what their ambitions were, and what responsibilities they wanted in the reorganization.

After the general manager had considered all this information, his opinion was that with one exception, there was sufficient strength present in the senior ranks of the organization to accomplish most organizational objectives. However, he also judged that "there was overlap as to who wanted what" and that he "wouldn't be able to satisfy everyone." The resulting organization decided on by the general manager was a complex product of his assessment of organizational priorities, current strengths and development needs of existing personnel, and the stated career preferences of each of these managers.

The diagram of the staffing actions in Figure 5.7 is presented as a matter of record. However, the formal diagramming of staffing changes fails to capture the real substance behind the archival record. For example, the move of employee E1 from one function (F1) to another (F1*) reflects little but a change in job title. The moves of employees E2, E3, and E4, however, were more significant. The manager previously responsible for the pulp side of the mill (E2) was appointed temporarily to a position of Area Manager with overall responsibility for the coordination of Production, Distribution, and Marketing for the whole mill. E2 was "replaced" in a lateral move by the manager (E3) who had previously been Production Manager–Papers. E3, in turn, was "replaced" by the manager (E4) who had previously been the Paper Mill Superintendent. Finally, a senior manager who had previously been in charge of Employee Relations (E5) had a large production operations job added to his portfolio of responsibilities.

These changes in the organization were complex and often difficult to understand. Not even the managers themselves were able to develop an accurate appreciation of how these organizational arrangements would eventually sort themselves out. The changes associated with the reorganization and the assignment of different managers to different positions implied both a reconceptualization of the way the administration of the mill was configured and a reassessment of the career status and career trajectories of the employees involved. Although some moves could generally be regarded as ones of succession, no job

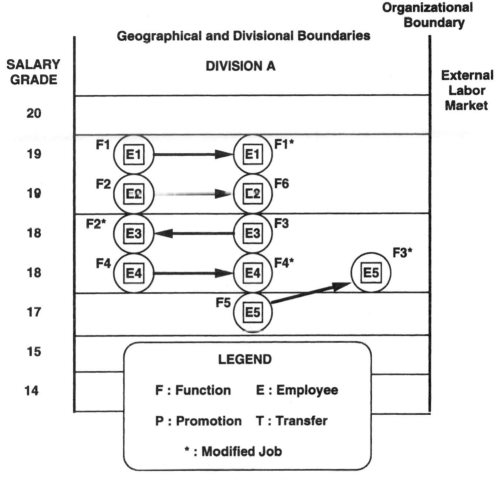

Figure 5.7. Vacancy chain 66.

was unaffected by the reorganization. The labeling scheme used in Fig. 5.7 shows an approximation of the job changes resulting from the reorganization and the reassignment of the members of this senior management team. The position of Area Manager to which employee E2 was assigned was a completely new position resulting from the reorganization. Employee E3 was moved to a modified version of the job previously occupied by employee E2. Employee E5 was "promoted," as his current responsibilities were combined with those previously assigned to employee E3. Finally, employee E4 was given additional responsibilities that previously were in the domains of the jobs previously performed by employee E2 and E3.

Some of these moves were clearly temporary, as they represented preparatory moves prior to other significant changes in responsibility. For example, while employee E2 performed his new coordinating function, he also spent time becoming more familiar with the operation of the paper machines in the mill. Within three months of this reorganization, this senior manager was promoted to another position in another Region to tackle a challenging assignment there. Other moves signaled significant development experiences. For example, the reassignments of the previous Production Manager–Papers (E3) and the Employee Relations Manager (E5) represented major changes in responsibility.

These changes are very organic in nature and consequently cannot be described with mechanistic precision. The difficulties in fully appreciating these changes experienced by outside observers were also shared by the persons directly involved in the reorganization. These jobs could not be defined in exact detail, as each job evolved and changed as a function of emerging problems and the developing skills of individual managers and their collective capacity to work together. Subsequently, there will be further ongoing adjustments and struggles among the participants as they adjust to their new responsibilities and attempt to find collective ways of addressing different parts of shared problems.

The reorganization of assignments presented in Figure 5.7 clearly considered two interdependent sources of uncertainty in the staffing task. Because of the senior and collective nature of the tasks facing this group of managers and executives, neither jobs nor persons were taken as given. Jobs were defined and redefined within some overall appreciation of the task accomplishments required to sustain production from the large pulp–paper mill complex. Persons were regarded as presenting different sets of skills, capacities, and experiences that could be applied to a shifting array of jobs. Moreover, assignments of persons to vaguely defined jobs were judged to produce important outcomes that would not become clear until the consequences of assignments could be experienced and observed. Assignments of persons to jobs both produced substantive performance outcomes and encouraged the development and display of managerial skills. Altogether, there was considerable good-faith experimentation associated with a succession of incremental reorganizations and reassignments.

REVIEW OF FOUR- AND FIVE-MOVE VACANCY CHAINS

Medium-length vacancy chains may be considered to be far more representative of stereotypical ILM processes than the minimal vacancy chains of one- or two-person moves reviewed in Chapter 4. Medium-length vacancy chains manifest stronger preferences for persons already employed within the ILM, as initiating vacancies produced two, three, or four additional vacancies as a consequence of this managerial selection preference.

Structurally, few differences were found between minimal (especially two-move) and medium-length vacancy chains. In particular, few differences in objective characteristics such as the numbers of such chains, hierarchical grade of origin, hierarchical grade of termination, and span of grades covered were found for the samples of two-move and three-move vacancy chains studied. Together, these two types of vacancy chain (i.e., two- and three-move) accounted for 56% of the 71 vacancy chains subject to detailed examination. Vacancy chains consisting of four- and five-person moves represented a further 18% of the 71 vacancy chains sampled. Vacancy chains consisting of one- through five-person moves therefore constituted approximately 85% of those investigated through interviews with the managers involved. These vacancy chains may therefore be considered to represent the primary vacancy chain features of ForestCo's ILM.

Stereotypical models of ILM operation consider vacancy chains to be concerned with the maintenance of ILMs through progressions of employee moves along lines of progression. While this progression was certainly a widely shared feature of many vacancy chains observed, this description underrepresents the variety and complexity of issues associated with such progressions. Staffing activities were rarely considered separate from more general issues confronting ForestCo's managers. As competitive conditions changed, as new products and processes were developed, as external political and regulatory demands both changed and increased, staffing decisions and the vacancy chains that linked them emerged as primary tools for the accomplishment of organizational change and adaptation. The relationships between vacancy chains and organizational adaptation showed few consistent distinctions between antecedent and consequent actions. At times, pressures for change led to the establishment of new positions that in turn triggered further adaptations in the redesign of jobs and modifications of established career paths. In other circumstances, the occurrence of vacancies reduced constraints that had previously limited the implementation of change, and adaptation occurred opportunistically in the redesign of vacant positions and the criteria used to select among candidates competing for assignment to those positions. Several "vacancy chains" occurred sequentially through time, but in fact represented several concurrent person-moves as whole departments were reorganized.

The language and constructs of managerial decision making may be used to describe this blending of vacancy chain processes with those of organizational change and adaptation. Vacant positions represent choice opportunities that become associated with larger organizational issues, such as the performance of the organizational unit(s) providing the context within which the position is located. The performance requirements of specific positions were rarely separated from wider organizational issues. Consequently, the procedures and outcomes of the staffing process were strongly influenced by contextual factors. Although no managerial level was insulated from pressures for change and adaptation, more senior managers typically had wider responsibilities than those located at lower levels of the organizational hierarchy. Thus, there was a tendency for broader organizational issues to "bleed" or "seep" into the choice opportunities represented by vacant positions at more senior levels of the organizational hierarchy. A not uncommon way of framing potential actions as a response to these and other issues was to consider vacant positions as the means of accomplishing new or redefined organizational functions. Selection of a person to perform those functions then became the staffing task. However, there were also many instances in which the availability of persons, and the skills and capacities they represented, also influenced the expectations of functions that could be performed.

As illustrated in several of the vacancy chains described herein, few organizational issues could be contained with one staffing action. When several positions were task-interdependent, changes in one position often required changes in other positions. Thus, issues that directly affected one department or one function typically resurfaced in several of the sequentially linked staffing choices associated with a vacancy chain. In other circumstances, especially when candidates were selected from organizational units other than the one in which staffing was initiated, additional issues more germane to the unit now experiencing a vacancy would enter staffing choice opportunities. Multiple contexts for multiple staffing choices provided opportunities for larger issues of organizational adaptation and change to modify job design and employee selection. The longer the vacancy chain, the greater the possibility for an increased variety of contextual issues to emerge and influence staffing choices.

The organizational scope of contextual issues brought into any staffing choice opportunity depended on the decision frame of the manager deemed responsible for the staffing action. As already mentioned, more senior managers typically had greater autonomy to act within the boundaries of their own authority without oversight by their immediate supervisor. However, these senior managers also experienced greater task interdependence with other managers and organizational activities. In addition, senior managers were more aware of competitive and survival pressures originating from outside the corporation. Larger, more complex issues considered in staffing choices could rarely be settled by a single staffing action because of interdependencies among tasks. Hence, a sequence of linked staffing actions was often required in order to put in place an administrative apparatus that could deal satisfactorily and more or less completely with these wider issues.

During the time of this study, vacancy chains in the professional occupations of Forestry illustrated most readily the seepage of wider organizational issues into emerging vacancy chains. Both formally (vacancy chain 33) and informally (vacancy chain 35), staffing choices were strongly influenced by external factors. In the design of positions and the choices of persons to occupy vacated positions, the organization engaged in strategic staffing, as functions deemed crucial to the survival of the corporation influenced staffing decisions. These choices had profound implications for reconceptualizations of skills and experiences required for career advancement. Lines of progression, career paths, and career opportunities were changed. As a consequence, these choices were contested by persons with vested interests in previous appreciations of what constituted established lines of progression.

Related perspectives also appear to capture the overall themes embedded in medium-length vacancy chains associated with the development of first- and second-line supervisors and implementation of strategic staffing. In the larger production units of ForestCo's organization, there were general lines of progression from the senior levels of the hourly workforce, to first-line supervisor positions, and then to second-line supervisory positions. These general lines of progression were not formal requirements of local staffing systems. Rather, custom and practice had established general patterns of succession within the "man-management" functions of these production units. For several of these patterns, progression to Area Supervisor positions, or to General Manager positions of smaller units, typically required four or five moves. Thus, when Area Supervisor or General Manager positions became vacant, the subsequent vacancy chains followed these patterns and produced four- or five-move sequences. In the instances of strategic staffing surveyed, a single move would normally not be regarded as sufficient to signal a new strategic direction for the organization. However, when an initial staffing selection was reinforced by other moves and each signaled a move away from traditional practices, then organizational change could be implemented more readily.

Other medium-length vacancy chains were concerned with more focused aspects of organizational change and adaptation. For example, the unifunctional, geographically dispersed sales workforce that was organized into a large number of smaller organizational units was able to contain its concerns within the sales organization. In this case, organizational conditions encouraged a centralized approach to staffing in which divisional issues and concerns were considered within the private planning deliberations of one senior manager, or possibly two. This centralized perspective avoided the public debates and questioning of managerial actions experienced elsewhere, but nevertheless permitted problem formulations and potential solutions limited only by the imagination of the person(s) responsible for the management of that division.

Medium-length vacancy chains represent both modal and longer versions of the bulk of sequentially linked staffing actions found in ForestCo's organization. As the term "medium" suggests, however, they were not the longest vacancy chains encountered. In Chapter 6, descriptions of long vacancy chains comprised of staffing sequences of six-, seven-, eight-, and nine-person moves are presented. Chains of this length were initially considered to be most derivative of stereotypical models of ILMs. Chapter 6 explores their nature and seeks reasons for their relative infrequency.

6

Long Vacancy Chains

INTRODUCTION

Long vacancy chains are one set of outcomes that may be derived from stereotypical models of internal labor markets (ILMs). Once triggered by an initial vacancy, long vacancy chains are consistent with models of ILM operation in which occupancy of a relatively stable system of jobs is maintained by repeated appointments of persons already employed within that ILM to fill successive vacant positions. In this stereotypical perspective, long vacancy chains originate at higher levels of the organizational hierarchy and continue until a lower-level port of entry is encountered and a new employee is hired from the external labor market (ELM). There are few external pressures for organizational change or adaptation that encourage reorganizations as a function of vacancies being experienced in departments. Thus, there is little if any job absorption or job dissolution to "prematurely" end the extended course of vacancy chains once they have been initiated.

In ForestCo's organization, the sample of "long" vacancy chains includes those that involve moves of six or more persons. In our interview sample of 71 vacancy chains, 11 (15.5%) were classified in this category. Of these, 7 were six-person vacancy chains, with the 4 remaining chains containing either seven (1 chain), eight (1 chain), or nine (2 chains) person-moves. A summary of these longest vacancy chains is presented in Table 6.1.

It can be seen that 6 of these 11 quite long vacancy chains originated in the range of salary grades (i.e., 11–15) in which most vacancy chains began. This proportion (54.5%) is smaller but not greatly different from that for the whole sample. There is some modest evidence, however, that a few of these longest vacancy chains did originate at higher organizational levels. Of the longest vacancy chains, 3 originated at the three highest levels of origin found in the total sample. In particular, the 2 vacancy chains having nine person-moves (i.e., 48 and 65), the longest sequences of related staffing actions observed, were those that originated at the most senior levels of the organization. Levels of termination for these long vacancy chains were also not remarkably different from those in the total sample. Of these 11 chains, 8 (72.7%) terminated in the active area of the hierarchy bounded by salary grades 11–15. None terminated above this range, and three terminated at much lower levels of the hierarchy. Although limited by small sample size, these preliminary data suggest only modest support for interpretations that point to consistency between the long vacancy chains found and stereotypical models of ILMs.

As with shorter vacancy chains, more detailed investigations of long vacancy chains can be completed only by means of information obtained from the managers who were

Table 6.1. Summary of Six- to Nine-Move Vacancy Chains

Vacancy chain number	Salary grades[a]	Occupation or function	Initiation of vacancy	Staffing actions
		Six-move vacancy chains		
3	11–15	Accounting	New position	Succession/job absorbed
4	14–16	Sales/Accounting	Retirement	Succession/development
13	12–14	Forestry/Engineering	New position	Reorganization/succession/development
14	13–15	Engineering	New position	Reorganization/succession/development
28	11–15	Employee relations	New position	Succession/development
44	TT–11	Employee relations/clerical	Resignation	Succession/development
68	15–24	Managerial	Retirement	Reorganization/succession
		Seven-move vacancy chains		
1	4–11	Sales Support	Retirement	Succession/hire from ELM
		Eight-move vacancy chains		
69	14–19	Administration/Accounting	Retirement	Succession/development
		Nine-move vacancy chains		
48	7–26	Management/Accounting	Retirement	Succession/reorganization
65	13–29	Executive/supervision	New position	Succession/reorganization

[a](TT) Indicates a move from a temporary position.

responsible for the staffing actions that continued to extend and finally terminated these chains. The caution raised in previous chapters regarding overall interpretations of extended staffing sequences applies particularly strongly to interpretations of long vacancy chains. Long vacancy chains are sequences of related staffing actions in which the original conditions that initiated the vacancy chains are usually proximate, in both time and organizational location, to the first or possibly the second subsequent staffing action. As the sequence of staffing actions continues, however, the contextual conditions surrounding the first few moves become more distant from subsequent staffing actions. Consequently, any effects that originating conditions may have on immediately subsequent staffing actions are likely to be vitiated in later staffing actions. Staffing actions toward the end of long vacancy chains are more likely to be influenced by other, more local causal factors entering the decision domains of the persons responsible for staffing. As a means of identifying these factors and investigating potential distinctions between the vacancy chains defined somewhat arbitrarily herein as "long" and the shorter vacancy chains described in Chapters 4 and 5, three illustrative long vacancy chains are presented in greater detail. An initial speculation is that these extended staffing sequences can be distinguished from shorter vacancy chains in terms of the microdetails encountered at each staffing node of each vacancy chain. Thus, detailed descriptions of the multiple conditions that led to these long sequences of staffing actions are presented in the sections that follow.

"LONG" VACANCY CHAINS: ILLUSTRATION 1

Background Information

Figure 6.1 diagrams vacancy chain 1, one of the longer vacancy chains encountered at ForestCo. This vacancy chain consists of seven related person-moves. In this sequence of seven related staffing actions, all the employees associated with this vacancy chain shared a functional concern and technical expertise in providing sales support for the lumber mill operations. These employees provided the documentation for the transportation, billing, and subsequent accounting associated with the sale of ForestCo products to both domestic and international markets. They provided a sales support function within the organization, but also liaised with production to ensure that sufficient product was available for shipment as required. They had to be familiar with the technical requirements of shipping

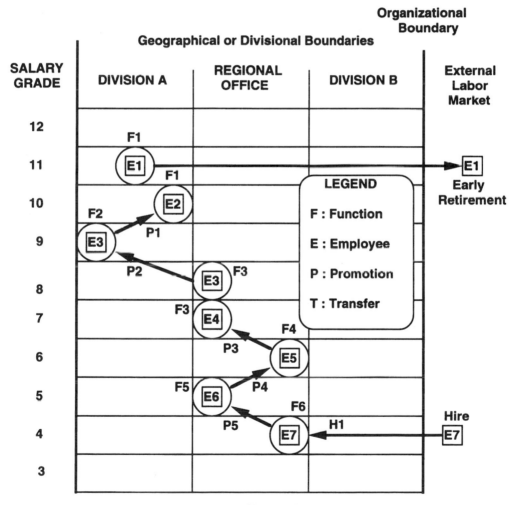

Figure 6.1. Vacancy chain 1.

ForestCo products, such as various dimensions of lumber, by rail or sea or both, directly to customers or through customs brokers. For the most part, these jobs were moderately specialized. Technical knowledge of company products, shipping requirements, shipping companies, and customs regulations and associated record-keeping required to execute the accounting functions were not generalizable to other firms—except possibly other forest product companies. Even then, other forest product firms would not necessarily ship the same mix of products, would not have had the same customers, and would not have had similar relationships with customs and lumber brokers in the market.

Simple Description of Vacancy Chain 1

Vacancy chain 1 originated with the early retirement of employee E1, a Transportation Supervisor. The position (F1) vacated by employee E1 was filled by employee E2 by means of an administered staffing process. However, E1 vacated the position/function of Transportation Supervisor at a salary grade level of 11, whereas E2's appointment was to the "same" position/function (but also with a new title) at salary grade 10. Thus, the salary grade level of the position vacated was not identical to that of the position filled. Employee E2's previous position, that of Documents Supervisor (F2), was filled by an interdepartmental transfer of employee E3 from the Regional Office to the Division. The selection process was one in which the vacant position was posted and several candidates applied and were considered for the appointment. At the Regional Office, a cascade of vacancies took place as employee E3's position (though again at a lower salary grade level) was filled by employee E4, whose position was filled by employee E5, whose position was filled by employee E6—all internal appointments within the Regional Office. The final vacancy, that of position/function F6 made vacant by the move of employee E6 to fill position/function F5, was filled by the hire of employee E7 from the ELM.

As described here, the actual vacancy chain appears to offer several similarities to a stereotypical vacancy chain. Although this vacancy chain did not originate at the highest level of the organizational hierarchy, there was a more or less orderly process of staffing actions that terminated with the hire of a new employee from the ELM. The original vacancy was balanced by an eventual hire, thus maintaining the organizational complement. As noted above, however, two of the moves in the vacancy chain did not occur against a fixed framework of positions. In both position/function F1 and F3, the position filled was a salary grade level below that of the position vacated. As noted before, this arrangement is not uncommon at ForestCo. In this organization, the classification of positions in terms of salary grade offers some degree of flexibility, as the salary grade of a position is seen to be partially dependent on the qualifications and seniority of the person in the position. Although this practice violates the tenets of formal bureaucracy found in many modern governmental organizations (DiPrete, 1989), the flexibility does permit subsequent "promotions" as recognition of increased skill and diligence without the requirement of a formal move from one position to another.

Situational and Contextual Factors

Balance of Stability and Change. What is not recorded in Fig. 6.1 is that immediately prior to the early retirement of employee E1, two other senior retirements had also recently occurred. The Sales Manager who supervised the Transportation Supervisor position/function F1 originally occupied by employee E1 had himself been in his current position for less than eight months, as he had recently replaced the previous Sales Manager, who had also taken early retirement. In addition, one other member of this relatively small sales support group (the Sales–Production Coordinator) had also recently retired. Thus, the replacement of the Transportation Supervisor/Traffic Coordinator position F1 took place in a department in which much change had recently occurred.

Against this background, the Sales Manager attempted to reconcile two potentially conflicting requirements: the need for stability so as to maintain efficient operations and the need for change to adjust to the new, lean and mean competitive philosophy spreading throughout the organization. As a significant factor in his consideration of these tensions, he was aware of the ongoing need to provide the documents necessary to ship products, to bill customers, and to raise revenue. These tasks were viewed as departmental imperatives—they were tasks that had to be accomplished on an as-needed basis. Delays were regarded as intolerable. Responding to this imperative, the new Sales Manager quickly arranged to cover the not unexpected early retirement of the previous Transportation Supervisor (E1) by advancing the experienced employee (E2) who had previously been the Documents Supervisor. In making this appointment, it was critical to maintain continuity of operation. The Sales Manager believed that he could not wait for the results of a competitive posting process to produce an approved candidate. Moreover, he believed there were very few if any alternative candidates who had the requisite technical knowledge to move into what he described as a "turnkey" operation. Thus, expediency dominated the manner in which the resulting appointment was made. There was a strong supposition, but no guarantee, that this method of matching people and positions produced the best possible selection from those who were potentially available. The method used satisfied concerns for administrative expediency, but not necessarily those for market efficiency.

Having made this staffing decision, the Sales Manager turned his attention to how he would fill the vacancy in position/function F2 produced by the promotion of E2, the previous Documents Supervisor, to position/function F1. Philosophically, this manager had already begun to think in terms of the "new broom" perspective beginning to sweep through both the division as a whole and his own small department. Since his own appointment some eight months previously, he had examined very carefully whether the work associated with this position still needed to be done or could be done in a more efficient way—perhaps by combining it with tasks currently performed by others. He concluded that he could not eliminate the work associated with the position, nor could he assign the work elsewhere without risking serious morale and overwork reactions. The work and position, he concluded, were a necessary and integral part of the requirements of his organizational patch.

If the work and the position could not be eliminated, then he had to consider how to fill the resulting vacancy. In addition to thinking about work requirements over the past eight months, he had also given substantial consideration to the talents and capacities of his subordinates. Because of recent retirements, three of the positions in his group (including his own) were now filled by persons who had not been in those positions a year previously. The few remaining staff members who had not been promoted were in jobs with significantly fewer demands than the one now vacant. It was his judgment that none of these employees was capable of making the jump from his present job to the vacant position. He therefore undertook a formal search for a suitable appointee to the vacant Documents Supervisor position.

Managerial Influence, Standard Operating Procedures, and Organizational Adaptation.   In deciding to undertake a formal search through the posting process, this manager

was required to engage ForestCo's standard operating procedures (SOPs) for job definition, job posting, candidate application, and candidate selection. These procedures were
formally managed by the personnel specialists in the division, and the Sales Manager had
only modest discretion as to how the process unfolded. Previously, this manager had
avoided a competitive posting process for the appointment of the Transportation Supervisor (employee E2 to position F1), as he had judged the process to be too time-consuming
given his urgent needs to fill the vacant position. The length of time taken in the subsequent staffing process supported his previous claim of delayed appointments when the
posting process was used, as it was three months from the initiation of the posting process
until the second appointee (E3) was established and working in his new position (F2) in
the department.

Although the Sales Manager had only modest influence on the form and duration of
the posting process, he appeared to have considerably more influence on the outcome of
the standardized selection procedures. This manager exercised influence on the critical
features of the job to be posted, the elicitation and solicitation of potential candidates, the
weighting of candidates on the various job dimensions, and ultimately the choice of the
eventual appointee.

The Documents Supervisor job initially vacated by employee E2 was nominally the
same as the Documents Supervisor job eventually filled by the appointment of employee
E3. The job had the same title, the same job number, and the same salary grade. Within
ForestCo, however, there was no formal check to ensure that the content of a job remained
exactly the same over the time span of a single incumbent, nor was there a check to ensure
that the job content did not change when incumbents changed. Thus, when the job of
Documents Supervisor was posted, there was no requirement that the description of the
job to be posted be identical to the description of the job filled by the previous and now
departing incumbent. To be sure, there were strong similarities between the two—but the
task of writing the new job description allowed job evolution to occur. Although there was
no direct evidence that the Sales Manager acted to modify the job definition in this
particular instance, such job modifications were not uncommon in many other staffing
situations. What was known was that this particular Sales Manager was interested in
changing the way the department operated:

> Employees need to understand that a new manager's standards can be different. This is
> what I've been confronting ever since my arrival here.

In particular, the Sales Manager wished to emphasize the collective, team perspective he
believed should be a concomitant of the new managerial philosophy he wished to implement:

> If a person doesn't fit, if they're not a team player or don't have an appropriate attitude,
> there's a penalty with respect to efficiency in getting things done as a group.

and:

> I looked for someone who is willing to do the work and jump in and help others when
> their work is done.

Job modification and evolution of this nature was generally regarded as a critical
element of organizational adaptation. There were few managers who regarded prior job
definitions as fixed and sacrosanct. Particularly within operational departments and
divisions, job definitions were seen as means to accomplish practical ends. Job classification, the technical means used to classify jobs into broad salary grades, was reluctantly
accepted as a means of establishing general parity between the pay rates for jobs at

ForestCo and similar jobs elsewhere. However, the overall logic and detailed order of the relationship between job demands and the pay system for the organization as a whole were not issues that local managers thought to be either relevant or important for their departments.

The organizational system at ForestCo permitted, and at times encouraged, a process of job evolution that was sensitive to the press of organizational needs as seen by the occupant of the job/position, the supervisor of the person in the job/position, and others who interacted with, and placed demands on, the person in the job/position. The concept of a job was extraordinarily elastic, as there was often a drift of job responsibilities and activities so that actual job tasks frequently evolved from those originally used to select job incumbents. While these adaptive responses occurred informally all the time, formal recognition of these discrepancies occurred (1) when jobs and responsibilities were reorganized and job titles and salary grades were changed; (2) when a single job was regarded such that both the job and its occupant were placed in a higher salary grade; and (3) when the job occupant was changed and the previous job definition was modified to meet the new, emerging requirements. In the latter case, these changes might be recognized formally in new job descriptions or salary grades or informally in the weight given to selection criteria. If we now return to the posting process used to select a new appointee for position/job F2, we can see that the relatively new Sales Manager had an opportunity to influence how work would be done in his department by redefining jobs and shifting the emphasis among the components of the functions, responsibilities, and relationships of the Documents Supervisor job.

A second potential source of managerial influence on the staffing system was through the elicitation, solicitation, and screening of candidates for the position the critical features of which the Sales Manager had just confirmed. The Sales Manager used his network of contacts in the organization, such as previous supervisors, coworkers, and friends, to elicit candidates:

> I personally phoned the supervisors I'd known from my Head Office and Regional Office days, and asked them if they knew of anyone who would fit, and if they did, to let them know the position would be posted.

He also solicited selected candidates:

> I'd also had experience with _____ and knew she had the appropriate background. So I contacted her, and drew to her attention that this position was coming available.

Although the Sales Manager had some influence over the definition of the job, and which candidates applied for the job, he relied on more formal SOPs to screen and evaluate these candidates. A total of 11 applications were received, and six of these were initially eliminated on the basis of the criterion of insufficient experience with the technical demands of the job. The five applicants remaining on the shortlist were interviewed by a panel of three middle-level managers: the Sales Manager, the Employee Relations Supervisor, and the Production Manager at the mill. All five shortlisted candidates were interviewed on the same day for the same length of time. Standard questions were put to all candidates, and a common rating scheme was used to compare each of the five candidates. In terms of the competition for the job, the formal procedures used met commonly accepted criteria for equal opportunity. The competition was fair in its reliance on multiple raters, common criteria, and equal treatment.

It is much less clear, however, that these procedures were necessarily free of all social bias. The 16 criteria used to evaluate candidates included four concerned with technical qualities: aptitude for numbers, computer skills, documentation experience, and product knowledge. Most of the remaining criteria were social in nature and could be best assessed through prior social interactions in a work setting. Examples of such attributes were: self-starter, able to work with minimal supervision, general attitude, stable emotional makeup, and supervisory abilities. Candidates who were known to members of the panel therefore had greater opportunity to demonstrate either that they possessed or that they lacked these qualities. This selection "system," with its dependence on prior social knowledge, therefore, had a tendency to confirm preferred candidates rather than to identify superior candidates not previously known to members of the panel. Not surprisingly, the chosen candidate was the person the Sales Manager had worked with previously and whom he had invited to apply for the position. As he subsequently commented:

_____ was the only one that I knew personally who'd be able to do the job.

Confirmation of the salience of the social criteria in selecting the chosen candidate occurred later when the Sales Manager noted that the previous Documents Supervisor had

made an offhand comment about having to work with his replacement—and he'd prefer to work with _____ because of her previous work experience.

In addition, he also reported that a junior member of the group, who had also been a candidate for the vacant position, but who had been eliminated because of insufficient experience, had commented that she knew the chosen candidate and liked her. Because she liked her

it was easier for her to accept _____ in the job she herself didn't get.

This detailed analysis of a particular selection decision does not necessarily imply that the person chosen was not the "best" candidate. What it does suggest is that determination of the best in organizational situations is often problematic: Jobs are not always well defined, selection criteria do not always clearly map onto job requirements, and raters' confidence in their knowledge and understanding of candidate attributes can vary considerably across candidates. Under these conditions, the procedures used by the Sales Manager are judged not to be inappropriate. The pragmatic mixture of personal influence, SOPs, and personal and collective judgment meets a reasonable test of a competitive, market-based appointment. Nevertheless, there is no guarantee that the best candidate was ipso facto selected.

Managing a Line of Progression.   The appointment of employee E3 to position/job F2 left a vacancy (F3) in the Regional Office. The organizational unit to which this position belonged was larger than the divisional unit and was supervised by a manager who had been in his current role for approximately ten years. This person managed a set of specialist functions that supported the Accounting and Documentation activities for sales at a Regional Office level.

Two sets of factors appeared to influence the manner in which this manager responded to the vacancy. First, the manager still had clear recollections of the early 1980s, when there had been major cutbacks. He reported that in 1982 he had "lost half of his people" and that he felt he was doing "more with less." He believed that the technical aspects of his business had changed dramatically over the previous eight years. In fact, he saw organizational change as an ongoing process, as the measurement of costs, accounting procedures, and reporting requirements were continually being updated through new computer systems and applications. Given his general appreciation of the very demanding situation in which he found himself, this manager was not interested in finding additional ways to make his life difficult. Thus, when the vacancy occurred, he did not automatically look to find new ways of organizing his unit. Similar pressures for change were a more or less frequent occurrence. New and increased demands for control were frequently received from both line management and Head Office as employees there sought to apply techniques arising from the application of new computer technology.

The second factor that influenced this manager's reaction to the vacancy was the size of the unit he managed. He was responsible for a staff complement of more than 30 persons, with several functions being duplicated across different product groups. His organizational unit possessed both breadth (two different product groups, two different functions) and depth (five levels in one function, three levels in the other). Thus, the array of jobs in this organizational unit meant that there was significant opportunity for orderly lines of progression to occur.

These two factors combined to predispose the manager of this unit to quickly make three related staffing appointments under his own authority. The position previously occupied by a Senior Documentation Clerk (F3) was filled by the appointment of employee E4, who had been an Intermediate Documentation Clerk (F4). In turn, the position previously occupied by employee E4 was then filled by employee E5, a Documentation Clerk (F5). The position previously occupied by employee E5 was then filled by employee E6, whose job title was Accounting Clerk (F6). The only deviation of this sequence from that of a stereotypical vacancy chain was that job/function F3 was downgraded from salary grade 8 to salary grade 7.

In making these appointments, consonant with implementation of mobility along a line of progression, the manager of this unit observed that all three employees, E4, E5, and E6, were well qualified for their new positions. All three had experience in providing staff support for different export markets, had demonstrated aptitude for different computer systems, and had demonstrated good work habits. They had had the opportunity to acquire breadth of experience and to demonstrate performance in different jobs because another Documentation Clerk in another product group had taken maternity leave in the past year. In rearranging temporary assignments, the manager knew that employees E5 and E6 had already performed at the next level of responsibility and were therefore known quantities. Age, seniority, and experience attributes of employees E4, E5, and E6 followed orderly progressions: Employee E4 was older and had more seniority and more experience than either E5 or E6. Thus, these appointments represented a very orderly progression within the organizational unit. In this manager's opinion, a competitive staffing process would have been a waste of time, as it would merely have confirmed what he had already done expeditiously with minimal expense. Moreover, by promoting from within, he had demonstrated his allegiance to his subordinates. He had rewarded them for exhibiting good corporate citizenship and had demonstrated to them and other subordinates that "the system works!" In orchestrating this sequence of moves, the local manager fulfilled many of the quid pro quo requirements of the ILM model presented in Fig. 1.2.

Having made three internal appointments, the manager of this unit then faced the task of filling the "entry-level" position, F6. With no one available in his unit, he was forced, reluctantly, to post the position in the Regional Office. This manager's reluctance to post the vacant position originated from his beliefs about external appointments:

> Going outside is the toughest. There's a large scope, but nothing is really known about those who apply. You have to rely on your gut instinct even more than inside appointments.

He received five applications—four from temporary employees and one from someone in another departmental unit. He screened these applications and was not certain he wished to appoint any of them permanently in his department, as none appeared to offer a suitable fit with his requirements. At least two appeared to be overqualified, and the others had career aspirations different from those that he felt he could realistically offer. While he was still considering whom to appoint, however, he received an application from someone outside the company who had heard about the job opening from a ForestCo employee. This new applicant came highly recommended from this employee, whose opinion the manager respected:

> Some of my best hires have been people who've been recommended by someone, not a relative but a friend, who works in the organization.

He evaluated her qualifications, interviewed her, and confirmed her as the new appointee in job/position F6.

One Vacancy Chain, Two Approaches to Staffing

Two quite different approaches to staffing can be found in this one long vacancy chain. The Sales Manager in Division A faced a very different organizational situation than did the Accounting and Documentation Manager at the Regional Office. In the division, the organizational pressures associated with being new, and the personal motivation to modify the organization so he could better establish his own influence on organizational performance, led that manager to follow a line of progression for one appointment and then to use the competitive, market-oriented posting system to select a suitable candidate for the position that then became vacant. This manager's initial preference was to fill organizational positions using the competitive procedure associated with posting, but he reluctantly had to follow an implicit line of progression initially because of the urgency associated with filling a vacant position and the small number of persons likely to be able to meet immediately required levels of performance.

The wider search associated with the posting of the second vacancy identified the best candidate as someone from the Regional Office. Her appointment switched the vacancy chain process from the divisional unit to the Regional Office. Here, the breadth and depth of potential candidates meant that a series of moves along an orderly line of progression was both possible and desirable. Searches for suitable candidates for the positions that then became vacant were limited, as the manager responsible for this unit had high confidence that department-specific skills were readily available within his department. Philosophically, the department manager was oriented to managing a flow of increasingly experienced employees over an organizational climbing frame composed of a stable set of jobs. His implicit benchmark for staffing levels was at pre-1982 levels, before his organizational complement had been cut in half and before more modern office automation, in the form of computers, had been introduced. It is unlikely that this manager would seek, on his own initiative, to cut positions. This attitude is in contrast to that of the Sales Manager in Division A, who professed to always seek methods of operation that would lead to increased levels of performance.

This detailed review of a long vacancy chain illustrates that a concatenation of two quite different vacancy chains produced what appeared to be a single, long sequence of staffing actions. Conceptually, this vacancy chain manifested several features of long vacancy chains that derive from stereotypical models of ILMs. Although the manager responsible for the first two vacancies in this chain was predisposed to more competitive forms of staffing, his awareness of the urgency associated with filling the initial vacancy and the availability of a skilled and knowledgeable successor to the employee whose departure created the initial vacancy led him to use an administered staffing procedure. As neither of these conditions applied to the subsequent vacancy, this manager used the posting system, which then switched the locus of staffing choice to the manager of the Regional Office, who faced a very different organizational situation.

Here, several factors combined to produce a series of relatively small moves along a well-established line of progression. First, the manager's purview or area of authority/ responsibility included a unifunctional departmental unit that contained several closely similar positions that differed slightly in organizational level and work focus. These positions emphasized technical knowledge that was specific to the department. There was little requirement to import new knowledge from outside, as most technical expertise was developed by performing the work required. Second, these positions had a largely internal orientation. They focused on internal procedures that had changed considerably in recent years as a consequence of new office technology (in the form of computers) and changing corporate requirements. The manager of this department sought protection and control from disturbing aspects of his organizational environment. Staffing was used as a means to increase local control rather than to adapt to changing circumstances. There was little requirement for the exercise of strategic staffing. Third, because of prior temporary assignments, there were strong precedents as to which persons were regarded as successors to vacant positions. These employees had invested energy in learning the requirements of their new positions, and their likely performance was known. The requirements for local decision making were present, and there were few pressures for staffing to meet requirements for change.

Thus, even though vacancy chain 1 involved one posting appointment that led it to evolve over two separate departments and managers, it nonetheless represented a close approximation of the operation of a stereotypical ILM.

"LONG" VACANCY CHAINS: ILLUSTRATION 2

Background and Context

As a means of providing further evidence on the detailed operation of the longest vacancy chains found at ForestCo, vacancy chain 3 is also described in greater detail. As was mostly true of vacancy chain 1, the functional content of the work done by most of the employees who participated in this aspect of ForestCo's ILM again concerns the Accounting function. A schematic of this vacancy chain is presented in Figure 6.2.

The series of staffing actions shown in Figure 6.2 occurred against a background of two significant changes in the organization. First, a relatively large reassignment of responsibilities took place when a senior general manager quit to take a vice-presidency at a competing organization. In the subsequent reorganization, at least 12 positions were reassigned—including the recent appointments of many of the managers responsible for the decisions that comprise the vacancy chain reported here. Second, in one particular unit, a decision was made to consolidate the operations of three sawmills. One mill was shut down, and the management of the remaining two mills was consolidated under a single group of senior managers. The specific effects of these prior changes on this vacancy chain cannot be determined with precision. The staffing actions described here are therefore best regarded as second-order consequences of the two primary changes just noted.

This particular vacancy chain was initiated by two considerations: the opening up of a new position in Division C, which at the time was just completing a major rebuilding,

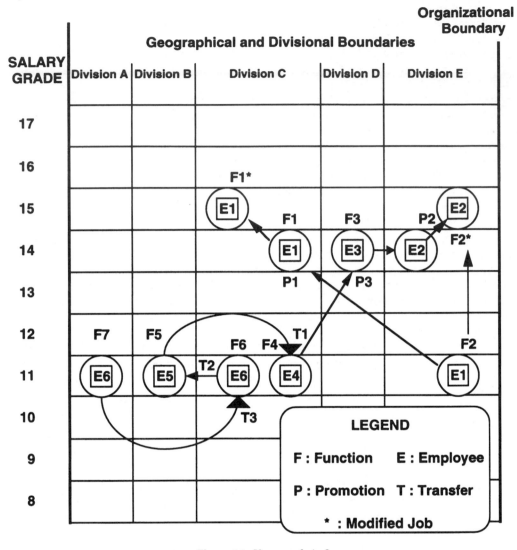

Figure 6.2. Vacancy chain 3.

and an increasing recognition in Division E that employee E1 was "stuck," as he had been in his present position for "too long" a time. Employee E1 was a "good financial manager" who wanted to consider other opportunities for personal career growth in the organization. Moreover, E1 was no longer regarded as an appropriate fit with his present job. His performance was regarded as lackluster for someone of his organizational position—and it was for this reason that his current salary grade was low compared with those of comparable positions in other divisions of the company. This person was still regarded, however, as possessing the capacity to produce and as having the potential to develop further. One serious drawback to further advancement of this manager was that he had not yet had any direct mill experience.

An opportunity to "solve" the organizational fit and personal development problems associated with employee E1 came about when the Mill Manager in Division C looked for suitable persons for a short-term Project Accountant position there. Such a person was needed to refine the accounting measures that would guide the marketing and production decisions in the relatively new value-added production philosophy being implemented in the new mill. Once these systems had been implemented, the person most familiar with those concepts would be advanced to the Sales Manager position—thus further integrating marketing and production, a requirement of the new operating philosophy.

The move of employee E1 to the new position F1 thus occurred because of both the demand–pull pressures from the requirements of the new job and the supply–push pressures from the existing job and personal situation for that employee. An administrative move therefore represented an expeditious way of meeting both pull and push requirements. As noted in Figure 6.2, the initial move to the Project Accountant position (F1) would soon be followed by either a transfer at the same salary grade level or possibly a promotion at a higher salary grade level to the designated position (F1*) of Sales Manager.

Once employee E1 had been moved, the manager of Division E was finally able to begin the program of upgrading he had wanted to implement for some time. Progress toward this objective had been frustrated by the lack of fit between what he saw as the "new" requirements of that position and its previous occupant E1. Now that employee E1 was transferred to another division, however, the manager of Division E could more readily implement his desired program of organizational change. Determined to find the best candidate for this upgraded function [(F2): Financial Manager–Division E], the manager of Division E posted the position vacancy throughout the company. Eight employees with relevant experience applied for the position. The mill manager talked at length with other managers and supervisors about the qualities of the candidates who had applied and short-listed four of them. He also established a selection panel composed of himself, two mill managers (because the new position was heavily dependent on obtaining cooperation from mill managers), and an employee relations representative. This process resulted in the choice of employee E2. This selection confirmed to others that employee E2 was "being groomed for the fast track." In addition, the elevation of the position salary grade of the Divisional Financial Manager position from level 11 to level 15 was rationalized by the Divisional Manager employee's viewing employee E2 in that job as being "worth a lot more in that job" than had been the case with employee E1. However, the adjustment of position classification as a function of job occupant was done in two stages. The first appointment was a lateral transfer of employee E2 to an interim position at salary grade 14 in Division E and a subsequent promotion five months later within the division to the Divisional Financial Manager's job (F2*) at salary grade 15.

The departure of employee E2 from Division D left a critical vacancy [(F3): Divisional Accountant] there. Again, the position was posted, four of the 14 candidates who applied were interviewed, and the successful candidate, E3, who had previously been the Accounting Systems Supervisor in Division C, was appointed. This employee was judged to have come from a "good" background, as his previous supervisor was generally regarded as one of the best managers in the company for the development of his subordinates.

However, this move created another vacancy in Division C. Again, a combination of circumstances influenced the outcome of the posting process used to find a replacement for employee E3, who had previously occupied the Accounting Systems Supervisor position (F4). A review of the candidates who applied for this position included employee E4, who was then working in Division B and, like employee E1, was regarded as a person who no longer fit his job and his supervisor. This employee had struggled long and hard to obtain his accounting degree and had apparently lost much of his self-confidence in that struggle. Independently of his job requirements and his quest for professional certification, however, he had developed a substantial knowledge of computers. He was chosen partially because of this added expertise, which would be more useful in his new position (Accounting Systems Supervisor) than in his old position (Cost Accountant). He was also chosen for this position because it was judged that he needed further development and could be in no better place to develop his skills than under the direct supervision of the manager of Division C, a person reputed to be the best developer of accounting talent in the company.

The new vacancy in Division B was also posted, and a younger female employee (E5) who had previously been a Cost Accountant in Division C was selected—thus leaving a third vacancy in this chain in this division. Again, the position was posted, but no applications were received, partly because the immediately prior series of moves had almost exhausted the possibilities for further developmental moves in this functional specialty. However, the supervisor responsible for this appointment, who was the same mentor who approved the appointment of employee E4, was aware that another division in another part of the country was in the process of shutting down. He inquired about potential talent, visited this operation, and interviewed three potential candidates. One was invited to visit the local division and on the basis of interviews was eventually appointed to the Cost Accountant position (F6). Her previous position was discontinued in line with the impending closure of Division A.

Competition for Development and Advancement

What appears to be most significant about this vacancy chain is the relatively large number of vacancies that were posted and that resulted in interdivisional moves. Although the vacancy chain was initiated by both a new position and a push from an existing job–person assignment that was not working well, all subsequent moves were made using the competitive, market-oriented procedure of posting. For the Accounting function at this level in the organization, employees were making the transition from initial demonstration of technical competence, and initial supervision of clerical staff, to accepting responsibility for either part or total performance of the Accounting function for a division. Experience and accreditation requirements here were critical, as all these employees had either an accounting degree or a professional accounting certification.

Extensive use of a competitive, market-based system for selecting employees for positions leading to further development and advancement worked for this occupational group, as the basic skills and competencies required for superior performance were similar across all these jobs. In addition, there were relatively large numbers of technically trained employees in a reasonably large array of similar jobs, but few were concentrated in any one division. Because the function performed by these specialists was that of support for the multiple production/distribution units in the organization, these persons worked in several different, geographically separate, divisions. Under these circumstances, progression through a succession of career tournaments (Rosenbaum, 1984) appeared to be both an effective and an efficient process for ensuring that high-talent employees in this occupational specialty were put in positions of progressively increasing responsibility. The overall function apparently served by this vacancy chain was a temporary sorting out of candidates in the Accounting specialty area. Some of the moves were associated with substantial and substantive increases in responsibility (e.g., employee E1 from position F2 to position F1 and then to F1*; employee E2 from position F3 to position F2*; and possibly the move of employee E3 from position F4 to position F3). These moves were also associated with relatively large increases in salary grade. However, the three other moves that comprised this vacancy chain were ones that represented more jockeying for additional experience and positions from which real advancements could be made in the future. Such promotions were not guaranteed, but would depend on the additional measures of performance in and potential obtained from these developmental assignments.

Developing Nontechnical Requirements for Advancement

Although formal accreditation was viewed as a necessary condition for appointment to, retention in, and advancement from these positions, other candidate attributes were also regarded as critical. Interviews with the different divisional managers indicated that personality and interpersonal skills were also important:

> You can have all the degrees you want—but if you don't fit the team, you won't get the job.

When pressed to provide further details of the nature of this fit, these managers noted that "accountants have to work with others in the mill." They also talked about candidates having "a similar disposition to the rest of the group," being "quietly aggressive," and "being willing to create an enjoyable and exciting place to work" for those with whom they worked. In addition, assessments of future promotability were also important:

> I want to hire people who can move two to three groups higher. Not everyone can go to the top. They may have the potential but not be able to act on it. They've got to have demonstrated talent to advance.

As has been noted, the consistent use of the posting system to manage the career stream described in Figure 6.2 is seen as a functional response to the need to have a number of qualified candidates, spread throughout a number of different divisions, compete for jobs at the next higher level. Because technical qualifications obtained through academic and professional learning needed to be leavened by actual work experience, breadth of experience was obtained through a series of interdivisional moves. As previously noted, the last three moves in vacancy chain 3 involved similarly qualified employees moving at the same salary grade level among different divisions with different cultures and different product emphases. It was not clear whether these moves represented promotions when considered as moves against a framework of fixed organizational positions. Nevertheless, each person went through a public, competitive process to obtain his or her appointment. Legitimation, rationalization, and institutionalization of these types of move were clearly part of the developmental philosophy of the manager in Division C, who noted:

> Crossbreeding is the way to develop people here—that way they don't become obsolete.

The organizational experiences deriving from the interdivisional cross-breeding of these fledgling managers were seen to fulfill two functions. First, these assignments facilitated the development of critical skills in the new supervisors and managers assigned to different divisions. Second, the performance of these aspiring managers in these assignments provided senior managers with extensive evidence of the competitive suitability of these candidates. This information would become very important in future assessments of these employees when they became candidates for other, higher-level vacancies that would occur in the future.

Organizational Obligations to Employees

A second feature of this vacancy chain worthy of comment concerns both the attitude toward, and the treatment of, employees E1 and E4. Both these employees were manifesting a lack of fit with their current positions. One was characterized as "dying" and the other as being "stuck." In contrast to more hardheaded managerial styles and employment systems in which problematic appointees are "fired, not rehired," two managers were willing to take a risk with employees whose advancement opportunities had atrophied because they were stagnating in their current jobs. Both employees had lost the trust and confidence of their immediate supervisor. Firing them was not regarded as an attractive option, given the still vivid experience of the layoffs in the early 1980s. Consequently, each was given a further opportunity to demonstrate his potential contribution to the company. As the manager of Division C remarked:

> ForestCo owes its long-term employees a chance.

Indeed, this same manager noted that he knew employee E4 and knew of the "personality clash" he was having with his present supervisor. He saw the move of this person from Division B to his own division as being "a positive move for both divisions," as a long-term employee was to be given a chance to demonstrate a combination of skills: the accounting accreditation obtained outside the job, the application of this knowledge with active support by the company, and the computer skills that the employee had initially developed as a personal interest. Thus, for both employees E1 and E4, subsequent career moves appeared to be as much a consequence of push out of a previous lack of fit as a pull move initiated to serve immediate organizational interests.

It is clear that the organizational culture at ForestCo was generally supportive of employees who were not working out in their present positions—whether this lack of fit came about because of personality clashes with a particular supervisor or for personal reasons. However, such accommodations were limited:

> When people go through a hard personal time, the company is pretty understanding. But it's a time thing. There's a limit as to how much help is available because the job is number one. They've got to satisfy the mill manager. Employees have to roll up their sleeves and not let the problem drag on.

Nevertheless, the organizational commitment to employee development appeared to be considerable. These attitudes were supported by the humanistic comments of some managers—"There's more to life than work," "Work priorities are changing to include family considerations, particularly if people have kids"—as well as by the longer-term, functional consequences of supportive behaviors:

> Understanding and forgiving are valuable stances in the long run. People appreciate the support and want to work for you. They have to like and respect you. If you don't have that— you don't get very far with them giving you their best.

In this latter comment, it is clear that the obligations managers felt for their subordinates carried implicit, reciprocal demands for employees to repay these considerations at some future time. Actions that provided development opportunities were invariably intermingled with implicit obligations for additional work from subordinates. Additional, successful work also carried the promise of increased intrinsic and extrinsic rewards, which in turn led to increased employee motivation. As practiced at ForestCo, staffing was not concerned solely with limited, short-term organizational priorities. While managerial obligations to subordinates were not entirely without potential self-interest, pursuit of organizational efficiency was effectively leavened with humanistic, though paternalistic, concerns for fellow employees.

Two Vacancy Chains, One Occupation, and Two Modes of Development

The first two long vacancy chains selected for further, detailed description were both associated with the occupational specialty of Accounting. Vacancy chain 3, the first chain illustrated in this chapter, described a series of relatively small, close moves along a line of progression that included divisional and regional members of semiskilled accounting staff. Vacancy chain 1 was concerned with career development of employees at higher levels of this occupational specialty. While selection of these two vacancy chains for detailed description was motivated more by the depth and extent of information available than by the area of expertise involved, their association with the occupational specialty of Accounting is not surprising. Of the 11 "long" vacancy chains, 5 were associated with this occupational specialty.

Accountants have an important and distinct identity in ForestCo's organization. ForestCo displays many features of the machine bureaucracy: Close financial control of production and sales activities is a significant feature of "what it takes to be successful in this business" (Mintzberg, 1979). At the more senior levels of each division or mill, Financial Managers are responsible for the overall measurement and evaluation of wealth-producing activities. Reporting to these senior managers are Divisional Accountants, Project Accountants, and Accounting Systems Supervisors—all of whom have substantial responsibility for the design, modification, and professional standards of systems used to collect and use financial information.

Below these positions, employees are required to operate the systems designed by their supervisors. Their responsibilities do not include the exercise of independent professional judgment. For salary grade levels 11 and below, accounting positions are regarded as being more technical, specialist, and clerical in nature. For employees not possessing a professional accounting designation, advancement is possible only through a small range of salary grades, as demonstrated in vacancy chain 1. Without either academic qualifications or professional certification, advancement beyond salary grade 10 is difficult.

For the Accounting occupational group, therefore, there are two career streams: a clerical, specialist career structure that is heavily based on prior job experience and a career stream for those with academic and professional qualifications that leads to supervisory and managerial positions. These two career streams "touch" or partially overlap at salary grade levels 10 and 11. These grade levels are the highest levels attainable for nonaccredited accountants, but are considered entry-level positions for candidates with accounting credentials. Only those employees who obtain professional credentials off the job are able to move from the predominantly clerical, "bookkeeping" lines of job progression in the lower levels to the more professional and more competitive career development at higher levels. Administered appointments represent the predominant mode of staffing at lower levels, whereas posting is used extensively for the competitive selection and advancement of senior-level careers.

"LONG" VACANCY CHAINS: ILLUSTRATION 3

Initiation of the Vacancy Chain

Vacancy Chain 28 concerns a series of moves of persons in the employee relations function. As documented in Figure 6.3, this series of staffing actions began with the creation of a new function/position F1 (Employee Relations Supervisor) at a new mill and a promotion of employee E1 out of his previous function/position F2 (Divisional Employee Relations Supervisor) located at one of the Regional Offices. This position and four others were subsequently filled through moves representing a mixture of employee development and current organizational job requirements. The only feature of the vacancy chain presented in Figure 6.3 that can be considered to differ from those of a stereotypical vacancy chain is the downgrading of job/functions F3 and F4. In each instance, the job filled was at a lower salary grade than the one vacated. There follows a more detailed discussion of this vacancy chain and the staffing issues associated with each move.

The initiating move of employee E1 was not especially problematic. It was generally understood and accepted throughout the organization that the new mill had priority when it came to filling positions. In addition, most persons regarded moves to the new mill as potentially exciting and challenging. Candidate E1 was well known throughout the relatively small professional world of Employee Relations specialists and was just com-

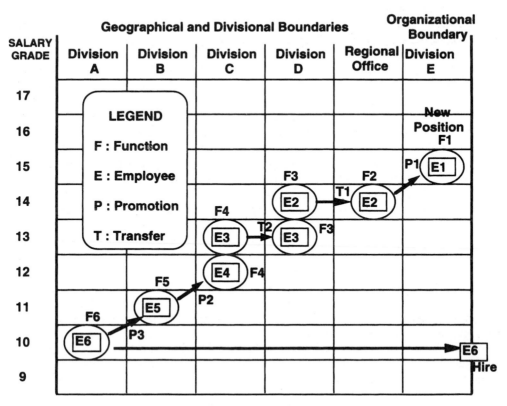

Figure 6.3. Vacancy chain 28.

pleting a developmental assignment at the Regional Office. The new position fitted his developmental needs, and his past experience indicated he would be an excellent candidate for the newly created position. With this opportunistic match of job and candidate in place, together with the company custom that few positions at salary grade 15 level were posted, the new job assignment was made quickly and easily by means of an administrative assignment.

Competition for Scarce Development Opportunities

The next staffing situation, that of F2 eventually filled by the appointment of employee E2, was different from the immediately preceding one. Employees chosen for this level of posting at the Regional Office were usually being groomed for further development and advancement:

> The [Industrial Relations] Administrator position at Regional Office is designed for a young, bright, high-potential person who has been at a mill for two to three years. Once they've been here for a couple of years they then go back to the mill having had opportunity to broaden their view and experience and hopefully being more effective in the trenches. This is a grooming stop for IR people we want to track.

Because of the critical, rare, added-value nature of this assignment, candidates chosen to occupy this position were selected carefully and competitively. The position was posted so the supervisor could "get a sense of what was out there that [he] might not be aware of." Five candidates applied, and "two were written off and not interviewed." Preliminary assessments of these two candidates indicated that they were looking for promotions, whereas the dominant consideration for this appointment was the training and development that would occur as a consequence of the assignment at Regional Office. Three candidates were given further, serious consideration. The supervisor of the vacant position carefully checked the qualifications and performance records of these three remaining candidates with their current supervisors and peers. He did not initiate a panel review, however, because he was currently involved in labor negotiations and had little spare time to invest in "wasteful" searches. In fact, the Regional Manager had more or less made up his mind which candidate he preferred:

> _____ was the only one I interviewed because he was the only one seriously being considered. Besides, time was of the essence here.

He also sought reassurance and affirmation that his choice was "correct." He spent considerable time validating his choice by talking with "all the practitioners in the field" to see "if the fit was good." Not surprisingly, the chosen candidate was reported as having received "unanimous support," and the supervisor reported that "there was no doubt in [my] mind that [the candidate] would be more than able to do the job." Additional factors that apparently influenced the manager's choice were the candidate's development needs and the company's training needs. In terms of individual development, it was the candidate's "time to get the job;" in terms of corporate needs for training, the candidate was experienced and had demonstrable talent. At the time, he represented the best bet for the investment in the training that would accompany his assignment to the new position.

Mixing Developmental Opportunities with Adjustments in Operating Style

The appointment of employee E2 to the Regional Office produced a vacancy in Division D. This position was a hands-on employee relations position in a Logging

Division. The vacant position was posted primarily because there was no obvious candidate in an existing line of succession, and the local manager believed that the competition associated with posting was beneficial both for candidates and for the organization as a whole.

Five candidates applied, and four were short-listed and interviewed for the position. Although each candidate was interviewed by several interviewers, it was clear that the Divisional Manager had both a strong personality and a vision of how he thought the division should operate. In particular, he was attempting to implement a shift in emphasis in his division from industrial relations to employee relations. This shift in emphasis and focus had been supported by E2, the previous Employee Relations Supervisor in that division. The Divisional Manager wanted to develop a system of management in which employee grievances were handled as much as possible by the employees' immediate supervisors on a one-on-one basis. He wished to reduce, and preferentially avoid altogether, institutional or rule-oriented procedures for resolving differences between employees and management. His view of the "new" role required for employee relations was that the staff person should act more as a referee in disputes between supervisors and subordinate hourly employees. That is, staff should be willing to give employees a fair hearing, to develop their trust, and to gain credibility with employees as well as with first- and second-level supervisors.

Although the job requirements for the vacant position were spelled out quite formally, the manner in which these requirements would be interpreted and subsequently acted upon was a critical aspect of the selection process. This being the case, the Divisional Manager conducted two additional interviews with the candidate who was finally chosen—to assure himself that the candidate could indeed meet his vision of how employee relations should develop in his unit and also to signal unmistakably his requirements for successful performance. The Divisional Manager was particularly concerned that the new appointee support his initiatives in developing a different labor relations climate in the division because the candidate had come from a sawmill to a logging operation in which the conditions of work were quite different:

> In the mill, the machine dictates the process and the individual has little effect on the system. They're reactive.

In contrast:

> Employees who work in the woods are more individualistic and free-flowing rather than living in a system. Here, the equipment only does what a man makes it do. The men are active masters of their equipment.

The additional interviews also fulfilled some initial training function, as the Divisional Manager and the candidate discussed a variety of problem scenarios and talked about how they should be handled in the emerging employee relations climate. In passing, it is noted that the position vacated had been assigned previously to salary grade 14 but was filled at salary grade 13. As mentioned before, such downgrading of a position was regarded as relatively normal practice at ForestCo, as it allowed managers to reward subordinates for subsequent good performance by awarding them a "promotional increase resulting from reevaluation of present position to a higher position group."

The appointment of employee E3 to Logging Division D created a vacancy in Sawmill Division C. According to the supervisor responsible for this job, the position "wasn't posted because [employee E4] was part of a succession plan" that had been discussed informally among the more senior managers for the past year. This employee was "due to get more exposure," and the timing of the opportunity coincided with the employee's maturation and a recognition of his need for further development. While this rationale may have well been valid, the local supervisor also commented disparagingly on the merits of the posting system:

> Most often, posting is a pain in the ass. You feel you have to interview all candidates even though you already know who and what you want.

It is impossible to determine whether a different manager, one having a different evaluation and orientation toward posting, would have managed this staffing action any differently. What is known is that the administered staffing action taken by the local manager was in line with his predispositions. His rationalizations for the manner in which he chose to staff the vacant position were consistent with his voiced prejudices.

Employee development and succession may well have been the primary factors that influenced the manner in which the prior staffing action was performed, because a similar story was told by the manager of Division B. When he and the manager of Division C first discussed the assignment of employee E4 to Division C, they also discussed the question of who would be rotated through these positions to fill the resulting vacancy. The moves of employee E4 to Division D and employee E5 to Division B were not seen as a simple, sequential progression, but rather as a pair of concurrent appointments. These appointments were designed both to broaden and develop the skills of employee relations professionals and to improve the employee relations competencies available for application in the workplace.

The manager of Division B was an enthusiastic supporter of the posting system. However, when he "received a call from Regional Office" to confirm the specifics of moves that had previously been discussed generally, he did not insist on using the posting system. Nevertheless, he did check on the suitability of the proposed appointment of employee E5 to his division, through lengthy discussions with both the candidate and several managers who had previously supervised this employee. After confirming that the proposed candidate "was best qualified and best able to fit the group," the local manager accepted the initiative of the senior professionals in the region who were managing this series of rotational assignments for their eventual successors.

The technical feature of employee relations jobs in the forestry industry was used to justify the predominant use of administrative appointments for these two vacancies rather than posting or conducting a search of the ELM. The tension between posting and administered appointments was evident in the responses of different employee relations specialists to the procedures used in this vacancy chain. Nominally, employee relations specialists were responsible for the operation of the posting system, and many professed an ideological commitment to competitive, corporate-wide searches for suitable candidates. In contrast, line managers often wanted to manage their patch independent of outside interference by staff specialists. Within the employee relations specialist group, attachment to posting was uneven. Specialists closer to classic appreciations of ILMs, such as those involved in the practice of industrial relations associated with unionized hourly employees, appeared to be more comfortable with administered appointments. Employee relations specialists who were more concerned with the manner in which ForestCo managed its employment system for white-collar, salaried employees appeared to support posting procedures more strongly. The use of two administered appointments in staffing the industrial relations/employee relations occupational specialty described in vacancy chain 28 was perhaps acknowledged with greater justification than might have been the case for other occupations.

Competition for Entry into Professional Lines of Progression

Again, movement of a person from one position to another created a vacancy. In this case, the appointment of employee E5 to Division B left a position vacant in Division A. However, because almost all divisions in this region were involved in this sequence of staffing actions, the latter vacancy represented the end of the line in terms of further rotational moves. Consequently, there were no succession plans for others to move into this division, and the position was posted. Notices of the vacancy were distributed first within the company and, shortly thereafter, in the local media. Five applications were received from internal candidates, and each of these applicants was reviewed by a three-person selection panel. Although one candidate "was head and shoulders above the others," he still was not considered to possess the minimal requirements for the position. In contrast to this candidate, the four other applicants were characterized as "wanting to know what they had to do to get into the field."

Faced with this less than satisfactory situation, the Regional Supervisor responsible for this functional specialty in all divisions in the region decided to expand his search to the ELM. More than 100 candidates had applied in response to the external advertisements, and each was prescreened on the basis of education and industry experience. These attributes and the technical knowledge that came with industry experience were judged to be critical requirements for any applicant. Apparently, many applicants were surprised by the extent of technical knowledge required to be an employee relations specialist in this industry. Safety regulations, union rules, and company policies were all quite technical and extensive. It was judged that applicants from outside the industry who were unfamiliar with this technical information would be unable to function without a prolonged training period. Once the applicant pool of over 100 potential employees was established, a shortlist of eight candidates were interviewed by the Regional Supervisor. At this point, a second selection panel was formed, and this panel interviewed the top two external candidates and the top internal candidate from the previous search. The Regional Supervisor provided justification for this extensive search:

> We wanted to know what was out there in the field. Outsiders provide a baseline of the best there is out there compared to what's available inside.

The second selection panel discussed their evaluations of the three final candidates with the Divisional Manager and let the final selection outcome emerge from discussions between him and each candidate. One of the external candidates was chosen and appointed to the vacant position.

REVIEW OF "LONG" VACANCY CHAINS

At the beginning of this chapter, "long" vacancy chains were characterized as being consistent with stereotypical models of ILMs. From this perspective, employees advance through a succession of increasingly demanding jobs along stable, relatively well-established lines of progression. Vacancy chains originate with the creation of new positions or exits from existing positions or both. In staffing vacant positions, managers express a strong preference for existing employees who have developed the organization-specific knowledge and skills judged to be required for successful job performance. Thus, vacancy chains are extended by repeated selections of candidates from other related organizational positions. Such vacancy chains are expected to terminate with hires into positions representing ports of entry from the ELM into the ILM. As candidates and jobs are both relatively well known, it is also expected that staffing would be executed primarily by administrative appointments rather than by competitive posting.

The three long vacancy chains just presented by and large met these expectations. Each long vacancy chain selected for more detailed review was associated with succession and development along a specialist, unifunctional line of progression. The representativeness of the overall sample is partially revealed in this subsample. Of all 11 long vacancy chains from ForestCo's organization, 9 were associated with professional occupational specializations such as Accounting, Employee Relations, Engineering, and Forestry. In these chains, internal, technical concerns for job performance and capacity to learn from developmental opportunities dominated selection criteria. There were some external pressures, but no large or extensive pressures, for organizational change and adaptation. Except for two employees associated with vacancy chain 3 (diagrammed in Figure 6.2), few other staffing actions produced large increases in the hierarchical level of employees being appointed. Most moves were of candidates either being promoted one grade or being transferred at the same grade.

A mixture of administered appointments and posting was used to identify and select candidates to vacant positions. Although the first appointment in vacancy chain 28 was accomplished through an administrative process, the next two appointments were made through use of the posting system. However, the next three appointments, which extended this vacancy chain beyond an average length, were not posted but were also made through an administrative process. These latter appointments provided the senior managers of this occupational specialty with the control they needed to manage several concurrent developmental assignments required to implement a succession plan. In all three of these illustrative long vacancy chains, plans for the development and assignment of employees within an occupational specialty were judged to require a more centralized and controlling form of staffing. It was argued that if the posting system had been used, there was no guarantee that the previously designated successor would be chosen. For these reasons, longer vacancy chains were often associated with the implementation of development and succession plans through administrative processes.

What is most interesting about this review of specific long vacancy chains is less their specific characteristics than their relative infrequency. Long vacancy chains are not common. Approximately 85% of the vacancy chains uncovered in the first sample were shorter than the admittedly arbitrary length of six moves used to designate stereotypical vacancy chain length. For the two samples of vacancy chains, "long" vacancy chains represented only 10% of the total. Only occasionally did combinations of conditions encourage the emergence of long vacancy chains. More often than not, vacancy chains that were initiated at various levels of ForestCo's hierarchy encountered conditions that limited the spread of further vacancies through the appointment of existing employees. The majority of vacancy chains studied terminated either because the originating vacancy occurred in close proximity to an established or opportunistic port of entry or because vacated jobs were either dissolved or absorbed.

Long vacancy chains were more likely to occur when they were located in larger systems of jobs related by the similar skills and knowledge required for superior job performance. In addition, longer sequences of employee moves through related jobs were facilitated when a single manager, or a unified managerial group, had the authority for a managerial purview over the system of jobs. Although a few long vacancy chains were comprised of several concurrent assignments associated with reorganizations, most long vacancy chains emerged in situations in which there were few pressures for change to an existing relational system of jobs.

Review of Part II

Chapters 3–6 have examined the operation of ForestCo's internal labor market (ILM) from the perspective of vacancy chains found in the organization. In this context, vacancy chains have been interpreted as sequences of related staffing actions in which there has been a "person-move" of some kind in which the organizational status of an employee was changed. Typically, these moves were ones in which employees moved from one position to another inside the organization. Other moves involved the exit of an employee from the organization, such as when an employee quit, or a move from the external labor market to an employed status, as in an employee hire. Person-moves inside the organization were mostly "promotions" or "transfers," as employees moved from one position to another with a higher or equal salary grade ranking. However, interpretations of promotions and transfers based solely on mobility between salary grades could be ambiguous, as there was only a loose coupling between salary grade and salary level. Also, initial job gradings were often regarded as preliminary, and further increases in both status and pay often followed initial "probationary" appointments. Moreover, job gradings were not always assigned independently of the qualities of the person assigned to the position being graded. Finally, the framework of jobs and positions in ForestCo's organization exhibited considerable dynamism as jobs were created and absorbed as a function of local adaptations to changing products, technologies, and environmental conditions.

Although vacancy chains were found to originate almost anywhere in ForestCo's organization, each originating vacancy typically produced several other vacancies elsewhere in the organization. With an average vacancy chain length of just over three person-moves, each originating vacancy typically produced two additional person-moves. Although it is true in a general sense that all staffing decisions and actions are greatly influenced by the context in which they occur, it is true in a particular sense for vacancy chains. Approximately two thirds of all vacancies and staffing actions were dependent on the immediate outcomes of previous staffing actions that led to those particular staffing opportunities. A full appreciation of either a sequence or any one of these latter person-moves can best be gained by a more detailed examination of the local contextual issues that framed each prior staffing action. Appreciation of the linkages among context, decision, and organizational actions permits one to conceptualize how employment systems accomplish system-level functions such as maintenance, adaptation, and change.

The vacancy chains described in Chapters 4–6 present a perspective on the micro-processes by which ForestCo's organization was both maintained and changed. A summary of the issues found in the vacancy chains described in detail in Chapters 3–6 is

Table R.1. Summary of Features of Vacancy Chain Length

Organizational feature	Vacancy chain length		
	Minimal	Medium	Long
Adaptation and change			
Interdependence of persons and positions	X	X	X
Vacancies as opportunities for change	X	X	X
Organizational redesign		X	X
Implementing new Styles and cultures		X	
Staffing new positions	X	X	
Strategic staffing	X	X	
Absorption of jobs	X	X	
Opportunistic hires	X		
Dislocations in career structures		X	
Managing lines of progression			
Organizational obligations to employees	X	X	X
Executive succession		X	X
Professional development		X	X
Competition for development		X	
Developing supervisors from hourly ranks	X	X	
Rotational development	X		
Replacements close to ports of entry	X		
Promotions within position	X		
Unique skills	X		

presented in Table R.1. The purpose of this table is to summarize the various issues uncovered in those chapters and to indicate the types of vacancy chain in which these issues surfaced. Consideration of these issues suggests that the various issues intertwined with the evolution of vacancy chains can be captured under two primary but linked themes: the system-wide need for organizational adaptation and change and the more local concerns for the management of lines of progression. There is an active tension between these two themes, as they represent the conflicting requirements for system adaptation and system stability. Linking these two themes but also representing the point of conflict between them are concerns associated with the maintenance of or dislocations in career structures. While there was a tendency for some issues to be found more frequently in either minimal, medium, or long vacancy chains, several issues were found in vacancy chains of all lengths, and many issues were found across at least two of the independent groupings of vacancy chains segmented by length.

Issues of organizational change and adaptation are revealed when we consider the extensive dynamism in ForestCo's organization as represented in the numbers, types, and structures of jobs in each departmental and divisional subunit of the organization. Job creation and absorption are intricately intertwined with the capacities and availabilities of skilled staff. Job classifications, descriptions, and salary grades are often interdependent with the qualities of the persons assigned to positions. Organizational change is frequently driven by a recognition that new job functions need to be performed, and staffing occurs as a consequence of this conceptualization. However, prior vacancies and prior person-moves also provide opportunities for local adjustments and changes in job definitions and the structures of organizational subunits. Different moves in the same vacancy chain often reflected the reciprocity of planned and opportunistic change.

Because of the dynamism and interdependence of jobs and persons, the managerial function of staffing has to balance, in real time, several competing objectives. Many of the staffing situations encountered by ForestCo's managers required them to balance forces for stability with those for change. When a relatively large proportion of employee–job assignments were new, the opportunity for organizational change was great, but the stability and dependability of unit performance could be at risk. Forces for change could originate from direct relationships with agents in the external environment, such as regulatory agencies, suppliers, customers, and competitors. Forces for change could also originate from elsewhere inside the organization, such as new personnel policies designed to cut costs and reduce manpower complements. Change could also originate inside a unit, such as when a random clustering of retirements exhausted the stock of staff in the development pipeline. The severity and origin of these forces for change influenced managers' choices as to both the manner in which they searched for candidates for vacant positions and the weight they gave to different criteria used to assess these candidates. Jobs could rarely be defined independent of the contexts in which they occurred. Local contexts therefore influenced the selection of criteria used to select candidates. Bureaucratic, and hence universalistic, models of employee selection had limited application in a proliferation of local contexts and assessments.

Because of the interdependence of persons and jobs, a second "balance" required in organizational staffing was that of the timing of organizational needs and career and skill development. When job requirements could not be changed and filling the jobs was regarded as urgent, less than ideal job assignments were occasionally arranged because individual employees had not yet had sufficient time to develop the skill-set required for a particular job. In other circumstances, job requirements would be finessed in order to accommodate organizationally relevant development needs of key employees. In related cases, job requirements would be similarly satisfied rather than maximized to meet the personally derived career needs of employees. For example, employees would be given "a second chance," and reassignments would be made to provide transfers for employees who needed relief from stressful work and family situations.

The dynamism of an evolving array of jobs and an evolving array of candidates for various positions in contexts characterized by evolving competitive demands limited the application of top-down models of rational human resource planning. Considerable intellectual creativity and flexibility were required of managers making staffing judgments. Only rarely did managers consider staffing as problems with one degree of freedom, namely, the selection from among an array of candidates for a fixed job. More frequently, and particularly in the case of senior appointments, managers considered external demands as potentially negotiable and arrays of both jobs and candidates as variable. The manner in which managers developed simpler models of staffing choices to deal with such complex and confusing choices remains a most interesting question. Not all changes required by environmental or competitive conditions were clearly seen and understood by the organizational units affected by these changes. When these processes unfolded over long time periods, local managers adopted an incremental approach to staffing. Jobs with unclear and evolving definitions would be filled by administrative assignment with employees whose qualities were well known. In these circumstances, job definitions were often strongly influenced by the known capacities and skills of long-term employees. As the outcomes of preliminary person–job assignments became clearer, subsequent job descriptions became more definitive. In turn, these jobs would then often be filled competitively through the posting process, in which job requirements drove selection criteria for appointees.

Side by side with these incremental approaches to organizational change were those that embodied processes of strategic staffing. In these situations, an evolving contextual condition and an organizational opportunity would become contiguous and coincident. For example, environmental requirements for ForestCo to respond differently to public criticism of its forestry practices were not acknowledged until they coincided with the early retirement of a Senior Forester in the firm. Because of tradition and institutional pressures, previous incremental change had not occurred. When an opportunity to re-define this position presented itself, however, the subsequent selection and assignment challenged the logic of the previous line of progression, which shaped, even if only implicitly, the development sequence assumed to be required of candidates for that function. The sequence of moves in this limited progression had great substantive and symbolic value for others in the corporation and presaged a transformation in the orienta-tion of the company to environmentalist stakeholders.

So far, it has been argued that an examination of the issue content of many of the vacancy chains found at ForestCo provides insight into the manner in which system-level functions of adaptation and change are obtained in ILMs. This argument is extended in the following discussion of the statistical and structural properties of the vacancy chains in our sample organization.

Economic models of organizational functioning suggest that the most economically efficient assignments of persons to jobs are best obtained through competitive processes. Neoclassical interpretations of this fundamental model assume that the administrative mechanisms for obtaining economic efficiency are not cost-free. Many ILM features, such as lines of progression and limited ports of entry that limit competition, are nevertheless economically functional, as they reduce the high administrative or transaction costs normally associated with finding the "best" person for a particular job. The existence of relatively long lines of progression can be rationalized with models of economic efficiency if prior experience in a related job is regarded as a necessary and sufficient condition for future job performance or if there is competition at each staffing opportunity in the vacancy chain. In salaried employment systems, the former condition is unlikely to be realized, as stable arrangements of jobs rarely obtain when organizations have to respond to environmental change. Moreover, if there are extensive staffing competitions at each staffing opportunity, delays and associated administrative costs would be substantial. Therefore, traditional models of ILMs manifesting long lines of progression and few ports of entry have little application to salaried employment systems because these features restrict the processes of organizational adaptation and change.

A more appropriate model of organizational adaptation is suggested by the vacancy chain data presented in Chapter 3, which demonstrated that most vacancy chains consist of relatively few person-moves. Distributions consisting of many short vacancy chains are consistent with models of organizational adaptation obtained largely from incremental processes. In this perspective, vacancy chains originate at all levels of the organizational hierarchy and also terminate at all but the highest levels. Jobs are created, merged, and absorbed to suit the needs of organizational adaptation and change. Moreover, job defini-tions are interdependent with the skills and capacities of employees assigned to those positions. When manifesting these attributes, salaried employment systems embody great flexibility and adaptability. Thus, the data, indicating as they do a relatively large propor-tion of short vacancy chains, reinforce an interpretation of ILMs as systems that encourage adaptation and change as much as efficiency of operations.

A second feature of ForestCo's salaried ILM, namely, that any vacancy has the potential to be a port of entry into the ILM, permits frequent, multiple comparisons of ILM candidates with those from the ELM. Competition between employees already within ForestCo's ILM and candidates from the ELM occurs in short, focused bursts when there is an assessment that the quality of internal candidates is insufficient for the jobs to be filled. This competition is not a universal attempt to find the best candidate, but a local assessment of the capacity of available candidates to meet reasonable performance expectations. Under these conditions, searches for appropriate candidates are expanded when prior searches fail to produce acceptable results.

Such search mechanisms are themselves adaptive to assessments of returns likely to result from further expenditures of effort. Vacancies are filled either by administrative (i.e., noncompetitive) assignment or by the more competitive posting system as a function of local circumstance. The opportunity for employees to compete for vacant positions is partially controlled by managers' circumscribing the geographic and organizational extent to which posting occurs. The greater the extent of posting, however, the less control the responsible manager typically has over the consequences of staffing. Selections of candidates from elsewhere in the organization switch the opportunity to act to another manager. Thus, posting typically produces conflicting objectives. On one hand, posting increases the extent of competition and the likelihood that a superior candidate will be found. On the other hand, posting decreases the range of a manager's control over the flows of personnel in the organizational unit for which he is responsible. Posting encourages internal competition appropriate for organization-specific skills. When the development of these organization-specific skills is regarded as critical, however, administrative staffing provides the stability and management control required for such developmental processes to occur. The managerial discretion associated with the manner of making assignments to a dynamic system of jobs permits flexibility in the speed of response to staffing vacant positions. Indeed, multiple models of staffing are applied as a function of each manager's interpretation of local conditions.

Organizational staffing is required to meet multiple objectives. Current and future performance of organizational subunits, adaptation to changing organizational circumstances, and the organizational and personal career development needs of organizational participants usually factor into most staffing judgments. The emphasis given to any one of these objectives depends very much on assessments of local and contextual conditions. In dynamic environments, no single model of staffing is likely to be universally applicable. Multiple models applied as a function of local circumstance provide a flexible approach suitable for accomplishment of organizational change and adaptation. Unfortunately, the means used to obtain these pragmatic outcomes also produce conceptual confusion. No single, normative model of staffing is appropriate when used as an integral component of organizational adaptation and change.

A significant theme of this review of vacancy chains is that such perspectives encourage a view of the adaptability and flexibility of ILMs and employment systems. In this perspective, flexibility is predicated on interpretations of local contextual conditions that frame each staffing action. Part III presents a comprehensive review of the factors that entered the decision frames of ForestCo's managers as they struggled to define and respond to staffing opportunities.

III

Staffing Action Perspectives on Internal Labor Markets

The third perspective on internal labor markets (ILMs) to be presented in this book examines ForestCo's salaried employment system through the lens of the staffing processes found in that company. As the detailed discussions of vacancy chain processes presented in Part II made clear, staffing decisions and actions are an integral component of a complex set of managerial cognitions and actions. Managers are responsible for the attainment of multiple, interdependent objectives by deploying the human, technical, financial, and physical resources available to them. Most simply, staffing is the administrative mechanism through which persons of different talents, capacities, and experiences are assigned to interdependent jobs the execution of which results in departmental performance. Staffing is an integral component of the managerial job and is also embedded in the larger social, corporate, organizational, and temporal contexts that frame managerial actions.

Because the attainment of objectives is rarely independent of the processes by which they are attained, managers confront many choices of means they may use to meet departmental and organizational goals. Staffing is often much more than a simple decision process designed "to hire one or more applicants for employment and not to hire others" (Guion & Gibson, 1988). Managers exercise considerable discretion over the types and interdependencies among the jobs in their departments, the manner in which persons are sought to fill those positions, the criteria used to assess candidates, and the subsequent treatment, protection, and training of recent appointees. This set of activities is far more complex than those discussed in the very extensive literature produced by academic social scientists, consulting research psychologists, and personnel specialists over the past 50 years, which assumes that staffing decisions are almost invariably defined as questions of personnel selection (Guion, 1993; Schneider & Schmitt, 1986). While recent reviews of current issues in personnel selection argue for change in the conceptualization of personnel selection (Schmitt & Borman, 1993), there has been only modest progress in extending the traditional selection paradigm to full consideration of the rich complexities of staffing as it is practiced.

For these reasons, the staffing perspective on ForestCo's ILM presented in Part III follows a series of nested viewpoints similar to the schema presented in Fig.1.1 for the overall plan of this book. In that schema, staffing was presented as occurring in the context of vacancy chains, which in turn occurred in the context of the overall employment-system

169

of ForestCo's organization. Moreover, it was argued that activities and phenomena conceptualized on any one level were interdependent with activities and phenomena conceptualized at each other level. Appreciations of ILMs developed from employment system perspectives were interdependent with those conceptualized at levels indicated by vacancy chains and staffing actions. Similarly, staffing as a key component process of ForestCo's ILM cannot be appreciated independently of the temporal and situational features of the context in which it occurs. This interdependence is true for staffing considered generally as well as for individual managers who confronted choices on how to proceed when faced with a vacant position. Managers were profoundly influenced by aspects of their situation. Their general attitudes toward different staffing philosophies, their appreciation of other problems and issues that should be considered in conjunction with evolution of the staffing process, their choice of a selection method, and the criteria they used to evaluate candidates were all influenced by their assessments of their organizational context.

Chapters 7 through 11 present contextually based perspectives on managers' self-reports of why they acted as they did in staffing vacant positions in ForestCo's ILM. Chapter 7 considers both the situational and the temporal aspects of the general context in which the staffing function was performed during the time of this study of ForestCo's ILM. Initially, Chapter 7 describes the general factors that influenced managers to choose either the posting system or administrative appointments as their preferred method of identifying and selecting candidates for vacant positions. These general considerations may be viewed as built-in features of the tension between administrative and competitive means used to select candidates for vacant positions. At times, however, managers also chose one method rather than another because of their appreciation of local circumstances. To put these circumstances in historical perspective, Chapter 7 also includes a discussion of ForestCo's recent economic past, which affected both the objective reality of the firm's demography and the perceptual filters through which vacancies were seen.

Chapters 8 and 9 present more detailed descriptions of how staffing was accomplished through either administered appointments or the posting system. These descriptions elaborate on the choices confronted by managers who engage in staffing activities. For example, Chapter 8 describes the dilemmas associated with the use of administered appointments, especially those associated with managing lines of progression and of accomplishing staffing when either jobs or persons, or both, are not well known. Similarly, Chapter 9 describes various difficulties encountered in implementing a competitive labor market process, as manifested in ForestCo's posting system, for the selection of persons to vacant positions.

Chapter 10 complements the discussions presented in the chapters by describing the contextually derived criteria used by managers to select persons for positions. It describes the many different signals, surrogate measures, and biases used by managers to infer the capacities of candidates to perform in prospective jobs.

Chapter 11 considers further staffing issues derived from extensions of the temporal context beyond the selection of candidates. In stereotypical treatments of staffing, in which staffing is viewed primarily as personnel selection, staffing activity ceases once candidates have been chosen. This was clearly not the case, however, for ForestCo's managers. Managerial concerns regarding future organizational performance, managerial reputations, and the well-being of both chosen and unchosen candidates influenced postselection managerial activities. Moreover, as many staffing choices provided chosen candidates with opportunities for further challenge associated with their experience of demanding work, managers often acted to facilitate employee development beyond any recent appointment. These five chapters may therefore be considered to present staffing activities as linkages between past corporate and managerial experiences, through the procedures and criteria used to assess candidates in the present, so they might be prepared for not-yet-experienced organizational futures.

The material presented in Part III may also be regarded as being qualitatively different from the discussions of vacancy chains presented in Part II. In Part III, much greater use is made of the many voices of ForestCo's managers explaining why they acted as they did. In this presentation, staffing is viewed as a generic organizational activity—not one shaped and circumscribed by the particular features of a specific staffing action in a specific vacancy chain. Thus, Part III presents a general overview of staffing as it was practiced in the salaried employment system of ForestCo's organization. The intent of this descriptive presentation is to confront the predominantly normative views of human resource management predicated on rational, bureaucratic models of organizations.

Staffing Practices as Internal Labor Market Processes

Internal Labor Markets as Contexts for Staffing

INTRODUCTION

The introduction to staffing practices presented in Chapter 1 discussed the development and application of scientific principles to personnel management, which has occurred both before and since World War II. Both then and now, development of more sophisticated personnel procedures has progressed most readily under assumptions closely associated with rational, bureaucratic forms of organization. That is, organizations are most appropriately viewed as closed systems in which explicit goals provide unambiguous criteria for choosing among alternatives, including those that involve the selection and assignment of persons to positions. One feature of such models is the "strong vacancy chain assumption" (Miner, 1987), in which jobs are both temporal and causal antecedents to the selection of persons.

In partial contrast to closed-system models of organizations are natural-system models, which consider organizations as organic systems that embody emergent social structures and collectivities. Actual behavior, as indicated by employee activities, interactions, and sentiments (Homans, 1950), may be quite different from that nominally prescribed by formal, rational models of organizations. Organizations are viewed as "organic systems imbued with a strong drive to survive, to maintain themselves as systems…their structures grow out of the natural abilities and interests of participants and enable the collectivity to benefit from the human resources of its membership" (Scott, 1992, p. 25).

A third perspective on organizational functioning is the open-system model. This perspective views an organization not just as a formal structure or an organic entity, but as a system of activities interdependent with each other and with other environmental agencies and resources. Organizations are integral with the environments in which they operate and are required to continually adapt their internal processes to sustain exchanges with agents outside the organization. Organizations are dependent on flows of personnel, information, and resources for their survival, and distinctions "between organization and environment may be shifting, ambiguous, and arbitrary" (Scott, 1992, p. 25). Each perspective focuses attention and emphasis on different aspects of organizational functioning. No single perspective is best suited to developing all appreciations and understandings of organizational activities. Open-system models focus attention on the interdependencies between organizations and the situational and temporal context in which organizational activities occur.

Because organizations display both inertial and adaptive properties, the consequences of past experiences are frequently found in current conditions and practices. Therefore, this first section of this first chapter describing staffing at ForestCo presents an analysis of the firm's immediate history, which apparently had a profound influence on subsequent managerial staffing actions and decisions. The description that follows traces the consequences of the deep recession experienced by this firm and its industry some seven or eight years previously. It elaborates on the manner in which the context of the employment system of this firm influenced subsequent, critical orientations toward staffing. Thus, this first section may be regarded as a more detailed extension of the background context for ForestCo's internal labor market (ILM) presented in Chapter 2. This extension, however, moves beyond purely structural attributes of the firm's employment system to considerations of background norms, values, and assumptions that shaped current selection practices.

THE EFFECTS OF ORGANIZATIONAL HISTORY ON STAFFING

Multiple prior events and histories conditioned the selection component of the staffing process at ForestCo. These events and histories shaped the general organizational context within which staffing occurred. Past experience arising from a particular corporate history influenced the rules and procedures used to staff positions, the biases and prejudices of both individual managers and groups of managers in divisional units, and employee dispositions to present themselves as candidates for vacant positions. The following sections describe the recent history of this particular corporation together with the consequences of this experience for the immediate context within which staffing occurred at the time of our study.

The Experience of the Recession in the Early 1980s

An extraordinarily distinctive feature of the staffing practices of ForestCo in the late 1980s was the continuing influence of the events that traumatized the organization in the early 1980s—some seven or eight years previously. Approximately half the managers interviewed expressed some opinion or awareness of the devastating effects of the global recession of 1981–1982, its consequences for the forest products industry, and the subsequent cutbacks in employment at ForestCo. The large reduction in employment levels for the organization as a whole involved significant reductions of almost all organizational units:

> Since 1981, we've scaled down from 96 to 41 employees and have maintained a steady level of employment at that level.

> We had 39 people then and now we've got 17 and they're doing the best they can.

> I had over 60 people working for me in 1982—in two different groups. I had to fire half my people and I now work with a staff of 32.

> Salaried positions have lost status because of the layoffs and hassles that were experienced in 1982. We laid off 65 people then.

> We had 90 people in 1981—now we've got 45.

> In 1981–1982 we used to employ 500 people—now we're down to 250 and producing more timber than before. Also, we used to employ 100 men in the booming grounds. We now process the same volume as before with the same technology but with only 30 people.

These individual experiences conditioned managers' view of their present staffing responsibilities and their emotional orientation to those tasks. Fundamentally, these managers told us that if we wished to understand why they did what they did, we first had to understand "where they were coming from." Their individual and collective histories with the recession of the early 1980s were both a significant component of their current context and the lens through which they viewed current choices and options. Such views are consistent with open-system models of organizations. In particular, orientations toward current staffing were framed by managerial experiences in the past. As one experienced manager wryly commented: "I wasn't born this way!"

Critical Reactions to Vacancies

The consequences of the experience of the recession were several. As revealed by the previous comments, many managers believed that their units were running lean and that they had insufficient staff to do all the jobs that they thought needed to be done:

> As a result of downsizing, we've had to learn how to be lean and stretch our comfort zone as to what is the minimum required to do a job.

At the same time, they continued to feel pressure that staffing levels not be increased. Operationally, this pressure meant that vacant positions should not automatically be filled with a replacement and that ways should be found to consolidate positions and to reduce staffing levels. As a consequence of the recession and the massive change experienced in the industry, ForestCo's managers were required to adopt a Model II approach to staffing (see the section entitled "Choice of Selection Systems," p. 183, below). That is, selections of persons were based on assessments of their capacities to perform a broad array of functions and not just for a specific job. Few jobs were regarded as unchangeable, and many staffing actions were initiated in contexts in which detailed job specifications were not necessarily precursors to employee selection. To a significant extent, jobs were arranged around the capacities and abilities of existing employees:

> We had to get rid of 10 people because of 1981–1982, and since then there's been a hiring freeze. Any new hire has to be approved by [ForestCo's President].

While such practices were regarded as necessary in the first few years of the decade, their continued application some seven or eight years later was increasingly being questioned. Several managers reported discomfort with the current administrative procedures, which limited growth in staffing levels. Many were acutely aware of the trade-offs between the reduced costs of lower staff complements and organizational inefficiency that resulted from work overload:

> When I get a vacancy, I check to see if the work needs to be done and if the job has to be filled. When a job is time-consuming and demanding, I can't expect existing staff to share the workload. I feel we're lean and mean as it is—and if I overwork my people I wouldn't have a winning position in the long run.

It was clear that the personnel policies initially put into effect in 1982 to establish, and then to maintain, a lean and mean organization were still operative in 1988–1989 when this study was begun. However, there were signs that these policies were increasingly regarded as being less appropriate, as business conditions had changed. From an open-system perspective, staffing policies designed to address problems that resulted from changed circumstances should be expected to change again once those external conditions no longer obtained. There was some evidence of inertial tendencies in personnel policies and a resultant lack of fit between current policies and circumstances:

> Whenever a vacancy comes up, we have to get authorization to get the position filled again. If it's an established position, it's just a formality to get approval. In 1982, each position had to be looked at very carefully, but now it feels more like a waste of manpower and valuable time to go through the chain of signatures to get an approval. I can understand senior management wants to maintain the intent of always thinking very cautiously about expansion—but we shouldn't have to fight to get a position filled.

The tension between keeping staffing levels to a minimum and yet maintaining a productive workforce were manifested in managers' either questioning or adhering to previously articulated staffing policies. In several instances, there was resistance to the current application of the survival policies initially established in 1982. This resistance emerged most strongly in those departments that had seen changes in demography and that now required renewal of retiring personnel through new hires.

Organizational Demography: Mobility, Training, and Motivation

Prior to the major recession experienced primarily in 1981–1982, ForestCo's employment system exhibited a relatively stable demography. That is, the flows of new employees into the organization, and their mobility through and eventually out of that system, balanced to produce both a stable workforce complement and stable distributions of employees by age, grade, and length of service (Keyfitz, 1973). The new personnel policies (illustrated in Fig. 2.4) changed these flow rates, as they involved early retirements, unprecedented layoffs, limitations on hiring, and the training and reassignment of employees with long service and good performance. Changes in employee flows had a significant long-term impact on the consequent organizational demography. First, supervisory and management ranks were thinned by accelerated retirements and layoffs. Second, a hiring freeze limited the inflow of new employees. As an intermediate-term consequence of these changes, the overall organizational demography became limited in range. There were both fewer older employees and fewer junior employees. With the continuation of these policies throughout the remainder of the decade of the 1980s, the demographic profile shifted to an older, longer-service distribution:

> The effect of 1981–1982 was that through downsizing, we have older average ages at the entry-level staff jobs.

> In 1981–1982, the middles got wiped out here. We kept a few low ends and the seniors, but the hole has never been filled. There have been no moves because of the cutbacks.

> The cuts didn't impact on us at first—but they got us the second time around. We were able to keep most of our senior people, but we had to let almost all our juniors go.

By the end of the decade, there was an increased rate of retirement among the older employees who had managed to survive the cuts earlier in the decade. At the same time, there was a shortage of trained younger employees with the capacity to move into key organizational positions.

> Since 1982, we've been able to control our growth in employment to a great extent. The only new positions we've authorized are those that could be justified by immediate business

needs such as growth in U.S., Ontario and Japanese markets. In these areas, it was essential to get a few new people in to support that business growth. However, elsewhere, very few trainees have been brought in, and there's a demographic dip of experience because of the past seven years.

Other managers also reported on various aspects of an imbalance between the demand and the supply of skilled, trained, and experienced personnel. Often, this imbalance was seen as a gap in the range of skills needed to operate the large, complex administrative system of the organization:

> When we took a good look at our accounting group, we realized there was a gap. We had quite a few individuals with professional qualifications and lots of people with no qualifications at all—but we had nothing in the middle.

Moreover, changes in demography, together with tight control to ensure that only work with an immediate payoff was done, yielded little opportunity to train and develop candidates for future supervisory and management positions. For many managers, this lack of opportunity was the most damaging feature of the policies implemented in response to the recession:

> We haven't been grooming anybody for upward mobility. All our development positions were wiped out in the recession.

Because all the vacancies that would ordinarily have occurred in the middle of the decade were brought forward in time, and concentrated in an 18-month period in 1981–1982, there was both a lack of training and a lack of opportunity in the organization over the remaining six or seven years. These deficiencies produced a stagnant workforce with potential supervisors and managers having little opportunity to learn from experience in a series of more challenging jobs:

> There's been virtually very little movement since the early 1980s, and as a consequence we haven't had to do much formal succession planning. *The five to six year recession period killed us in terms of junior employees getting enough grooming in operations.** We now do it informally—and occasionally talk about who will possibly move up the ladder.

Lack of mobility was seen to deaden the variety, interest, and intrinsic motivation obtainable from work. The prospect of no new jobs deadened motivation even further, as there was little incentive to develop skills for jobs only vaguely discernible in the future:

> Major changes are needed because *it's boring to do the same job for seven or eight years.* Managers need a new shake and a better-rounded perspective. Now we don't have the bodies to develop into middle management.

Stagnation and boredom in this organization could also push high-quality employees interested in self-development and advancement to leave the organization to search out opportunities elsewhere in the industry. The ones who remained were loyal, but limited by the lack of opportunity and challenge they had experienced in the past seven or eight years:

> I was real concerned there was nobody in the organization to fill that role. Basically, this happened because of the lack of turnover in the '80s and *many of the good accountants left for opportunities elsewhere.* The ones that stayed got stifled at lower levels because of lack of promotions.

---

*Here and in several following excerpts, emphasis is added to what were, of course, transcripts of oral interviews.

In addition, for those who remained with the organization, there was little incentive to develop and obtain accreditation for professional skills from off-the-job education:

> We used to require all our accounting staff to work on getting their degrees and professional qualifications. But when the purge came, all that went by the board. After that, *most just seemed to be content with what they had. There was little competition for positions, so people saw little point in working for their degree.* There were few places to go, and people became frustrated sitting in one position for a long time.

All these factors—stagnation, lack of training and development, and loss of motivation—have had major implications for the quality of candidates whom managers considered for vacant positions. This situation is amply indicated by the following illustrative comments:

> Presently, the quality of supply of possible candidates being uncovered by the posting system is relatively weak.

> There aren't enough people in the organization who have had breadth of experience.

> I believe the division is vulnerable—we'll end up needing people who won't be available.

> This is a time for us to upgrade skills to meet the need of the new mill—computers and human relations, for example. But many of our existing employees just don't have what we're looking for at this time.

> The department is just too tight—and I've got a lot of concern regarding the depth of the people here. They just don't have a broad enough experience and we may end up with nobody qualified to do the work. For example, the _____ supervisor is 62 years old and nobody is being groomed to take that position. When the person underneath that supervisor is not yet anywhere close to qualifying for the job, that's potentially damaging for employee morale.

The recession of the early 1980s had a major impact on both the immediate and the subsequent demography of ForestCo's organization. As staffing is concerned with the flows of persons into, through, and out of the human resource system of the organization, these demographic effects had a strong influence on the immediate contexts within which subsequent staffing activities occurred. The recession directly influenced the mobility opportunities for several significant groups of employee. Corporate responses to the recession limited employee opportunities for further training and development, thereby restricting their motivation on their current jobs and lessening the incentives for them to develop additional skills for future jobs.

In addition to the ongoing consequences of organizational stagnation, the actions taken to help the organization survive the deep recession in the early 1980s also had a delayed effect on the retirement rate in the later years of the decade. With few retirements for the past several years, there was a relatively large group of older supervisors and managers ready for retirement in the later years of the decade. Just as the members of this older cohort had begun to retire, a sharp increase in the succession rate of younger supervisors and managers was required. Because of the previous stagnation associated with the lack of mobility, however, few of these younger employees had received much breadth of training and experience. At the time of this study, several of the managers responsible for appointments to these vacated positions experienced a significant increase in the degree of uncertainty and risk associated with organizational staffing:

> Because we'd used up all available people when we reorganized three years ago, and then several senior managers—all of a similar age—started to retire at about the same time, we had nobody prepared. Essentially, those retirements created a shambles.

As a reaction to this increase in uncertainty and risk, other managers decided to become increasingly proactive and to act so as to limit their vulnerability associated with impending retirements:

> We decided it was time to train up/down/across for succession in the organization. With the impending retirements of [three senior managers], we realized we weren't ready to replace these men. If we wanted to promote from within, we'd have to get started on broadening senior managers' experience.

> We now need holes for training in the organization for fast-trackers to step into.

As this brief history of ForestCo indicates, an open-system perspective on organizations suggests that staffing actions cannot be separated from the historical and economic context within which they occur. Current staffing actions taken to accomplish organization-wide objectives are profoundly influenced by concrete consequences of past actions, such as the supplies of experienced personnel available within current demographic distributions. Current staffing actions were framed so as to offset part of the negative, long-term consequences of policy initiatives taken several years previously.

The Effects of History on Current Staffing

Not surprisingly, managers' appreciation of these prior conditions influenced how they thought about, and how they acted to staff, positions that were currently vacant. The general perception that there was a poor match between the demands arising from the key positions becoming available and the qualities and flows of the internal supply of candidates influenced managers' views of the payoffs resulting from searches for either internal or external candidates. Representative of the views of ForestCo's managers as a whole are the following comments of one manager, who linked the current consequences of using either an administrative or a competitive, market-based process for staffing to the context framed by the past experiences of the firm:

> All of our jobs are first posted on the inside—giving first opportunity to existing employees. Depending on the scope of the position, we post in the division, region, or corporate-wide. When we recruit, we search either provincially or country-wide. Recently, posting has been futile. There are lots of positions available and all of our divisions have vacancies to fill. I call my counterparts in other divisions, and there's no one available. Much of this is because of the cutbacks in 1982.

General appreciation of the values of either an administered approach to staffing or use of the posting system was conditioned by current circumstances. This conditioning could lead to a reversal of previous priorities. For example, the prime directive of the early 1980s to refrain from staffing if at all possible and then to consider only internal candidates was ignored by some managers who currently viewed outside searches as a necessary complement to opportunities for internal succession:

> I'd hired _____ one year earlier, and during that process I'd come to realize the restrictions regarding the availability of people in the company. Too many of our people have limited skills and abilities. Their major shortcoming is that they're not appropriate for succession. They're not able to go one or two steps beyond their present position. Also, people are unwilling to relocate. So, when this new vacancy came up, we advertised both inside and outside the company at the same time.

Facing a different situation, another manager decided that if he searched outside his immediate department, he might have to terminate the employment of that recruit if his mill did not survive its impending closure. Thus, he squeezed his internal requirements and appointed an insider who appeared to be satisfactory at best:

> This is an old sawmill with a stagnant work force. Given that the future is shaky—we're
> in a survival mode. Also, given that our previous hire from outside didn't work out, we
> didn't have a lot of choice as to who to appoint to that position. We didn't want to go
> outside—and there was no one else inside who was as qualified as _____, the person
> we appointed.

Another manager who was able to take a longer-term perspective, probably because the survival of his operation was not in question, reacted by increasing his requirements for the selection of new entrants to his division:

> Basically, this operation is going through a regeneration of an older demography. We've
> hired 20 people in the past year and are being much more selective than we were in the past.

This review of the effects of organizational history indicates the importance of that historical context for the conduct of present staffing activities. One significant experience, the recession in the early 1980s, continued to influence organizational practices up to the end of that decade. As a reaction to the recession, ForestCo actively intervened in the operation of its ILM by severely limiting hires from the external labor market (ELM) and initiating large flows of personnel out of the organization in the form of early retirements and layoffs. At the same time, there was an increase in internal flows, as mid- to senior-level employees were assigned to new positions that consolidated the duties and responsibilities that had previously been assigned to more than one job. Once these flows of human resources had taken place, little further movement was experienced until later in the decade, when normal retirements started to occur again. In the meantime, the primary change taking place was attributable to the passage of time. In addition, there were no flows of human resources, such as inflows and development of younger recruits. Consequently, ForestCo's overall workforce grew older.

It is not clear how these experiences influenced managerial preferences for either a more competitive or a more administrative process for staffing vacant positions. Some managers were aware that the dislocations in the normal patterns of job mobility through which talented employees were developed and trained meant that the quality of the internal supply was limited. Some managers were predisposed by this circumstance to intensify their search for candidates from the ELM and to increase their standards. Other managers, however, believed that they had an obligation to their present subordinates precisely because of their shared experience of the recession. They had little inclination to hire from the ELM, as these recruits could face layoffs if the business performance of their division was not especially promising. This concern with avoiding the experience of further layoffs emerged as a second significant consequence of the experience of the 1981–1982 recession.

The Effects of the Recession on Managerial Values

A second effect of the deep recession in the early 1980s and the resultant extraordinary actions taken to survive both during and following this economic threat was on the values and attitudes of managers themselves. To survive the recession, managers were required in some cases to fire and in some cases to request the early retirement of a substantial number of their colleagues, subordinates, neighbors, and friends. Evidence obtained from interviews indicates that these layoffs represented a traumatic event for many managers. This trauma continued to influence staffing practices in the latter part of the decade some seven or eight years later. The most pronounced consequence of this experience was that few managers wished to revisit the psychic pain of these firings. Consequently, they were reluctant to increase their complements to a level that, should there be a future slowdown in the industry, might require them to lay off staff. Moreover, they were reluctant to take risks in their selection of candidates—as some believed that their own job security could become vulnerable if the widely (and accurately) predicted economic slowdown of 1990–1991 were to occur. Such social-system considerations had a profound effect on the sentiments and relationships among ForestCo's salaried employees.

Different managers had different reactions to these experiences. In 1988–1989, some managers continued to accept the policies initially promulgated in 1981–1982, as these policies provided a partial retreat from a potential personal responsibility to fire other employees:

> This department's structure has been stable for the past ten years—though I have fewer people working for me now. With cutbacks, my staff was reduced from 25 to 13—a major impact. Because of this, I'm very cautious with respect to hiring, even though I could easily use another person in this area.

Other managers made do with their reduced complements and accepted the fact that some jobs wouldn't get done. One manager also made use of expensive overtime to avoid future firings:

> I had to fire half my staff and reorganize the work of this whole department. I never want to have to fire 30 people again. I'd rather run lean and pay overtime for a while than hire someone I may have to fire later on. Even though this is more expensive, and some jobs don't get done, I don't want to go back to that terrible experience.

Another manager used temporary term contracts so as to avoid hiring and then laying off permanent employees. In doing this, he also protected himself from the psychological difficulties he would experience if he were again required to terminate permanent employees:

> We need to put extreme care in how we hire people. As a larger corporation, we attract higher lines of people. It's not about the money, because ForestCo is not the top payer in the industry, but more in terms of work output. I'm very reluctant to increase my headcount, and I handle expansion through contract employees. Staffing is much more conservative now.

Managers reported that because of their experience with the previous recession, they were now less inclined to take risks associated with hiring employees:

> Because of the recession, I had to release people who'd been around for quite a while—people who should have been promoted. This was devastating for both the company and the individuals concerned.

> I won't hire unless I'm absolutely sure there is a place for them in the long term.

Employees were also cautious about accepting moves that could increase their vulnerability to layoffs. This phenomenon was particularly acute at the interface between the employment system for hourly employees and that for salaried supervisors, who were normally drawn from the ranks of experienced hourly workers.

> The resistance [on the part of hourly workers to apply for supervisory jobs] comes out of the scar tissue of the early '80s. Their hesitation comes from seeing so many people let go and the corporate guilt that comes with that. Hiring supervisors for relief work now is different than it was before the early '80s. People are very reluctant to move now.

Clearly, the experiences of the early 1980s conditioned the way managers viewed their approach to staffing. Few middle managers had the balanced perspective offered by one senior manager:

> A lot of our new hires just don't relate to the experience of the early 1980s. My major
> concern from that period was about who was not moving in the organization. Many people
> haven't gotten over that experience. It was a tough thing to do. It wasn't expected that
> ForestCo would terminate so many people. As a result of that experience, we've become
> more sensitive to our employees and have accepted the challenge to stay lean. This is a shared
> concern because nobody wants to have to throw people out the door again. But I do feel
> employees now understand the realities of our business and our role as global competitors.

Managers and their subordinates have tended to close ranks as a response to the
actions undertaken by the corporation to survive the devastating recession of the early
1980s. Although the overall quality of potential supervisors and managers has decreased,
few middle- and senior-level managers reacted by searching out superior candidates in
the ELM. Rather, a majority of managers reacted so as to protect both their remaining
subordinates, and themselves, from potential future threats. Rational evaluations of potential benefits from the use of either administrative appointments or the posting system
were themselves moderated by the personal values of the managers engaging in those
exercises. Again, there is evidence of conflict between the rational requirements of pursuit
of organizational objectives, the sentiments of local managers, and the conditions required
for maintaining the social system of ForestCo's organization.

The Effects of Regionalization on Staffing Practices

A more general feature of past organizational history and its impact on current
staffing practices at ForestCo was the reorganization implemented in 1982. The establishment of three integrated regional production units focused attention on the profitability of
each production division in the regions formed at that time. While this reorganization was
not as pervasive as the cutbacks in employment and did not have as great an impact, it
nevertheless reoriented the way managers thought about the interdependencies, and
therefore the personnel flows, within and between units. In particular, the reorganization
changed the boundaries within which local unit managers attempted to compute trade-
offs between unit objectives and those of wider organizational constellations:

> The effect of 1981–1982 has been that we've fallen into a regional rut. Prior to then, there
> was a fair amount of movement around the company. Since regionalization, people only care
> about their region.

Other managers worked within the boundaries of even smaller organizational units:

> Whenever possible, we try to staff from people available within the division.

Reasons offered for the focus on regional and divisional personnel varied. For example, some appeared to result from modest expressions of divisional self-interest:

> I get lots of calls from other managers asking me to "take this guy—help us." It's the way
> the division takes care of divisional needs and its people. This isn't pressure as such—more
> in the realm of suggestion.

Other managers adopted a local focus to their staffing because they believed the
orientations developed in other parts of the company, particularly those in other geographic locations, were not necessarily transferable to local operations:

> We've hired 20 people in the past year and are being much more selective than in the
> past. I have some concern about bringing in someone from the other side of the island, as I'm
> not sure the knowledge they've gained there will transfer to the local operation. I have a
> hunch there's less of a work ethic here—and consequently there's more pressure on our

supervisors than elsewhere. This is particularly true for logging operations. It's not unusual to get employees saying they won't do something because it isn't safe. This is a very tenuous judgment call—and local people are aware of our precedents on calls like this. There's no way a supervisor could learn the subtleties from outside the local situation.

Finally, some supervisors and managers believed that they had more accurate and reliable information on local candidates than on those coming from other parts of the company:

We talk about succession at the regional level and that provides an arena to find out information about potential candidates. If people are in the region, they're known. Outsiders are not known. Often, people try to get rid of their problem children by encouraging them to move into another region. However, we've got our own lines of communication to sister production lines in other regions. The idea is to call someone you respect to get good information.

These effects of regionalization are judged not to be overwhelming—and would no doubt exist as a general phenomenon no matter what organizational form had been adopted. Moreover, there was some evidence that some managers had recognized and were addressing the potentially negative consequences of a divisional and regional focus:

Last year, there were several good jobs that became available. When the staffing of those positions had been completed, there was some disillusionment that managers were favoring their own region. Now there's some sensitivity to this issue, and we're trying to search more widely for suitable candidates.

The picture emerging from this description of ForestCo's staffing practices is that of a complex social system, as appreciated from an open-system perspective. The experience of the intense recession in the early 1980s led to a reorganization that changed the real and apparent interdependencies within the organizational system. As immediate and longer-term consequences of the reorganization were judged to be not entirely aligned with current objectives, modifications to policies were being sought. This search is clearly consistent with a view of ForestCo as an adaptive social system that is interdependent with the context in which it is situated.

While open-system models of organizations provide a critical and necessary perspective on ForestCo's managerial values and orientations toward staffing at the time of our study, rational and natural models also provided complementary and overlapping perspectives. There is at present no fixed model of staffing, although customary practice continues to reinforce traditions that are increasingly being questioned in today's competitive environment. As discussed in the sections that follow, there is a rather awkward overlap between different models of staffing, the selection of selection systems, and appreciations of the three background perspectives of organizational functioning: closed-, natural-, and open-system models.

CHOICE OF SELECTION SYSTEMS

Embedded in perspectives on organizations are established views on organizational selection and staffing. Snow and Snell (1993) have recently described three conceptual models of the staffing process that, in their view, approximate the past, present, and future of staffing practices in business organizations. The constellation of assumptions and perspectives they label Model I represents a traditional, historical focus on staffing, which considers individual employees being chosen to perform individual jobs. Snow and

Snell's Model II represents a more contemporary focus on organizational strategy, which integrates linkages between jobs, the organization as a whole, and their relationship to the business environment in which the organization competes. In Model II, there is less emphasis on current, individual jobs and their relation to current organizational objectives. Instead, candidates are chosen more for their general capacities to implement emerging organizational strategy than for their immediate fit with a specific job. Model III is "presently more theoretical than applied" (Snow & Snell, 1993, p. 449), but differs from the other two models in its assumption that competitive strategy originates from the interests of organizational participants rather than from the employment of organizational participants to implement a previously established strategy.

The background assumptions of both Model I and Model II underlying organizational staffing are derived from rational perspectives on organizations, as employee selection is presumed to be guided by formal organizational goals. These two models differ, however, in their definition of the selection situation. In Model I, organizational rationality is manifested in detailed specifications of individual jobs and the development of analytical procedures to match employees' attributes to the requirements of these jobs. These assumptions are similar to those associated with the strong vacancy assumption (Miner, 1987) noted above and discussed in detail in the Introduction to Chapter 3. The dependence of employee selection on formalized job specification leads Model I conceptualizations to be most compatible and consistent with stable, bureaucratic models of organizational rationality. Model II conceptualizations of staffing view employee selection as being subordinate to strategy implementation. Jobs are not considered to be independent entities, but are viewed more as organizational roles interdependent with those of other organizational participants and the current competitive situation. Implicitly, the Model II perspective contains assumptions more of the open-system type, in which staffing can be incorporated into the processes of organizational adaptation in the context of a changing environment. Model I also differs from Model II in the unit of analysis chosen as the selection criterion. Model I assumes that individual job performance can be measured validly and reliably, as each job performance maps aggregationally and rationally onto organizational performance. Model II assumes that organizational performance can be measured validly and reliably, but that several combinations of job performances rather than a unique set of job performances can produce desired levels of organizational performance.

Model III differs from both Model I and Model II in that it assumes an emergent quality to the competitive strategy of the organization for which staffing is being considered. In Models I and II, competitive strategy is presumed as a given that organizational participants are required to accept. In Model III, competitive strategy emerges from interactions between features of a changing competitive environment and the talents and capacities of key employees. Staffing criteria are therefore not constrained to the detailed requirements of a stable job, as in Model I, or to the requirements of a relatively stable strategy, as in Model II. Instead, staffing criteria in Model III place much greater emphasis on appreciations of candidates' broad skills, which can be deployed flexibly and rapidly as strategies are developed and pursued opportunistically. In Model III formulations, candidate selection and strategy development processes are recursive and interdependent. Candidates are hired or promoted to develop and implement strategies that are not necessarily established before the candidates are hired or promoted! Thus, Model III fails to satisfy the local microprescriptions of rationality inherent in the closed-system Model I, but can be interpreted as rational in the context of more open-system, environmentally adaptive characterizations of organizational functioning.

At the heart of the concept of an ILM is a tension between the selection and assignment of employees to jobs through competitive market dynamics and their selection and assignment through an administered, bureaucratic process (Doeringer & Piore, 1971). ILM models derived from unionized industrial employment systems are those in which a nondiscretionary application of bureaucratic rules, such as seniority, determines which employees are considered for more skilled and better-paying jobs. In many contemporary ILMs, however, particularly those characteristic of salaried employment systems, there are either few rules regarding the selection and assignment of employees to particular jobs or flexible interpretations of the administrative rules that may exist. When there is opportunity to exercise discretion, managers can choose to emphasize either administrative rules or competitive, market-based procedures for selecting employees for organizational positions.

An examination of the potential tension between competitive, market-based procedures and administrative rules is problematic, as there is no unequivocal assessment of the extent to which adherence to one "polar" perspective necessarily inhibits pursuit of the other. For example, competitive, market-based assignments are typically determined through administrative procedures designed to identify and evaluate a selected sample of suitable candidates. Therefore, the potential tension is not between market mechanisms and administrative rules, but between the consequences inferred from following the execution of two different sets of administrative procedures or actions. Administrative actions intended to produce competitive, market-based consequences can be considered to be intentionally designed to make explicit comparisons between potential candidates. Purely administrative rule-based actions can be considered to be preformed decisions prescribed by standard operating procedures (SOPs) (e.g., promoting the person next in the line of progression) or decisions based on localized managerial judgments.

In the latter scenario, it is often assumed that the person selected through SOPs would have been the same person who would have been selected through a competitive process had one actually been activated. Under this assumption, the economic advantage of the SOPs is that they save the time and energy associated with the explicitly competitive selection process. The risk associated with utilization of such administrative rules, of course, is that the person selected may not necessarily be the one who would have been chosen if a market based, competitive process had been followed.

Normatively, both competitive and administrative procedures are intended to implement an economically rational model of organizations. As a means of exploring this feature of ILMs, let us first consider the neoclassical economic model for labor in firms. Individuals and employers are presumed to be economically rational and to act in their own self-interests. Variations in the supply and demand for labor are reflected in price adjustments that lead to changes in wage and salary levels. Wages and salaries reflect, though probably not perfectly, the relative value of employees' contributions to the organization. Thus, as employees develop scarce and increasingly valuable skills, they receive increases in salary that are more or less appropriate to their new duties and responsibilities. The great attraction of this model in appreciating the internal labor dynamics of firms is that if firms had ILMs such as these, they would produce employee assignments that closely approximate those that are the most economically efficient. Economic efficiency, in turn, contributes positively to the firm's capacity to survive in a competitive marketplace. Increased chances of survival permit the development of improved and more valuable skills and careers and improve job security and reduce the risk of job loss.

The ideology of competition also has a positive value for natural views of organizational functioning. Because the social hierarchy typical of most organizations results in some employees being paid more than others, the legitimacy of the processes that produce unequal social outcomes is an important consideration. In North America, where the institutions and values of capitalism are pervasive, the increased wages and salaries of employees are often seen to be more legitimate when some employees have been assigned to higher-paying roles through a competitive process. From both rational and natural perspectives, competitive, market-driven arrangements therefore have the potential to be valued positively by employers and employees.

There are administrative limits, however, that preclude the wholesale application of competitive principles for the internal assignment of employees to positions within organizations. First, in the search for the best employee for any job that becomes vacant, usually only a few candidates are considered, for any wider search could be extraordinarily costly.

Second, a wholesale rationality encounters the cognitive limits on complex problem-solving (March & Simon, 1958). Typically, in the rational model of economic decision-making, candidates must be selected and assigned to vacant positions on the basis of an assessment of their likely present and future performance, along several dimensions (e.g., current work output, future work output, capacity to innovate and improve work productivity, capacity to maintain working relationships, capacity to implement the training and development of subordinates), both in those positions and in positions that may become vacant in the near future. While these assessments are not considered problematic within the context of a traditional model of staffing (Guion, 1993), the complexity and uncertainty associated with economic evaluations of different alternative assignments is usually much too great for rational computation. Consequently, managers rely on organizational customs (e.g., prior experience in a given position is regarded as prima facie evidence of suitability for other positions) and SOPs to help them make staffing choices.

A third feature of organizational staffing that influences the mode of search is that the firm and the employee alike sink substantial investments into their employment relationship. There is a substantial payoff to both the firm and the employee from on-the-job training, learning by doing, and general organizational experience, but these investments are generally not transferable to other firms. Employees with experience in the organization are generally regarded as being more valuable, as they are believed to possess the capacity to produce more than would a candidate with comparable skills brought in from the ELM. Thus, both firms and employees have vested interests in maintaining long-term employment relationships in which current employees often constitute the pool of candidates for vacant jobs. Searches are limited, then, to those current employees with experience, knowledge, and skills relevant to the job to be filled. The limits to the economic benefits of employee competition derive from economic assessments (i.e., costs) of the administrative procedures required to accomplish organizational competitions. ILM features such as limited ports of entry and lines of progression may therefore be viewed as rational responses to the administrative economics of operating organizations (Williamson, 1975).

Taken together, these features of organizational staffing indicate that while there are many potential economic advantages to operating competitive, market-driven ILMs, there are also many restrictions that limit implementation of such systems. These restrictions are reduced by the development of administrative rules, SOPs, and customs that represent expedient and approximate solutions to the economic problems of organizational staffing. Such administrative rules also serve other goals. For example, administrative rules permit and encourage the development of an internal organizational environment that limits uncertainty for both employers and employees. In more secure environments, supervisors can manage their units with increased confidence that their future plans are likely to encounter conditions more or less similar to those that they forecast. These plans are particularly important for assignments that represent investments in the training and development of their staff. Having the capacity to follow through on promises, intentions, and personal guarantees is an important part of a manager's ability to elicit the cooperation and support of his subordinates. Second, having SOPs available to deal with complex problems permits decisions to be made expeditiously. There are few delays in assigning qualified employees to unanticipated vacancies, and there are fewer interruptions in the work flows of departments. Administrative rules that support administrative efficiency may also support economic effectiveness. Administrative customs and rules also emerge to serve the social systems embedded in rational organizational arrangements.

As administrative rules limit the implementation of competitive, market-driven models of organizational staffing, economic restrictions also limit the potential outcomes of a purely administrative model of staffing. The core problem with staffing according to bureaucratic rules is that no set of rules can be sufficiently comprehensive to cover all likely exigencies and yet be sufficiently wieldy to be administratively efficient. As the general business environment is often unstable, many organizations are constantly adapting to changes in overall economic conditions, changes in products and markets, changes in technology, and changing legislation. In environments such as these, bureaucratic rules are usually very crude instruments for fine-tuning efficient administrative arrangements. For example, managers are rarely able to control voluntary quits, as employees often leave for what they believe are improved chances elsewhere. Given this circumstance, staffing plans predicated on organizational loyalty such as investments in training have no guaranteed realization. On a larger scale, line managers and human resource specialists may have to react to restrictions in promotion prospects caused by flattening hierarchies, demographic imbalances, and cutbacks. As such exigencies are encountered, purely administrative models of staffing, in which selection is based on bureaucratic rule, reveal built-in restrictions that limit their effectiveness.

The picture of organizational staffing that emerges is that neither of the polar extremes—a competitive, market-driven system or one dominated by administrative rules—is likely to work well. Most organizational staffing will represent a blend of both approaches. Increased influence will be given to one type of system or the other as a function of the circumstances that exist. These circumstances in turn will be those germane to each firm or organizational unit at the time the staffing action is being contemplated. Managers are not unaware of the benefits of market processes in general as a source of legitimacy for their actions. Market processes also bring benefits to the organization as a whole. Many managers are also acutely aware, however, that pursuit of organizational goals may at times limit their individual capacity to meet local objectives. The tension between these two perspectives—administrative vs. a competitive, market orientation—contributes to the view explored here that organizational staffing represents an interesting and contested domain for students of organizations.

Given these trade-offs and choices, it is not surprising that a significant feature of staffing in ForestCo's organization was the discretion available to each supervisor and manager to choose the process or procedure through which selection decisions could be made. Although different processes could produce the same selection decision, for the most part different staffing procedures were judged to produce different results—in terms of both the candidates considered and the person finally selected. Moreover, independent of substantive outcomes such as the candidate actually selected, different staffing procedures could also produce different consequences for the values and maintenance of ForestCo's organization. Thus, a significant feature of ForestCo's ILM concerned the choice of selection systems by the firm's managers. In the sections that follow, these aspects of ForestCo's ILM are examined in greater detail.

Internal Searches: Posting versus Administrative Appointments

In deciding how to staff vacant positions, ForestCo's managers could choose between two primary processes: an administered process in which the responsible manager selected the new appointee without recourse to a formal selection procedure and a posting process in which job vacancies were advertised, qualified candidates were invited to apply, and a formal, quasi-public, evaluation process was engaged to select the "best" of the qualified applicants.

The administrative process under the unit manager's direct and often private responsibility is consistent with a traditional managerial view of organizational functioning. While managers could follow administrative rules and SOPs in selecting candidates for vacant positions, the lack of opportunity for public scrutiny of the manager's decision rationale suggests that there are few guarantees that managers would invariably follow organizational prescriptions. On the other hand, posting processes manifestly exhibit a competitive, market-based ethos. These procedures encourage a wide dispersion of information regarding vacant positions, such as the salary grade associated with each of these positions and the minimal qualifications required of candidates. Posting also allows interested candidates to exercise their initiative and apply for vacant positions. Finally, in most posting exercises, selection among candidates is typically done in a quasipublic manner, with a panel composed of several managers being responsible for the selection decision. With information and responsibility shared among candidates and managers, the posting system is a significantly more open and public process than selection made through an administrative decision.

At ForestCo, the nominal staffing model specified in the company's policies and procedures is that of a posting system. However, exceptions to this pro forma posting process are also permitted within ForestCo's staffing policy. First, posting is not required for all vacancies above salary grade 14. Second, when a fully qualified successor has been previously identified in succession plans, that person can be appointed immediately and directly (see Fig. 2.3). Appointments, especially those that are promotions and that satisfy these criteria, implicitly follow a line of progression. The successful candidate's experience and performance at previous jobs is assumed to provide the background and training most likely to yield a high-performing employee in the position that is currently vacant.

When these two polar approaches to staffing—posting and administered appointments—are considered in finer detail, a more realistic appreciation of staffing emerges. As a mechanism for staffing vacant positions, posting nominally encourages "each employee…to seek out and realize individual career goals." However, supervisors and managers not unexpectedly have their own priorities and objectives, such as administrative efficiency and expediency, current and future unit performance, and their own self-interests to meet in staffing vacant positions. For example, when the review of a large number of candidate applications is likely to be time-consuming, managers might restrict the extent to which positions are posted. Also, as supervisors could have likely candidates in mind for vacant positions, they could encourage those candidates to apply. While employees nominally have an equal opportunity to apply for a vacant position for which they satisfy minimal requirements, some employees could be advantaged if their personalities, as well as their work capacities, were already known to, and possibly preferred by, the manager responsible for staffing the vacant position. In other cases, a manager could have in mind a fully qualified, preselected successor to replace a departing employee. However, as managers might occasionally wish to establish the suitability of their preselected candidate in the minds of other managers, including the staff professionals in Employee Relations, they could use posting procedures to confirm the legitimacy of a predetermined appointment.

Similar motives are even more likely to surface when posting is not used. Nominally, at least, the grounds for not posting are that there is a "qualified candidate" or a "fully qualified successor" available. An interesting question, then, is: What constitutes, and who determines, the qualifications of the identified successor? Managers may have been recently appointed to a particular division and not be familiar with the qualities of available candidates. Alternatively, they may have excellent knowledge of their immediate subordinates but not be fully familiar with the qualities of employees who are subordinates of other managers in other organizational subunits. Even though managers may choose not to use formal posting procedures, they could nevertheless search quite widely, though informally, for suitable candidates. In searches of this nature, employees would not necessarily be aware that they were being considered for a potential promotion.

The procedures used to staff positions can take several forms that mix and match attributes of both administrative and posting selection processes. For each approach to staffing, several variations are possible, depending on both the perceived and the actual attributes of the situation confronting the unit manager. Moreover, a simple classification of selection processes as either using posting or not would not necessarily capture the extent of the search undertaken for the most suitable candidates. For example, use of a posting procedure, which generally indicates an open search process, might incorporate a limited focus on only one or two "qualified" candidates, thus limiting the degree of competition for the position. Alternatively, posting might not be used, but there could be a substantial informal search for the best candidate by the responsible manager. Appointments resulting from such administered processes could in fact be quite competitive, but not necessarily be seen as such, as these processes would not be open to public scrutiny.

Within ForestCo, posting procedures were viewed as most closely emulating the requirement of competition for positions. However, posting also served several of the requirements of the organization as a natural social system. Managers who chose employees for vacant positions through a posting procedure, and the employees so chosen, could claim that the employees' new status had eventuated through the legitimate means of an open competition. This claim to legitimacy was extraordinarily important for several parties to the transaction. For the manager, the due process associated with the posting procedure supported any future claim that he had chosen the "best" person available. Such claims could be insurance for the manager's reputation should the appointee's future performance not meet general expectations. For appointees, the competitive dynamics of the posting procedure reinforced their confidence that they "deserved" the new position as they struggled with its demands. For coworkers, especially those who were also candidates for the vacant position, acknowledgment that another candidate had "won" the appointment through a relatively fair and open competition enabled them to accept and cooperate with the new appointee more readily.

Although there were several positive outcomes to the use of the posting procedure, there were also several perceived costs. First, the posting procedure took time to execute—often as much as three months or longer between notification of the original departure and the establishment of the new appointee in the vacated position. When work demands were high and unremitting, use of the lengthy posting process was seen as a luxury, when an administered staffing decision from the responsible manager could be made in two or three days. If the latter course was followed, there would be relatively little disruption in the coverage of positions necessary to obtain the unit's required output. A second potential cost of posting is that the procedure itself emphasizes a formal, more bureaucratic approach to staffing in which candidates are assessed against a formal statement of job duties and responsibilities. Many managers resisted this predisposition to formalize job definitions, as they were more concerned with adapting jobs to the capacities and qualities of the best person for the organizational unit. In doing this, ForestCo's managers adopted a position on organizational staffing somewhere between Model II and Model III of Snow and Snell (1993).

In addition, many managers wished to consider candidates for a succession of jobs, but did not always believe that the person most suited to the job currently vacant was necessarily the best person for jobs likely to become vacant in the medium-term future. For managers who were technical specialists, a further "cost" of the posting procedure was that it required them to use human relations skills such as interviewing and counseling. Several of these managers were unfamiliar with and unpracticed in these skills. Finally, posting was regarded as a "waste of time" in those situations in which the manager believed that he knew about all alternative candidates and that there was "an obvious choice" just waiting to be made.

Positive Functions of Posting

The preceding discussion has been presented from an overall perspective of assessing the contingencies associated with each staffing situation and then rationally choosing a suitable selection procedure. While such rational calculations were implicitly a part of much of the staffing system studied, individual managers also had prejudices and biases that predisposed them to use, or avoid, the posting system. As the following quotations indicate, different managers viewed posting quite positively for a variety of reasons. First, posting was viewed as a process that gave management an opportunity to widen their search for the best candidate. A widened search presumably provided access to better candidates than the limited searches normally associated with administrative appointments:

> Posting gives management an opportunity to potentially find a better candidate than the predetermined choices.

> We get better employees because we can look throughout the organization.

Second, the widened search prescribed by posting also implied that a broader cross-section of ideas, capacities, and experiences could be brought into the operation of the department with a vacant position. Posting therefore often facilitated the importation of new ideas:

> Posting helps cross-fertilization of ideas in the company.

Third, the posting process was supported because it informed employees about potential opportunities elsewhere in the corporation:

> People aren't aware of opportunities if there's no posting.

Fourth, the posting process allowed employees to advance their personal interests in being considered for different positions and different career directions. For many of ForestCo's managers, the requirement that subordinates had to work to demonstrate their interest in advancement was quite appropriate. Persistence in the face of adversity was regarded by many as a desirable managerial quality:

> Without posting, employees just wouldn't be able to indicate their interest in movement. As people go through the process, they have the opportunity to share themselves and to get their name out to different areas.

These four evaluations of posting are consistent with neoclassical economic models of organizational functioning. The scope of competition was increased when employees were enabled to advance their candidacy. Posting was also seen to fulfill requirements of natural models of organizations. For example, the active pursuit of advancement was judged to facilitate the development of employee loyalty and motivation, which in turn benefitted the organization:

> Posting supports expanding knowledge and possibly more loyalty. If we stopped posting, employees would lose an opportunity to grow and expand their knowledge. This would eventually impact on us, because when they're confined they become frustrated, and the organization would consequently pay.

For these reasons, several managers were strong supporters of the posting system and advocated its use widely throughout the corporation:

> Posting has very few drawbacks, and it would be a sad day if they ever terminated the process.

While individual managers had considerable opportunity to exercise choice in the staffing procedure to be used in each particular situation they confronted, many supervisors and managers were already strongly predisposed to the posting system. In contrast, a few managers expressed contrary predispositions. Most managers, however, were very much aware of their discretion in selecting a selection system and argued for a conditional implementation of different staffing practices.

Conditional Choices among Selection Systems

Although many managers saw virtues in the posting system, they also believed that posting was administratively inefficient. In addition, it could restrict their freedom in terms of fitting jobs and roles to the qualities of the person they wished to promote or hire. If there was someone already available in a line of progression, posting was regarded as being contrary to the self-sustaining system of the firm's ILM. Under these circumstances, posting could inhibit motivation and put local investments in employee training at risk. The time required to conclude a staffing process using the posting system was particularly bothersome:

> I like posting systems. It's important for employees to know what is open and why it's open. Generally I post. But I'm reluctant to post if there's someone in the mill who might fit. If there is, we usually take a look at each other and attempt to assess if that person is right for the position and the position right for the person. Sometimes, it's a matter of time management. It takes at least a month from opening to closing a competition. Also, if we're going to post, we must describe the position and the required qualifications real well.

> Posting is fair and democratic—but not always efficient. The time required to post can slow the process of hiring. However, you never know where an appropriate candidate can come from.

Again, both rational and natural models of organizational functioning were invoked by ForestCo's managers in arguing for posting. Rational concerns of efficiency and effectiveness, especially issues of delay, were used to consider alternative staffing procedures more favorably. However, managers also wished to maintain the positive functions of the organizational social system. They were unwilling to pursue rational objectives to their limit if doing so implied a substantial decrease in the positive natural, social features of the collectivity of the firm.

Evidence for similar dual considerations was manifested in other illustrations. For example, other managers pinpointed more directly the tension between managed lines of progression—in which the flow of employees' development could be controlled—and the uncertainties associated with more random, competitive draws of candidates from other divisions. As a system for employee development, posting was seen to cut both ways. The attraction of excellent candidates from other divisions also implied that a manager's own candidates might be raided by other divisions:

> We generally post positions. If you have a good succession plan, posting is the icing on the cake because you can confirm you've already got the best candidate in place. But posting can interfere with training for succession. Managers are inhibited from investing in employees who are likely to leave their division.

Different perspectives on the potential for conflict between posting and succession planning were raised by other managers. Several argued that posting should be used truly for selection purposes and not to confirm an already selected candidate. While processes of validation and affirmation rather than selection could help the preselected candidate, these "false" representations would lessen the overall legitimacy of a valuable organizational procedure. Managers who attempted merely to ratify their preselection wanted support for the candidate of their choice without running the risk of exposing that candidate to a competitive scrutiny by the manager's peers:

> Posting is fine except where there is a succession plan. We shouldn't be locked into posting if there is a natural successor for the job. If we post, and the successor gets the job anyway, it just creates cynicism. On the other hand, successors get turned off if they don't get the next assumed position in the progression. The manager should decide if a position gets posted or not. If you're not seriously looking for someone, don't put people through the ropes.

> It's only right to post if there are realistic candidates in the organization. Otherwise, posting just creates damage to morale and creates false hopes.

Posting was also not without its further drawbacks. Posting necessarily required a more formal specification of job roles and job requirements than did administered selection decisions. As a bureaucratic procedure, the posting process had the potential to increase the degree to which position definitions were formalized:

> It's also real important to pay attention as to how the position is described in the posting. It's very important to state clearly what you want and what the work really is.

Increased formalization could marginally restrict the opportunity to redefine a job to suit the skills and capacities of a particular candidate. Here, the pull of conflicting perspectives is more between Snow and Snell's Models I and II. Traditional, stable, and more bureaucratic views of organizational staffing are challenged by contemporary requirements for flexibility and adaptation.

For these reasons, most managers employed a conditional approach to their use of the posting process. Senior positions in particular were generally regarded as not providing an appropriate opportunity to benefit from posting, because these job definitions were more dependent on candidate characteristics than were those at lower levels of the organization's hierarchy. Posting, with its emphasis on rational, bureaucratic, job-based approaches to staffing, was judged to be less suitable when position definitions were secondary to the capacities of the persons charged with developing and implementing corporate strategy:

> I'm a real strong advocate of the posting system. I believe everything should be posted—
> with the possible exception of senior management positions.

Still other managers questioned the quality of candidates uncovered by the posting process. In their view, a well-organized ILM with well-managed lines of progression would produce few if any candidates who would benefit from appointments outside these lines of progression. Therefore, if a manager was reduced to posting to find superior candidates, those who responded to postings could have unrealistic expectations regarding their suitability for advancement:

> I value posting, but I doubt it provides a unilateral ability to make the right choice. It
> tends to bring forward all the ambitious players.

More generally, the decision to post or not to post occurred as a consequence of corporate policies and the exigencies that applied in each staffing situation. ForestCo's managers exhibited little ideology in their attachment to either rational or natural models of their organization. Their evaluations of contingencies associated with use of one staffing procedure or another were often local and pragmatic:

> When we get a vacancy, we usually call around, based on "mechanical" criteria, and ask
> people in other divisions or in the industry to find out who's around. Posting depends on the
> urgency to fill the position and whether or not there's someone already available for the
> position. Here we must post if the position is under group 9. We don't post the highest
> superintendent positions because there's a smaller field to pick from and the candidates are
> known.

Nevertheless, in more instances than not, it was presumed that administrative staffing decisions could be made most easily, and the decision to use posting was often a residual. That is, posting was used when other methods of staffing positions were judged to be unsuitable. Administrative expediency, based on local rationality, tended to dominate the criteria used to select one staffing procedure over another. When local searches failed to produce a satisfactory candidate, the envelope circumscribing both the search and the "rationality" of the staffing consideration would be enlarged:

> We considered if there was a person on-site who was ready for the position as a
> consequence of relief assignments. There was a potential candidate—but he was unsuitable.
> Therefore, we initiated the posting process and looked outside the division.

Because of different local conditions in different departments and divisions, traditions and customs that supported one staffing scheme or another became established in localized parts of the corporation. Some managers critical of the posting process provided persuasive, logical arguments as to why posting was not suitable for the conditions that applied in their particular organizational unit. For example, representatives of one unit argued that the size and geographic dispersion of subunits, combined with highly specialist knowledge requirements, meant that the ILMs of their division were best managed from a centralized source:

> Because of the nature of the U.S. organization, we hardly ever post positions there. First,
> there's a wide geographical dispersion of branch operations with wide functional splits in
> each branch. Second, the nature of product knowledge varies enormously from one product
> group to another. So, within each branch we have some small lines of progression which are

managed locally. But system-wide, overall direction comes from a small executive team that is very knowledgeable about everyone in the system. They make the decisions.

Other criticisms of the posting system derived from perceptions of biases built into the posting procedures themselves. Because it was difficult to assess future performance with great confidence, some managers preferred to take candidates who were known quantities. At times, this preference for local, better-known candidates could conflict with organizational priorities to open vacant positions to applications from previously hired, permanent employees. The self-interests of local managers were not always the same as those of the specialists from Employee Relations, who were more interested in the maintenance of the larger rational, and natural, social systems:

> Even when positions are posted, it's the "better knowns" who get the jobs. The system would work better if we could post within and have more freedom to go outside the organization when we're not satisfied with what's inside. I wasted a lot of time, energy, and money because I had to post the position and go through the whole process to hire someone who was less than [a temporary employee] I already had.

Finally, some managers viewed the posting process as an infringement on their "right" as individual managers to select and appoint subordinates as they saw fit. As the following quotation indicates, one manager resented the restrictions associated with procedures designed to serve organization-wide needs, namely, the requirement that he use the posting process, and indicated that he intended to appoint whomever he wanted no matter what the results of the posting process indicated!

> Posting is often a pain in the ass. You feel you have to interview all candidates even though you already know who and what you want. Posting is ideal for new jobs, but for old jobs we usually know who's available. Posting doesn't take care of the real candidate. The fact is, you get who you want so why go through the exercise, because it looks fixed and not everyone gets a shot at feeling good.

Such perceptions were in the minority, however. Most managers saw both positive and potentially negative consequences resulting from noncontingent uses of the posting system.

Both rational- and natural-system perspectives on organizations pervade the thinking of ForestCo's managers as they consider what to do when confronted with a vacant position. Even if only one philosophy, such as a rational perspective, dominated the manner in which ForestCo's managers framed their selection decisions, such uniformity would not necessarily provide them with unequivocal decision criteria. Personal managerial objectives could conflict with the objectives of the local organizational unit, and both could conflict with the objectives associated with larger organizational units or even those of the firm as a whole. In addition, choices of staffing procedures that addressed concerns of efficiency and urgency could be different from those that addressed effectiveness. Complicating these choices even more, however, were considerations associated with maintenance of the organization as a social system. Issues of incentives, motivation, commitment, and legitimacy appeared to be associated very strongly with staffing activities. While rational and natural models of ForestCo's organization produced similar or compatible guides to action on some occasions, they did not always do so. Often, analyses and appreciations of choices among staffing practices and procedures based on either rational or natural assumptions pointed to different action recommendations. Neither philosophy, rational or natural, dominated. What emerged at any particular staffing choice was therefore the result of an amalgam of assessments influenced largely by each manager's definition of his or her local situation.

Standards of Performance and Searching Outside the Firm's Internal Labor Market

While approximately three quarters of all of ForestCo's appointments involved the reassignment of existing employees, the remainder consisted of direct hires from the ELM. There would normally be appointments from the ELM for entry-level positions and for jobs requiring skills and capacities not regularly developed within the organization. Thus, jobs requiring specialist professional and scientific knowledge but little organizational experience would more likely than not be staffed by means of outside appointments. Also, jobs that required basic, standard skills that would be similar across many different organizations would also be filled from the ELM. However, these positions would not be the only ones filled by hires from the ELM. From time to time, managers might not find internal candidates with the required skills and capacities for appointment to a vacant position. In such situations, managers would have to balance the potential advantages of an external appointment against the damage such an appointment might do to their maintenance of an existing line of progression. External appointments typically disrupted upward mobility along lines of progression and diminished the motivational functions of ILM operation. The closer such appointments were to traditional entry-level positions, the less disruption was likely to occur. However, making an external appointment at the more senior levels of a line of progression might cause many employees to miss out on the promotional experience normally associated with a series of moves along that line of progression.

In ForestCo, the procedures for making external hires were very similar to those for internal appointments. External hires could be obtained through the administrative decision of a single manager or through the competitive evaluation of candidates who responded to advertisements or the enticements of executive recruitment firms. Generally, external appointments tended to be more open and competitive. External appointment processes more frequently mirrored posting procedures than they did administrative processes. Administered appointment processes had little application to hires from the ELM as there was no built-in knowledge of candidates. It was usually necessary to follow more elaborate and detailed procedures, such as those incorporated in posting practices, in assessing the qualities of previously unknown candidates.

As ForestCo's managers had a choice of which staffing procedure to use when considering internal appointments, they could also choose whether to make or buy the next occupant of a vacant position. That is, managers could search either for a successful candidate already employed at ForestCo or for a candidate from the ELM. Guiding this search were considerations derived from both rational and natural models of organizations. The obvious fact that managers even considered hiring from the ELM could also be taken as evidence for an open-system perspective. Although most managers generally preferred candidates from inside the corporation, they were willing to search the ELM when no suitable candidate was found inside the firm. Initiation of external searches was dependent on assessments of internal conditions:

> I'm generally supportive of posting, as I do think it's appropriate first to try to advance ForestCo employees. It's sensible to draw possible candidates for higher jobs from those who are already employed here. We first move employees within the division and then either assign them or post on a broader base. If no one's available, that's when we go outside.

This perspective seemed to apply quite widely throughout the corporation. That is, when candidates from inside the corporation, whether accessed through administrative means or through the posting system, failed to measure up to the internal standards of the person responsible for the appointment, then a search of the ELM would be mounted.

While it is relatively easy to base a model of the choice between staffing from internal sources and staffing from external sources on known, valid standards of performance, it was often quite difficult to actually make choices. The judgment to stick with an internal appointment, when the manager was not certain that the internal candidate was satisfactory, could produce its own existential dilemma:

> He looked to be the best, but I doubted if he was ready to go outside. I decided to give him the benefit of the doubt and take the risk. I knew more about him than I would about any outsider. I have to take him at his word he'll do everything he can to make this move work out. It's a matter of basic trust.

The reasons that "the best of those available" might be found not to meet minimal standards could vary from appointment to appointment. Often, however, traditional sources of supply would be regarded as unsatisfactory when the manager of the organizational unit wished to implement a change in custom and practice:

> Four internal candidates applied for the position. I interviewed them all but wasn't comfortable with any of them for various reasons. Mainly, they lacked experience and I feared they couldn't handle the job. I couldn't see that any of them would make a difference.

The dilemma associated with the inside/outside staffing choice was compounded in that actions to appoint someone from outside the corporation had their own associated risks. In particular, the manager could incur the resentment of overlooked internal candidates and lose their loyalty, commitment, and motivation. In this illustration, natural-system issues associated with the sentiments and relationships between superior and subordinates dominated the appreciative framework of the manager responsible for the staffing action. In the simplified rational model of organizations based predominantly on economic exchanges, credibility and trust are unnecessary requirements. For many Forest-Co managers, however, such social considerations were critical requirements for the accomplishment of unit and organizational objectives:

> When I looked at the best of the internal candidates, I could see he was the wrong person. He couldn't do more than the technical aspects of the job. So, my message was loud and clear that as far as I was concerned, none of the internals was appropriate. By turning down internals, I didn't win any friends. This could affect my reputation and make my credibility suspect, as ninety percent of the time we fill positions with internal candidates.

As the majority of appointments were made from internal sources, with occasional appointments going to outside candidates, managers could assess internal candidates against the standards of the ELM. In the language of one manager, the best of the candidates in the ELM provided the baseline standard against which internal candidates should be assessed. Here, both rational- and open-system considerations influenced staffing choices. ForestCo's internal system of rewards, incentives, and performance requirements was framed by parallels to the employment systems present in its environment. If ForestCo fell behind competitors in providing attractive employment conditions, employees would leave for employment opportunities elsewhere. Public awareness of ForestCo's employment conditions was inferred from the company's success in attracting the best of those available in the ELM. The possibility that ForestCo's standards would drift out of line with market conditions was revealed through such benchmarking:

> We posted the position and also advertised in [the two local newspapers]. We wanted to know what was out in the field. Outsiders provide a baseline of the best that is out there compared to the best that is available inside.

Maintaining this balance between the efficiency of internal appointments, especially administered appointments, and the effectiveness of finding the best through external searches often led managers to pursue quite convoluted staffing procedures. Neverthe-less, occasional external appointments ensured that outside standards were part of the context for internal staffing arrangements:

> We posted internally and received five applications, but only one was suitable. So we advertised outside and received more than 100 applications from there. Eight of these were interviewed—and two deserved further consideration. We then reinterviewed the only suitable candidate from the internal posting plus the two outsiders, using a different panel. We wanted to make sure these candidates had baseline criteria, would be suitable to the division, and had future growth potential.

Within ForestCo, there appeared to be an assumption that if internal standards were not actively maintained through complicated, time-consuming, and expensive proce-dures, there would be a tendency for performance standards to drift slowly downward. This trend could be abruptly reversed when a new supervisor was appointed, as it was expected that newly appointed managers were more likely to change established staffing assignments:

> What typically happens is that when a new department head comes into a division, they evaluate what they inherit in terms of what they like or dislike, and prioritize what they're going to do. It's easier for people to accept change when there's a new boss. When they get comfortable with someone, and then after three or four years he wants to make a change, the typical response he's going to get is, "we've always done it this way."

But even new managers found it problematic to implement different standards. Part of the difficulty was that new managers inherited a history of performance reviews that had legitimized the previous standards in the formal records of an employee's history with the corporation:

> In my ten years with the company, performance appraisals are the thing that's handled least well. I've had to release people who'd been around for quite a while. When I looked at their performance reviews, they stated that these people should be promoted. But according to my standards, they weren't even close. This is devastating—both to the company and to the individual.

One of the reasons that organizations have difficulty with internal standards and struggle with the acceptability of internal candidates is that there is a natural inclination for managers to take the easy way out. Given the subjectivity of many standards of performance, managers preferred to give problem employees the benefit of the doubt regarding their current performance. In particular, given the contextual dependence of performance, there might still be a chance that an employee would perform better in another organizational situation. Consequently, some managers preferred to transfer problem employees elsewhere rather than fire them. Such reasoning is consistent with the rationality underlying Snow and Snell's Model II, in which personal qualities could be at least as important as, if not more important than, detailed job requirements in determining employee selection. It is also consistent with social-system requirements, as managers were reluctant to initiate actions that could threaten their subordinates' trust in their judgment.

> We do good succession—but we'd better be really committed to it or people will go nowhere. It's our job to ensure employees stay on track. We don't do a good job with reviews on an annual basis, as there's no way of enforcing performance standards. There are many factors which cause people to avoid making judgments about stuff that isn't clearly defined. Negative feedback is not done in writing because of questions in the system regarding human rights and fear of lawsuits. You have to watch out for people who try to transfer their performance problems.

Formal definitions of performance, and the degree of latitude granted to employees whose performance was below standard, varied with each local situation. Apparently, such standards were also influenced by the examples modeled by occupants of the executive suite:

> Culture regarding performance standards changes with economic times. [A senior executive] is tolerant, and so others follow his lead.

One of the other reasons that managers had difficulty with standards was that negative evaluations were a source of trouble for the supervisor. Many managers thought it best to let sleeping dogs lie. Provocation of loyal employees, even if their performance was questionable, could mean subsequent problems for the manager of that unit. The manager's ability to maintain his authority could be vitiated if his subordinates believed he was imposing "unrealistic" performance standards on them. In situations such as this, interpersonal conflict could escalate. Consequently, managers believed they could be "tarred with the trouble brush" if they failed to avoid conflict.

This was a tension to which practicing managers were not infrequently susceptible. While they often wished that they could increase the performance standards in their organizational unit, organizational customs and practices maintained an inertia that limited what was possible. One way of signaling the need to implement higher standards of performance without inducing overt resistance was to emphasize verbal rather than written appraisals. Even verbal appraisals, however, required managers to be extraordinarily skillful at assessing of persons and situations. Clearly, it was not easy to put negative, difficult-to-accept judgments in a context that encouraged improvement:

> It's a bitter pill to hear that you need to improve. Most people feel they're doing a great job unless they are told otherwise. Some people have been given verbal appraisals that are more truthful. In order to do a better job of performance appraisals, you have to know where the person can improve and talk in terms of improvement. The difficulty for most people is that it's a matter of framing the experience in terms of giving feedback.

A mechanical difficulty with maintaining standards at ForestCo was that employees or their immediate supervisor often moved before the employees had fully internalized the experience of their current position. Performance assessments were often postponed, not done, or based on incomplete progress along the learning curve of the new job. This is one side of the paradox of competitive, market-based systems of staffing. Demand–pull staffing systems, in which the posting of job vacancies initiates applications from employees, permit movement of employees before they have paid off local investments in their training. Such mobility occurs largely from the initiatives of the departments that post vacant positions and employees who propose their candidacy for those positions. The supervisors and managers who have invested in employee development, and who have borne the organizational costs of their training, have relatively little control over the exit of subordinates from their unit to another part of the organization. Again, notions of rationality associated with the maintenance of the overall organizational system could conflict with the self-interest or the local rationality of a unit manager:

> More than ever, there's a need for technical competence. People get their education and gain experience through their work. I'd like to have people spend more time at the same job. But, just as I get people to the point where they're paying for themselves, they move. This is not great for the division.

Yet despite this drawback, posting permitted a wider basis of competition than a heavy reliance on administrative appointments would allow. In turn, this wider competition helped maintain organization-wide performance standards. Thus, posting both encouraged and undercut performance standards.

Internal norms for appropriate performance standards were often taken to be as good as a manager could get. Even so, the advantage of going outside was that a manager could benchmark his internal performance norms against external standards:

> If you have a good succession plan, posting can be the icing on the cake. In terms of the people who respond to postings, often you're taking the best of a bad lot. Every so often, people come out of the woodwork and you get somebody who's excellent. We don't pay enough attention as to how people measure up against higher standards.

Several managers acknowledged that a generic problem/issue for them was the maintenance of appropriate performance standards—especially when organizational norms suggested that they should accept the best from among the internal candidates who were available. One partial solution was to ensure that their subordinate supervisors knew how to deal with "below-standard" employees.

> One question I ask everyone I'm considering for a vacant supervisory position is how a manager should deal with a below-standard employee. I'm looking for people's ability to create corrective procedures versus punishment.

A continual challenge for ForestCo's managers in their choice of staffing methods was their assessment of any gap that might occur between an internal candidate's likely performance and wider organizational standards. The size of the performance gap clearly varied as a function of two separate judgments: one concerning the candidate's likely performance and the second concerning the level of the normative standard. If a subordinate—one who was already working in an organizational unit—was judged to meet "normal" organizational standards, efficiency considerations of staffing would most frequently lead the supervisor to make an expeditious administrative appointment. However, if the supervisor judged that locally available subordinates were unlikely to meet required standards, or if the local manager had other reasons for posting positions, a wider but internal search, one using the posting system, would be initiated. External recruitment was used most often for entry-level positions and for other jobs for which a judgment had been made that internal candidates were unlikely to meet desired performance standards.

Thus, the choice of selection systems was characterized by a preoccupation with performance standards. When these standards could be met, administrative appointments were used. When they were questioned, and past experience indicated that suitable candidates could be found elsewhere in the organization, posting was used. When the candidates from these wider searches were known and judged to be lacking in some respects, external recruitment would be undertaken. Not all managerial decisions followed this pattern, but it appeared to be the implicit model followed within ForestCo's salaried staffing system.

In summary, managers select different procedures (and possibly different candidates as a consequence of using those different procedures) as a function of both their personal biases and the situational exigencies that apply during each staffing consideration. One way of viewing these considerations is from the perspective of an economically rational manager who is interested in both the pursuit of explicit objectives and the maintenance of the social system embedded in ForestCo's organization. Rational- and natural-system assumptions were used most frequently to provide rationales for the selection of selection systems. However, current values and assessments of choices available to managers considering staffing actions are solidly located in an open-system perspective, in which the organization is viewed as being previously and currently interdependent with its local environment.

SUMMARY

This chapter has examined the general contextual features that influenced staffing activities in ForestCo through the lenses of three conceptual perspectives on organizations and associated staffing philosophies. Each conceptual lens provided a different appreciation of the issues that should be considered in an examination of staffing. When organizations are viewed as *rational*, almost deterministic systems concerned with the accomplishment of specific, explicit objectives, staffing is reduced to the technical concerns of individual assessment. When organizations are viewed as *natural* systems, staffing issues widen to include concerns with organizational maintenance, including career development and individual motivation. When organizations are viewed as *open* systems, the dynamic interdependencies between organizations and their environments become the primary focus of attention. All three of these macroperspectives inform micropoints of view of the administrative procedures through which staffing is accomplished.

While rational and natural perspectives on organizations informed managerial debates and choices between staffing philosophies, open-system perspectives were judged to be of profound importance. The factors judged to have the greatest and most lasting impact on staffing issues in ForestCo's organization derived from changes in the larger economic environment. At the time of our investigation of ForestCo's ILM in the late 1980s, the most significant and specific contextual influence on staffing derived from the firm's experience with the recession of 1981–1982. This experience led to the implementation of personnel policies that continued to have effects seven and eight years later. In addition, the experience of the recession had a profound effect on the values that guided the choices manifested in staffing decisions. Many managers believed that their involvement in the extensive layoffs of the early 1980s had violated both their previous expectations and values and those of their subordinates. As a consequence, managers and supervisors tended to become more inward-looking in their search for candidates for vacant positions.

Managerial reactions to these experiences were partly driven by rational concerns to catch up on the training and development that had not been done in the middle of the decade. In addition, the layoffs and hiring restrictions associated with the survival tactics of the recession had a major impact on the demography of the organization. In the late 1980s, the full consequences of this changed demography were being felt as the "demographic bulge" in the age distribution approached the 55–65 retirement phase. Increased retirements, coupled with a shortage of skilled and experienced persons in the development pipeline, meant that managers were often short of skilled persons with the capacity to advance to key jobs.

The most powerful effect of the recession and the layoff experiences in the early 1980s was in terms of a lingering psychic guilt and pain. Many of the supervisors who survived what some had described as the "holocaust" of the recession believed that they had been co-opted into policies and actions that were inconsistent with their personal values as ForestCo managers. Collectively, there was a diminution in the degree of shared trust, which restricted the opportunity for further cooperative and collaborative relationships in the organization. Managers actively sought ways to limit any further deterioration in this shared trust, which they regarded as a crucial and necessary aspect of organizational life. There was therefore an active tension between managerial interests in maintenance of the organization as a social system and the necessity for change felt from open-system requirements for the organization to adapt to changing economic conditions.

In discovering and reporting on these significant contextual effects for staffing, we found evidence for substantial interactions between ILM phenomena conceptualized at the level of the whole organization and the individual staffing behaviors of ForestCo's managers. At the macrosystem level, ForestCo's dependence on its economic environment meant that it could not survive the world recession of the late 1970s and early 1980s without major internal change. The staffing policies subsequently developed and implemented to enhance corporate survival had a profound effect on the balance of employee stocks and flows and on managerial values in the latter part of the decade of the 1980s. As external conditions continued to change, however, the utility and suitability of earlier policies were increasingly questioned. Concerns that were originally conceptualized as necessary to the survival of the employment system produced changes in the microbehaviors of staffing actions that were being called into question almost a decade later for their detrimental effects on another aspect of system survival. The conceptual lens of ForestCo's ILM provides a useful, powerful, and longer-term perspective on the adaptability of organizations as multitiered social systems.

The conceptual frameworks provided by different models of staffing and organizational functioning were used to provide a preliminary appreciation of the philosophical and administrative choices available to ForestCo's supervisors and managers for their staffing of vacant positions. Actual staffing practices varied between two polar positions: competitive, market-based comparisons obtained through the use of a posting system and administrative decisions made under the authority of the manager responsible for staffing the vacant position. Examination of the reasons for the choices of staffing procedures made by ForestCo's managers and supervisors demonstrated a variety of individual philosophies and value systems. Rationales for the choices that were made illustrated frequent tensions and conflicts between competing philosophies. Posting procedures were seen to increase choices available to both managers and employees and to widen the range of opportunity within the corporate-wide employment system. However, posting could also interfere with the implementation of local rationality on the part of individual managers. Posting was seen to reduce the capacity of managers to manage lines of progression and to realize returns from investments made in training. In addition, exigencies associated with individual staffing situations also influenced the manner in which the staffing of individual positions was carried out. Overall, ForestCo's managers exhibited both rational- and natural-system orientations, with neither perspective being dominant. Indeed, there was at times an active tension between the two perspectives that was resolved through argumentation, bargaining, and organizational politics.

This chapter has presented an open-system perspective on organizational staffing, arguing that managerial predispositions and actual conditions influence the choice of selection systems. These choices have been presented primarily in terms of two polar positions: selection based on a locally administered process and selection based on use of a posting system. The next two chapters present further details of each choice. Chapter 8 presents an extended description and discussion of staffing as an administered process. Chapter 9 presents a similar treatment of staffing accomplished through the processes of organizational posting.

8

Staffing as an Administered Process

INTRODUCTION

As elaborated in Chapter 7, ForestCo's managers used two primary approaches to staffing: administered appointments and posting. In the posting procedure, the requirements of vacant positions were posted at various locations throughout the corporation and qualified candidates were invited to apply. Administered appointments were those that did not use posting. Typically, administered appointments were made by the manager immediately responsible and accountable for the performance of the person appointed to the vacant position. We argue that administered staffing was used primarily as a means of managing mobility along lines of progression, especially when the details of both vacant jobs and candidates were relatively well known.

Within ForestCo, there was a discrepancy between normative prescriptions and actual behavior regarding staffing processes. The normative staffing model implicit in ForestCo's formal policies and procedures (as stated in Figs. 2.2 and Table 2.3) is that of the posting system. In these formal policies, administered appointments are to be made only when posting is judged unsuitable. That is, ForestCo's managers and supervisors have discretion regarding which staffing method they may use depending on their evaluation of their situation. In particular, the posting of vacant positions should not extend beyond the immediate geographic area if relocation of employees would be particularly costly, and posting should not be used "where a fully qualified successor has been clearly identified in Region, Group or Department succession plans." Surprisingly, given posting as the pro forma staffing model, ForestCo's managers judged that exceptions to normative policy were justified more frequently than the ostensible routine occasions when the posting system was used. Approximately two thirds of the actual staffing decisions studied at ForestCo were not posted, but were made through some type of administrative appointment process. This chapter therefore examines administered staffing processes in some detail. The implicit rationale for the considerable use made of the administered appointment process is considered first, and the details of such staffing procedures are then described.

ADMINISTERED STAFFING AS UNCERTAINTY REDUCTION

A majority of ForestCo's managers cited several reasons for preferring administrative staffing appointments. Given the normative policy of posting vacancies, managers most often expressed preferences for administered appointments as reactions to the limitations of the posting process. In a positive vein, they saw posting as providing them with a wider choice in seeking to fill vacant positions, because it enabled them to look at candidates beyond the envelope of their usual corporate interactions. This widening of competition for vacant positions permitted cross-fertilization of ideas, as knowledge from one part of the organization was brought into other departments by interdepartmental transfers. Posting was also seen to provide a positive motivational climate, as it made employees aware of opportunities elsewhere and enabled them to nominate themselves as candidates for vacant positions.

Against these positive recommendations for use of the posting system were those that pointed out its limitations and therefore implicitly argued for a system of administered appointments. In providing these rationales, managers were not unaware that they were often arguing for their local interests as organizational agents against a corporate-wide policy. A prudent way of justifying extensive use of "exceptional" procedures was to couch them in terms of "safe" arguments. For example, posting procedures took time to execute, and administered appointments were therefore recommended if work demands were urgent. A second safe argument for not using posting derived from the legitimate exceptions when there were identified successors for vacant positions. Another limitation was seen to be that the posting system encouraged candidates to nominate themselves for vacant positions. Self-nomination, some managers argued, was consistent with ambition but not necessarily with competence. Also, the bureaucratic procedures associated with the administration of posting required the specifications of the posted job to be spelled out in great detail. In some departments, such job specifications were difficult to draw up, as reorganizations and job redesign were often under way. Finally, several managers argued that posting interfered with their management of lines of progression. Posting could reduce investments in training, as candidates could be attracted elsewhere before their training was complete or before they had paid back their dues to the department that trained them.

Overall, administrative appointment processes allowed managers greater control over the various exigencies associated with staffing. This increased control decreased the uncertainty that managers experienced with their jobs and enabled them to better meet their self-interest as managers. Managers argued that administered staffing enabled them to meet the interests of their subordinates and others with whom they were interdependent. By using administrative procedures, managers could actively maintain a hands-on approach to the management of the human resources under their direct responsibility.

In expressing this preference for administered appointments, ForestCo's managers exhibited a traditional approach to management—one quite consistent with their immersion in a traditional, mature industry. They believed that if they were to be held accountable for the performance of their units, they needed to control the resources that were to be used to obtain that performance. In their view, the most important of these resources were the capacities and working relationships of the employees under their authority. These managers were keenly aware that in most sectors of this industry, especially those producing standard wood-related products such as dimensional lumber, pulp, newsprint, and packaging, competition was based primarily on price and quality. It was their job to cut costs and to increase the value-added component of their output. These managers believed that they faced more than enough uncertainty in the price and demand fluctuations of their product markets in this cyclical industry. They therefore wished to control, insofar as reasonably possible, the additional but unanticipated uncertainties associated with their assignment and utilization of human resources.

For these managers, reduction of this uncertainty meant that they could anticipate and plan for future exigencies. They were aware of current and emerging changes in technology, changes in product markets, and so on, and understood that they often had little control over these factors. They believed, however, that they could exert greater control over the current and developing human resources in their units. In particular, they wished to develop the scarce skills and knowledge needed to maintain and operate their units in the future. They looked to manage an organizational system in which employees had the capacity to develop these needed skills and were also motivated to develop these abilities. In an idealistically simple world, one concerned solely with uncertainty reduction, these managers would have preferred to manage their organizational units free from outside disturbances. They realized that doing so was impossible and rarely desirable. They knew that their own career development and advancement would come from assignments in different divisions. They also knew that their units could benefit from the transfer of employees who had been trained and developed elsewhere. Therefore, their approach to staffing manifested the tension between certainty, with its associated lack of flexibility and innovation, and uncertainty, which limited their capacity to implement plans that helped them train, develop, and use key employees and their critical skills. While they accepted the requirements for innovation and change, and understood organizational requirements for flexibility, they nevertheless preferred organizational arrangements in which rational, logical plans could be developed for the accomplishment of unit and organizational objectives.

Within situations characterized by more or less uncertainty, managers and supervisors were mostly interested in using and developing the skills that they believed would be needed to operate their units in the short- and medium-term future. They believed that these skills were best obtained by assigning subordinates to positions in which their current capacities would contribute to current performance. But they also wished to challenge their subordinates so they would develop additional skills and capacities that would in turn contribute to future unit performance. Individual employees were also motivated to develop additional skills and to learn from on-the-job experiences, as they realized that their own self-interest and career advancement depended on their demonstrating these competencies. From the perspectives of many individual managers as well as some well-placed subordinates within ForestCo, administrative staffing systems that produced predictable matches of jobs and persons were preferred. Administrative appointments provided managers with an improved opportunity to expose employees to the development and training required for current and future skills. In addition, the managerial control associated with administered appointments gave managers and their subordinates increased confidence that their investments in work would result in future rewards.

Many salaried employees occupied roles in which they were both managers of subordinates and subordinates of other, more senior managers in the organizational hierarchy. Preferences for administered staffing arrangements were stronger when employees considered themselves as managers rather than subordinates. Administered staffing decisions provided employees in managerial roles with power and influence over subordinate careers.

Employees in subordinate roles, in contrast, often felt that their careers were constrained by administrative staffing arrangements. Their mobility was more dependent on the frequency of vacancies in their immediate organizational locale than on the larger number found in a wider organizational domain. In addition, their future mobility was also more dependent on the judgments of their immediate supervisors.

Administrative staffing increased local managerial control. As managers, employees enjoyed the consequent empowerment. As subordinates, they disliked the consequent dependency.

Jackall (1988) has written at length on corporate culture and has noted that the construct of "fealty," or personal obligation, often characterizes relationships between managers and their subordinates. ForestCo managers appeared to be no exception. Interpersonal relationships built up over a long-term career in this organization were extraordinarily important for the maintenance of cooperative relationships among networks of employees and managers. Actual favors, or even the appearance of favors, were important lubricants to social relations that enhanced managers' and their subordinates' shared trust. Dependable performance from subordinates assigned to key jobs, and dependable cooperation in political coalitions, were important commodities in the social and economic exchanges of this corporation. Among other outcomes, administered staffing arrangements yielded loyalty, fealty, and dependability, which helped to offset sources of corporate uncertainty.

Administered Appointments, Skill Development, and Employee Motivation

Against this background characterized by the need for dependable plans in the face of organizational uncertainty, ForestCo's managers attempted to balance the range of interests represented by the current and future performance of their unit, the needs and wishes of their subordinates, the requirements of other managers, and higher-level organizational objectives. Publicly, ForestCo's hands-on managers supported and encouraged two primary outcomes of internal labor market (ILM) operation: skill development resulting from employee mobility and the maintenance of employee motivation to develop and acquire the skills that would be needed in the future. These objectives represent a blend of rational- and natural-system perspectives. Skill development is a rational means of accomplishing overall organizational objectives. Arrangements that reinforce employee motivation are both rational means of accomplishing organizational objectives and social mechanisms that help maintain the social system of the organization:

> I look at what's best for both the organization and the individual concerned. We know the company is going to need skilled people in the future, and I'm responsible for providing opportunities from within the organization. People need something to look forward to. There's frustration for both the industry and the company if there's no movement, and stagnation if people and divisions lock themselves in. People work harder if there's somewhere to go.

> It's important to move people. They need training which should consist of exposure to different operations. It improves their promotability.

Many managers believed that the best way of meeting the motivation and training requirements of organizational functioning was to promote from within. Although the injunction to "promote from within" could be taken in the strict sense to mean that positions should be filled with ForestCo employees rather than from the external labor market (ELM), the expression was used primarily to indicate promotion from within an organizational unit or a line of progression. Implicitly, "promotion from within" meant that peers and subordinates with whom these managers had established positive relationships were to be favored with mobility. These managers were therefore predisposed to an administrative approach, rather than a market approach, to staffing, as they wished to promote colleagues and subordinates they knew from within their current units:

> Promotion from within is a strongly held value of mine. I try to develop an overall awareness of people around me so I have a better sense of what the organization needs. When it's time to replace people, I have a better sense of what kind of person would fit. Poor fit leads to poor efficiency.

> When the position became vacant, I checked to see if there was someone who was ready for this job as a result of doing relief there or in other types of relief work. It's important to promote from within.

Different managers interpreted "within" differently, as a function of their level in the organizational hierarchy and of other organizational identities. Although this construct was not investigated intensively, "within" appeared to be interpreted most frequently as including the organizational unit for which the supervisor or manager was directly responsible. Other staffing options, including wider searches outside, were considered only if no one was available from within the unit:

> I definitely consider my own staff first. It's only if no one is available that I go outside to look for candidates. Promotion from within is a personal and organizational value.

In discussing the cognitive frames through which they viewed staffing choices, ForestCo's managers often invoked the imagery of job ladders with specific people-moves as the primary means of meeting organizational objectives of skill development and employee motivation. They believed that skills required for the successful future operation of their organizational unit were best obtained by subordinates' learning as a result of being required to perform well in a succession of related jobs. In addition, they believed that the best indicator of having learned the required capacities was demonstrated performance in a similar or related job. Thus, lines of progression were an integral component of the way ForestCo's managers thought about the task of human resource management. Indeed, lines of progression were institutionalized in the rational decision frames applied to staffing decisions.

Because issues associated with the management of employee flows along lines of progression were often associated with administered staffing decisions, this important aspect of ForestCo's staffing system is examined in greater detail in the next section.

LINES OF PROGRESSION

A significant element of any model of ILM operation is the concept of a line of progression. As described in Chapter 1, lines of progression consist of clusters of jobs related by a hierarchy of skills and capacities, in which performance of lower-level jobs develops the skills required for higher-level jobs. Lower-level jobs usually require skills available from the ELM, and higher-level jobs require skills developed in performing lower-level jobs. As employees leave upper-level jobs through retirement, resignation, or movement to other lines of progression, there is employee mobility up the line of progression. Such mobility is often denominated a "career path," as it describes the various jobs or job categories through which employees could advance as a function of their record of experience and performance. The rules and procedures used to determine who moves along such lines of progression can vary considerably, as detailed in the first section of

Chapter 7. Nevertheless, the concept of a career path or a line of progression was an important background idea for the purposes of administrative staffing.

The concept of a line of progression served more than one function in ForestCo's organization. Lines of progression were rational, technical means of maintaining the complex arrangements of organizational roles. ForestCo's organization and a large number of arrays of organizational roles were presumed to exist for longer periods than the immediate career options of any one person. Organizational role interdependencies were viewed as being relatively stable even though different persons moved from role to role. The concept of a line of progression enabled managers to think about relatively stable organizational arrangements even as employees retired or quit and were replaced by promotions, transfers, and new hires. Ideas about lines of progression helped managers maintain the dynamic equilibrium of the organization. Incorporated in ideas regarding lines of progression were concepts of hierarchy. Ideas of career progression and advancement up the organizational hierarchy reinforced the existing social order because of their association with notions of earned status and reward. Ideas regarding lines of progression legitimized existing social arrangements with their hierarchies of power and authority (Jacques, 1990).

Approximately one third of all the staffing actions surveyed were considered to follow "the normal line of progression" in which managerial attention in selection processes focused on aspects of skill and career development. In these staffing actions, an appointment was seen as a transition from a prior accumulation of experience to a new beginning in the new job. These appointments often had a large material and symbolic significance for the person being appointed, as well as for others who participated in, and those who were observers of, this status passage in the corporate environment. Whether or not posting occurred, new appointments were generally regarded as outcomes of competitive contests for increased status and reward. As an ending to a prior phase in the mutual dependency between the appointee and the organization, the new appointment often represented a reward for having served well in the prior position and for having developed the additional skills and capacities that could be transferred to the new job. Moreover, previous task interdependencies and relationships between superiors and subordinates were invariably changed as a consequence of appointments of employees to different positions and roles. As beginnings, new appointments represented opportunities for further challenges, new experiences, and the development of additional skills and abilities that presumably would also lead to further rewards.

Formal, Well-Established Lines of Progression

Although the general outlines of such a human resource system were appreciated by almost all corporate participants, only a small proportion of all appointments occurred along well-defined lines of progression. Few managers were able to provide clear descriptions of an established line of progression that existed independently of the employees currently assigned to the different positions in the department or unit. On those occasions when a line of progression was described with assurance, it typically was in either a scientific or a technical area that relied upon specific knowledge and experience initially obtained and accredited outside ForestCo's organization.

Mobility along a line of progression can occur in two primary ways (Stewman, 1975). In the traditional bureaucratic model, a position or job precedes the assignment of an employee to that position. Typically, the hierarchical rank and the salary associated with the position are based on some assessment of the skill and responsibility requirements of the job. In these administrative systems, progression occurs as a vacancy chain process that proceeds down the hierarchy in a succession of promotions or transfers. Systems such as this are occasionally referred to as "pull" systems, as employees are pulled upward one after another through the hierarchy to fill the immediately senior vacancy.

An alternative "push" model of organizational mobility obtains within an organizational hierarchy in which the rank of a position is influenced by the qualities and capacities of the person occupying that position. In these systems, mobility occurs as a consequence of employees being given higher status or rank, frequently because they have developed additional skills, capacities, or qualifications. As the organization gives formal recognition to these developments, the person rises in rank and the position occupied by that person reflects that increase in status. Thus, mobility in these systems is "pushed" by the accumulation of skills by candidates in their previous and lower rank.

The definitional bases for lines of progression are different in pull and push systems of mobility. In the pull system, structural relationships between jobs define the line of progression independent of the attributes of each job occupant. In the push system, the line of progression is based primarily on individual attributes. In ForestCo, both conceptual schemes were used interdependently to establish the cognitive frames within which internal organizational mobility was understood. Within ForestCo's salaried employment system, the clearest descriptions of lines of progression, presented in Figure 8.1, were those that most closely resembled push models of organizational mobility. That is, a line of progression was defined most clearly when the steps along the line were defined more by attributes of the person than by the specific characteristics of the job that person held. The clearest definitions of lines of progression were presented by ForestCo's managers when the complications of actual jobs were distanced from the titles and ranks derived from employee characteristics. For example, the titles Programmer Analyst I, II, and III were informal ranks that corresponded to moves through different salary grades rather than different jobs. As far as an outsider could tell, a Programmer Analyst I with one year of experience had the same job title as, and performed tasks similar to those performed by, a Programmer Analyst III with three years of experience. In addition, it was difficult to distinguish between the projects assigned to one or the other. Informally, however, these differences in experience and rank were well recognized and understood—especially by those employed as Programmer Analysts.

Although the clear lines of progression for researchers, programmers, and technicians emphasized individual characteristics more than specific jobs, not all moves up the line of progression occurred independently of specific positions. Past practice was occasionally invoked to establish a precedent in which an appointment to a particular position was associated with a particular rank in the occupational line of progression. For example, the

Senior Research Associate	Senior Program Leader	Technologist
Research Associate	Senior Journeyman	Senior Research
Senior Research Chemist	Programmer	Technician
Research Chemist	Journeyman Programmer	Research Technician
Chemist	Programmer Analyst III	Technician II
	Programmer Analyst II	
	Programmer Analyst I	

Figure 8.1. Illustrations of clearly defined lines of progression. Read from bottom to top; each line of progression is independent of others.

first three moves up the line of progression for Programmer Analysts were nominally of one year in each grade, even though later moves to more senior positions followed a less formal timeline and were based more on demonstrated skill development and acquisition. However, the development of more general administrative and supervisory skills was not independent of the demands required of certain positions. Thus, some higher-level moves up this line of progression were partially influenced by the opportunities made available because certain positions became vacant. That is, a pull-type vacancy chain process was more influential at the senior levels of these lines of progression and partially displaced the push model used for lower ranks.

In occupations as these, an employee's status was not automatically determined by the grade of the position to which the employee was assigned. Employee rank and career status were therefore managed by senior specialist-managers in the occupational group. For example, the senior manager who looked after the careers and assignments of Programmer Analysts performed such a function. In managing mobility along this occupational line of progression, he indicated that he was "concerned about moving people too fast and setting a precedent of jumping too many grades in the period of a year." As a general rule, he tried to keep his staff in their jobs for a minimum of a year and noted that in career development, "patience is a virtue." Nevertheless, occasional circumstances indicated that a faster progression was justified for "those who demonstrated extraordinary performance and potential."

Such arrangements gave managers considerable power and control over subordinates. Employee progression, and associated development opportunities, were therefore quite dependent on the supervisor's judgment. In making these judgments, supervisors were required to balance criteria that derived from both rational and natural perspectives on organizations. They had to balance organizational requirements to "keep employee costs in line," to maintain an assignment system that both developed and utilized critical skills, and to provide sufficient incentives to retain employees with critical skills.

Quasi-Formal Lines of Progression

Less formal lines of progression than those illustrated in Figure 8.1 appeared to operate in various other areas of the organization. These lines of progression were also not associated with specific jobs, or even job titles and ranks, but were more general notions of customary moves that facilitated the development of the capacities that could be used in future assignments. For example, in labor relations:

> The _____ position at Head Office is designed for a young, bright person with potential. They come into Head Office after they've been in a similar position for three years or so in the mill. After they've had their Head Office stint, they go back to the mill having had the opportunity to broaden their views and experience and will hopefully be more effective in the trenches.

Similar general but not formal notions of initial lines of progression that would facilitate training also appeared to be held by managers in marketing and distribution:

> All sales people must do inside sales first before they can move up or out. If somebody is keen to get into sales, they get hired at the entry level, which is inside sales—but if at all possible they do time in the warehouse first.

> I usually have two trainees in the department who get exposure to all areas of marketing. It's only fair they should get the full spectrum so they can move upward in the organization. It's not predetermined as to when someone will move up, but when moves happen, they're the first to be considered.

And in the engineering field:

> The construction engineer position is like a finishing school for engineers. It requires more formal education with an emphasis on administration. They get road construction experience and then move to a more technical job that has less administration. Our intention is to develop people towards the position of divisional engineer.

Quasi-formal lines of progression such as these, rather than the more formal hierarchies that characterized the occupational structures of scientists and technicians, guided the thinking of managers as they considered the development and training needs of their staff. Within these quasi-formal occupational job structures, it was not uncommon for certain positions, often entry-level positions for professionally trained staff, to be used for developmental opportunities. Typically, an employee would be assigned to a generic position. From that base, the employee would then be assigned to various projects on an as-needed basis. In these training and development positions, the salary grade assigned to the position depended partially on the experience and capacities of the person assigned to that job. As the employee gained experience and developed additional skills, the classification of the job would be changed to reflect assessments of the value being produced by the person in the job.

This feature of organizational staffing was well recognized and institutionalized in the formal corporate staffing records and the compensation practices of the corporation. For example, the form used to record changes in employee pay and status notes at least two different reasons for salary rate change: "promotional increase resulting from movement to another position in a higher position group" and "promotional increase resulting from re-evaluation of present position to a higher position group." The former change is consistent with a traditional pull vacancy chain, in which an employee moves from one position to another that became vacant. However, the latter change in the classification of the person in the same job to a higher salary grade permitted managers to recognize and reward the accumulation of experience in that job without waiting for an appropriate vacancy to occur. By being enabled to elevate the status and reward received by a subordinate, but to do so without the need to change the subordinate's job assignment, managers could better control the flow of incentives and rewards to those subordinates who demonstrated superior performance in their initial job assignments. These moves, in which both the employee and the job were regraded, represented approximately 14% of all substantive moves that occurred in the corporation.

Implicit Lines of Progression

In ideal-type conceptualizations of ILM operation, a line of progression is typically job-based, as mobility is considered to occur from one job assignment to another in a relatively well-established sequence. In contrast, views of career development are based on the skills and capacities of employees. Management of an ILM or a human resource system requires an integration of these two perspectives on job mobility. At ForestCo, a striking feature of a majority of the moves contemplated by the managers was that they considered individual development explicitly against an implicit background of potential lines of progression. Individual employees were seen particularistically in sharp detail. Jobs were seen more vaguely and abstractly. Job functions became more specific, and developed more detailed outlines, when they were considered with a specific job occupant in mind. Vague and implicit lines of progression became more specific when considered for a particular employee as a particular manifestation of a generic pattern. Within

ForestCo, lines of progression were rarely considered independently of the employees who were being considered for future assignments. Most frequently, the need to fill a particular position, together with the development needs of the employees who were being considered, evoked potential lines of progression and development in the minds of managers considering possible appointments.

These general notions of lines of progression and succession typified the way For-estCo's managers conceptualized the task of staffing organizational positions. Thus, when managers were questioned as to what they did, and why they did what they did, vis-à-vis a specific appointment, their responses were often couched in terms of succession, groom-ing, and career development. But these concerns for development were framed by their appreciation of a context of organizational needs. As the following quotation illustrates, managers implicitly attempted to control both immediate and future staffing assignments in seeking to balance organizational (job) requirements and the individual (development) needs of employees:

> Formal succession plans are done in writing on a semiannual basis in this division. The senior managers get together, review existing personnel, and strategize what the needs of the organization will be, who best would fit those needs, and what needs to be done to upgrade the person so they will be ready when the opportunity comes.

This general approach was manifested most often in specific local situations. For example, there was a general expectation that an employee hired for a job in a sawmill would eventually move to a logging operation to round out his experience. However, the exact nature of the position to which a person would be assigned at a logging operation was not specified. The particulars of such a move would be worked out when a vacancy arose in a logging division and a specific candidate was being considered for assignment there:

> This is a training position. We'd expect that the person we hire here would move from the sawmill to logging to gain more experience.

Thus, general notions of career development and associated lines of progression were most often evidenced in specific plans for specific employees to meet the particular needs of the department for which a manager (or a colleague) had staffing responsibility:

> It was predetermined that _____ and _____ would be destined for those jobs. They were given the necessary training to get into those positions. Because they'd been trained, knew the systems, and know the different businesses, there's less chance of them being snowed by their employees.

If future events could not be guaranteed, contingent plans and possibilities were developed to give managers and their subordinates increased assurance that assignments and development opportunities would continue to arise:

> _____ went into [another manager on long-term disability]'s job in the old mill in order to gain experience. He's the acting superintendent. If the manager on LTD doesn't return, we'll keep _____ in production in order for him to get the operating experi-ence he needs.

These development plans often stretched well beyond immediate organizational needs. Career development was occasionally planned for several years into the future, even though there was no guarantee that such plans would necessarily be realized:

> _____ came as a trainee and eventually became a department foreman. He was interested in manufacturing and was given an opportunity to have on-line experience as a shift foreman, to get his feet wet in the mill, and to learn to understand the supervisors. He's

been preparing for this job [Processing Superintendent] for two years. He needs another four or five years' grooming and would then be considered for further succession.

Managers also talked about their specific plans for specific individuals in their own departments:

During this year, _____ will be groomed for my position and will help me get through the workload now pending. _____'s key task is to create and implement a five-year management plan for this function. He needs this year to develop a network of working relationships in the Region. We expect him to get close to the land and the people.

Given these prior considerations for development and future assignments, it is no surprise that when positions became vacant, managers preferred the control offered by administered appointments. They avoided the possibility that prior development work would be undercut by the less controllable, market-driven approach of the posting system. Moreover, administrative appointments, being appropriate in the context of the need to develop skills and capacities, typically produced even more administrative appointments. In the internal, managed logic of administered appointments, current appointments link realized past development experiences with the potential for future opportunities. If the system is to produce any reasonable set of credible expectations, future assignments are also likely to be biased toward administered appointments. The internal logic of an administrative system reinforces the close-linked determinacy of sequences of administrative appointments. Managerial motives to control career and skill development thus acted against the use of the market-oriented posting system of staffing.

Nevertheless, as was described in Chapter 7, posting also offered many potential benefits to the organizational system. Thus, there was an active tension between the two primary means used to staff organizational positions. While administrative appointments were more frequent than those made through the posting system, the viable alternative of posting constrained wider use of administrative appointments.

Limits to the use of administrative appointments were most evident when the knowledge and informational requirements for administered staffing could not be met. Administrative appointments generally require the person making the appointment to be familiar with the requirements of the job to be filled and the qualities of the person being assigned to the vacant position. In particular, administrative appointments implicitly require that the supervisor have the staffing authority to make judgments regarding the likely performance of the chosen appointee in comparison with the expectations of performance from other potential appointees. While comparisons against these background standards were rarely made explicitly in administered appointment processes, their presence was sufficient to lead supervisors to make administrative appointments when both jobs and candidates were relatively well known. In the sections that follow, the manner in which knowledge of jobs and candidates was obtained and the manner in which this knowledge influenced the use of administered appointments in the staffing process are examined in further detail.

KNOWLEDGE OF JOBS

In comparison to other business firms, ForestCo can be characterized appropriately as a relatively stable organization. ForestCo is a well-established firm that operates in a mature industry. In the past 20 years, there have been few major changes in either technology or markets faced by this firm. Such pressures for change as have been experienced have come from the general economic environment in the form of increased competition and from vocal environmentalist stakeholders who have challenged the legitimacy of ForestCo's traditional rights and methods of harvesting wood fiber. This general context, as modified by the recent history of the 1981–1982 recession described in Chapter 7, frames the following discussion of the factors that influenced how jobs were "known" for the purposes of administrative staffing.

Fine-Tuning of Organizational Roles

Many of ForestCo's managers were constantly on the lookout to fine-tune and adjust the ways in which their units were staffed and managed. A substantial proportion of the managers interviewed regarded vacancies as opportunities to reconsider, and to adjust, the task roles and assignment structures of their organizational units. One manager compared this phenomenon to the game of checkers or chess. In these games, pieces can be moved more readily in the middle and endgame, as there are more open spaces available to which pieces can be moved. As with checkers, there are more degrees of freedom in the assignment of employees to job functions when more than one position is vacant. Consequently, vacancies were often viewed as opportunities to reframe and modify the task roles associated with persons and positions in organizational units.

At the time of this study of ForestCo's ILM, there was continuing pressure to cut costs and manage production with fewer employees. Many managers were vigilant for opportunities to amalgamate positions and to improve organizational effectiveness and efficiency. They also looked to place their subordinates in positions that would both challenge their existing capacities and contribute to the development of increased personal capacity. It was clear, however, that in readjusting job functions and roles, ForestCo's managers used their knowledge of candidates, jobs, and candidates-in-jobs to find appropriate job assignments:

> Each time a position needs to be filled, the job description should be reevaluated. A vacancy is an opportunity to reorganize so that functions and available people make a fit. There's a tendency to fit the job to the person. The person needs to grow, so the job grows to accommodate the person. You can't fill the vacant position with just anybody—because the departing person had unique abilities which caused the job to change.

In redesigning job functions and roles, managers gave primary consideration to the capacities of available candidates. Jobs were regarded as more flexible and malleable than the personalities, skills, and capacities of employees:

> In order to survive, we have to manage increasing production with fewer people. Functions have to be amalgamated. Any time a position becomes vacant, the job description needs to be reevaluated. Because people lack flexibility and are limited in what they can do, we take advantage of opportunities to reevaluate what we're doing and to place people in places where they can expand their capacities.

The bureaucratic model in which jobs are considered to be relatively stable and employees are chosen to fit the requirements of established positions was representative of a minority of the staffing situations encountered in ForestCo. The content of specific jobs and the relationships among sets of jobs in an organizational unit were often regarded as temporary arrangements. These arrangements were considered to be part of an evolutionary dynamic that was in constant flux. In considering how to fine-tune organizational roles, managers attempted to integrate their appreciation of changes in technology, product markets, and organizational strategy with different arrangements of persons-in-jobs.

Person-in-job assignments were the primary elements in the calculus of staffing. Different configurations of these units, in turn, were used to assess the extent to which the interdependent objectives of local departmental goals and career development could be met.

Additional Jobs

Despite widespread recognition of the need to fine-tune the organization and to consolidate jobs so a smaller number of more skilled employees could meet the requirements of increased production, these actions were not always possible. Staffing had its own rhythms. Although most departments were downsizing, other departments were growing as new units replaced old. Also, selected functions grew in importance because of technological and strategic change:

> As the new mill got into regular production, and as the old function expanded to encompass all aspects of quality control, it became clear that _____ couldn't manage this expanded function alone. He couldn't keep up with the demand for his services, so a new position was created.

Often, a manager would need to build up his staff to cover the departure of very experienced subordinates. Thus, new jobs were often spun off from existing jobs or created from the overlapping functions previously attached to other jobs:

> _____, the General Superintendent, is retiring in two years. He's a Trojan worker and very experienced. Because we were concerned about succession, we created two positions—one to cover most of _____'s old job and a new position to cover Computer Maintenance.

New positions were also created as a function of changing technology that was often developed in response to new legislative requirements. New measurements of various consequences of operations, particularly fiber utilization rates or pollution indicators, became required as the general public, and the provincial government, placed ForestCo's operations under increased scrutiny:

> There's been a shift to different skill-sets to meet the needs of new production systems. We need technical information that responds to changing legislation. Every time the government passes some new legislation, we end up having to create a new position.

Both organizational fine-tuning and the introduction of new jobs to compensate for the loss of particularly skilled staff were regarded as manifestations of evolutionary change in the organizational affairs of ForestCo. This feature of organizational life was well captured by one manager:

> Reorganization can be evolution or revolution. People make jobs fit them, and therefore the organization is always changing to fit the people. We tend to hire for holes, but jobs are not rigidly defined. We're dealing with constant change. We have to manage so skills don't get stagnant.

It is clear from the foregoing discussion that ForestCo's staffing system rarely followed the detailed, atomistic rationality embedded in the Snow and Snell (1993) traditional Model I of staffing, in which jobs precede causally and temporally the selection of employees. Pervasive organizational change severely limited implementation of staffing systems in which individual employee selection was based on detailed specifications of stable jobs. The scope of considerations used to select candidates for positions extended well beyond the immediate job to be filled. Job definitions were often subordinate to employee capacities and abilities. Candidate requirements derived from immediate vacancies were often modified by anticipated requirements for further moves several years in the future.

Reorganizations

The need to respond to pressures for organizational change was often an essential precursor to the staffing actions and vacancy chains found at ForestCo. Approximately a quarter of the staffing actions and vacancy chains studied were associated in part with a reorganization of job duties and responsibilities. When such a reorganization happened, managers rarely had a complete appreciation of what sets of roles would be under their supervision and authority in the near-term future. In many of these instances, reorganizations were not temporary periods of change and uncertainty in a predominantly stable world, but ever-present attributes of organizational life:

> We've constantly been in a state of reorganization because the woodroom is being remanned and restructured.

Often, this state of affairs meant that managers had incomplete understanding of who would be working in the departments for which they were responsible. Under these conditions, specific, detailed planning of employee mobility along lines of progression was next to impossible:

> I can't tell you exactly who'll report to me when we've finished this because we're right in the middle of creating our new organization.

Staffing also occurred in situations of intense organizational change. Within the context of new equipment and technology, new persons in new roles had to develop new ways of working together. Revolutionary change was occasionally thrust upon ForestCo's managers, requiring them to reorganize most, if not all, of the jobs in the units under their control. Reorganizations that required multiple staffing decisions and assignments were often very complex staffing problems:

> This function has changed radically in the past 18 months. This is a whole new way of making lumber—and there are lots of people here in new jobs learning from on-the-job training on how to fit in the new technology.

Managers invariably had to shuffle people and positions when major reorganizations took place. General roles emerged from considerations of task demands. But the fine-tuning of who would do what, and the manner in which linkages and interdependencies would be established between these roles, was done by relying on detailed knowledge of candidates and their idiosyncrasies and capacities:

> This is a time of transition for the new mill. We're now in the process of shuffling superintendents to accommodate the changes. We had a meeting of department heads to discuss "here's who we have and here are the roles." The players fell into slots based on what they'd been doing in the previous organization.

So far, substantial evidence of the dynamism of everyday managerial life as it related to staffing has been presented. However, not all the managers interviewed were preoccupied with change. Several of the staffing actions studied involved the appointment of an employee to an existing position for which the duties and responsibilities were not changed. Change was so pervasive in some units, however, that it could not be ignored. In other units, a manager's responsiveness to externally imposed change was more open to that manager's discretion. Overall, both the actual amount of change and the managerial sensitivity to change appeared to directly influence each manager's choice of staffing procedures.

Managers who chose to ignore the possibilities of redistributions of tasks and responsibilities in the face of vacancies tended to regard vacancies as disturbances of a desired, stable status quo. These managers exhibited less interest in problematic aspects of human resource management. They regarded staffing as an application of standard operating procedures to replace, as well as possible, the skills and capacities of the person who had just left a position vacant.

In these stable situations, as well as in situations in which the local manager was sensitive to the phenomenon of change, knowledge of candidates was a critical factor in determining the fine-tuning of organizational roles.

KNOWLEDGE OF CANDIDATES

Managing mobility along lines of progression in salaried ILMs requires a relatively stable hierarchy of jobs and positions as well as a broad knowledge of potential candidates and their capacities to develop further knowledge and skills. For many of ForestCo's managers, candidate attributes and capacities were generally regarded as being more stable and dependable than the types of job likely to emerge in the medium-term future. Stable and enduring candidate capacities were therefore often regarded as the starting point, if not the primary attribute, in matching people and jobs. This approach to selection presents a modified view of the Snow and Snell (1993) model of strategic staffing described in Chapter 7. Because job requirements were often unstable, and the relationship between candidates and current and future strategies could not be specified precisely, the logical rationale required in selection processes gave much greater emphasis to enduring candidate characteristics than to immediate matches of job requirements and candidate skills.

In general, candidates were expected to have previously performed jobs that were similar, or related, to those to which they might be assigned. If a manager could demonstrate this relevance of experience, he could demonstrate in an immediate and practical way that he was not exposing himself, or the performance of his unit, to unnecessary risk. This capability is another feature of the tactics of uncertainty reduction presented at the beginning of this chapter as the predominant rationale for administered staffing decisions. The defensibility of administered staffing decisions depended on managers' being familiar with candidates and their records. In many cases, managers and supervisors were familiar with candidates because they had worked together in the past—though not necessarily in the department in question. These past associations meant that some candidates were advantaged in their competition for vacant positions, as their capacities and personalities were well known to the manager(s) making the selection decision. The following sections review the arrangements through which candidates became known to persons responsible for staffing positions through administrative, nonposting decision processes.

Prior Experience as Relief for Predecessor

Fitness for succession was often tested by assigning a potential successor to work temporarily in the position to which that person's assignment might be contemplated. This working as a relief was a relatively common occurrence at ForestCo, as potential successors often replaced their predecessors while those persons were temporarily away from their regular positions. Absences for vacations, temporary assignments elsewhere, and sick leave were often used opportunistically by managers and supervisors to see how well a potential replacement might function in a new role. Such a relief assignment permitted a manager to assess the degree of fit between the candidate and the position. When there was a history of previous assignments, managers were assured that their subsequent administered staffing selections would work out well and with little risk:

> _____ was not a risk because she'd done this job on several previous occasions on a relief basis.

When an employee had performed a prospective job, even if only for a short while, and no glaring problems had emerged, the choice of whom to appoint when that job subsequently became vacant was already established in the manager's mind. Indeed, the notion of a precedent no doubt also entered the minds of the subordinate who had done the relief work as well as others who had observed the trial assignment:

> Having been on vacation relief, it was an obvious choice that _____ should get the job if we were picking an insider.

The advantages of these trial jobs as a means of assessing the likely performance of a prospective appointee in a new position were several. The manager responsible could assess the capacities of the prospective appointee in the now vacant position with some degree of reliability. The candidate was also aware of the demands of the new job and presumably had already learned some of the requirements of that position. The performance of the candidate-in-job was also visible to other candidates and interested and affected coworkers. All in all, these arrangements signaled a prospective move and allowed negative evaluations to surface before the appointment was confirmed. Given these benefits, some managers initiated programs of job rotation as a systematic means of evaluating different people in various job assignments:

> _____ came from [another division] and was well known to people here. We have a rotational program for [occupational group] types we'd begun two years ago. As part of that process, _____ had liked us and we'd liked him. In fact, when he was here, he'd filled in for [the previous occupant of the vacant position] while he was away and fitted in very well. When the position became vacant, _____ was the logical candidate.

Indeed, opportunistic assignments occasionally worked out so well that they could become institutionalized into accepted lines of progression:

> I'm deliberately trying to build a particular culture here. I want aggressive, ambitious, and hard-working people. _____ had already demonstrated these qualities in her previous position. So there was a built-in bias for a program of internal development which resulted in _____ following what is becoming a well-established line of progression.

Even if temporary assignments were not undertaken as part of a systematic attempt to assess potential candidates in jobs, the demonstrated capacity to perform that occasionally emerged from happenstance assignments often helped temporary employees get permanent jobs:

> I'd hired _____ to do the job temporarily, while I interviewed other people. I didn't do an extensive search—but I did look and found no one who was as good as _____. So I offered her the job!

ForestCo's managers provided multiple illustrations that candidates who had previously worked on a temporary basis, perhaps as relief when the regular incumbent was away either for vacation or for health reasons, were clearly advantaged when being considered for permanent assignment to a vacant position:

> I like to deal with people I know and have seen operate. _____ had previously been a temporary in _____'s position and was the logical choice.

> _____ had been put in the position temporarily and had shown a desire to excel. He had some knowledge and was quickly learning what needed to be done. He'd done holiday replacement and had some training from [the manager of the unit]. He got the job!

Some managers were very aware that candidates often developed expectations of succession once they had done relief work. But the experience of relief work, independent of performance while temporarily in the job, was insufficient to convince these managers that experience alone guaranteed the subsequent selection of the temporary assignee. Nevertheless, there was often a strong presumption that relief employees were the logical candidates for succession:

> Even if there's a potential succession here, we still look around for possible candidates. It isn't good for people to feel there's no competition for vacant positions because they'll end up feeling there's no chance to ever get a higher position. However, we lose credibility if a successor doesn't get the job, especially if they're talented.

The option of making relief assignments or rotational assignments appeared to offer many benefits to managers concerned with the management of lines of progression. Temporary assignments permitted ready, valid evaluations of potential appointments. However, if these arrangements were not used as part of an overall program of competitive testing, but instead were used to affirm only one of several possible appointments, managerial autonomy could be lessened. Relief assignments also produced informational outcomes for employees. Employees found out in advance whether they liked the job or their potential coworkers in a department and developed some idea of how well they might perform the prospective job. However, employees could also develop unrealistic expectations regarding their prospects for future appointments, which could have demotivating potential if those expectations were not subsequently fulfilled.

Direct Contact

Other candidates could become well known to prospective supervisors even though they had not worked temporary relief assignments as a subordinate to the manager with staffing authority. Candidates with favorable reputations were viewed as likely to provide at least acceptable performance and to be less risky appointments. Known quantities were strongly preferred—even if potentially superior but riskier candidates might be obtained from the wider search associated with the posting process:

> _____ had been in the Region doing log quality control work. We'd had direct involvement with him. His appointment meant minimal risks on both sides because he was a known quantity.

> We selected _____ for the job because there was a lot of local knowledge of _____ as a worker here. Also, she had knowledge of pulp and paper operations—which was judged to be very important.

At times, a supervisor's personal knowledge of a candidate could be used as sufficient self-justification to dispel any qualms others might have about a prospective appointment:

> _____ was well known to me [the manager making the decision]. Those who had reservations were people who didn't know _____ well.

In citing this quotation, we emphasize the functions served by a strong affirmation such as this. The supervisor is able to allay his own dissonant apprehensiveness that the chosen candidate might be unsatisfactory in some respect. Strong affirmations also help create an organizational climate that protects chosen candidates from the doubts and reservations others might have about their competencies.

In summary, then, candidates were often known from prior work in the department or organizational unit to which they were to be assigned. In many instances, this knowledge was assignment-specific, as the prospective candidate had worked previously in the position for which he or she was being considered. In other instances, even if no job-specific information was available, selected candidates were still well known from direct, personal contact with the supervisor making the staffing decision.

Indirect Knowledge and Recommendations

Even if a candidate was not known to a prospective supervisor, a recommendation by a friend of the candidate—perhaps someone whom the supervisor also knew and respected—was often seen as providing trustworthy information about the prospective appointee's qualities. The potential advantages of social networking for access to jobs in ILMs appear to be considerable:

> Risks are minimized with recommendations. I feel free to look at potential candidates recommended to me. Friends of friends recommend people. I only look at them if they're highly recommended.

Recommendations from others appeared to be particularly important for hires from the ELM. Recommendations from persons regarded as having values and perspectives similar to those of the supervisor responsible for the proposed appointment were particularly helpful when there was less information available to assess the performance potential of candidates:

> Going outside is the toughest form of hiring. There's a larger scope of candidates, but nothing is really known about their capacities. You have to rely on gut instinct. Some of my best hires are people who've been recommended by someone who works in the organization—not a relative, but a friend.

Of course, when recommendations came from peers and colleagues who were also members of the panel of interviewers for the selection, they undoubtedly carried greater weight than recommendations from subordinates:

> Of all the people I recall we short-listed for that position, _____ stood out because of his experience [at another mill]. I didn't know anything about him, but [two other members of the panel interview team] knew him well. They both had a feel for who would fit the group, based on their personal knowledge of each candidate.

Clearly, supervisors shared information about candidates with other supervisors. This informal network of information and advice about prospective candidates did not operate across all departments of the organization, but tended to concentrate in localized areas in which a group of supervisors confronted similar problems and shared aspects of a common fate. Both within and among these networks of advice and recommendation, supervisors would recommend candidates to others who posted vacant positions. Similarly, they would let others know of upcoming vacancies in their departments and inquire about prospective candidates. Depending on the relationship between two supervisors, and their appreciation of mutual obligations, a recommendation could be free or unencumbered. For example, a recommendation could consist primarily of information, with no implicit or explicit obligation on the part of the recipient to accept the recommended candidate:

> When I've posted a position, I've had lots of experience of managers calling to promote someone to me. They say, "I just wanted you to know that this person is available for consideration." This is much more likely to happen when a supervisory position becomes vacant.

At other times, however, there could be an implicit obligation:

> _____ had mentioned [a candidate] to me. They'd met at professional functions. After talking with _____, I felt I should interview this person.

Informal recommendations were often made by supervisors who nominally acted to meet the development needs of their subordinates. As a corollary, supervisors would receive calls from employees in other parts of the organization who were familiar with candidates. These calls could be framed as calls designed to accomplish the further development of deserving candidates or as calls from "honest brokers" whose stated interest was the best possible matching of people and jobs:

> People often call on behalf of employees they feel need a move and ask us to take a look at them. Regional Office called on behalf of _____ because he had the criteria we'd listed in the job posting.

Supervisors also acknowledged that they themselves occasionally recommended their subordinates to other supervisors as a means of facilitating career development. They supported promotional moves for those of their subordinates who they felt were ready for a move elsewhere:

> _____ left us in September 1989. He'd been in his past division for eight years doing an excellent job and had lots of potential. I felt he could do more and encouraged him to broaden his scope. With my endorsement, he went to _____ and got a promotion.

Supervisors also made sure that employees who had previously been their subordinates were made aware of upcoming vacancies in their departments and encouraged them to apply for vacant positions that were posted. Prior subordinates were known qualities in that they had established knowledge, skills, and experience:

> I try to keep in touch with those who leave my department. I called _____ to tell her about the position I was going to post and to ask her if she would be applying. We all want to hire people who have the tools to do the job.

Even though senior managers might occasionally call other supervisors on behalf of their subordinates, the managers and supervisors who received these calls rarely acknowledged the existence of any personal pressure to go along with their boss's "recommendations." In ForestCo at least, local managers appeared to have considerable discretion in how they managed their patches. Moreover, most managers were well aware of the potential mixed motives behind a recommendation:

> Various people recommend others or offer their opinions regarding candidates for positions. I consider what they tell me, but I'm quite cautious in doing so because the motives of the individual doing the promoting aren't always clear.

When receiving a recommendation so strong that it sounded more like a marketing promotion, receivers of the information often tested to see whether the recommender was getting rid of damaged goods:

> Another thing that happens is that people call promoting their employees. If the caller isn't the applicant's present boss, I suspect the caller's motives. If the caller is just passing information, rather than actively promoting, I'm less suspicious.

In summary, managers seeking to staff vacant positions and candidates seeking positions are inextricably bound up in their prior histories. Direct personal knowledge of candidates, especially knowledge of candidates in job situations, was viewed as a particularly reliable indicator of future behavior. Many of the staffing and selection decisions in ForestCo's salaried employment system were intertwined with social processes and could not be resolved through immediate, technical procedures. Contextual factors dominated because direct knowledge of the work histories of candidates was often seen as the most valid and reliable guide to future performance. Moreover, because staffing decisions were frequently seen as extensions of past behavior into a future beyond the immediate vacancy for which candidates were being considered, stable, enduring candidate characteristics were often viewed as more reliable indicators than were technical matches between current individual attributes and immediate job requirements. Knowledge of candidates was often seen as both a necessary and sufficient condition for administered staffing processes. Managerial preferences for the increased control available through administered staffing led them to experiment with temporary, relief, rotational, and developmental assignments that provided them with information on potential candidates. Through both design and happenstance, these processes that functioned as precursors to the processes of selection often began long before vacancies occurred. Thus, these precursor processes provided information that advantaged known employees as potential candidates in administered staffing.

SUMMARY

Although posting processes are presented as the normative, implicitly preferred method of staffing in ForestCo's formal personnel procedures, administered staffing decisions in which managers made selections and appointments dominated actual practice, being used much more frequently than posting processes. Administered staffing processes were often considered to be the preferred means of making selections. In many instances, posting was employed only when administrative practices were judged to be inappropriate.

Managers often chose to use administered staffing decisions rather than posting processes [to select among potential candidates and to appoint subordinates to vacant positions] because these administrative processes provided them with greater certainty and control over staffing outcomes. By using administrative means, managers gained greater control over the mobility of their subordinates along lines of progression. By controlling these employee flows, managers were better able to obtain assignments that provided opportunities for subordinates to develop the skills and capacities required for future organizational performance. Managers were also able to demonstrate that they could deliver on organizational rewards of additional status and compensation. These demonstrations in turn helped each manager create and maintain an organizational climate supportive of subordinate motivation and managerial control. Together with the other outcomes just described, these factors produced local situations in the larger organization in which managers believed that they were able to maintain, and possibly improve, the performance of the organizational units for which they were responsible.

In exercising their discretion over different means of staffing vacant positions, and predominantly choosing administrative staffing over the nominally prescribed posting process, ForestCo's managers acted to increase their local influence and control over organizational relationships. While this increased control can be construed as a rational response to uncertainties that reduce the accomplishment of career development, an alternative interpretation is that ForestCo's managers acted to serve their own self-interest. Staffing lies at the heart of wider organizational processes through which status and financial rewards are distributed to employees in a collective, competitive game. By choosing administered staffing processes, managers had greater opportunity to increase the dependency of their subordinates on their superiors' goodwill. In such social systems, fealty or subordinate obligations to managers also provided each manager with increased influence and power. Both rational- and social-system models provide explanations for the dominance of the administrative means of staffing over that of the more competitive, market-based system of position posting.

Although managers most often presented rational interpretations consistent with bureaucratic models for their predominant use of administered procedures to select and staff organizational positions, their execution of these processes was rarely straightforward. In the salaried component of ForestCo's ILM, lines of progression were rarely seen to exist independently of the persons being considered for appointment. Although managers could articulate a small number of scientific and technical lines of progression that they were responsible for managing, paradoxically they defined these career ladders primarily by the qualities of the candidates they were considering, not by the jobs to which they were to be assigned. For these lines of progression, jobs mostly consisted of variable project work rather than regular responsibilities and stable roles. Even for those positions for which there was greater stability of job definitions, however, the unit of analysis used to assess the career development and organizational performance outcomes of potential assignments was that of persons-in-positions. Only in lower-level jobs in stable, managerially controlled units were conceptions of jobs considered separately from consequences considered to arise from particular persons in particular jobs.

This interpretation of staffing is strongly inconsistent with established models of employee selection based on rational, bureaucratic models of organizations. The predominant perspective of industrial/organizational psychology used to develop and study personnel psychology regards job specification as the causal and temporary antecedent of employee selection. Employees are assessed in terms of their knowledge, skills, abilities, and other attributes requisite to high levels of performance in a specific job. These selection criteria are derived from job assessments without regard for the employee who might be assigned to that job. The selection task is not necessarily easy to perform, but it is possible to develop procedures through which one can arrive at consistent, reliable, relative assessments of candidates.

However, when there are many more possible combinations of persons-in-positions (in which jobs are partially reframed as a function of who is considered to be in them), the calculus of employee selection and appointment becomes a nontrivial judgmental task. Instead of there being only one degree of freedom, namely, variability in employee characteristics, there are two sources of variability: the arrays of actual and potential jobs to be filled and the characteristics of candidates considered for assignment. Many administered appointments studied were reported as requiring quite complex judgments of different arrangements of persons and organizational positions. Mechanical methods of matching personal attributes to stable job requirements were regarded as being too simplistic for these subtle and complex requirements.

An interesting question that deserves further research concerns the manner in which reliable staffing and selection decisions can be made when they involve complex judgments such as these.

Administrative appointments requiring a match between a job and the chosen candidate require the supervisor making the appointment to have knowledge of both the requirements of the job to be filled and the qualities of candidates being considered for that job, as well as other contextual information that could qualify outcomes anticipated from different candidate–job pairings. A significant finding from this study was that even in this traditional and well-established firm in a mature industry, there was considerable job change. Jobs were continually being created and abandoned. Job definitions even for long-lasting jobs were often in flux. This phenomenon was partly attributable to the circumstance that many of ForestCo's managers were constantly reevaluating the organizational structures and arrangements of jobs in the organizational units for which they were responsible. Vacancies produced by the moves of employees to positions elsewhere in the organization, and vacancies produced by exits to the ELM, provided opportunities for managers to redesign organizational arrangements.

A second problem that also deserves further research, therefore, concerns the cognitive models that managers use to define new and different jobs. To this author at least, it is astonishing to find that the conceptual construct of a job is at the center of the phenomenology of corporate life, yet we apparently have no a priori theories of how concepts of particular jobs are created and defined.

Paradoxically for Snow and Snell's Model I of personnel selection, which is representative of the traditional selection paradigm used in industrial/organizational psychology, vacancies were both immediate precursors to selection decisions and the stimuli to change job definitions. Thus, the stable job requirements implicitly required for implementation of a traditional selection model were most often and most recently undercut by the appearance of vacancies—the phenomenon on which traditional models of personnel selection are most dependent. The limitation of traditional models of selection arises from their lack of consideration of other organizational processes related to organizational adaptation and change.

In ForestCo, the degree of change in the nature of jobs and task interdependencies therefore produced an organizational situation in which there were very few established, job-based lines of progression. A consequence that emerges from these features of administered staffing is that in managing lines of progression, ForestCo's managers emphasized individual characteristics and development needs against an implicit background of actual and potential organizational positions. Lines of progression were rarely seen as moves from one specific position to another. Instead, more general appreciations of types of move from one job class to another governed the ways in which ForestCo's managers arranged for the development of skills and capacities of particular employees. In this way, ForestCo's managers were able to avoid many of the logistical difficulties associated with obtaining a fixed pattern of assignments in a dynamic organizational environment. By adopting this general posture to organizational mobility, they were able to maintain considerable flexibility in the assignment of employees to key organizational positions.

Administered staffing decisions were used to meet requirements of both rational- and natural-system conceptualizations of ForestCo's organization. Rationally, administered staffing decisions were concomitants of the management of flows of employees along lines of progression. Lines of progression were rational means for the accomplishment of skill development and maintenance of employee motivation. From natural-system and institutional perspectives, lines of progression also served to reinforce the hierarchical and bureaucratic nature of ForestCo's organization. They legitimized the substantial power and control of managers over subordinates and supported a replication, if not an exaggeration, of external social rankings inside the organization.

Following this examination of administered staffing processes in ForestCo's organization, Chapter 9 presents a description and assessment of staffing accomplished through the posting process.

9

Organizational Staffing and the Posting Process

INTRODUCTION

The preface to Part III introduced ForestCo's internal labor market (ILM) from the perspective of staffing decisions and actions and in doing so presented three background models of organizational functioning. These three are the rational-, natural-, and open-system models (Scott, 1992), which provide different vantage points and sets of assumptions that can be used to frame interpretations of organizational activities. Rational models are consistent with perspectives that emphasize bureaucratic rationality. In these models, the individual job performance maps aggregationally onto overall organizational performance and the accomplishment of established organizational goals and objectives. Natural models are those that emphasize social system aspects of organizations. Maintenance of the social system of the organization is considered to be important in conjunction with issues such as individual motivation and maintenance of work group identities. Open-system models of organizations are those that consider organizations to be interdependent with their environments.

Overlapping these models is another set of descriptive and evaluative frames (Snow & Snell, 1993) through which one can assess different approaches to staffing actions and decisions. These frames were described more fully in Chapter 7. The first frame (Model I) represents a traditional, historical approach to staffing with its focus on individual jobs. This frame is consistent with rational, bureaucratic models of organizations and is usually viewed as being most consistent with the closed-system model of organizations, which assumes stable and established goals. The second frame (Model II), which shares characteristics with both the natural- and the open-system model, focuses less on jobs and more on persons, as employees are chosen not for specific jobs but rather for their general capacity to implement current and emerging corporate strategies in a dynamic, shifting environment. The third frame (Model III), noted briefly in Chapter 8, will not be discussed extensively here, as it presents more a potential future for staffing than an opportunity to contrast past and current perspectives on staffing.

In the presentation of posting that follows, posting processes are presented, paradoxically, as manifestations of Model I (i.e., job-dominated) forms of employee selection that in fact primarily address concerns associated with natural-system views of organizations. The linkage of Model I perspectives on employee selection and staffing with natural-system frames is unusual, as traditional emphases on individual jobs are usually seen as being derived from rational, closed-system perspectives on organizations. By the latter perspectives, the legitimacy of assignments obtained from selection processes is regarded as the primary outcome of the posting process. Such legitimacy is usually viewed as a by-product of the process through which one obtains rational, substantive outcomes (i.e., selection of suitable employees). I argue that the uncertainties experienced in making rational staffing decisions—such as the variability associated with alternative forms of organization, job definitions, staffing assignments, and role and performance inter-dependencies—all limit the attainment of specific, rational objectives. The aforementioned linkage thus implies that managers are more interested in developing robust assignments that have the capacity to meet a wide range of future performance exigencies. Managers therefore seek enduring administrative and social systems that are unlikely to fragment in the face of future challenges. When administrative and social arrangements are regarded as legitimate, there is less likelihood of system breakdown. The primary function fulfilled by posting procedures is the legitimation of the outcomes of various role assignments that result from application of socially accepted competitive selection processes.

There are several sources of social legitimacy associated with posting processes, other than specific, job-based criteria for selection. As noted in previous descriptions of For-estCo's staffing procedures, posting is a generic staffing process in which candidates apply and compete for appointment to vacant positions. Posting necessarily involves the use of administrative procedures, but these procedures are characteristically open rather than closed. The initiative to compete, and to be considered, for the vacant position lies with each employee/candidate who asks to be considered for an advertised vacancy, rather than with the supervisors and managers who make internal administrative appointments. In addition to offering increased openness of opportunity, appointments made through posting processes are also subject to greater scrutiny by other managers and professionals in Employee Relations. These characteristics—candidate initiation; relative openness of the competition and evaluation process; and participation by other managers, which limits the exercise of arbitrary authority by managers making selections—all increase the social legitimacy of outcomes obtained through the posting process.

Although only one third of the staffing actions studied at ForestCo used some variant of a posting process, these appointments, and the procedures that led up to them, had considerable value to the company. Appointments made through the posting process, as well as the ongoing vacancies advertised throughout the corporation, manifested an ethos of competition in the organization. The symbolic value of these competitive appointments helped maintain an institutionalized belief that advancement was based on relative merit and had to be earned. Appointments to positions of higher status and reward helped maintain a motivational climate in which employees at all levels actively or nominally strove to accomplish organizational objectives. Moreover, by striving to perform in the present, these employees developed the abilities and capacities that would permit them to compete for even more attractive and more highly remunerated appointments in the future.

This chapter presents a description of posting as these processes were implemented in ForestCo's organization. However, before both primary and secondary features of the posting process are discussed in greater detail, a stereotypical staffing appointment that used this procedure is first described for readers who are unfamiliar with posting systems.

A STEREOTYPICAL POSTING PROCESS

Typically, a vacant position is one that an incumbent has left or that has been newly created. If a reorganization or organizational fine-tuning is taking place, it is likely that the vacated position will not match exactly the position to be filled. In this case, a modification of a previous position or a new position would be targeted for staffing. Once the general features of the position to be filled have been determined, the person who would normally supervise the new appointee, perhaps with the advice of the manager of the unit in which the position is located, as well as with the advice from Employee Relations, would develop a more detailed description of the job and the minimum requirements desired of applicants for the position (Levine, 1983).

Details of jobs and applicant qualifications would be circulated to various parts of the corporation and publicly posted for two or more weeks on notice boards or computer bulletin boards (Moravec, 1990) reserved for that purpose. When employees in other parts of the corporation see these postings, they can decide for themselves whether they would be appropriate candidates and whether they wish to compete for the vacant position. Those who do submit their applications. As applications are received, or shortly after a reasonable number have been received, or after the deadline for receipt of applications has passed, the applications are reviewed. If a large number of applications have been received, they are screened and a shortlist of likely candidates is prepared.

The applications of short-listed candidates are usually reviewed in greater detail, candidates are invited to a selection interview, and their work references are checked. Selection interviews can be conducted one-on-one or by a panel of interviewers. Typically, if the interviewing is done by a panel, some preparation for and organization of the interview process is required. Following the interviews, further reference checks could be done, or the recommended candidate could be asked to meet with others for a further confirmatory interview, or both. If the recommended candidate continues to meet the generally understood requirements of the position, the appointment is offered to that candidate.

In ForestCo, the Employee Relations function managed the process through which positions were advertised throughout either some or all divisions of the corporation. Employee Relations also ensured that the form and content of advertised vacancies followed standard guidelines. In addition, Employee Relations managers often provided training and guidance on employee attributes and selection judgments to line managers who were ultimately responsible for the final appointment to the vacant position.

This overall review of the posting process is similar to that offered by one of our managerial respondents:

> We posted and interviewed those on our shortlist. Then we advertised outside the company and interviewed the shortlist of those we uncovered from that search. Interviewees were ranked according to their responses to standard questions related to job criteria. We used average scores developed on the basis of weightings attached to the questions we asked. We then sent our recommended candidate to our consultants for aptitude evaluation.

Like any stereotypical account, this description provides little insight into the subtleties of the process and few detailed explanations of the various issues confronted by managers and candidates as these processes unfold. This chapter therefore presents a fuller account of issues and preoccupations of managers who used the posting process to staff vacant positions at ForestCo.

THE FUNCTIONS OF THE POSTING PROCESS

While the posting process can be described and will be described as a specific method of eliciting candidates for a specific organizational position and then selecting from among them, the process itself also serves broader organizational purposes. Awareness of these functions shaped and conditioned the use of the posting process. The sections that follow explore these contextual factors and their impact on the use of the posting process to staff organizational positions.

Posting as Opportunity

Posting was viewed as the primary means of signaling and communicating the message that there were competitive opportunities for career advancement in ForestCo's organization. Competition was valued not only for its implications of efficient market allocations, but also for the legitimacy and "honesty" of assignments made through competitive mechanisms. In addition, posting was seen as informing all employees that higher-level positions were continually becoming vacant and that competition for those positions helped maintain a focused motivational climate within the organization:

> Posting is good. It creates an equal opportunity world in that all get a crack at opportunity—which I think is a fair way to go. Posting is also a good communication tool— it can give people a feel for what's happening in the organization. It keeps the labor market in the company honest and competitive.

In signaling equality of opportunity, the posting process was seen to fulfill several functions. For one, posting enabled ForestCo's employees to indicate their interest in being considered for advancement and to learn about opportunities in parts of the organization with which they were unfamiliar:

> Posting is good because people need to know about opportunities. Posting creates more choicefulness for the employee.

Posting also provided managers with information on a wider variety of candidates. Through posting, the ILM process developed a broader scope. Potential candidates learned about possible jobs, and managers wanting to staff jobs learned about a wider array of candidates:

> My general view of posting is that it offers an opportunity for us to identify and meet who is available in the organization that we're not already aware of.

Even managers who normally preferred to staff positions through administrative means could find some virtue in an occasional posting. Use of posting benchmarked the implicit standards of candidates already in the line of progression against those of candidates in other parts of the firm. Moreover, reviewing the ratings and recommendations received by other managers also helped managers develop a collective sense of corporate-wide standards:

> Posting allows you to check out your opinions of someone against a wide base of competitors. It also allows you to get some appreciation of how other managers evaluate their candidates.

In summary:

> Posting is excellent. It allows people to signal they're interested in movement. It allows managers to see candidates they otherwise wouldn't have any knowledge of—especially

> those from other Regions. It allows for open testing of candidates and also gives you a chance to see what a really good candidate looks like.

Thus, there are many apparent benefits to the posting process. However, few of ForestCo's managers made unreservedly positive comments about the benefits of the posting process. Posting was rarely seen as a straightforward process. Each manager who initiated a posting process was aware of costs associated with the use of this administrative procedure. Implementing the posting process incurred the expenditure of both time and energy. In addition, managers who accepted candidates as a result of the posting process also assumed a larger set of responsibilities and obligations associated with their choice of, and responsibility for, the new appointees.

Potential Drawbacks to the Widening of Opportunity

The most frequently cited drawback to the posting process is a corollary of one of the features that lead to its success, namely, that employees repeatedly applied for posted positions. While their doing so was generally desirable, it often caused problems when the managers responsible for the selection judged many of the repeat applicants to have inappropriate or insufficient skills. Consequently, these managers often regarded a review of repeat candidates as a waste of time. They believed that these repeated evaluations represented inappropriate use of their scarce and valuable time and in addition generated awkward interpersonal relationships. They also felt that repeated rejections of marginal candidates undercut their implicit claims that the system was fair and undid their efforts to build a robust and legitimate social system. Interestingly, these managers often blamed other supervisors for not previously having communicated to these candidates that they should not apply. Few of these managers acknowledged that one corollary of a competitive selection process was a surplus of candidates for available positions. Indeed, as the following quotation illustrates, some managers assigned responsibility for repeated applications by poor candidates to the Employee Relations function, which was seen as the primary advocate of the posting system:

> We keep getting repetitive applications from the same candidates in response to postings. Candidates don't get told in honest enough terms they're not suited for the job—so they keep applying. Posting pressures you into interviewing even those people who don't have a real shot at the job. Screening isn't as stringent as it should be. I want personnel to send me guys they think will really make it. Nobody likes to say "no"—as it has the potential to discourage applications, which in turn affects personnel standards.

> A significant drawback to the posting system is that jobs are opened to people who have no business applying.

This position contrasted with that of other managers who saw a positive purpose of posting as the encouraging of applications from potential candidates. Significantly, perhaps, this encouragement occurred at the interface between the hourly and salaried employment systems. Traditionally, hourly employees had little need to advance their candidacy for better positions because the seniority rule provided little discretion as to who would advance. However, when experienced hourly employees were the primary source of supply for salaried positions such as production supervisors, encouragement of "new" behavior was called for:

> We wanted to see every candidate who applied because we wanted to encourage them to present themselves for opportunities as they came along. We wanted to get the message out to all hourly people with different backgrounds that they could become staff.

If "unacceptable" candidates were told not to apply, the posting system would not be seen to be open. Instead, it would resemble the administered staffing system with its paternalistic, centralized control of candidacy for vacant positions. Inappropriate applications were part of the costs of administering a more open, competitive staffing system. A few managers recognized the requirements for maintaining a competitive posting system and accepted the administrative costs that came with the benefits obtained from a widening of opportunity:

> I don't have any problems with our posting system—but I do find there are a lot of games being played. The result is that a lot of time is wasted because a lot of people who don't really have sufficient qualifications apply for posted positions. But without posting, I wouldn't know who's available in other divisions. All in all, it's better to have the posting system because it gives people an opportunity to better themselves and makes visible those who're interested in advancement.

Managers were aware that in order to maintain the legitimacy of the posting system, the competition for positions had both to be fair and to be seen to be fair by the candidates involved. Most managers recognized that it was important to maintain the integrity of the posting system, even though they offered few unconditionally positive statements about the posting system.

Responsibilities, Requirements, and Obligations

Grumblings about "unqualified" candidates aside, the primary concern voiced by ForestCo's managers was that the administrative process of posting should not be used if the process was not truly competitive. The core concern was that all aspects of the posting process should not only be legitimate but also be seen to be legitimate. That is, an open process should produce an honestly arrived at outcome. There were two aspects to this voiced concern for organizational legitimacy. First, the competitive process should not be used to legitimate a predetermined outcome. If this was done, and then made public, one of the primary functions of the posting system for the organization as a whole would be destroyed. Second, the posting system should not be used to produce an outcome that would have resulted without the process. In sum, the process itself should be seen as legitimate:

> If we've already got the right people in the organization for the available position, we should promote from within. If you already know who you want for the position, don't go through a charade. We do that occasionally—and it bothers me and leaves a sour taste in people's mouths.

Use of the posting system thus implies a wide array of concomitant responsibilities to be assumed by the persons managing the posting process. Managers need to follow a disciplined approach to the posting process if there is not to be a wide distribution of negative effects, even small ones. With an accumulation of negative effects, the legitimacy of the entire staffing system, including the authority of senior management, could come into disrepute. Because so much authority is assigned to occupants of senior-level positions, the process through which certain persons attain those positions must be seen as legitimate.

Posting was a means of widening the search for suitable candidates and the results of that search therefore could not be known until the search was complete. Thus, the implied requirement that posting should be undertaken only if there was more than one realistic candidate for the job could not always be met. A manager could believe that his search would likely reveal several superior candidates, but he would have no guarantee that it would. Nevertheless, if the number of applications from unsuitable candidates was to be minimized, the job requirements needed to be realistic and spelled out in considerable detail:

> It's only right to post if there are realistic candidates for the job already in the organization. Otherwise, posting just creates damage to morale. It creates false hopes. If you're going to post, you need to pay lots of attention as to how the position is described in the posting. You need to state clearly what you want and what the work is really about.

Even if this condition was met, the reasons for selecting one candidate rather than another still needed to be communicated to all persons involved in the selection process:

> It's wrong to post if you have a candidate in mind for the position. If you do post, it's very important that feedback be given as to why someone wasn't chosen.

In posting, it was important that the majority of candidates applying for a vacant position not become cannon fodder for the process itself. That is, an opportunity should not be a chimera, but should be felt to be realistic. If more than a small minority of employees felt that their applications served merely to legitimate the appointment of preselected candidates, they would quickly become cynical, lose motivation, and question the legitimacy of established procedures. Responsibility and obligation are part and parcel of the posting system. Management has "a responsibility not to take candidates for granted":

> We're committed to respond to every candidate who applies for a position, even if they don't fit. We try to tell people why they didn't get the job, but usually it's because there are much better people available. We go through so much effort initially to hire someone, we owe them an explanation as to why they didn't get a subsequent job they applied for.

Maintaining the legitimacy of the whole organizational system requires that employees be continually motivated to learn and develop new skills. The competitive dynamics of the posting system are a necessary corollary of appointments made through administrative procedures. The occasional use of the competitive staffing process invoked by the posting process provides an outside discipline, as well as checks and balances, to organizational staffing through administrative means.

No specific examination was made of the degree to which values embodied in the staffing process were consistent with, and complementary to, wider organizational values. But a few managers clearly made a connection between a fair, competitive staffing process at the microlevel of analysis and adaptation at the level of the organization as a whole:

> Whatever selection process we use, we should look for the best so we can adapt to future demands. We should undertake a thorough search and all things should be equal in the interview process so all candidates stand on the same judgment ground.

Given the advantages as well as the potential responsibilities and obligations of the posting process, a few managers expressed mixed and negative opinions about their use of posting. One manager hoped to finesse the system—to have his cake and eat it too—by invoking the posting system but hoping no one would emerge who would challenge his preferred candidate. Clearly, this manager was stretching the responsibilities and requirements articulated by other managers:

> We hoped no one else would apply for the job because we already had _____ in mind for the job. Actually, _____ had the job in his back pocket because he can train others to do what he does now and he's really great with the environmentalists.

A second supervisor wanted to rebel against the requirement that he post a position because he knew that his preferred candidate for a secretarial–clerical position, a temporary employee, had a lower staffing priority than other permanent candidates likely to respond to a position posting. In his opinion, the effort and expense put into the posting process were a "waste" because the process did not yield the candidate he wanted. From his singular perspective, the legitimacy functions of the posting system were immaterial:

> All that money put into the posting process was wasted when I was required to advertise the position. I had to go through the whole rigmarole just to hire someone [a permanent employee] who was less than [a temporary employee] I already had on site.

In summary, the posting process was viewed as a key element in the staffing of organizational positions. The primary function of posting was that it served as a foundation of the legitimacy of the whole social hierarchy of the organization. Even though a majority of organizational positions were not filled by the posting process, occasional use of the process nevertheless backstopped and reinforced the legitimacy of all appointments. The benefits of the posting process can be readily undercut if its internal requirements are not met and the process is used in illegitimate ways. A process with legitimacy as its primary function is most vulnerable when it is used in a manner inconsistent with its primary value.

Following this discussion of the rationale for the use of the posting system, the next section describes the specific administrative procedures used to implement a posting process. As will be seen, the details of the procedures themselves are at least as important as, if not more important than, the substantive person–job outcomes produced by the process.

THE POSTING PROCESS

As with any administrative procedure, the staffing of organizational positions through the posting process contains many phases and possible subroutines. In this section, the main phases of the posting process are described in greater detail. In particular, attention is focused on the primary conditions that lead the selection process to switch from one subroutine to another.

Initial Reaction to a Vacancy

Vacancies can occur with varying degrees of surprise, as exemplified by a vacancy that arises because of a long-anticipated retirement, because an older employee indicates that he intends to take early retirement by the end of the next month, because the manager of a unit contemplates a reorganization, or because a key employee leaves suddenly to take an urgent posting elsewhere in the corporation or with another organization. More often than not, managers faced multiple, concurrent configurations of these and other circumstances. Thus, no two sets of staffing circumstances were ever identical, even though there were often strong similarities among groups of staffing initiatives.

Except for long-contemplated vacancies in which the vacating of a position by a key employee was the triggering event for a reorganization or for a planned succession, a frequent reaction of managers to an impending vacancy was to look first for a potential line of succession. As described in Chapter 8, the dominant concern evoked by the staffing opportunity was to find a preestablished line of progression or to fashion, perhaps idiosyncratically, a new line of progression. In the latter case, succession, and possibly progression, would emerge from the particular confluence of the talents and capacities of known potential appointees and the range of demands to be met by the occupant of the position to be filled. In general, managers had a strong preference for creating and affirming order in the flows of employees through key positions and often felt that they were best able to do this through administered appointments. Although individual managers differed in their preference for either administered or posting staffing processes, a majority of managers considered posting only after they had assured themselves that there was no suitable, preferred, and available internal candidate within potential lines of progression under their direct control:

> When the vacancy came up, the first thing I did was to check to see if the work needed to be done and if the job had to be filled. I then considered if there was someone already on site who was ready for the position. I couldn't find anybody even though I've been looking at my staff since I started this job eight months ago. So we posted the position and got 11 responses.

The preference for internal candidates is strong and persistent. As one manager reported, virtue can be found somewhere in the qualities of available internal candidates, even when these employees initially appear to be staffing dead ends:

> We considered four hourly craft men and decided that not one had what we wanted. I decided to send all of them for psychological testing to see if that would help clarify what the problems were with respect to each candidate. According to these tests, _____ was unsuitable, but later when I had a chance to see _____ in action, I realized he was doing exactly what the tests said he couldn't do. So I dumped the test results and approached _____ about the position because he had the most raw talent and it was time to get serious about investing in his training.

Few managers either believed that they were or behaved as though they were completely autonomous in their review of internal candidates. Several managers noted that they consulted with their fellow managers, Employee Relations representatives, and immediate subordinates about the identity of potential candidates. The social and political system of the organization was clearly capable of exerting influence and at times constrained the manager's autonomy in managing the staffing of positions as he wished. Thus, one divisional manager was thwarted in his attempts to get his local line managers to perform their own personnel functions:

> I was convinced we didn't need an Employee Relations Supervisor position, but I got no support from my local managers and none from the Region in this initiative. So we advertised in the Vancouver papers and got over 100 applications.

A second manager responded to his staff's concerns that new blood was required by inviting applications for a vacant supervisory position from both experienced hourly employees and any young engineer available in the external labor market (ELM):

> After discussing it with my staff here, I went around the mill and talked to a few of the more senior employees we felt could be possible candidates. As a result, we had four employees apply for the position. We also advertised in the newspaper for a young engineer—but nobody applied.

Initiation of the posting process was therefore not an automatic response to the first recognition of an impending vacancy. Administered appointments were preferred, especially when the manager had the authority to rearrange the assignments of his subordinates, including control over both the position to be filled and the person to be assigned to that position. Under these conditions, managers often used administered appointments to maintain a line of progression. If these conditions could not be met, or there were other pressing reasons to search more widely for potential candidates, then the posting system would be activated.

Position Posting: Who Applies and Who Is Considered?

Once it was decided that position posting was the staffing procedure to be followed, the job description was reaffirmed or changed, and notices of the impending job competition were sent to selected or all posting points throughout the organization. In the case of very specialized positions for which it was known beforehand that no one with the required qualifications was available, advertisements were placed in national newspapers and professional journals. The job description, together with the statement of applicant requirements, influenced who applied for consideration for appointment to the vacant position.

For readers who are unfamiliar with posting notices, we present an illustrative position posting from ForestCo's organization in Table 9.1. This job description and posting notice, and many similar others, were prepared through posting procedures similar to those described below:

> We sent a copy of the job description and posting to Head Office, who circulated it both on the mainland and on the island. We had eight internal applicants and three externals who found out about the job from friends in the organization.

As illustrated by the "DUTIES" section in Table 9.1, these job descriptions could be quite comprehensive. Even if a large number of candidates believed they could meet these requirements, the extensive listing of other desired qualifications noted in the "QUALI-FICATIONS" section in Table 9.1 could be used to screen this larger number to produce a shortlist of preferred candidates. Although Table 9.1 and the foregoing brief account of it are representative of mainstream posting activities, managers also told numerous stories about idiosyncratic features of the posting process that influenced who applied and who was considered. In the first example cited above, "friends in the organization" told outsiders about the vacant position, even though the posting was originally intended only for internal candidates. As it happened, none of these applicants from outside the company was interviewed, but their candidacy was nevertheless given some consideration.

Other idiosyncrasies in the posting process also occurred from time to time. For example, on one occasion, a mistake (whether inadvertent or not) limited the number of candidate applications received:

> Somewhere a mistake was made, and the position was posted at group 13 instead of group 14. The Regional office thought we were downgrading the job and didn't correct the mistake. We received five or six applications, but none of them was suitable. We had to argue for a reposting of the position at group 14. Some of the people who hadn't applied for the job at group 13 felt uncomfortable applying for the job at the new grouping because they didn't want to be seen as money hungry.

On another occasion, the actual use made of the posting process apparently violated the ground rules presented and discussed above. For example, the posting process was used occasionally when there was a clearly established favorite for the position. Although it could not be established that other potential candidates withheld their applications, there was reason to believe that they indeed did so:

> As part of the process of rotating various people through these occupational positions, _____ had liked this mill and the people here had liked him. In fact, when he was here

Table 9.1. Illustration of a Representative Position Posting

NOTICE OF POSITION AVAILABLE

Date issued: April 8, 1988 **Closing date:** April 22, 1988

Position:	Regional Forester
Location:	Region Woodlands
Duties:	Under the direction of the General Manager, Woodlands, and in consultation with the Company Chief Forester and Assistant Chief Forester:

- develop, assess, and recommend long-term harvesting and silviculture programs
- recommend approval of annual harvesting and silviculture plans and five-year logging development plans
- guide and monitor the execution of the forest management program and coordinate forestry activities between divisions and other Company organizations
- communicate forest management objectives, standards, policies, and standard practices and participate in their development and revision
- advise on forestry related matters, including new government acts, regulations, policies and tenure administration
- direct the preparation of the Management and Working Plan for Tree Farm License XX and coordinate the public involvement process. Process amendments and revisions
- direct the preparation of annual reports and activities related to the TFL Subsidiary Agreement and Audit procedures
- arrange for technical training programs and for the transfer of technology from Woodlands Services and elsewhere
- communicate with special interest groups through speeches, letters, and TV/radio appearances
- administer special forestry funding programs

Qualifications:

- University degree in forestry preferable, with emphasis on forest resource management including silviculture. Must be a Registered Professional Forester (B.C.) with at least 5 years experience as a ForestCo Division Forester, or related experience.
- Effective communicator (oral and written), with experience in dealing with the news media, senior management, government agencies, and the general public.
- Self-starter committed to the long-term forest management policies and objectives of the Company and the Region, and capable of directing the preparation of a responsible and defensible Management and Working Plan.
- Able to work with a minimum of supervision and capable of providing professional guidance to Woodlands Divisions and Woodlands General Manager on matters pertaining to forest land management, and items relating to forestry objectives, policies, standards, and procedures.
- A good administrator concerned with protecting ForestCo's forest land base and providing direction/guidance for developing and controlling the Company's forest management activities to meet the requirements of Management and Working Plan and other legal and contractual obligations.
- Proven ability to coach and train junior foresters, evaluate performance, and recommend and coordinate training and development of forestry staff.
- Understand the principles of allowable annual cut and fiber-flow calculations and be able to demonstrate leadership in choosing and defending within and outside the Company the appropriate harvest level for the Region.

Salary: Within Position Group ZZ

> on temporary assignment, he'd filled in for [the previous occupant of the position now vacant]. Therefore, when the vacancy came about, _____ was the logical candidate. Although the position was posted company-wide, there were very few [three] applicants because most people knew _____ had applied and was the logical choice for the job. Because of this, I used a very informal selection procedure, as _____ was head and shoulders above all other candidates.

From time to time, managers also made sure that employees they had known and worked with applied for positions that were posted. A person who, as a past subordinate or coworker, had been personally advised to apply for a position often became the preferred and selected candidate. Even so, candidates were aware of modest risks associated with opportunistic applications and asked for special consideration of their applications. As illustrated in the following quotation, a personal and informal relationship previously developed between the supervisor and a subordinate permitted the subordinate to be considered for a vacant position without her candidacy potentially disadvantaging her in her current position. Moreover, because she was a known and probably preferred candidate, she was also advantaged in the competition for the vacant position:

> We posted the position and 12 people applied—of which seven worked on the manufacturing floor. Out of courtesy, I talked with everyone on the telephone. Several of them were quite good, but I chose to meet with the three or four candidates who had sales experience. I also called _____ and asked if she would be applying because we knew she'd be able to handle herself and there were no concerns about her capacity to handle the job demands. She asked that her application be kept confidential until such a time as a shortlist was established, as she didn't want to jeopardize her chance of movement, as she was coming out of a line of progression. In the end, I chose _____ because of her sales experience.

The influence of managers on the staffing process works to both hinder and advance their self-interests as well as the effectiveness of overall corporate mobility. For example, managers can entice applications from good-quality candidates in other divisions, and managers in other divisions can offer inducements to retain a key employee, even when the employee has been offered a promotion elsewhere. In the following instance, the "market" features of ForestCo's ILM are readily appreciable. Managers of two different divisions wanted a talented employee, and the employee was able to enhance the managers' perceptions of his competitive value by making each manager aware of his potential value to the other. Moreover, because the employee chose not to move, the results of this competitive interplay led the manager of the department with the vacancy to reconsider the potential value of applicants to whom he had not before given serious consideration:

> We wanted to hire _____, who was a mechanical engineer with exceptional qualifications. He stood out from the rest, and we felt he could really improve the department's performance, as we needed help in settling conflicts regarding the technical aspects of purchasing. We brought him in from [another Region] to talk with him, and he said he wanted to talk with his supervisor first. We were disappointed when _____ was "coerced" by his boss to stay where he was. It's too bad that department was so selfish. However, with this rejection, we went back to the files. Time was now of the essence, and we reconsidered all the people we hadn't really thought about before.

Opportunism also occasionally modified the operation of the bureaucratic procedures associated with the posting process. For example, when one organizational unit had an oversupply of candidates and another had a shortage, it made sense for the one unit to share its job opportunities with candidates from the other unit:

> Six people applied for the job. We weren't happy with any of the applications, and the interviews confirmed that these were not right for the job we wanted to fill. Then we heard

that [another mill] had over 100 applications on file from people who wanted into production trainee jobs. After [the other mill] had taken who they wanted, they shared the abundance with us, and we found an excellent caliber of applicants there. Our successful candidate came from that batch of applications.

At other times, a combination of persistence and serendipity influenced the choice of who got the inside track to a vacant position:

_____ has worked for this sawmill before but had gotten laid off when the recession hit. He'd stayed in town and had gone to work for a local computer company and was known for doing good repair work. About a year ago, he applied for another position and got it. At the time, he indicated he was interested in the Production Trainee position, but was unaware of when an appointment like that might come about. So when this vacancy [for a Production Trainee] came up a short while ago, we posted the position and had the panel interview him. He was such a good fit, we decided he was the man for the job and didn't consider anyone else.

Once ForestCo managers had decided to consider candidates outside the lines of progression that were nominally under their direct or partial control, they were willing to consider candidates from a variety of sources. Interestingly, the decision to search outside nominal lines of progression freed them from local obligations associated with loyalty and career development. Once the decision to search outside the unit had been made, and managers cleared that cognitive hurdle, they focused their attention on organizational needs and attempted to identify and appoint the best person who could be obtained from any source. In keeping with notions of adaptive search, when local searches were relatively unsuccessful, managers were more accepting of unusual searching and matching processes. Under these conditions, opportunism and serendipity were more likely to be evident:

We posted the position, advertised across the country, and used headhunters, but nobody responded. Out of the blue, the mill manager got a letter from _____, who used to work for us a few years ago. He'd run into family problems and went back to his home country to sort them out. We'd heard he was moving back to Canada, but had no idea he'd be looking for a job with us. We talked with him when he was in the area and thought he'd be an ideal fit. We were lucky.

Opportunism can come into play if the manager has freedom and discretion to take advantage of previously unforeseen, but potentially favorable, circumstances. For example, if managers have discretion to hire without already having established the normal bureaucratic requirement of a vacant position, much greater flexibility in staffing is possible. The following anecdotes illustrate Snow and Snell (1993) Models II and III of strategic staffing, as persons are hired to both implement and develop corporate strategies that have not yet been fully articulated:

It happened we bought a line of products from the company _____ was working for at the time. He was well known and considered a valuable person to grab while you can. So we hired him from this other company without any specific position being vacant.

Managerial discretion and capacity to be opportunistic, including the opportunity to perform strategic staffing, were directly related to the scope of the manager's job and his level in the organizational hierarchy. Very senior managers could add to their staff complements much more easily than lower-level managers, who worked within a more rigid budgetary system:

I'd been looking to fill this position for some time and had considered hiring a recent MBA for the job. But most of these didn't have experience and also had little credibility in this

industry. While we were considering various candidates, the senior manager received a call
from _____ about another matter. _____ had worked with us previously and
had both the appropriate experience and lots of credibility. He was available, and we talked
him into a two- to three-year assignment. It was serendipity.

In summary, several factors can be seen to influence the number of applicants who
apply for and are considered for a posted position. For the most part, candidate applications were largely shaped by the job description and applicant requirements. From time to
time, however, both managerial and candidate self-interests also found expression in the
social and political milieu of the organization that framed the posting process. Finally,
managerial discretion and autonomy permitted serendipitous appointments to be made.
Strategic and opportunistic staffing did take place, but typically at more senior levels of
the organization.

Prescreening Candidates and Preparing the Shortlist

Once a job had been posted and candidates had applied for the vacant position, a
selection process was used to identify the candidate who would be appointed to the
position. This section describes the procedures used to prescreen candidates, together
with the processes used to identify the short-listed candidates who would be subject to
more thorough and careful evaluation.

Although it had been part of the original intent of this study to collect systematic
information about the numbers and characteristics of all candidates considered for vacant
positions, this venture turned out not to be viable. Administrative appointments, in
particular, were often made on the basis of managerial judgment—and few managers
either could or would disclose the internal thought processes and personal speculations
that resulted in their selection of a particular candidate. Thus, for more than half the
staffing appointments studied, it was impossible to obtain an "objective" count of the
candidates given either informal or serious consideration for appointment to the vacant
position. For appointments that were posted, however, a more formal record of candidate
applications was often more readily available. Even so, few of ForestCo's managers were
in the habit of keeping detailed archival records of past staffing actions for appointments
made through use of the posting system. Once the staffing decision had been made and
implemented, the details, but not necessarily the generalizable lessons of the past, were
put aside, and attention was concentrated on future issues and actions.

For the sample of appointments for which objective information on the numbers of
candidate applications could be obtained, prescreening was almost always done when
more than ten candidates applied for the vacant position. Efficiency considerations of the
screening process generally led managers to reduce to five or fewer the number subjected
to more detailed evaluation. Occasionally, more than five candidates would be interviewed, but that usually occurred when the manager or his staff or both had other
agendas, such as wishing to learn more about candidates generally available in the unit.
For example, the manager quoted below used the interim results of a posting process to
interview a sample of his subordinates in order to obtain information that he could use
subsequently to explore potential lines of progression in his department:

> I reviewed all applications and decided initially to talk with all the internals, since they
> were all largely equivalent in terms of their education and experience. By doing this, I had an
> opportunity to get a gut feel for who's coming up in the company and where potential future
> fits might be. I didn't interview the externals because there was enough quality internally.

In situations such as this, and in those in which there were fewer than seven or eight applicants, it was not uncommon for all applicants to be subjected to more detailed review—usually by means of an interview and occasionally some psychological testing. When there were more than eight or ten applications, this set would usually be reduced to a shortlist of five or fewer candidates.

Efficiency considerations that led managers to prescreen candidates, and to short-list those to be interviewed, derived partially from the perception that it was often difficult to schedule an interview program by a panel of senior managers. In addition, other agendas could occasionally be exercised through the interview process:

> We interviewed everyone so as to give all of the candidates an opportunity to learn about how competition for jobs occurs. But we ran into criticism as to why everyone was interviewed. The union called it an inquisition. When candidates freaked out during the interview, we moved to a less structured format, as some applicants clearly didn't know how to play the interview game.

The criteria used to eliminate these candidates from further consideration were clearly part of the fabric of the competition for jobs. As one might expect, multiple criteria were used overall, but past experience and satisfactory performance in a related position were cited most frequently:

> Initially, there were three internal applicants whom we interviewed and found not to be suitable for the position. So we advertised in the local newspapers and got 40 applications, which we screened on the basis of experience and education. We interviewed ten by telephone and finally interviewed eight in person.

> We had eight applications, and four didn't make it past the initial screening. Candidates were eliminated immediately if they didn't have sawmill experience.

In keeping with the more public competition associated with posted jobs, prescreening of candidates was usually done by persons other than, or in addition to, the manager responsible for the position:

> We posted the position and got eight applications, which was fewer than we expected. The Assistant Superintendent and the Employee Relations Supervisor jointly prescreened these applications by pooling their collective knowledge of the candidates, using past performance review reports, their resumes, and word of mouth. We found we couldn't eliminate any of them because they were all on a par, and so we interviewed all eight applicants.

Efficiency considerations also influenced the mode of prescreening when candidates were recruited from regional, national, or international ELMs. Reference checks and telephone interviews were seen as inexpensive ways of screening out less qualified persons and focusing attention on the few candidates likely to be successful:

> Headhunters provided profiles of ten potential candidates, of which two were highly recommended. Two of us did group telephone interviews to short-list the candidates. If necessary, we called them back to ask more questions. We weren't prepared to fly all of them in for initial interviews, and we were able to develop a shortlist of three candidates. The interview team we used was experienced and therefore needed a less disciplined approach.

There was no established format for prescreening candidates. Managers were often quite creative in taking advantage of recent developments in communications:

> Three of us were involved in the staffing decision. We discussed what type of person we would want for the position and created an image of what we were looking for. We posted the position and received about 15 responses. We made up a criteria sheet and faxed it to each out-of-town applicant and told them there'd be a telephone interview during which they

were to address each of the criteria and to indicate how they'd met them. We didn't ask them
specific questions, but expected each candidate to make a presentation of himself in relation to these guidelines.

Once the initial screening based on relatively specific job descriptions and associated
knowledge, skills, abilities, and other attributes had reduced the set of candidates, the
overall selection process moved into the traditional domain of academic and professional
staffing and selection issues. In this phase, the requirements for implementation of rational
competitive models of selection were viewed even more strictly. At ForestCo, however, the
primary method of evaluating candidates who made it to the shortlist was the selection
interview. In the next section, we describe the dilemmas confronted by ForestCo's managers as they struggled with the rational requirements and realities of this selection
procedure.

THE SELECTION INTERVIEW

Within the widely distributed staffing actions characteristic of a decentralized organization, ForestCo managers had recently begun to experiment with, and to implement,
various interview processes. There were two major features of this centrally sponsored
experimentation: rational decision analysis and the panel interview. The term "rational
decision analysis" denotes the use of a formal decision technique that is taught in a
commercial program on rational problem-solving and decision analysis. The term "panel
interview" denotes the panels of interviewers increasingly used and accepted by ForestCo's managers to assess the capacities and qualities of job applicants. As use of these
techniques was often controversial and problematic for ForestCo's managers, each technique is discussed in greater detail.

Rational Decision Analysis

Embedded in the recent history and culture of Employee Relations at ForestCo was
acceptance and implementation of a formal method of rational decision analysis for
employee selection. This formal method, based on the work of Kepner and Tregoe (1965),
had become institutionalized in many parts of the company as the technique to match
candidates and jobs. The K-T methodology would be generically familiar to most students
of organizational analysis, as it presents an ordered and systematic technique to meet what
(Kepner & Tregoe, 1965, p. 14) characterize as a general organizational phenomenon:

> Managers tend naturally to deal with problems, causes, and decisions without con-
> sciously realizing which is which, or where these fit in the process of thinking a problem
> through. They do not distinguish between what's wrong that needs correcting, what brought
> the problem about, and what actions to choose to correct it. As a result, they waste a great
> deal of time and money in their problem solving.

Not surprisingly, Kepner and Tregoe offer a solution to this deficiency in the form of
an action sequence for problem analysis and decision making that has been taught
through commercial programs to many thousands of managers, including a substantial
number at ForestCo. The K-T procedure should be quite familiar to business students
taking their first course in decision analysis. It consists of seven generic steps that translate
into seven specific actions for the employment interview. Table 9.2 illustrates such an
application.

A form of rational decision analysis was almost always applied to each vacancy

Table 9.2. Application of Rational Decision Analysis to Employee Selection

Generic decision analysis	Application to selection interview
1. Set objectives against which to choose.	1. Decide on job demands and requirements.
2. Classify objectives as to importance.	2. Classify requirements into those that are necessary (MUSTS) and those that are desired (WANTS) and weight/rank these objectives.
3. Develop alternatives from which to choose.	3. Identify candidates to be evaluated.
4. Evaluate alternatives against the objectives.	4. Evaluate candidates on necessary and desired requirements.
5. Tentatively choose the best alternative.	5. Tentatively identify the best candidate.
6. Assess possible adverse consequences.	6. Evaluate risks associated with choice.
7. Control effects of final decision.	7. Plan/initiate actions to reduce possible risks.

posted. The criteria derived from the demands and requirements for each job were translated into selection criteria, and these in turn were assigned relative rankings or weights. Thus, one artifact of using the K-T method was a grid or matrix in which candidates were assigned to columns, job requirements (and their associated weights) were listed in rows, and the score entered in each cell represented the evaluation of the designated candidate on that particular job requirement. Thus, the final judgment of each candidate was represented by the sum of the candidate's weighted scores on the job dimensions, and the relative ranking of each candidate was obtained by comparing the sums of their weighted scores, as illustrated in Table 9.3.

A comparison of the original posting notice in Table 9.1 shows close but not identical correspondence with the criteria used to evaluate candidates in Table 9.3. As expected, the specifications of the job to be filled mapped closely onto the criteria used to discriminate among candidates. Of course, the weightings of the job requirements were not included in the job posting notice. This study has not been especially concerned with differences between job descriptions and schemes used to evaluate candidates for those jobs. Nevertheless, it is to be noted that the four most heavily weighted candidate criteria accounted for approximately three quarters of the weightings total and were related directly to technical and professional expertise. For this particular job at this particular time and place, the softer managerial skills of effective communication and coaching and training together amounted to approximately 15% of the weightings total.

Managerial Evaluations of Rational Selection Procedures

Many of ForestCo's managers were most comfortable with concrete, physical objects such as logs, trucks, and machines. They often had little interest in or inclination or opportunity to develop sophisticated interview skills. The formalization of the interview process into a standard operating procedure gave them a way of structuring and handling what they often experienced as soft, uncomfortably subjective, information. A second advantage of using a programmed approach to employee selection was that it established a base standard for the thoroughness and quality of the competitive process through which applicants to posted positions were selected.

The following managerial descriptions are representative of the application of this mainstream method of a selection interview process. First, job criteria were used to develop a series of questions to be used in the interviews used to assess candidates:

Table 9.3. K-T Procedure for Evaluating Candidates

		Candidate number			
Objectives (criteria)	Weight	1	2	3	4
Effective communicator with media, senior management, agencies, and public	4				
Self-starter	5				
Capable of preparing a responsible and defensible M&WP	7				
Capable of providing professional guidance to GMs and divisions regarding forest land management objectives, policies, standards, and procedures	8				
Good administrator concerned with protecting ForestCo's forest land base and providing direction/guidance for developing and controlling activities required to meet M&WP, legal, and contractual objectives	10				
Ability to coach/train Junior Foresters, evaluate performance, recommend and coordinate training and development of forestry staff.	3				
Understand principles of fiber-flow calculations and able to demonstrate leadership in choosing and defending, within and outside the Company, the appropriate harvest level for the region.	9				

> The first thing we did was to prepare the job description. From that we developed 18 questions for the interview—with the ER supervisor helping me in that process. We posted the position and got eight applicants.

Once the questions had been established, the interviews were conducted, and each candidate was ranked on the previously established criteria:

> Three people did the interviews, and each interviewee was ranked according to their responses to standardized questions which related to the job criteria. We averaged these weighted scores and looked carefully at the numbers.

> In the interviews, we used the paint by numbers sheets and rated each candidate on the qualities required for the position.

> All of our decisions were based on who stacks up against whom in a standard K-T analysis.

Despite the mainstream acknowledgment of the possible benefits of this structured approach to an evaluation of candidates, many managers expressed misgivings about use of this system. One feature of this formal system is that it biases managerial attention to those attributes that can be formalized and quantified. It tends to focus attention on immediate, concrete requirements and is less appropriate for issues of style:

> It's very difficult to do average weight decision making, because the system biases you in terms of how you look at someone. Different projects have different demands—so if I look at experience and weigh that heavily, I may miss someone who is a quick learner. Candidates like that are more important in terms of future placement in the long run.

> K-T is good for a focus on technical strength, but it doesn't tell you much about the style and personality required to fit the organization's needs.

Other managers believed that the system became an end in itself and that concentrating attention on the immediate process often precluded a possible reconsideration of the ultimate objective of the staffing exercise:

> There's a potential danger in using the formal system in that people can get too invested in the system itself and miss something significant because they're too focused on getting through a series of questions. There's also the possibility we could weight the criteria incorrectly. It's not uncommon for the gut to say one thing and the numbers to say something else.

Although most selection interview processes were characterized as being used fairly and with integrity, the potential for personal bias was acknowledged. It is not clear that this potential is necessarily a bad thing for the organization as a whole. The formalized K-T method contains its own biases. Unless the intent and consequences of individual managerial influence are known, it is impossible to assess the claim that managerial biases and manipulations are inappropriate. Nevertheless, several managers believed that the potential for personal bias was sufficient for them to recommend against using the K-T process:

> I don't like to use the grid for assessing candidates using the K-T process because if you don't get the answer you want, you manipulate the scores and the weightings to get the answer you want.

> A problem with K-T ranking is that everyone has their own interpretation of what they're actually ranking.

As with most complex social processes, ForestCo's managers developed a pragmatic, flexible view of the "approved" method of selecting candidates. Many were not averse to using the system, but they retained a realistic, occasionally skeptical view of the reliability and validity of the K-T procedure:

> Though I use the K-T method of evaluating candidates, I don't give it a lot of weight. On a day-to-day basis, I see a lot more than what a K-T analysis can.

> I use K-T analysis, but it's much more useful when you've got large numbers of potential candidates. Then, it's easier to choose fairly and equitably. There's a few downfalls to the system, but it's dependent on the criteria that panel members say should be weighed. On the whole, panelists use the system with integrity, but it's hard not to form first impressions. Feelings get in the way when you know people already. Invidious comparisons will always happen.

Given a system for evaluating candidates, the second problematic issue confronting ForestCo's managers was that of who was to perform these evaluations. The mainstream custom was to use panels of interviewers, but as with the K-T methodology, managers were often ambivalent about this recommended practice.

Panel Interviews

It has been argued previously that one of the primary functions of the posting process was to confer legitimacy on selected appointees. While the actual outcome of the selection process was important, the process itself had functional consequences for the maintenance of the social system of the organization. It follows that the social legitimacy associated with a selection and appointment decision would be enhanced by the participation of a larger group of organizational members in the decision. Typically, these members were likely to be attached to overlapping but different social and organizational networks. Assuming that the selected candidate did not prove to be an unmitigated failure, the bestowed imprimatur of approval (which originated from a consensus within the selection panel) would strengthen the legitimacy of the specific appointee and likewise reinforce the legitimacy of the selection system in general. Thus, the perceived strengths of panel interviews were that they reduced the potential for individual bias and increased overall confidence in the selection:

> Panel interviews are the only way to go. There's safety in consensus. You measure each candidate against well-established criteria. It's fairer to the candidate—especially if there's been a wide range of contact with him and biases have built up.

> When individual interviews are done, there's room for doubt regarding the right decision. With panels, there's more people involved and the greater the likelihood there'll be more confidence in the final decision. Panels help you avoid bias.

The process of interviewing using a set of panelists helps apportion the interview task. It gives each interviewer an improved opportunity to listen and to record the answers given in response to the questions asked:

> We like the panel interview process because it limits biases during the interviews, gives us a time to think, make notes, and observe the candidate. You can be a keener listener because you're not busy anticipating the next question. You get to experience different points of view which eventually emerge in the scoring system. If all scores are the same, we're more secure in the hire.

A further benefit of interview panels is that they can serve as training in employment interviewing for others who are less experienced:

> We try to do panel interviews for almost all jobs. We avoid having just one person make a decision because it's useful to get different opinions which lead to fairer evaluations and eliminate bias. It shakes the "who's prettiest?" approach to hiring. Though it's time-demanding, I believe in the process, as participation in the panel is a training process in itself. However, I do insist that at least one person who serves on the interview team be familiar with the panel process.

As pointed out by this comment, the composition of the interview panel can have important consequences for the outcome of the interview. At least one manager was scared off by the potential for conflicting views within the panel:

> Panels are not so good because it's hard to get agreement about criteria. There may also be disagreement with the majority as to who should get the job.

But most managers believed that selection decisions were better when there was a diversity of opinions and perspectives available:

> A panel is the best vehicle for interviewing, but you must involve those who will be responsible for the position—they know best what to look for. Personalities must be kept out. Dangerous biases come into play when one or more of the panelists have personal investments in seeing someone get the job.

> Often what screws us up is selecting the wrong people for the panel. It doesn't work when people on the panel have mutual biases and the wrong person gets selected.

Managers who used selection panels believed that in most instances, three was the "magic number" of panelists. More than three panelists had little impact on increasing the diversity of perspectives brought to bear, but increased the likelihood of internal conflict. Collusion of panelists with the same point of view and the introduction of personal bias were more possible with fewer than three panelists. Moreover, a number of panelists greater than three was judged more likely to "scare off" potential applicants and thereby defeat the objective of widening opportunity and increasing competition for posted jobs. Thus, a flexible capacity to meet the personal concerns of candidates in the panel interview was often seen to be important, as was the opportunity for a majority opinion when two panelists disagreed:

> There should be three people on each panel. Three is the magic number. It doesn't scare people off. Biases are eliminated. It pushes you to find clarity regarding what is important and how the important items would be weighted.

> The value of panel interviews is that interviewers can complement one another and trigger each other's thinking. You can salvage the interview if one person is ineffective. The main concern with the panel interview is that it can be very intimidating, and this may be counterproductive when you're trying to find out as much as you can about a candidate. It's easier to help someone get comfortable so you can find out more about them in a nonpanel situation. There must be enough flexibility during the panel interview process so the interviewer can change the line of questioning if needed.

As noted above, the primary reason for not organizing panel interviews was that considerable time was required to get a set of busy managers together for one or two days to engage in the panel process:

> We don't always use panels—sometimes because scheduling all those people into one or two days of meetings is difficult.

> We don't like panels because it's demanding to try to get everyone together. Panels affect candidate comfort; the room setup doesn't allow for physical closeness.

From time to time, other managers indicated that they would be less willing to participate in a set of panel interviews if they believed that the chosen candidate had been selected already. Under such circumstances, they indicated that they would be reluctant to facilitate an attribution of legitimacy to an appointment that was in fact made without an honest process. If the process wasn't honest, they would be placing their reputations at risk with no offsetting gain.

Because staffing decisions and candidate selections were subject to agency effects, expressed evaluations of any managerial technique could possibly misdirect attention away from the self-interests of the manager/agent. For example, one reason cited for not using panel interviews was that when they were used in conjunction with the formalized K-T analysis, the employment interview became inflexible and impersonal. However, the alternative formulation noted below, namely, a selection based on an informal lunch, could also produce a biased result. A demonstrated capacity to handle such social requirements could possibly provide information on social similarity, but would not be a reliable source of technical job information!

> We don't do panels. We tend to meet informally over lunch in a small group. Panel interviews never worked because they're too mechanized—like handwriting analysis. It's better to play it by ear and get information in different ways.

A more rational argument against using panel interviews was that they failed to give candidates a clear appreciation of the person to whom they would be directly responsible. From this perspective, the selection interview was viewed as being a vehicle for convincing candidates of the attractiveness of a likely job offer, rather than selecting among competing candidates. Implicit in this characterization of panel interviews, however, is again the possibility of an agency effect. Panel interviews can limit managerial autonomy, and arguments against panels could also, either unwittingly or by design, strengthen a manager's bias toward local autonomy and control.

Panels aren't necessary. It's easier to do one-on-one interviews. That way, the candidate has an opportunity to know who they're going to work for. The team approach is a distraction.

One additional reason cited by a senior manager for not using panel interviews derived from his judgment that only he had sufficient skill and sensitivity to assess the candidates for a senior position:

I chose one-on-one interviews because this was a senior position and there was no one else in the division who was competent to judge what I really needed. I interviewed all those who applied. I did this because there was an undercurrent from the two appointments that had been made here previously. Other staff felt they weren't able to compete. If I'd known some of the people who'd applied, I'd have interviewed them by phone. However, it was useful to check them out and to give them an opportunity to practice being interviewed. It's relationships which keep the place going. Justice, which is trying to keep everything fair, has no uniform definition.

This was an anomalous comment, however, as consensual decision-making appeared to be associated quite often with appointments to the most senior positions.

In general, ForestCo's managers approached the use of panel interviews in the same practical manner as they approached other issues. If the procedure offered them some net advantage, they used it. They exhibited no ideological commitment to any procedure that they judged to be of marginal benefit. Thus, if a particular staffing situation presented them with little opportunity to realize the potential advantages of panel interviews, they would find faster, easier ways of satisfactorily solving their staffing problems. Their use of panel interviews was clearly conditioned by the exigencies they faced in each situation. There was considerable folklore regarding the conditions under which panels did or did not make sense:

If a selection is to be based primarily on *technical abilities*, you don't need a lot of people involved in the selection process.

Panel interviews are a waste of time for *clerical jobs* because most female clerks are short-term with the company. Panel interviews are more appropriate for *career types*.

When it comes to selecting someone from *within the mill*, one-on-one interviews are sufficient because there's a lot of base information about each candidate already available. Panel interviews are more appropriate *for outsiders*, where there's a need to protect against biases.

There's not much support for panel interviews for *entry-level positions*, but they do help managers get a better feeling for who they're getting. Just seems to be a costly process given the high rates of turnover.

Clearly, ForestCo's managers had considerable freedom to use a variety of selection techniques. Although corporate policies were generally supportive of K-T analyses and the use of panel interviews, local managers were accustomed to working in an organizational context characterized by a philosophy of "let the managers manage." In an environment such as this, they enjoyed considerable local autonomy in their choice of primary procedures to use in selecting their staff and used procedures that suited their pragmatic characters.

The choice of selection processes was rarely concluded with the decision to use or not to use a selection panel. In quite a number of the staffing situations examined, the mainstream techniques of K-T analyses and panel interviews were supplemented by still further confirmatory activities. These activities and procedures are described in the next section.

RATIONALIZATION/CONFIRMATION OF JUDGMENT

The final activity associated with the selection of a candidate to be appointed to a vacant position occurs when the manager reaffirms his provisional selection within his social and political network and checks his own judgment against the judgment of relevant others. Not all managers engaged in these activities, but these consultations were mentioned with sufficient frequency to deserve further consideration. Most frequently, when managers sought affirmation of their judgment, they had the provisionally chosen candidate meet with their supervisor so as to obtain his approval for the proposed appointment. Also, from time to time, candidates would be sent to talk with other senior managers and coworkers:

> The team making up the interview panel seriously reviewed three candidates and made their recommendation to the Regional Manager, who then spoke with the candidate. If there isn't a single preferred candidate or if the candidate is from another Region, the Regional Manager wants to meet the candidate. I feel it's good to get my boss's point of view.

By involving others in a selection decision, managers were able to diffuse their responsibility for the appointment should the decision eventually turn out to have been a poor one. Also, a concern for maintaining cooperative relationships with other managers in the organization meant that a manager who was politically sensitive checked to see that he wasn't stepping on someone else's toes:

> I talked with several other managers about my likely choice to get any additional information I could on his qualities. I also talked with his present boss and wanted to know if he thought this was the best move for him or did he have other development plans in mind. Essentially I wanted their approval, to confirm the decision I'd already made, and to maintain political relationships with them.

ForestCo managers used a mix of standardized procedures and other confirmatory techniques to arrive at a staffing choice with which they were confident. There were no formal rules to guide this mix of procedures. Rather, each manager was free to assess his own situation and to determine his standards for the proposed appointment. Supplementary and confirmatory procedures could include psychological testing, further interviews with future coworkers, or a further interview with the manager's immediate supervisor or the divisional manager:

> We went through a lot of structured procedures because we wanted to compensate for lack of experience on the part of the three people doing the interviews. We also paid attention to our gut feel after the formal interview was over. One candidate stood out—so we rationalized that a second round of interviews wasn't necessary. We sent him to the consultant for aptitude tests.

> The supervisor does the first interview. If the supervisor approves of a candidate, the manager does a second interview and makes the final decision.

Although confirmatory interviews were occasionally used when a panel of interviewers had made an initial selection, such interviews were more likely to be used when a panel had not been involved. Thus, confirmatory interviews were used as compensating mechanisms to backstop selections that were more strongly influenced by the preferences of a single manager:

> I called a headhunter for this job and outlined the criteria for the position. I knew of _____'s name and wanted the headhunter to find out where he was and who else was available. I found four potential candidates from this process, and after interviewing these four candidates I discounted three of them. That left _____ as my recommendation. I

had him interviewed by three other senior managers to see if they thought he was OK too. Then I had him go out and talk to the people in the mills and the marketing departments. All agreed he was the right guy. If anyone had any concerns, they would have been checked out in addition to the regular reference checks we do.

Confirmation of judgment permitted managers to live more comfortably with their choices. It also enabled them, should a selected candidate fail, to argue that this failure should not reflect on their individual judgment, as significant others had also participated in the selection decision. As noted previously, few candidates were perfect, and managers needed time to rationalize their acceptance of anything less than the ideal candidate. Thus, the ambivalence and cognitive discomfort stemming from a candidate's not being "an expert in everything" could be assuaged by affirmation. Candidates could be placed retrospectively in a cognitive frame dominated by positive attributes:

> _____ came to the fore when I talked with other managers and supervisors about him. He's considered to have good judgment. He's been given training and exposure. We watched how he had handled dealing with the public, and always he did well. The other guys we considered just weren't as good. He was a good, industrious candidate. He doesn't know paper, but he knows as much as anyone else. Even though he's been around for 27 years and has lots of operations experience, he can't be an expert in everything. I'm satisfied with my choice.

Thus, as evidenced by this brief review, confirmation of preliminary selection judgments by others who had not participated directly in the selection process was an important ingredient of staffing decisions and actions. By consulting more widely, managers and supervisors who had immediate responsibility for selection decisions were able to broaden the legitimacy of the preliminary selection. These processes also enabled them to diffuse their personal responsibility by co-opting other senior managers into the selection decision.

This wider round of consultation can also be viewed as a rational response to the requirement for efficient staffing procedures. Responsibility for executing the selection procedures is delegated to the small number of managers and personnel specialists most knowledgeable about the immediate job requirements and selection procedures. Once these procedures have produced a preliminary decision, approval is sought from higher-level managers. Framing the selection procedure as a two-stage process focuses the involvement of the senior managers on a smaller number of prescreened candidates. Within ForestCo, these two-stage processes were rarely required by more senior managers. Most often, these two-stage processes were initiated by the lower-level managers with direct responsibility for the selection of their subordinates. These lower-level managers chose to affirm their choices with their superiors so as to increase the legitimacy of their preliminary selections and to increase the buy-in of other organizational participants whose own work performance could be affected by that of the new appointee.

SUMMARY

A competitive, market-based approach to the matching of employees and jobs grounded all other approaches to staffing, even though a majority of staffing decisions were not made through use of the posting system. The primary functions of the posting system derived from outcomes that resulted from the procedures of the posting process itself, rather than the different substantive outcomes which resulted from using posting rather than other staffing processes. Social constructions of the salaried employment system at ForestCo employed posting as the primary manifestation of a social system that provided equal opportunity to its participants. Posting procedures were represented as being fair and honest, as employees could demonstrate their interests and initiative and freely apply for positions for which they were qualified. The posting system communicated potential opportunities to employees and also informed supervisors and managers about employees who were available and who wished to be considered as candidates for vacant positions. By widening the formal consideration of self-initiated candidates and requiring reviews of these candidates by other supervisors, managers could establish the background standards against which administrative appointments were made. In addition, managers were also able to compare their evaluations of specific candidates with those made by other managers. Posting therefore provided some approximation of the openness required for a competitive labor market.

Because the primary outcomes of the posting process were ones that supported and maintained the legitimacy of existing assignments, posting was implicitly prohibited unless its use could potentially produce a different substantive outcome. Posting was regarded as illegitimate when it was used solely to validate a predetermined outcome such as the selection and appointment of a favorite subordinate. Although such choices occurred from time to time, social norms among ForestCo's managers discouraged such deliberate misuse of the posting system.

A modest cost of the posting system was that appointments made using the administrative procedures of posting were relatively inefficient. It often took a long time to execute appointments, and managers involved in the selection process often had to consider multiple applications from marginally qualified candidates who repeatedly applied for vacant positions. In addition, as posting also implied a responsibility to provide feedback and possible career counseling for unsuccessful candidates, managers spent increased time on organizational maintenance. Implementation of a staffing process through the posting system consumed scarce supervisory and managerial time and attention.

The mechanics of the posting process are clearly derived from rational models of organizational performance. Intraorganizational competition for more rewarding appointments mirrored rational economic models of ELMs. These notions of rationality, however, were conceptualized at the level of the employment subsystem containing at least one vacant job and several candidates for that job. But notions of rationality are various. Rationality is a slippery construct the operationalization and meaning of which can change depending on the level at which it is defined. Procedures designed to implement rationality associated with operation of an employment subsystem are not necessarily identical to those that pertain to the local interests of a departmental manager. Local objectives of administrative efficiency, rational from the perspective of departmental managers, could be bypassed by rational actions originating from other points of view. The wider consultation process permitted consideration of wider organizational issues that could displace local within-unit concerns such as mobility along lines of progression. Posting therefore tended to serve organization-wide issues more than the immediate concerns of a unit manager. Use of the posting system tended to diminish local managerial control, but paradoxically reinforced the legitimacy of the social system as a whole.

While the administrative procedures of ForestCo's posting system most closely approximated the requirements of an open-market system for assigning employees to different jobs, there were practical limits to the attainment of this objective. Jobs could not always be fully specified with formal precision, and the translation of job requirements into candidate qualifications was not always perfect. Information about vacant positions was not always posted company-wide, and opportunistic hires occasionally preempted implementation of posting processes. The use of formalized decision procedures in selection interviews undoubtedly helped inexperienced supervisors who were unsure how to evaluate candidates for vacant positions. Formal selection procedures, however, could potentially give increased emphasis to quantifiable attributes and qualifications at the expense of qualitative and stylistic attributes. Moreover, rational decision analyses could also displace and substitute for judgments based on day-to-day observations of candidate performances. Despite these concerns voiced by ForestCo's managers, posting was nevertheless viewed as a reliable and honest process for staffing positions.

Two final features of the posting process were also judged to facilitate and support the open-market features of staffing. First, posting within ForestCo was associated with the frequent use of committees or panels to interview and evaluate candidates being considered for positions. The use of interview panels opened the selection preferences of managers to scrutiny by their colleagues and generally improved the reliability of judgments made through these means. Panels were seen to improve the consensus on the qualities of candidates and to increase the legitimacy of appointments. Second, preliminary selection judgments were occasionally referred for approval to other senior managers who had not necessarily participated in the direct evaluation of candidates. These referrals and subsequent confirmations also increased the legitimacy of proposed appointments and, as well, protected the judgment of the supervisor responsible for the choice emerging from the selection process.

Thus far, two different staffing processes used in ForestCo's organization—administered appointments and the posting system—have been described and articulated. In neither case, however, has there been a detailed review of the criteria used to select candidates. There were few observed systematic differences between the selection criteria used in administrative processes and those used in the posting process. Information on criteria used to discriminate among candidates is presented as an organization-wide, process-free, aspect of ForestCo's ILM in Chapter 10.

10

Criteria Used to Evaluate Different Candidates

INTRODUCTION

Underlying almost all the technical advances in the development of employee selection since World War II is the strong background presence of bureaucratic rationality (Jacoby, 1985). The apparatus of objective science, with its emphasis on reliable, valid, quantitative description, has been used to develop rational decision processes for the accomplishment of two primary purposes: first, to select the persons best suited to specific, objectively defined jobs; second, to develop legally defensible procedures, and outcomes resulting from use of those procedures, that result in the hiring or advancement of some persons rather than others (Schneider & Schmitt, 1986). By its very nature, selection implies some form of discrimination among persons regarded as being different from one another. Because work and employment, and equal opportunity to share in these necessities of contemporary life, lie at the heart of a democratic society, methods and outcomes of employee selection are of major political and social importance.

Because of the adverse impact of many traditional forms of employee selection and their systematic detriments to equal opportunity, a number of legal statutes regulating employee selection were enacted in the 1960s and 1970s in both the United States and Canada. In the United States, these statutes initially prohibited employment discrimination on the basis of race, color, religion, sex, or national origin. Subsequent legislation also prohibited employment discrimination on the basis of age or physical or mental disabilities or handicaps. In Canada, preferential employment programs target women, visible minorities, aboriginal peoples, and persons with disabilities. Overall, this legislation has had a profound effect on normative treatment of employment to the extent that some analysts now argue that "legal policies currently are the most significant aspect of human resource management in general and of selection in particular" (Gatewood & Feild, 1994, p. 23).

Within the frame of a rational perspective on organizations, normative treatments of employment selection are based most strongly on the prima facie correspondence between candidate attributes and requirements for satisfactory job performance. Measures of both jobs and candidate attributes should be reliable, valid, and preferably quantitative to permit relatively sophisticated statistical analysis. In these normative presentations, the defensibility of any selection method is rooted in the correctness of the scientific procedures used to assess and to match jobs and candidates to provide forecasts of future work performance. Over the past 50 years, a huge number of studies have examined and developed normative theory regarding various highly focused and specialized aspects of employment selection. The primary methods used to develop this normative theory have been those of the experimental psychologist. Increasingly, studies have begun to examine actual staffing behaviors of managers in organizational settings, but comprehensive theories that relate theory to practice remain a relatively recent innovation (Perry, Davis-Blake, & Kulik, 1994).

This chapter reviews descriptions of criteria used by ForestCo's managers to make administered appointments. As the reader will discover, staffing practice in these situations fails to meet normative prescriptions—a finding for which there are several potential explanations. Those with strong attachments to normative theory could argue that ForestCo is a poorly managed company—hidden in the dark forests of the Pacific Northwest coast and shielded from the realities of contemporary urban life.

Others more sensitive to different national histories could argue that the legal and moral pressures to change employment practices are fewer in Canada than in the United States. Canada has fewer minority groups, and smaller numbers of each, than does the United States, with its relatively large black, Hispanic, Asian, and other populations and its history of civil rights struggles. Therefore, finding ForestCo's practices to be different from normative models based largely on the work of United States academics and social scientists is an artifact of national and regional sampling.

For both of these arguments, normative theories of employee selection would not be challenged by a study that finds little if any evidence of the implementation of these theories in practice. A third argument, however, is that normative theory is based on too restrictive a view of the background model of organizational functioning. Rational-system models present only one perspective on organizational functioning. Rational precepts are often most difficult to implement in practice. Normative selection theory is often not attained in practice because of limited information, costly search, and bounded rationality. The greatest challenge to normative selection theory derives, however, from natural- and open-system models, which present coexisting, complementary, and at times competing perspectives on organizations. Depending on the situation, the latter perspectives could explain why managers acted as they did when their actions appear to be contradictory to prescriptions derived from rational models, but such perspectives have no legitimacy in normative selection theory. Whether normative theory should remain as the dominant paradigm for employee selection or should be modified to take alternative perspectives into account is a political and legal issue. The following sections present material pertinent to that debate.

In ForestCo, whether appointments were made through the posting process or by means of administrative decisions, each selection process involved some evaluation of the extent to which candidates met the performance requirements of the position for which they were being considered. When positions were posted, emphasis on objective, technical job requirements was more public than in administered appointments. Perhaps because of this increased openness, the extent of each candidate's technical knowledge also appeared to be given greater emphasis. In both posting processes and administered appointments, however, technical job requirements represented only a portion of the criteria used to evaluate and compare candidates. In making staffing judgments, ForestCo's managers also frequently incorporated many other considerations in their selection decisions and complicated the staffing judgments they were required to make. At the same time, however, these "complications" produced a rich tapestry of interactions that wove together themes from rational-, natural-, and open-system perspectives on organizations.

One striking feature of the more than 3000 salaried positions in the ForestCo organization, in common with other large organizations, is their diversity (Baron et al., 1986). Generally, small groups of some types of job (e.g., Divisional Accountant, Divisional Forester, or Shift Supervisor) could be considered to be quite similar in terms of technical, rational considerations. But in their fine detail, no two jobs were exactly the same. Jobs that were almost identical from a technical perspective (i.e., the specific knowledge, skills, and other abilities required for satisfactory job performance) were often considered to require different qualities in the candidates applying for those positions. Most often, these different requirements derived from the immediate context in which a particular job was located. For example, ostensibly similar jobs could be located in different organizational units having different requirements for teamwork, cooperation, or complementarities with coworkers. In other instances, similar jobs could be located in different divisions that exhibited different dynamic balances between employee stocks and flows. Whatever the nature of these contextual features, the criteria used to evaluate candidates for jobs varied as a function of the contextual requirements associated with each vacant job. While specific technical criteria almost always had to be met in candidate attributes, other, more general organizational factors were invoked when two or more candidates were viewed as having met these minimal requirements. Whether or not a candidate met these general requirements was occasionally weighted at least as heavily as whether or not the candidate met the technical job requirements. Moreover, the general methods and approaches used to evaluate candidates in terms of these contextual criteria showed remarkable consistency across a broad variety of organizational appointments.

This chapter describes the general approaches used by ForestCo's managers to evaluate the suitability of candidates for jobs. The immediate cognitive frame for this presentation is that of a rational model of organizational functioning. That is, there was a conscious effort to assess the likely future performance of potential candidates in the vacant positions. In no instances in this review of ForestCo's salaried employment system were appointments made by unexamined rules such as automatic appointment of the most senior candidate. Even in those instances in which succession up a line of progression was the outcome, such successions were invariably assessed against alternative arrangements such as posting or searches of the external labor market. Nevertheless, managers used many other "rules" to infer likely future performance. Whether these rules were logical and rational is an open question. As shown in descriptions of managerial assessments, the evaluative frameworks or jobholder schemata (Perry et al., 1994) used by ForestCo's managers were also strongly influenced by natural- and open-system perspectives.

Delineations among rational-, natural-, and open-system perspectives in processes of employee selection are less clear in practice than in theory. In the sections that follow, a perspective that is predominantly rational, though limited in its application, underlies the implicit rules of thumb that ForestCo's managers used to evaluate each candidate's past history, including the generic construct of "experience." Other attributes of each candidate's past history that ForestCo's managers used included the employee's length of service and age. Collectively, these candidate attributes were used to infer candidates' readiness for the proposed appointment, a direct manifestation of a rational perspective. Age, however, though it can be considered an indicator of past experience, is also a social marker having perhaps greater relevance for the maintenance of social systems. The topic of age therefore provides a link between rational and natural perspectives on employee selection.

The second set of issues considered to influence employee selection, then, are those associated with maintenance of the organization as a social system, such as the management of lines of progression. For example, while advancement potential was often a critical selection criterion, the requirement to have some mix of stability and mobility in a departmental unit occasionally implied that candidates selected for certain positions were chosen more for their suitability for a stable, long-term organizational role than for the purpose of implementing their succession to a series of positions in a line of progression. Maintenance of lines of progression was an integral feature of a rational, performance-oriented entity and also required managers to consider the timing of individual moves in ForestCo's ILM. Thus, time in rank was also used as a pertinent indicator of candidate readiness to move. In addition, new assignments as rewards for past service and mobility were also factored into decisions regarding the assignment and appointment of persons to positions. Natural-system considerations supplemented and complemented the operation of ForestCo's ILM as a rational entity.

The third set of selection criteria derives from an open-system perspective on ForestCo's organization and its managers. Within the social system of the organization, employees were given greater focus and attention than were jobs or positions. Relatively stable individual characteristics, such as personalities and personal styles, were often used to project future individual capacities independently of the specific jobs to which a person might be assigned. In addition, the interaction between these candidate attributes and the social milieu to which a person would be assigned were often critical selection criteria. That is, candidates were often selected for the compatibility of their personalities and styles with those of other employees with whom they would have to work. Contextual factors also included features of the social life in the small towns in which a substantial number of ForestCo's plants and mills were located. In these small communities, work relationships often overlapped social and community networks. In addition, these small towns offered lifestyles quite different from those found in urban and suburban environments. Thus, the capacity of candidates and their families to adjust to life in these small communities became a relevant selection criterion.

The final set of selection issues addressed here are those associated with gender and sexual stereotyping. ForestCo is a traditional firm grounded in the social norms and history of several small communities in western Canada. While corporate policies regarding employment equity have evolved to meet the changing social values incorporated in provincial and federal legislation, the operating traditions of older line managers have adjusted more slowly. The accession of females to the firm's supervisory and managerial ranks is a relatively recent phenomenon. Organizational relationships between males and females are still problematic for a number of traditional male managers—and this difficulty apparently produces the potential for gender bias in personnel selection. In part, this aspect of employee selection derives from an open-system perspective, as local managers and the organizational units they manage reflect the social norms of the communities in which they are situated. It is also possible, however, to view gender and sexual stereotypes as illegal and improper interpretations of attempts to operationalize rational systems. Whichever conceptual lens one looks through to make sense of managerial actions, this perspective on ForestCo's organization is presented neither to condemn nor to condone, but to illustrate the complexity of personnel selection as it is practiced.

In this chapter, as in previous chapters, extensive use is made of the self-reports of supervisors and managers regarding the issues they had considered in making a recent appointment. Primary insight into their decision calculus was gained by retrospectively discussing those issues with them. Of course, such recollections are subject to postdecision rationalization. That is, there is likely to be a retrospective tendency to interpret the choice made more favorably and to evaluate the choices not made less favorably. In addition, managers are likely to be motivated to present themselves in favorable terms. Nevertheless, though respondents' reports are potentially biased in their evaluations of the extent to which candidates met selection criteria, they do not necessarily misrepresent the nature of criteria used to evaluate different candidates.

CANDIDATE CHARACTERISTICS AND PAST HISTORY

An Illustration of Candidate Characteristics

An initial illustration of the common features of selection criteria as used by ForestCo's managers is presented in Table 10.1. This exhibit summarizes the views of a manager who had recently chaired a selection panel for a vacant position in the unit for which he was responsible. Although this particular position was located in a logging division, the summary provides a point of departure for a more general discussion of how ForestCo's managers thought about, and discussed, the substance of the match between individual attributes and job requirements. For each candidate considered, the manager responsible for the choice provided a retrospective summary evaluation that provides initial insight into the manner in which he cognitively framed this choice.

This illustration is representative of many other summaries of candidate qualifications provided by managers at ForestCo. Most notable here is that seven of the nine candidates were evaluated on the extent and suitability of their "experience." The notion of experience as a criterion for candidate selection is problematic for this outside observer of ForestCo's internal labor market (ILM), as it is a universal attribute of all candidates. The term "experience" was invariably used as a generic construct to match candidates and jobs, even though there appeared to be many different kinds of experience. In this illustration, for example, the manager responsible for the appointment noted different experiences as qualified by "logging," "supervisory," "company," "operational," and "overall."

Table 10.1. An Illustration of Recalled Candidate Characteristics

---

Candidate 1: No logging experience and limited supervisory experience.

Candidate 2: Had no degree. Wasn't promotable. Could only be a bookkeeper.

Candidate 3: Had potential but lacked experience with the company and with logging. Her people skills needed substantial development. Her spouse was also employed by the company—and we would have had to make arrangements to find a position for him too.

Candidate 4: No logging experience, limited supervisory experience, limited mobility, limited promotability.

Candidate 5: No logging experience, too intellectual for the job, would get bored very quickly. He's overqualified and overly intelligent.

Candidate 6: Satisfied all minimum requirements. We had some concern about his people skills—but felt he was trainable.

Candidate 7: No operational experience. He's an older fellow who is very set in his way. He's not promotable and saw this position as a pre-retirement job. He's had no supervisory experience, and isn't a strong man physically. We didn't think he could handle the loggers.

Candidate 8: He's young, ambitious and personable. He has two degrees. He's good interpersonally and has lots of pulp experience. He lacks logging experience but I'm willing to teach him what he needs. The average age in the Division is 50—and he's just 30 years old. It's nice to have a young, keen guy on site.

Candidate 9: Lacks overall experience—but looks good. Being a single parent gives her a great incentive to achieve. If she'd had a couple of years more experience she would have been chosen.

A second attribute of candidates used to discriminate between those viewed more favorably and those likely to be screened out from further consideration was their advancement potential. Thus, candidate #2 was described as not being "promotable." Similarly, candidate #4 was characterized as having "limited mobility, limited promotability." Finally, candidate #7, who was characterized as being "not promotable" and looking for "a pre-retirement job," was contrasted with candidate #8, who was described as being "young, ambitious and personable." Other criteria used to differentiate among candidates often involved softer, social skills such as supervisory ability and ability to fit in with the team or the work group. Also, for some candidates, managerial inferences regarding their personality and dispositions were judged to be important. These thematic constructs used to discriminate among candidates are examined in greater detail in the following sections.

Experience as a Generic Construct with Specific Application

As partially illustrated by the immediately preceding example of a manager's characterization of the attributes of nine candidates, the term "experience" was often used to differentiate among candidates even though, by itself, the term has no operational meaning. Without operational definition, the term could be used to mean whatever the manager wanted it to mean. In such a case, "experience" cannot be verified by an impartial third party. Nevertheless, managers who used this term, *at that time and in that specific application,* appeared to understand what they meant by it and were sincere in their use of it. Moreover, these categories of experience were assumed to be meaningful to outside students of ForestCo's ILM, as they were used to "explain" why managers evaluated and chose candidates as they did. One interpretation of such usage is that it permits imprecision in the use of selection criteria. Such imprecision can be used to obscure the real reasons that specific candidates were chosen or not chosen.

Alternatively, imprecision could result from a lack of analytical ability. Lack of analysis, however, could in turn result from limitations associated with the recruitment, selection, and training of ForestCo's managers or from the inherent limitations of the task facing any person in such situations. Thus, one additional reason that this managerial language is so evocative is that the task of matching people and jobs is quite complex. As illustrated by the following quotation from a ForestCo manager, many believed that desirable qualities often could not be readily measured or described in words. Intuition and a gestalt sense of the whole appeared to be critical requirements for effective managerial action:

> He has experience which gives him an intuitive ability to recognize what practically has to be done. He can take what the boss wants and combine it with his own perspective and implement action plans.

The notion of experience was a useful way of talking about candidate potential—the capacity to perform in situations the details of which were not yet well known or understood. Thus, appreciation of a candidate's past experience also often considered how that person had previously demonstrated unrealized capacities. Although no manager put the idea into these specific terms, the central notion was that if a candidate had successfully met an earlier challenge, one involving the demonstration of previously unseen qualities, then there was an increased likelihood that the candidate could also meet future, vague challenges. Thus, managers used generic, universal attributes that had both specific and generalizable meanings regarding future candidate performance in the face of ill-defined problems. Such vague speculations are undoubtedly anathema to the proponents of detailed rationalism in organizational studies. Such cognitive orientations were highly functional, however, for situations characterized by considerable uncertainty. Indeed, this form of cognitive framing permitted ForestCo's managers to match broad, flexible considerations of candidates to possible but not yet realized organizational futures.

The programmed, rational application of the Kepner–Tregoe procedure described in Chapter 9 deals with this uncertainty and complexity by reducing the matching process to a small, manageable number of dimensions. Many of ForestCo's managers were aware that this technology of choice was a gross simplification of actual reality and preferred to rely on their judgment when intangibles were involved:

> _____ had ranked highest on the K-T scores—but [another candidate] was chosen because _____ had run into a few situations with the Ministry of Forests as a result of him being too blunt and autocratic. [The other candidate] was far more comfortable with public relations. He was seen as being confident, deliberate, and able to relate what is going on at the moment to his background experience in the industry. He's got a good track record, has been on the speakers' tour, and is seen as a doer.

Even though the second-ranked candidate was chosen in this illustration, the managers involved in the selection decision by no means implied that the K-T process is unusable. Instead, this anecdote was used as a cautionary story to suggest that the K-T process should be used with discretion. A key phrase in the foregoing statement by one of ForestCo's managers is that the successful candidate was "… able to relate what is going on at the moment to his background experience…." Background experience is the context within which managers interpret current events. Experienced managers stretched their appreciation of candidates to include both cognitive and visceral speculations about how each candidate might perform in potential situations. The appropriateness of the criteria used in person–job matches was more strongly influenced by speculations regarding future job situations than by those that applied in the present.

Thus, many managers commented that "gut feel" was an important component of the candidate–job matching process. Indeed, several managers relied more heavily on their gut feel than on the "numbers" that came out of a K-T analysis:

> There's a potential danger in using the formal system in that people can get too invested in the system itself and miss something significant because they're too focused on getting through a series of questions. There's also the possibility we could weigh the criteria incorrectly. It's not uncommon for the gut to say one thing and the numbers to say something else. When in doubt—I go with my gut.

Gut feel was advocated when candidate responses to questions in the selection interview were regarded as less than straightforward (Daniel, 1986). Managers were aware of the potential for demand influences in selection interviews that might lead candidates to provide what they thought were responses likely to be judged favorably by supervisors and selection panels. In addition, managers did not wish to bias their selections toward candidates with greater verbal facility:

> You need gut feel in order to know the truth. People aren't always truthful in interviews because they want the job and are afraid to jeopardize the opportunity to move in the organization. I believe people are closer to the truth if they talk in layman's terms versus talking like a textbook.

Also, gut feel was often invoked as the final check before making a recommendation for an appointment. At times, managers might engage in a period of reflection before committing themselves to an action in order to reduce their experience of cognitive dissonance. More often than not, however, this brief period of reflection constituted a final review of all their perceptions to ensure that this appointment was comfortable for them and made sense. Periods of reflection permitted both an integration of previously dissonant signals and an opportunity to prepare and possibly rehearse justifications for the selections made:

> I always pay attention to whether the choice feels right in my stomach. I walk through all the regular steps of posting, short-listing, interviews and personal chats, and so on, and then check my gut to see if I feel comfortable with what I'm about to do.

The argument presented thus far is that managers' evocations of candidate experience represent their attempts to consider, in general terms, the very wide array of potential situations each candidate might encounter and to speculate how that candidate might perform. It is unlikely that each candidate's performance is considered for all situations envisioned. Instead, candidate characteristics provide the stimuli for managers, and others on the selection panel, to consider situations in which the performance of each candidate might be at risk. If candidate performance is at risk, so too are the reputations of the managers responsible for the appointment (Tetlock, 1985).

Different candidate appointments presented different degrees of uncertainty and potential risk. Managers considered past performance to be a relatively good guide to future performance when they judged that candidates were likely in the future to encounter situations similar to those they had experienced in the past. Because many managers were familiar primarily with ForestCo, or occasionally with other organizations in the same industry, quite limited samples of past experience were regarded as generalizable to potential job requirements. For all its evocative potential, previous job experience could be used to restrict candidate requirements to those that had strong face validity in a self-replicating definition of ForestCo's organization:

> The most important criterion in selecting the individuals for the job is previous demonstrated expertise. It's critical that the persons appointed have grading qualifications—which can only be obtained after at least three to four years' experience in the job.

Although it is possible to fit candidate requirements based on years of past experience to rational, detailed job specifications, the number of potential candidates who possess the requisite combination of experiences could be very small indeed. Thus, one must wonder whether the requirements to have "coastal experience," "manage contract logging," and be "familiar with herbicides" in the following example were elaborated post hoc or were in fact used a priori to select the candidate finally chosen:

> We screened applicants on the basis of their years of experience and knowledge of forestry practices. We also wanted someone who had coastal experience, knew how to manage contract logging, and was familiar with herbicides.

Part of the difficulty of interpreting the term "experience" is that it can have multiple meanings. Unless there is an explicit qualification, there is an implicit assumption that the quality of experience equals the number of years of experience. However, qualifications regarding interpretations of candidate experiences were often implicit, and interpretations of experience were socially constructed by the persons involved in the selection process. While there is face validity to a process in which persons most familiar with job requirements and candidate characteristics select candidates for positions, there was no objective, external means of assessing the extent to which different candidates would likely perform in the job to be filled.

Considerations of the prior experience of candidates often included the application of technical knowledge in a situation that involved specific, interpersonal relationships—the one aspect of past experience that was not transferable from one situation to another:

> _____ had 10 to 15 years' experience in sawmill operations. He had a grading and tallying ticket. In addition, he was most knowledgeable about computer systems, particularly the details of the systems we use here. He knows how to put together orders for all world markets and is familiar with people like the truckers, longshoremen, etcetera who have to be dealt with daily. His personality is splendid, and he knows how to deal with people problems.

Past experience, then, was regarded as a key candidate attribute from which to infer capacity to do the job. Past experience was also important from time to time as an indicator that the selected candidate had paid his dues and that his judgments should be respected by his new coworkers and subordinates:

> Experience helps—the crews tend to test the engineers.

> _____'s experience gives him both credibility and authority. He's seen as an expert.

Finally, experience was used as an indicator that the candidate required little or no further training. Experience signaled that little time should pass before high levels of performance could be expected:

> This was a good appointment because he had lots of experience and was a turnkey person who could move in and do the job with minimal training.

Past experience was the initial indicator of a candidate's suitability for a position. Past experience was a catchall construct from which the particular skills and competencies directly related to a specific job could be inferred. While specific questions about past experiences could be asked, as in behavior description interviewing (Janz, Hellervik, & Gilmore, 1986), possession of skills was more likely to be inferred from occupancy of a position than from detailed examination of conduct in a role. That is, candidates were assumed to have developed the required skills and competencies in the course of the previous career trajectories associated with their length of service in the firm. Separately and together, past experience and length of service were used as indicators of future performance.

Length of Service and Past Experience as a Guide to Future Performance

Both administered staffing appointments and staffing actions involving posting required managers to be familiar with present and future jobs and the present and future capacities of potential candidates. Of necessity, managers were required to forecast near- and medium-term futures and to confront the management of time-based phenomena. This dynamic feature of organizational life was most prevalent in managers' use of past experience as a guide to future performance:

> _____ had built [another mill]—which had become the most successful mill in the Region. He not only started up the mill, but was also involved in the design of the mill. When we decided to rebuild [another mill], we wanted the most knowledgeable manager in terms of building and employee involvement to head the project. _____ knew the people, had done the job before, was in his 40s, and could well take the challenge. He had run mills before, so there were few concerns with him dealing with the union. He understood the environment. He was a natural fit.

Past performance was signaled by past experience as partially indicated by length of service. Long service in particular was often used as a shorthand and de facto measure of past experience, and implicitly of past performance:

> _____ has been with the company for 20 years and has a depth of experience.
>
> He's been at this division for 18 years.

Long service had meaning within this context because of its implicit associations of loyalty, depth of experience, personal learning, continued acceptable performance, and obligations for recognition. Often, however, a candidate's long service was interpreted in the light of supplemental observations of related candidate characteristics, such as the technical and craft experience already gained by the candidate and applicable in the new job situation:

> _____ has lots of experience. He knows this division and knows documentation and sales.
>
> _____ was by far the most experienced candidate. He was already the Divisional Forester at [another site].

The consequences of past experience often extended beyond considerations of immediate job performance. From time to time, a candidate's past experience was extrapolated beyond its application in an immediate assignment to future career possibilities. Such extrapolations were particularly important when candidates were making significant career moves. These moves included crossovers from one product group to another or from a single functional specialty to multifunctional roles and responsibilities:

> _____ has spent all his career in pulp and paper. He was sent to [a particular business unit] for grooming in the building materials industry. He had two years to get to know the business. He knew most of the people, managers' skills, and labor problems. He's the logical choice to run either one or the other of the two Regions.

Technical expertise and supervisory/managerial experience were the attributes most often cited by managers as having been inferred from the length of a candidate's tenure with ForestCo. The personal and social attributes associated with experience were also used as selection criteria. For example, the successful candidate's experience and reputation often helped others, especially other candidates, accept the legitimacy of the selection and appointment. This acceptance appeared to be especially important when nonselected candidates were to work interdependently with the new appointee, as their acceptance of the legitimacy of the appointment was an important feature of future working relationships:

> I preferred _____ because of her previous work experience here. [Another candidate] also knew _____ and liked her. Since she liked her, it was easier for her to accept _____ in the job she didn't get.

Thus, length of service together with the work experience associated with past organizational tenure was an important indicator of current and potential performance.

Age-Related Norms as Staffing Guidelines

Within conventional social norms, most adults begin their working careers in either their late teens or their early 20s. They gain experience with increased organizational or industry tenure—and they grow older. Thus, in many organizations, there is often a high degree of correlation between the age distribution of employees and that of their tenure with the organization. It is no surprise, then, to find that many organizations exhibit age norms in which accession to a given job or level in the organizational hierarchy is associated with a relatively narrow range of employee ages (Lawrence, 1987). ForestCo did not exhibit pronounced age norms across the company as a whole. Nevertheless, various managers used candidate age as an indicator of past experience and as a yardstick against their ideas of appropriate age norms to assess a candidate's fit with a proposed move:

> _____ was the right age [mid-40s] to be appointed to this particular position. If he'd been in his mid-30s, he would have been too young and wouldn't have had enough experience. Being too young is often related to the acceptability of a manager to the men under his supervision. It's difficult for young managers to be accepted if the people who work for them are much older. Older people resent being overlooked. When it comes to promotion, they particularly resist golden boys. In view of the range of ages in this operation, _____ is more acceptable because he's mature and experienced.

A candidate's age was used to signal different attributes depending on the immediate context in which it was interpreted. For example, chronological age could be used as a preliminary indicator of maturity, as an indicator of the amount and degree of career energy remaining, and as an indicator of the potential rigidity or flexibility of a candidate's attitude toward new career directions. Indeed, as the following quotation suggests, projections quite far into the future were used to test the appropriateness of certain age-related appointments:

> Age is a consideration, but not an overriding concern. As far as age is concerned, what I'm really looking for is maturity. I'm more concerned about candidates who are 45 years old and started here at a junior level. How much more can they give? How do they feel about reporting to a younger supervisor? How well will they adapt to starting at the bottom of another career ladder? Potential is very important. I'm most interested in whether they could move into my job in 10 years' time.

Most concerns about age and age–grade relationships were framed in relation to organizational investments in the training of particular candidates. Appointments had a dual character. The first facet concerned the extent to which lessons of past experience could be applied in the new job for which a candidate was being considered. The second facet concerned what the appointee would, or could, learn in the new job and subsequently apply in even more new jobs. This second aspect of internal appointments became quite critical if the candidates being considered for a position were approaching ages at which persons "normally" wound down their organizational careers:

> Age influences our decision making because we consider the potential for additional years of service and what kind of return of investment you'd get on your training and development.

If there were signals that candidates were unlikely to acquire new knowledge, or that other age-related considerations could limit the development and application of skills and capacities, then the value of training would be regarded with increased skepticism. For example, an anticipated retirement could make the development of skills and capacities less worthwhile and implicitly lower a candidate's expected value:

> If a person is 60 years old, he normally won't get the job because ForestCo isn't prepared to invest in someone who's not going to be around for the next 10 or 20 years. Only six people have left this operation in the past 10 years. The person we just appointed is 38—which is the right age for the job.

> If you're 55, it's unlikely you'll be hired as a trainee because it doesn't make sense to go through all the training at that stage of a person's life.

Age thus appeared to be used in specific age-related considerations, such as the implicit length of time over which a return from an investment in training could be expected. For many managers, however, age was an approximate signal that certain features of a candidate should be investigated more thoroughly (Rosen & Jerdee, 1976). Age per se was not necessarily a significant attribute, but rather an indicator of age-related characteristics such as maturity, knowledge, and physical capacity:

> Age is a factor only to the extent it impacts on the physical capacity to do the job.

Thus, some managers used the candidate's age as a preliminary diagnostic screen to identify further questions that would help assess more directly the candidate's capacity to perform:

> I wanted his replacement to be a younger [30s] engineer. Though age is a consideration, I'm mainly interested in what the person has to offer and for what purpose. When I did hire, I went for _____, who had been in the hourly ranks for 21 years and is very respected by the men. He's 52 years old, and it serves our purpose to hire him because he has solid knowledge of the kraft process.

While length of service and age were important indicators of past experience and suitability for advancement, other considerations such as inherent capacity to develop additional skills were also frequently invoked. In particular, managers were often concerned with contextual issues related to how they might manage lines of progression. Thus, issues of candidate stability or mobility following an appointment were often regarded as important criteria in selection decisions. Increased consideration was typically given, however, to candidates who demonstrated the capacity for further development, rather than to those who were expected to remain almost indefinitely in the position for which they were candidates. These and other issues related to the management of lines of progression are reviewed in the next section.

MANAGING LINES OF PROGRESSION

It is not easy to manage an orderly flow of employees through lines of progression. As noted in Chapter 7, there was a very large disruption of these flows as a consequence of ForestCo's experience of the 1981–1982 recession and the subsequent dislocations in the firm's staffing practices. These external exigencies wrought havoc with past patterns of career and skill development. To meet needs for opportunistic adaptation, yet provide dependable current performance, ForestCo's managers did not view all positions as requiring mobility. In most units, staffing was arranged to meet needs of both mobility and stability.

Managing for Both Mobility and Stability

Although future promotability was often the most important criterion in selecting from among several candidates for a vacant position, many managers were also aware that their management of the flows of employees into and through their particular operation required a mix of stability and mobility:

> I feel there has to be a balance of promotables and dependables who stay forever. I wanted someone who would stay longer and lend some stability to my group, since some key positions here require long-term knowledge. When I can, I like to have two or three long-term people.

Stability was important for several reasons. It was judged that skill development would occur more readily if trainees were exposed to more experienced persons rather than simply being left to "share their ignorance with other trainees." In addition, well-established and familiar personal relationships were critical for the performance of certain functions. If the occupants of these positions were to change frequently, the dependability associated with stable occupancy of these positions would be lost. Enduring, dependable personal relationships appeared to be key performance characteristics of Timekeeper positions and hands-on functions in Employee Relations:

> The Timekeeper position is not one of progression. It's more for someone who's interested in being competent and having a long-term stay. We want stability in this area, as the job affects all other jobs as well as the hourly employees' view of staff at ForestCo.

> We're really concerned there might be a shortage of ER specialists, and having the degree helps move people more rapidly ahead. But this is really a training position, and it's difficult to do the job properly when you've got two strangers assigned to the group. We need lots of continuity to do this job well.

Stability, or at least slow mobility, was a by-product of specialist requirements in other jobs and occupations. When full competency at a particular job required the long-term development of specialist skills, organizational planners recognized that an efficient life cycle of skill development, skill application, and then future advancement should occur over an extended time—one much longer than conventional organizational norms for other occupations:

> The job requires specific knowledge of the _____ system, and there's just not that sort of background generally available in the organization. Even if we had the training resources, it would take more than three years for a totally green person to become independent. So, we have to watch so we don't hire an overqualified person who's just looking at this as a stepping-stone. I feel I can't hold people back who want to get ahead—but mobility is a risk to the time and money invested in this specialist training. Ideally, I'd like a person who's interested in this function and wants to stay, someone who doesn't want to get ahead.

Against this background of a need for both stability and mobility, candidate suitability for future mobility was a more difficult evaluation. Assessing candidates on the basis of their potential for advancement was often problematic, but was a significant preoccupation for the supervisors and managers attempting to manage lines of progression.

Advancement Potential and Mobility along Lines of Progression

Advancement potential was a significant consideration in the management of lines of progression, as there was an ongoing need for new skills and capacities in the human resources of the organization. Much of the demand for new skills originated from the normal requirement to replace or develop the knowledge and skills lost through flows of individuals into other organizational units as well as out of the organization. Assessments of demand, however, were necessitated by far more complex adjustments on the part of the organization. Few flows of aggregate human resources across a large, complex organization such as ForestCo could be anticipated easily. Responses to demands and adjustments in flows were most often made when a staffing opportunity presented itself. In addition to these complications, new products, new markets, new plants, and new technologies were also large, external forces for organizational change. Thus, there was always a persistent, ever-present demand for new skills and individual capacities.

The need for a mix of stability and mobility was perhaps more appropriately seen as an occasional need for stability in certain positions against a pervasive background of a need for advancement potential. Advancement potential was therefore frequently a key selection criterion used to discriminate among candidates for vacant positions. When stability was not a critical requirement, a lack of advancement potential and interest in future mobility could quickly remove a candidate from any further consideration as a potential appointee:

> If a person's not transferable, they're not touched. They need to demonstrate persistence and a high level of common sense.

Inferences about advancement potential were based on expectations for candidates' capacity to learn and develop new skills and capacities as a function of their experience. Many cues and attributions were used to assess development potential, including evidence of persistent effort, common sense, and initiative. Evidence of apathy and a "poor attitude" also signaled the absence of advancement potential:

> We wanted succession potential. The one thing that stopped any further consideration was a demonstration of a poor attitude and apathy. We didn't want someone who would just do what was required and failed to demonstrate any leadership qualities.

Inclusion of advancement potential in the criteria used to discriminate among candidates was an acknowledgment of the dynamic nature of ForestCo's ILM. Most managers recognized that they needed to keep the human resource system of the corporation moving with a steady stream of staff into, through, and out of the organization. Moreover, these managers recognized that few perfect matches would be obtained between ideal job requirements and actual candidate qualifications. Therefore, they used judgments about each candidate's learning capacity to develop an appreciation as to how each might grow into the job:

> People aren't perfect. Even if they don't have all the required skills, but have the basic abilities, we must give them a chance to develop.

Advancement potential, including the demonstrated capacity to learn, was a key requirement of employees in ForestCo's ILM. Individual employees were expected to advance through the formal and quasi-formal lines of progression in the firm. However, the management of employee mobility along career ladders and lines of progression was often awkward, as candidates did not always appear to benefit fully from their prior experience in a line of progression. Neither the quality of persons brought in to do the work at the lower level of the line of progression nor the experience of work at these lower levels was judged to be sufficient to generate the qualities needed at supervisory and middle management levels:

> What happens is you end up hiring outsiders for bottom-level positions only. The bottom end doesn't add a lot to the organization, and therefore it's pretty useless to have new blood come into the organization only at the bottom. They don't have any depth to them. The result is they can't contribute to moving some of the staleness out of the old blood.

Movement along a line of progression often required that employees do more than learn from on-the-job experience. In several lines of progression, employees could advance beyond a certain level only if they had obtained a professional qualification:

> Positions can become blocked with people who can't go any further because they haven't pursued any further education. If they haven't gotten any professional designation, it's difficult to create a new position where it doesn't matter if the guy moves or not.

The need to keep lines of progression open was an important factor in selecting individuals for vacant positions. Managers often looked at potential candidates to see whether they could move at least two positions above their current assignment:

> An important consideration is that you put people into jobs who are promotable so that unpromotables do not plug positions that are part of the succession path.

Employees who failed to meet expectations, and who did not manifest their promise because they lacked persistent initiative in seeking new challenges and opportunities to improve the status quo, were handicapped in their candidacy for new appointments:

> Two of the candidates we considered were judged to be stop-and-go performers according to supervisors of their last two jobs. I don't want someone who finishes their job and then waits to be reassigned.

Other candidates were similarly disadvantaged with respect to advancement potential when they demonstrated an incapacity to exhibit the supervisory behaviors required of them following previous promotions:

> He has been unable to confront and maintain or even improve standards. He tended to shy away from union conflicts and nothing got settled. It was a constant battle, and he couldn't handle the stress. He just wasn't ready for supervision.

Appointments judged to be unsuccessful had repercussions not only for the manager's reputation and judgment, but also for the manager's current problems in managing an orderly flow of employees through various lines of progression:

> I didn't want someone in the position who would be in the way of others who would need to have the General Manager experience to move up the ladder.

However, employees also had their own expectations regarding "natural succession" in the line of progression, and they objected to actions that detracted from their expectations for further advancement:

> _____ was supposed to back up [her boss], but instead kept herself busy with mundane tasks to avoid taking on the responsibility. Consequently, when we brought in another person from outside, there was a lot of jealousy as she considered any job in her area as a privileged position.

Past experience in a line of progression was important for further advancement. But while past experience was often a necessary condition, it was rarely sufficient. Past performance and demonstrated capacity to learn and to advance were also necessary considerations. While an occasional position required stability rather than mobility, a widespread criterion of candidate acceptability was the potential of a candidate to advance beyond the vacant position for which he was being considered. In this instance, there was little evidence of the Peter Principle (Peter & Hull, 1969). Employees whose past progression and performance indicated that they might soon reach their level of incompetence were ostensibly not chosen, as their "final" move might block a critical line of progression.

Time in Rank and Time in Previous Position

Although notions of lines of progression were partially and generally in place in many parts of the organization, managing flows of employees through a sequence of changing jobs was not without problems. In particular, time in rank was an important component of the management of a line of progression. A time in rank that was viewed as desirable was one that fell within the range defined at one end by a minimum amount of time to learn the basic skills and to demonstrate a capacity to perform and at the other end by a maximum amount of time to avoid the stagnation and potential loss of motivation associated with lack of mobility. In many departments, these times had become institutionalized into customary norms for length of time in a particular job:

> We need to groom people for progression into important positions, which requires the development of skills. They need to remain in positions for two to five years maximum and then move on.

However, time in rank or position was not always managed easily. External exigencies often disrupted managerial plans for orderly mobility. For example, employees could be moved too quickly when several vacancies in a short time initiated movement along the line of progression. In this situation, employees could be yanked up the line of progression before they had developed sufficient experience, or a manager could be left with no candidates to consider for positions that later became vacant:

> We had two openings—one at the pulp mill and one in the sawmill. These positions had been used as training schools for accountants. But once one or two people at the top move, the chain starts and we lose good, experienced people and don't get suitable replacements. I wanted someone with experience—but because of turnover, we had no one to reorganize with.

The opposite phenomenon, namely, too much time in rank, made career advancement problematic in another section of the company:

> In order to give my people a change and a sense of personal growth, I decided to rotate my staff to expand their experience base. I also thought it would make them more eligible for promotion. It's expensive to do this, but it helps people develop a more positive attitude. These men will continue circling until someone above them leaves. I call this process "the 35- to 45-years-old training circle while sitting and waiting."

Recognition that someone had spent close to the "maximum" length of time in a particular rank often built up pressure to consider that person for further career opportunities that became available. Time in rank or position thus became a signal that a candidate should be considered ready for further development:

> —————— had been at the Regional Office for five years, and it was time for him to get hands-on experience and knowledge in Mill Accounting.

This pressure originated partially from an acknowledgment that it was time for further career advancement and also partially from an implied obligation to recognize and reward past service. Rewards for past service were an important component of the organizational system, which needed incentives for candidates to continue to be motivated to develop and apply the knowledge and experience that they had acquired.

Assignments as Rewards for Past Service

Because timelines of progression could not always be managed in an orderly way, managers often found themselves needing slack in the network of mutual requests and obligations associated with cooperative work relationships. When subordinates performed well in a particularly difficult position for a number of years, future moves were often arranged for them as a reward for loyalty and past service. These considerations were important as a means of keeping the system lubricated. Employees who were asked to take less than desirable assignments needed to expect future rewards for their compliance with the current needs of the organization:

> After seven years of service [in a previous job], he should be rewarded.

The initiative for moves made to reward past service could come from candidates who requested that they be considered for future moves:

> _____ had been around for a long time and had paid his dues. He was interested in a change in career and a break from what he'd been doing before.

The initiative for a candidate to be considered could also come from a manager who felt an obligation to a particular employee and who wished to maintain cordial relations in the unit under his responsibility:

> _____ had been in [an isolated community] for many years and was the Shop Foreman there for quite some time. The division felt they owed him for his long service in [the isolated community].

Of course, actions to meet obligations to loyal subordinates could also serve current organizational objectives to develop further skills and capacities in these employees:

> _____ is in his late 50s. He'd been at [a particular mill] for 20 years, and it was time for him to get a new look on life. We decided he needed to get some export experience he didn't get at [this mill].

The corollary of the Jackall (1988) notion of fealty in organizational life is that of an obligation on the part of a superior to meet the personal needs of those who demonstrate allegiance to the superior. Only in exceptional circumstances did mentors decline to provide their protégés with considerable opportunity to rebuild purposive and productive organizational lives. Normally, ForestCo's managers showed considerable appreciation for this facet of organizational life and often felt an obligation to support subordinates who had "lost their way" or needed further encouragement:

> ForestCo owes employees an opportunity to turn a new leaf. _____ was stagnating at [Mill A] and was experiencing a personality conflict with his boss there. He wasn't being stroked and felt he was under a lot of pressure. It's a challenge to get his confidence back and to move him up the ladder. I'd known him ten years ago at [Mill A], and we'd known each other quite well.

Management of lines of progression was not a straightforward process. The task was cognitively complex, involving the management of orderly flows of employees over time and into an uncertain future. Subordinate performances of past assignments were crucial indicators of future possibilities. Moreover, managers had to demonstrate continuing appreciation of their obligations to loyal subordinates if they were to maintain the viability of current and future mobility along the line of progression.

While immediate job knowledge and required skills, as well as advancement potential and a candidate's capacity to develop further, were pervasive selection issues, many selection decisions also included other considerations. These factors, which are described in the next section, were not representative of a majority of selection decisions reviewed. Nevertheless, they were described with sufficient frequency that to omit them from a discussion of selection criteria used in ForestCo's organization would be to describe ForestCo's ILM incompletely.

CONTEXTUAL FEATURES OF STAFFING ASSIGNMENTS

Thus far, two sets of selection criteria have been described. First, the past experience of each candidate was often used as an indicator of skills and capacities developed in that organizational setting. These individual skills were examined in relation to the likelihood that their possessor would apply them to future organizational problems. Second, selection criteria derived from issues associated with managing lines of progression were also used. This section examines a third set of selection criteria, namely, "other" concerns that derive from the organizational and environmental context within which staffing was taking place. The general issues of enduring candidate dispositions and candidate–organization fit are given first consideration, followed by a discussion of broader issues such as the fit between the community and a candidate and his family. Finally, information on how some ForestCo managers viewed gender issues and sexual stereotyping in their staffing of organizational positions is presented.

Enduring Dispositional Attributes

Because future scenarios were, of course, uncertain, ForestCo's managers often looked for enduring dispositional attributes of candidates to get some feel for how each candidate might respond in this uncertain future. Although assessments of knowledge, skills, abilities, and capacities for future development were important to their development of this appreciation, managers also looked for consistent patterns of behavior. An illustrative set of selection criteria was stated as follows:

> We need someone with patience and good potential for promotion. They should fit the chemistry and culture of the group.

ForestCo's managers often looked for outcroppings of a bedrock personality "that you could go to the bank with." The assumption in these assessments was that the candidate's personality would remain stable, even though the candidate might encounter enormously varying situations (Staw & Ross, 1985). In particular, the chosen candidate should have the personality and personal style that fit group work and teamwork:

> Personality was a very important aspect of this hire. Whomever we chose had to deal with others and be able to communicate with them. They had to be imaginative. Our business requires lateral thinking. They have to have drive and be self-starters. They'll be put into a team where their skills have to complement and blend with others who have different skills. We couldn't hire someone who preferred to work in isolation.

A large variety of enduring dispositional attributes were mentioned by ForestCo's managers. Skills and knowledge required for superior job performance were important selection criteria, but the managers responsible also sought additional candidate attributes that gave them further confidence that their appointments would be successful (Barrick & Mount, 1991).

> We're looking for maturity. Their temperament is important. Their personality has to be a team fit but they should also be able to operate independently.

Dispositional attributes were occasionally inferred from sparse evidence. Even though inferred dispositional attributes could initially appear to be unrelated to job requirements, managers were adept at relating them to the candidate's capacity to work effectively within the local organizational culture:

> One guy felt like too much Madison Avenue. He was too bright and flashy and too far apart from local style to get the guys on his side.

Occasionally, enduring dispositional attributes were voiced as the ideal, preferred characteristics of the candidate the manager would like to find. Certainly, the description of desired qualities noted below seemed to this academic researcher to be an unlikely combination!

> What we wanted was someone with the gray matter of an academic and the style of a millworker. Someone who could create a vision, who could organize thoughts logically and clearly.

Other combinations of qualities were perhaps more likely to be found than that just noted—but nevertheless difficult to find:

> We were looking for someone with a strong personality. We wanted someone who could take abuse and who would quietly and not too forcefully go about applying their technical knowledge.

The capacity to exhibit a consistent set of behaviors in uncertain, changing, and muddled future situations requires toughness and personal integrity. ForestCo managers wanted as good a guarantee as they could get that their selected candidates would persist in striving to meet high standards. They also wanted employees who had demonstrated a capacity to bring others along with them in their collective endeavor:

> We didn't want someone who was satisfied with the status quo. We looked for ability to analyze. A secondary ability was that they should be able to promote the project and be able to sell change. _____ had ambition and sufficient drive to see the project through. He doesn't use his mouth before his brains and doesn't measure progress through physical action. This is important here, as it will be a long time before we know if anything tangible may or may not happen as a result of the study.

Having a reputation cuts both ways. While reputations such as "being organized and methodical" or "trusted to have good judgment and to do a good job" were usually considered to be positive, negative reputations could also quickly exclude a candidate from further consideration. Moreover, as the following quotation illustrates, reputations related to enduring negative dispositional qualities were unlikely to be shaken by a single demonstration of positive performance. Apparently, there could be nothing worse than a bad rep in the social and political milieu of organizational staffing:

> He had a temper problem. He was very bright and could have done the job, but his reputation killed his chances. It's unfortunate, because once he's branded it'll be very hard for him to get rid of it. It's a long road to recover your reputation.

While enduring dispositional qualities such as a person's personality were typically considered in addition to demonstrated skills and personal capacities, candidate personalities were examined for their fit to the interpersonal requirements of the position to be staffed. A candidate's personality and interpersonal style were used as entries to more careful considerations of the potential match between the candidate's behavior and the personalities of the team to which he would be assigned.

Matching Team, Group, and Interpersonal Requirements

Even though ForestCo was a traditional organization in a mature industry with many instances of local forms of functional and specialist organization, most of these structural forms were being replaced by more cooperative, flatter forms of hierarchy and working relations. A few plants and special units were regarded as leaders in these trends. In these units, considerations of the capacity of the successful candidate to work cooperatively were regarded as being at least as important as technical job requirements (Chatman, 1989). In other situations, managers looked for a potential fit between the interpersonal skills of candidates and the specific organizational requirements for teamwork:

> Relations with coworkers are important job requirements. The overall quality of the job done in the mill comes from cooperative lateral relations, as we're trying to get experienced craft workers such as sawyers, edgers, and sorters to modify their behaviors and judgments.

Demands such as these implied that candidates with authoritarian personalities might find these new work situations to be relatively difficult:

> _____ is dogmatic and would have trouble in a role where he had to deal with operations people. He'd have no authority over them except through the mill manager. He'll have to find other ways of getting his point of view across.

Many managers extended the general job requirements defined as qualifications, knowledge, and skills to include specific behaviors and personal styles that they thought were appropriate to the situation they were trying to staff:

> Successful candidates must fit the team—both in terms of their personality and their interpersonal behavior. They can have all the degrees they want, but if they don't fit they won't get the job. By fit, we mean a similar disposition to the rest of the group, a sense of humor, a willingness to create an enjoyable and exciting place to work. We want to be able to throw anything at them and not get back a "not in my job description" response.

For the most part, ForestCo's managers exhibited a practical and pragmatic approach to organizational work. Few adopted the technospeak of contemporary human relations specialists. Rather, they saw the need for cooperative relations emerging from their own analyses of task requirements. If two or more persons needed to talk and work together to get a job done, then these people should demonstrate that they can work with others. From time to time, however, the language of the human resource specialist could be heard creeping into the plainspeak of practical men:

> The most important criterion was the person's fit into the team concept which we're creating at this mill. Everyone in the organization is required to work cooperatively as a unit. We're looking for individuals with the personality, attitudes, and awareness of group dynamics which enables them to work in groups. They should have the capacity to motivate both themselves and others to work within this cooperative framework.

This section began with a discussion of the extent to which soft, social skills were an important complement to the learning associated with career development and advancement potential. That theme is revisited here, as various candidate assignments were made precisely because the interpersonal requirements for business success would require appointees to develop different interpersonal styles of management. There is a strong survival subtext to these assignments. Candidates who failed to develop these skills were not expected to maintain a positive career direction. Managers acted to serve their vested interests in both the health of the overall employment system and the career development of subordinates and protégés (O'Reilly, Chatman, & Caldwell, 1991). Much of the sorting out of potential candidates was done by management's adopting a paternalistic approach to employee development:

> _____ is intense, and that's O.K. because that's part of competence. But he's overly stern. He had to learn to be not just a hard-nosed leader because people no longer buy that kind of leadership. He didn't understand delegation, so we put him into [Mill A], where he had to learn the business and to delegate if he was going to survive there.

In other situations, a candidate could be aware of serious deficiencies in his personal style and as a consequence look for an assignment that would help him develop more appropriate skills:

—————————— wanted to change from being an autocratic technical engineer because he'd lost out on a manager's job at [Division A] because of his poor people skills. He felt he couldn't change at [Division B] and that it would be easier for him to develop at [Division C].

Because many of the routes to middle- and senior-level management jobs were through specialist occupations that initially emphasized technical competence, a generic training issue for the organization as a whole was development of people skills in technically trained personnel. For most jobs in most firms in this mature industry, technical job demands could be readily met by job occupants. However, the application of specific technical knowledge in concert with persons having different technical specialties was often problematic. Thus, a generic development theme for the majority of supervisory and lower management levels was that of people skills. A capacity to obtain collaboration, cooperation, and integration of diverse, specialist skills was a pervasive concern and selection consideration.

Community and Family Considerations

Traditional models of managerial decision making, including the processes of staffing and selection decisions, typically present the choice among competing candidates as taking place at a single stage in the overall decision process. In these stereotypical conceptualizations of decision processes, all the criteria used to make the choice are considered concurrently. In contrast, selection decisions in ForestCo were often made in various stages over extended periods of time. Moreover, different criteria were occasionally used to select among candidates at different stages of the selection process. When candidates were under final consideration for appointment to a particular position, the selection criteria used to discriminate among candidates became oriented more to idiosyncratic attributes of the short-listed candidates than to the preceding standardized, bureaucratic procedure. For example, when all short-listed candidates readily met minimum requirements, a wider range of selection criteria would be used to identify the "better" of the candidates remaining in the competition. These criteria would emerge from more detailed and contextualized considerations of the position to be filled. It was usually at these later stages of the selection process that issues related to gender, marital status, and community fit were considered.

Very few biases in terms of gender or marital status per se were expressed by ForestCo's managers. When questions related to these attributes were asked as part of a selection process, they were usually framed in terms of managerial, unit, and organizational interests. That is, within the local frame of reference of organizational norms, customs, and procedures, ForestCo's managers reported that they were primarily concerned with identifying and selecting the best candidate as far as organizational performance was concerned. ForestCo's managers rarely exhibited concern with any larger social definition of social equity. This indifference did not imply that they were hostile to such social change, as there was almost no privately voiced resistance to corporate initiatives to provide equal opportunity throughout the corporation. Given this predominant attitude of indifference, only a few managers actively pushed to increase the promotion rate of female supervisors and managers.

Within their local frame of reference in the final stages of each selection process, ForestCo's managers looked for issues that might interfere with the patterns of mobility they wished to have their subordinates follow. They were attentive to potential restrictions on mobility that might emerge from particular features of a candidate's family situation.

They were aware that if they forced moves on their subordinates, and ignored the personal preferences of their employees and their families, proposed moves would be unlikely to turn out successfully:

> I've had the experience of seeing a coworker appointed to a job against his wishes. His needs weren't considered, and he had to live with that decision. So, I'd rather make sure the job opportunity fits the employee's needs too.

Even though candidates understood themselves to be moving along a line of progression, they might be reluctant to make certain moves because their evaluations of long-term opportunities were insufficient to offset the short-run disruptions to their family and lifestyle. Revealing their reluctance to move could adversely affect their future standing in the corporation and limit the staffing options open to their supervisors:

> I like to promote my people to different areas so they get a variety of experience. But a key problem I have is in dealing with the mobility issue. Times have changed and people are no longer prepared to just get up and move. Men now have wives who work and who consider their careers as important as their spouses'. Also, employees consider things other than their immediate career—taking care of old parents, kids and their schools, and so on.

Even though managers attempted to take candidate preferences into account in making administrative assignments, their primary objective was to meet organizational needs. A certain degree of slack was granted to subordinates in terms of meeting their personal preferences, but at some point a limit would be reached. Rarely did a manager have definite, preestablished limits, but as the following quotation illustrates, some managers did have quite definite ideas of how much slack they would grant their subordinates:

> Lifestyle issues are much more prevalent than they were ten years ago. The end result from my point of view is that they get two chances to go somewhere. If they refuse more than twice, they're likely to get terminated because my system depends on there being mobility.

In the small, relatively isolated mill towns in which ForestCo had major production operations, the capacity of a potential supervisor or manager and their family to fit the local community was of paramount importance. Again, local managers did not wish to invest in an appointment that was unlikely to continue for a reasonable term. No doubt based on their own experience, they were aware of how critical the general attitude of an employee's spouse toward living in these idiosyncratic communities could be:

> When hiring someone, we must be honest about life in [a mill town]. We bring in spouses to look around and set them up with access to information about the community. We go out to dinner to get more information about their opinions. Wives need information about the labor market in [the mill town]. There must be honesty in hiring—we must make a fair and realistic representation to potential employees of what it's like to live and work here.

Geographic relocation was a particularly awkward concomitant of mobility along some lines of progression. Operational experience in ForestCo's mills often meant taking assignments in the small-town hinterland that allowed readier access to the local forests. Small-town life appeared to be an acquired taste, and not all employees and their spouses could fit in with the local culture:

> Assignments to this community need people who are willing to work long hours and who are willing to get involved in local activities. We want family persons, so conflicts between family and work needs must be resolved if they're to be assigned here. You can't dictate to your spouse where and how she's going to live. If a candidate says "My wife will do what I want," we get worried because this may reflect how they treat other people.

Consequently, when managers were examining the top one or two candidates for a specific position, they would examine the issue of community fit very carefully. Occasionally, the attitude of the spouse could be a significant factor in the selection of a candidate, because the fit between one's spouse and the local community could detract from subsequent job commitment:

> _____ just quit and moved elsewhere. He'd been a little disturbed during his stay here because his wife didn't like the community. This is a common experience. This is an established community and the people here aren't hungry for new friends. You have to be outgoing for the town to accept you. I know _____ and his wife considered whether or not to make the move here, but that doesn't mean much. There's no guarantee that the person who's best for the job will necessarily be happy here. In general, we aren't prepared to settle for someone who doesn't want to be here because of his family situation.

One way to control the uncertainty associated with bringing in employees and their families who were unfamiliar with mill-town lifestyles was to prefer local recruits. They were already familiar with the local community and had well-established social ties that engendered stability and predictability—valued commodities in employee selection:

> He was a local boy, and we like to draw from the local community for many reasons. Our hiring costs are lower; he already knows his way around and doesn't have to adjust to local living conditions.

> His family is stable and he has ties to the area. It's important to fit the community where you live.

This general issue of fit between a candidate, his family, and the local community could occasionally spill over into the controversial issue of gender. Jobs traditionally filled by males were more difficult to fill with females because the socially prescribed roles in the small, traditional mill towns meant that there was less support from the local infrastructure for nontraditional female employment. Certain occupations were deemed to be "male" jobs. Moreover, assumptions about female roles likely meant that females would face extra demands in challenging the male-defined work world:

> When you create and think about staffing a position, you have to think about the environment. For example, we don't look for female superintendents. The cultural mix of [a mill town] is not representative of the national average—we're not even close.

There is little question that most managers were intentionally rational in their administration of staffing and lines of progression. This does not mean, however, that in a large corporation with delegated staffing authority managers were completely free of prejudices—particularly managers who were steeped in the history and traditions of the industry. One such prejudice, namely, that associated with sexual discrimination, is discussed in the next section.

Gender and Sexual Stereotyping

A general feature of life in ForestCo was that the values and attitudes of its employees had developed over a long history. Organizational life, particularly in the mills located in small towns, reflected the social customs and norms of their local communities. It is therefore no surprise that a company with its roots in the rough, tough life of the woods, unconsciously, and at times consciously, favored a male-dominated world. Female employees were increasingly considered acceptable—but in their place and in female-dominated occupations. Apparently, few supervisors and managers had given much thought to gender issues in employment decisions. As is already manifest in preceding examples, they accepted local social customs and consequently articulated biases of which they were often unaware (Heilman, 1983; Heilman, Block, Martell, & Simon, 1989). These biases evidently had great potential to produce different career patterns for men and women:

> Mainly women apply for jobs like this [Senior Documents Clerk]. The job's too clerical for men. Men are channeled into "real accounting jobs," or sales, marketing, and so on.

Perhaps as a response to such implicit sexual segregation, women did not apply for positions for which they believed they had little chance of being accepted. Taking note of the lack of female applicants could lead observers to draw inferences about the interests of females rather than the situation that produced the observed effect:

> When you put personality aside, you are essentially looking for the same thing in everyone. Gender isn't an issue—though we don't have any women in the department. They don't apply. I even told one woman about a job and she still didn't apply.

> I've been in this [Engineering] Division for 27 years and we've never had a female employed here—even though at one point we had to create separate male and female bathroom facilities. We don't get applications from women even though they could get into the processing plant. After all, they can push a broom there for $15 an hour.

In these traditional organizational and community environments, women were stereotypically assigned the family responsibility for child care. Thus, they were disadvantaged when they applied for salaried jobs that had unpredictable time demands. Responsibility for child care was seen to limit a candidate's capacity to perform outside the range of a "normal" single-site, eight to five office job. This view detracted from their perceived suitability for jobs requiring out-of-town travel:

> Femaleness is irrelevant [for a specialist occupational group]. I have one in [Region A], two in [Region B], and one in [Region C]. Sometimes they're more effective in their work with blue collar employees than are the men. Having kids may put limitations on their ability to travel. That's the major difference between single and married women.

Similarly, women were regarded as having less flexibility in terms of unusual and unexpected hours of work, which were regarded as normal requirements of lower-level salaried jobs:

> Women who have children are a problem because they're not as flexible in meeting last-minute demands of working overtime. Mothers with babies sometimes are a problem because they can't flexibly arrange their time to meet last-minute demands. We've no in-house day care.

Sexual stereotyping varied in the perniciousness of the assumptions made. While responsibility for child care could interfere with the performance of unscheduled work and out-of-town assignments, these effects were likely to be occasional and limited. Other stereotypes, however, presented broader and cruder assumptions that managers struggled to resist. Working in traditional small-town environments, these managers attempted to find a balance between what they saw as the reality of local social customs and their emerging sense that sexual discrimination was illegal and had little place in staffing decisions. For some managers, ingrained attitudes developed from many years of experience in this traditional industry showed through more politically correct affirmations. For example, despite his denials that gender did not enter into his frame of reference, one manager nevertheless voiced reservations that were undoubtedly present but unspoken in more situations than this:

> Gender doesn't enter into my staffing choice. The risk in hiring a woman is that she could have a baby after we've invested in her training. For a man, marriage usually settles them down. For a woman, she may have to leave because of parenting. Another risk is that she's stepping into a male chauvinist world. She's gonna have to handle the extra hassle of convincing others she can do the job well.

Many managers were aware that they should be increasingly open to non-traditional ways of staffing positions. There were inevitable tensions, however, between the modern, urban, equal-opportunity values of corporate policies and the operational implementation of these policies in remote organizational units. Consciousness of the appearance of discrimination certainly entered the mind of one manager who was reluctant to exclude a female candidate, even though he believed she had insufficient skills for the job for which she was being considered:

> I didn't like the candidates on the shortlist and I didn't like one proposed candidate because her accounting skills were inadequate. There was a concern that others might get the idea we didn't select her because she was a woman and traditionally we haven't liked to have women in logging.

It should be no surprise that there was confusion regarding the manner in which gender issues could and should be factored into staffing decisions. The reputations of supervisors and middle-level managers were dependent on the opinions of other managers—including representatives from both local divisions and units and those from corporate headquarters. Values embedded in local customs and traditions could conflict with an awareness of the political and social changes taking place in the wider society, leading some managers to vacillate in their staffing choices:

> I don't know if it was a sex bias or just happenstance, but when I pointed out to [Manager A] that he mainly had women in his section, he reconsidered who he was going to recommend for the position and appointed a male when a female had originally been his first choice.

More thoughtful managers acknowledged that considerations of gender could not be separated from other issues that had to be factored into the staffing decision. For example, one manager was keenly aware of the different interactions between sexuality and job performance for "inside" and "outside" jobs. He recognized the reality that sexuality could be used to persuade customers to place orders and had no moral aversion to saleswomen flirting with clients. He was sensitive, however, to the potential risks of male–female relationships overlapping those of salesperson and client. He was concerned about the risks to the career of his female staff as well as his own should the male–female liaison impair the client–salesperson relationship. In particular, he was still sensitive to the risks to his own reputation, as he had challenged the implicit sexual stereotyping of jobs in his division by appointing a woman to a position traditionally occupied by a man:

> This is not an industry that is easy for females to do well in. An average guy can make it at ForestCo, but this is not true for females. They have to be more than average and able to gain the respect of the men in a male-dominated industry. When it comes to inside sales, women can use their sexuality to their advantage if they so choose. But in outside sales, women can find themselves in compromising situations when they take a client for a drink as part of a selling routine. It's very difficult for women to gain respect when doing face-to-face contact work simply because of built-in prejudices that have been around for a long time. I feel it's a higher risk to take a female from inside to play an outside boy's game.

Also, of course, when there is greater heterogeneity in the workforce, sexual liaisons between employees are more likely to occur. As in any large corporation, ForestCo managers were aware that these relationships could develop and took pains to ensure that extracurricular relationships did not interfere with work relationships:

> We have to look out for coupling at work. _____ is dating a woman who works in a different area. If we can accommodate couples we will, but we have to keep them separate to avoid actual, and appearance of favoritism. I also want my subordinates to concentrate on their work and not on who they're screwing.

Another manager believed that there were financial as well as social barriers to the advancement of women. However, there is no objective evidence either to support or to deny this potentially litigious allegation:

> Another aspect of fitting the job to the person is money. If the person keeps doing more, they should get more money. If a female moves into a man's job, she doesn't get the same amount of money.

For the most part, sexual discrimination was an implicit background to the staffing of positions at ForestCo. As reflected in the social milieus within which ForestCo's plants operated, men and women were streamed into different types of jobs. Few women were employed in supervisory positions, partly because candidates were drawn from the ranks of the senior hourly employees who had been hired 20 or 30 years previously—and who were men. At the time they were hired, social customs and corporate traditions did not support the hiring of female employees into the ranks of hourly employees. In contrast to their absence from supervisory positions in mills, women were being advanced in several other areas of the corporation. They were advancing well in occupations with a strong professional identification, such as Accounting, Research, and Forestry. But universal equality of opportunity across all occupational groupings will likely remain an unrealized objective far into the future.

SUMMARY

Managing the human resource system of an organization requires a large number of decisions regarding whom to hire, promote, and transfer to a shifting array of jobs and responsibilities. In ForestCo, few jobs were identical, and many jobs required quite different skills. This being so, the processes used to select from among candidates also implied the selection of criteria used to discriminate among the candidates being considered for a single job. This chapter has presented a very wide range of criteria that were used to assess the likely performance levels of candidates in positions to which a successful candidate had recently been appointed. No attempt has been made to link specific selection criteria with general demand conditions derived from aspects of groups of jobs or sets of organizational conditions. Instead, this chapter has presented selection criteria used by ForestCo's managers and described in their own words.

The selection criteria used in ForestCo's organization may be organized into three clusters: characteristics inferred from each candidate's past history, candidate characteristics relevant for managing lines of progression, and candidate characteristics relevant to the specific situation or context of proposed assignments. While these sets of selection criteria can be interpreted as being derived from rational-, natural-, and open-system models of organizations, the language framework for this description and analysis is intentionally rational. In describing and explaining their recent selection actions, ForestCo's managers used constructions of social reality in which rational purposes drove their choice of selection criteria. Because most candidates being considered for vacant positions were already employed at ForestCo and had established career histories in that organization, managers viewed various attributes of each candidate's past history and used these attributes to infer the candidate's capacity to perform. In particular, they made considerable use of the construct of "experience" as a generic summary of candidate knowledge, skills, and abilities. These managers were generally familiar with the work demands of previous positions held within the ForestCo organization and believed that these experiences represented accurate and efficient signals of future capacities to perform. Associated with direct indicators of the candidate's past history were secondary measures such as length of service and age. Choice and use of these selection criteria are consistent with rational models of organizations, as characteristics used to discriminate among candidates derive from considerations of future organizational performance. These notions of rationality, however, are not necessarily closely associated with bureaucratic rationality, as future performance was viewed in general terms rather than as potential performance in a specific position that was currently vacant.

The second set of selection criteria examined were those derived from managing lines of progression. Balancing flows of employees was seen to be problematic, as managers attempted to obtain a mix of both stability and mobility to serve larger, more longstanding, organizational needs for skill development. These concerns in turn reflected back on candidate characteristics thought to indicate a candidate's capacity to develop and learn from progression. Again, secondary indicators of candidate characteristics, such as time in rank, were used to infer likely incremental change in future performance. Concerns with mobility and stability, advancement potential, and time in rank can be viewed as contributing to both rational and natural models of organizations. Managing lines of progression contributed to both the maintenance of the organizational system as a performing entity and its survival as a social system.

The final selection criterion cited as critical to the management of lines of progression was that persons be appointed to positions as a reward for past service. This criterion offers little to rational models of organizations, but is a central feature of social-system maintenance and survival. Thus, the second set of selection criteria, those associated with managing lines of progression, derived from both rational- and social-system features of organizations. The final set of selection criteria described in Chapter 9 were initially characterized as reflecting concerns with the local context of the staffing situation. Clearly, contextual factors such as candidate attributes matching team and group requirements are consistent with open-system models. However, notions of personality and enduring dispositions, depending upon how they were used, were reflective of either rational- or natural-system requirements. Finally, notions of gender and sexual stereotypes could be reflective of rational-, natural-, or open-system models, depending upon how such stereotypes were used in the evaluative frames of staffing decisions.

A significant feature of this chapter has been an attempt to capture and present the language of evaluation used by ForestCo's managers. A conscious effort has been made to present, as empirical data, the explanations offered by ForestCo's managers for having done what they did to staff organizational positions. This effort has therefore been an exercise in what Turner (1974) has described as "practical reasoning." The details of language have not been subjected to deconstructionist interpretations, although various attempts have been made to signal more obvious subthemes and implicit assumptions. Readers interested in comparisons of organizational fieldwork having an ethnomethodological flavor may wish to compare the evaluative language of a rough-and-tumble Canadian forestry firm in the late 1980s with that used by civil servants in Britain in the early 1970s (Silverman & Jones, 1976).

There are very few other accounts of the actual selection criteria used in staffing decisions comparable to the one presented here. Nevertheless, it is believed that the general features of the accounts used by ForestCo's managers to make sense of organizational staffing are generalizable to other organizations. If they are, then the normatively rational perspective on employee selection established as the critical component of staffing by industrial psychologists should be subject to critical examination. Both the general ILM context within which staffing occurred, and the particular historical and current features of ForestCo's ILM strongly influenced the manner in which selection criteria were evoked and used. The detailed specification of selection procedures contained in most academic textbooks bears little relation to selection as practiced at ForestCo.

There are several interpretations of this discrepancy. First, it is possible to argue that ForestCo employs improper or flawed staffing procedures. While there is no question that some managers would benefit from some training in contemporary selection methods, there is substantial evidence to indicate that few practical persons would behave differently from the managers described herein.

Second, one could argue that the behaviors of ForestCo's managers, while intentionally rational in their local context, are not representative of the behaviors of managers in most business firms. This is a potential explanation, but is inconsistent with this author's experience of other firms. Knowledge of other firms suggests that in their day-to-day staffing activities, ForestCo's managers are indeed representative of managers in many other large organizations.

The third interpretation of the discrepancy between mainstream accounts provided in most textbooks and the accounts presented here is that academic specialists have focused too closely on detailed job-based models of staffing. While the collective pursuit of a consensual paradigm for organization theory is admirable and has many positive features (Pfeffer, 1993), the background model of bureaucratic rationality appears to have only partial relevance for contemporary staffing practice.

11

Postselection Considerations of Staffing

INTRODUCTION

A corollary of the argument that operation of ForestCo's internal labor market (ILM) as a whole can be viewed from both vacancy chain and staffing action perspectives is that a full appreciation of organizational staffing should include consideration of the context in which staffing occurs. As noted in Part I, staffing actions and vacancy chains occur in the economic, social, and demographic history of the organization. Also, as noted in Part II, most staffing actions occur in the context of other staffing actions, especially prior staffing choices, that constitute that particular vacancy chain. Aspects of temporal context also influence staffing through requirements associated with managing lines of progression and assisting with the development of individual careers. Appreciation of these contextual influences on current choices encourages conceptual links between past experiences and potential future outcomes. Past experience frames current staffing choices, which shape the orientations of managers toward potential consequences of those choices.

From the perspective of bureaucratic models of organization, staffing is synonymous with rational, science-based models of selection. That is, the processes associated with staffing organizational positions are expected to follow a predictable temporal sequence of considerations, actions, and events that culminate in the appointment of a person to an organizational position. Once execution of that sequence attains its objective, the process is presumed to recycle to the next staffing opportunity. But few of ForestCo's supervisors and managers believed that their responsibility for the consequences of appointments ceased when appointees first began working in their new positions. Because supervisors and managers were acutely aware of the historical, social, and political context in which staffing occurred, many felt both an internalized responsibility and an external accountability for the success of these appointments. Their interest in ensuring favorable outcomes often led them to take action, once having made their staffing selection, to reduce even more the risks to the favorable outcomes they intended and hoped for when they made that staffing choice. This chapter, therefore, examines these follow-up or postselection considerations of staffing. This presentation and discussion is notable in that the issues it examines lie outside the frame of traditional, normative theories of staffing and selection.

As managers accumulated experience through their participation in multiple staffing decisions, they learned about the range of potential and often unanticipated outcomes that can result from staffing actions. This learning influenced their approach to subsequent staffing decisions. What a manager did following a staffing decision was partially dependent on what the manager had done before making that staffing choice. At ForestCo, accumulated experience led managers to develop characteristic orientations toward the responsibility and accountability associated with their staffing choices. These orientations constituted a filter through which the exigencies of each staffing decision were evaluated. Managers developed acute appreciations of risks associated with staffing, and these appreciations influenced the postselection actions and considerations of extended staffing arrangements.

As managers approached each staffing decision, they had multiple judgments to consider. These judgments included the nature of the job to be filled, the procedures to be used in identifying candidates for these jobs, and the selection and assignment of a person to the vacant position. Though a few managers responded to vacant positions in a reflexive, habitual manner, most managers interviewed appeared to follow a rational calculative analysis in deciding what to do. Pursuit of this rationality was neither simple nor easy. In managing the staffing of organizational positions, managers were required to balance the interdependencies between managing lines of progression and maintaining their subordinates' motivation. Complicating this pursuit of rationality even more were uncertainties associated with the social and political context of selection decisions (Jackall, 1988; Judge & Bretz, 1992). Managers themselves were not always confident that they knew how a particular appointment might work out. Nor did they always know the extent to which a particular selection decision could disadvantage the interests of other organizational actors. Moreover, in the political world of organizations, perception shapes what is seen as reality. Managers guarded their reputations. Whenever possible, they attempted to ensure that less than satisfactory outcomes not be attributed to their judgment and action (Tetlock, 1985). They avoided placing their reputations at risk.

A significant aspect of the intended rationality associated with staffing was the calculation of potential risks associated with anticipated actions. In the best of all possible worlds, managers would be able to find the ideal candidate for each vacant position, new job definitions would be a perfect fit with other jobs in the organizational unit, the timing of staffing moves would fit both the short- and long-term career development requirements of candidates, and there would be no adverse effects on the subsequent motivation of candidates not chosen for the position. But in no situation could these and other potential outcomes be guaranteed. Managers therefore attempted to assess the risks that might accrue if anticipated outcomes were not realized, and these assessments influenced staffing choices as well as the nature of actions taken after the formal selection and appointment process had been completed.

Although positivist, externally benchmarked interpretations of risk influenced the degree to which managers believed themselves to be responsible and accountable for staffing outcomes, not all respondents held such beliefs. A substantial proportion of ForestCo's managers, though not necessarily a majority of those interviewed, expressed little personal accountability for unsuccessful staffing. Failed appointments were regarded as either unimportant or attributable to factors outside their control. Apart from these exceptions, postselection actions were a significant component of many staffing processes.

The most prevalent explanations for postselection actions derived from managerial interests in maintaining the dynamic natural and social system in which they themselves were significant players. In particular, they were committed to the survival of the organization as an economic and social entity. Both in their selection decisions and in their subsequent actions, they attempted to replenish the skills that were lost as employees moved out of departments. They also looked for appointments that would develop skills complementary to overall organizational adaptation. Considerations of training and employee development were therefore the primary rationalizations for postselection actions. Managers were also concerned, however, that their subordinates readily survive the transition from being a new appointee to being a fully competent member of their department. Quite often, these concerns led managers to coach, counsel, and undertake preliminary reviews of new appointees to facilitate and evaluate these organizational transitions.

ASSESSMENTS OF RISKS ASSOCIATED WITH STAFFING

Approximately half the managers interviewed indicated some concern or appreciation for risks associated with their staffing actions. These managers described a variety of potential risks in the event that an appointment did not work out. This review collects these expressed concerns into four sets of issues: (1) managers' personal fears and concerns for their corporate reputations; (2) the potential disruptions in organizational performance; (3) the future career and well-being of the selected candidate; and (4) the consequences for the candidates who were not chosen. The first of these sets can be interpreted as issues associated with the self-interests of managers acting as agents in organizational settings and the second as issues associated with rational aspects of uncertainties associated with employee selection. Issues related to candidates' future careers and the motivation of candidates not chosen reflect concerns with the maintenance of the organization viewed primarily as a social system.

A fifth subsection describes the proffered rationales for not accepting responsibility for the outcomes of prior staffing actions. In doing so, it highlights the administrative and social complexities associated with attempts to design and implement rational organizational systems.

Personal Fears and Corporate Reputations

Managers occupy dual roles in organizational hierarchies. To their subordinates, they are the agents who articulate overall organizational goals. Managers represent an authority for organizational direction and are seen to be responsible for the performance and maintenance of their particular part of the overall organization. But all managers are themselves subordinate and accountable to higher authorities. Managers occupy roles as agents for owners and other stakeholders. As agents, managers are evaluated in terms of how well they manage the organizational systems for which they are responsible. In staffing, managers looked for positive outcomes, as would any rational agents who sought to implement the objectives that higher organizational authorities charged them with achieving. Managers also understood, however, that their performance as agents depended on how well they managed the employment subsystems for which they were responsible. Thus, less than successful staffing outcomes for which they were responsible could have a negative impact on others' perceptions of their performance and career potential. Consequently, two significant aspects of organizational staffing were those related to personal fears and corporate reputations.

Different managers expressed different levels of concern regarding the potential risks associated with their staffing actions. Not surprisingly, managers with a great deal of experience in staffing expressed less anxiety than those who had only recently taken on managerial responsibilities. A few of the managers in the latter category found staffing to be a relatively stressful task. Their concerns about the potential risks and outcomes of the staffing process reflected personal fears and insecurities associated with the process of choosing and appointing someone to a vacant position:

> This was my first hire at ForestCo, and while I was doing it I was very conscious I was dealing with a system that was new to me. For example, I didn't realize I needed Regional approval in order to advertise the position. I'm concerned there'll be other holes I'll stumble into. You don't know everything when you start this hiring business. You find out the rules along the way when you make a mistake.

Clearly, personal concerns and feelings of inadequacy were greater when the manager had no one to turn to for information and assistance. When guidance was available, the stress level appeared to be reduced:

> I wasn't given any training in the hiring procedures we use here. I'd like to have seen something written down, as this was my first experience. I did tell my manager what I was doing, and he gave me guidance when I was having some difficulties.

Other managers were also concerned about their personal well-being, but viewed this concern through the lens of their corporate identity and the consequences of a spoiled reputation for the credibility of their future actions. Clearly, reputational capital was important to these managers. It influenced the respect and credibility each manager had in his or her working relationships with significant but unspecified organizational constituents:

> If _____ fails in that job, I'll pay the price of dented reputation because everyone knows it's me who's developing the team here.

Other managers had quite specific constituencies in mind and were especially mindful of their reputations with their supervisor or with the local union:

> If this appointment doesn't work out, my manager will start to look at me more closely and maybe to question my judgment.

> If there's a bad hire, you lose respect. The unions here are very quick to be critical.

Some staffing decisions appeared to be more critical than others because of their real or symbolic significance or both. When managers were responsible for mill start-ups in which the style and traditions of new or rebuilt mills would be established, the assignment of candidates with inadequate skills could have substantial business consequences. Moreover, managerial actions that failed to follow tradition or that broke precedent were judged to be more visible and therefore inherently more risky than those of a more routine nature:

> The risk to me of making this appointment is that this is a critical period in a mill start-up. It's going to be hard on everyone for the next two years, because if there are any failures, fingers will be pointing out the mistakes. We're in a fishbowl, and this pushes me to be more cautious because there are lots of people out there watching the end result.

When managers felt their reputations to be at risk, they were motivated to take actions that reduced these risks. Thus, when one manager chose not to accept a number of internal candidates and instead appointed someone from outside the traditional pool of candidates, he was very conscious of the need to appoint someone whose subsequent performance would not detract from his at-risk identity as a manager who chooses wisely:

> In making this appointment, I turned down several internal candidates. I realize this could affect my reputation here and could make my credibility suspect. The impact on me was that I had to find someone visibly better than those I'd turned down. The person I chose couldn't be a lightweight because my credibility was at risk.

A different manager from the one just cited had faced similar circumstances, and he generalized from these experiences to an orientation that conditioned his view of staffing choices between internal and external hires. Candidates from outside ForestCo's ILM were not strictly comparable to internal candidates. Internal candidates were advantaged, as the implicit standards against which they were compared were less than those applied to hires from the external labor market (ELM). While it is possible to attribute these higher standards for external hires to the organizational learning and socialization already obtained by internal candidates, assessments of managerial risk associated with the two types of appointment undoubtedly also contributed to this discrepancy:

> I experienced no pressure regarding this hire. Nevertheless, I had to have a valid reason in my own mind for hiring an outsider. In general, outsiders have to be better than insiders. In the case of two equals, hire the insider and give them an opportunity to get training and prepare them for movement up the ladder. When I hire from the outside, I try to hire as much strength as I can get.

Other staffing decisions were considered notable because of particular aspects of who was chosen. The performance of candidates chosen by managers who challenged traditional sexual stereotyping of jobs could be subject to very careful examination:

> I'm confident she'll continue to do well in her work. She's a quick study and will soon be able to move into more senior positions. She's quickly overcoming the biases people have because she's the first woman in that kind of job.

In other instances, actual risks were increased because of differential mobilities between rather than within employment systems. For example, when hourly employees made a permanent move out of the hourly employment system, they lost the continued employment protection directly related to their company seniority. Because of this potential loss, promotions from hourly ranks to a salaried position had large downside risks. Should the appointment not work out successfully, a manager would either have to live with a less than satisfactory appointment or bear the reputational attribution of someone whose staffing judgment contributed to the job loss of a "loyal" employee:

> If we take someone from hourly into staff, they can't go back to hourly. We must be extra careful and take full responsibility for these selections.

Finally, a few managers saw potential risks to the appointment less in terms of personal reputation and more in terms of the skills and capacities that would no longer be available for deployment in the manager's unit. Unsuccessful appointments implied the loss of valued employees:

> I'm going to do whatever it takes to make the job fit the person. The risk I run is if I make the wrong move, then I'm going to lose [the person appointed] permanently.

Because of their status as agents in the organizational hierarchy, managers sought to maintain or improve their reputations as capable, dependable managers. They were aware of potentially negative consequences to their own careers and reputations if responsibility for unsuccessful appointments was attributed to their judgment and managerial capacity. Thus, they were motivated to avoid undue risk in making appointments and to act to better ensure positive outcomes following the initial assignment of a new appointee.

Potential Disruptions in Organizational Performance

In addition to concerns about the direct risk of decrements in their personal reputation, managers also recognized the possibility that an appointment that failed to work could also affect the performance of their unit. Such a failure would also affect their reputations as managers, but would primarily affect a different facet of their reputations as managers of personnel. From this point of view, staffing was regarded as a component of the line function of management, and risks associated with staffing decisions that did not work out well were viewed primarily in terms of their effect on organizational performance. At a minimum, a botched staffing assignment was viewed as a nuisance, as the time and energy in finding and training an inappropriate appointee would have been wasted:

> If she fails, we lose our investment in three months of training, and we'd have to go through a lot of work to find another person.

But not all consequences were so easily written off. Depending on the importance of the appointment, quite substantial risks to unit performance could be associated with poor selections:

> The price we may have to pay in choosing _____ revolves around crew morale, control, respect, decreased production, accidents, and grievances, which are a sign of weak supervision.

> If the new supervisor doesn't have the technical knowledge and the personal style to get cooperation from his subordinates, the work won't get done. This is critical, as we'd have downtime on the machines, lost time, and higher machine costs.

In a few instances, staffing was a component critical to the implementation of an organizational innovation. If the person appointed to the position associated with this new responsibility did not meet expected performance requirements, the project itself could be questioned and the desired innovation threatened:

> If this appointment doesn't work out, the rationale for the position will lose legitimacy, the idea will be seen as a failure for a while, and the [functional] area will lose a growth opportunity.

Other managers took a more distanced view of the risks associated with appointments that did not work out. Rather than look to local difficulties, these managers believed that poor appointments ultimately had a negative but marginal impact on the bottom line of the corporation:

> The key risk is that the new person will not perform at the existing level of performance regarding sales and profits.

Although the risks of an appointment not working out were translated into supervisory and organizational consequences, the most frequently mentioned consequences of a misjudged assignment were those that affected the selected candidate's career and well-being.

Career and Well-Being of Selected Candidate

When an appointment did not work out well, the candidate appointed to the vacant position was most frequently identified as the person whom future consequences would affect. Depending on the nature of the appointment, alternative appointments that might be available, and the manager's loyalty to the candidate, various outcomes could result:

> Mostly, it will be an inconvenience if _____ doesn't work out in this position. He can still stay where he is or go to another logging division. He could get moved into an equivalent job here, he could be terminated, or he could change his career path.

Acceptance of responsibility for their staffing actions led managers to develop a sense of obligation to find some solution to appointments that did not work out. The extent of their obligation was tempered, however, by their appreciation of the merit and worth of the candidate who had been misplaced. Managers would expend reasonable effort to find a match between employee and job, but if they considered the necessary effort to be too great, they would cut losses by finding a way to have the employee exit the corporation:

> If he's not a success, we'll either change the job or let him go. But we'll try to find a fit.

In most instances, though, letting an employee go was a last resort. Most managers expressed some degree of loyalty to their subordinates and had fallback positions already in mind should the appointment not work out successfully:

> If _____ doesn't work out, he'll be moved back to the field.

> If _____ doesn't fit operations, he'll simply be assigned to a senior technical position. This wouldn't be a waste, though, as he has immediate skills and gifts for the division regardless of long-term outcomes.

But even if a manager felt some degree of responsibility for the continued employment and development of a subordinate whose career had stalled, there were limits to what could be accomplished. Eventual outcomes depended on the vacancies available at the time an alternative assignment was being sought. There was no guarantee in this shifting, dynamic world of changing jobs and employees that future matches could necessarily be worked out:

> The risk is that I'll have to tell _____ he doesn't fit, and at the time there may be nowhere else for him to go.

The issues of time and timing were critical and unavoidable aspects of making managerial sense of the staffing process. Managing organizational units that faced changing market and task demands, changing technologies, and changing levels of skill and motivation required managers to develop dynamic views of current and emerging arrangements. Career development in particular was viewed as being time-dependent:

> _____ is doing well. She has to stay a little longer in her present position because so far we have had only limited experience with her. It's not time for her to move on yet because she's still fairly green.

> _____ has been doing well since he's been in that position because he's had the time he needed to get into the woodrooms.

Even if the exigencies associated with the timing of future moves could be worked out, some moves could take subordinates away from positions that could enhance their visibility in the corporation and thereby reduce their opportunities to experience considerable intrinsic satisfaction:

> The risk for _____ is that he won't be as involved in the new mill as he'd like to be. If this job doesn't work out, he'll miss out on what could be a glamorous and exciting assignment.

For such a candidate, the risks associated with an unsuccessful appointment could influence others' perceptions of career potential and possibly the person's actual career trajectory:

> If he doesn't fit this position, the consequences have more to do with his future potential.

At worst, for a relatively small group of candidates for whom the responsible manager felt little loyalty or responsibility, the candidate's job security was at risk:

> If this turns out to be a poor decision, we'll recognize it in his first six months here. If that's the case—he'll go.

Aware of themselves, aware of their bosses, and aware of the potential interruptions to a protégé's career, managers were also aware of their responsibility for maintaining the social system of their patch of the corporation. This included a responsibility for maintaining the motivation of candidates not chosen.

Consequences for Candidates Not Chosen

Managers were keenly aware that to choose one candidate for a position was to not choose all the other candidates. The construction that these unsuccessful candidates put on this experience—of being compared with another employee and not being chosen— could have deleterious effects on their subsequent motivation to perform. As the following quotation dramatically illustrates, at least one manager had little difficulty in prescribing his postselection agenda:

> What you have to do is give 'em the job if they deserve it and deal with those who are pissed off with your decision. They'll only be angry for a short time if they see the fairness of your choice and further opportunities for themselves. Any time you post a position, disappointment is an inevitable consequence. You have to follow through and talk to unsuccessful candidates about where their skills didn't match and how they presented themselves during the interview.

Smoothing the feelings of unsuccessful candidates, explaining the grounds for the selection decision, reaffirming the legitimacy of the choice, and providing coaching and ideas for subsequent interviews and further career development are all actions likely to be required when there is an open competition for a vacant position.

Different managers gave different degrees of emphasis to each of these postselection functions. For some, it was a primary concern to smooth the feelings of disappointed and occasionally angry candidates who felt that they had been overlooked:

> I need to talk with him and clarify why he didn't get the job. It should be easier for him to accept because this ended up being a lateral move.

> We still have to deal with _____, who's pissed off he didn't get the job.

Rationales for actions taken to smooth the feelings of disappointed candidates often overlapped with those that attempted to reaffirm the legitimacy of the choice. Justifications were a critical component of postselection discourse when candidates who were not chosen began to question their expectations about future upward mobility. Different groups of managers gave different degrees of emphasis either to smoothing feelings or to explanations designed to support the legitimacy of their choice. Legitimacy claims were at times based on explanations of their reasons for choosing the successful candidate:

> Now I phone people and tell them who got the job and why they were picked.

More frequently, however, legitimacy claims were based on the reasons that unsuccessful candidates did not get the job for which they had applied:

> It's important to talk with candidates and explain why they were not chosen for a particular position.

> We tell people who weren't chosen why they weren't appropriate for the position. This process of reporting back puts a lot of pressure on us to be clear and honest.

Occasionally, legitimacy claims were based more on the defensibility of the selection process than on its outcome:

> I used _____ [another manager] to help me with this selection. We came up with ten possibles. We did lots of courtesy interviews by telephone and explained why they weren't getting personal interviews.

Providing feedback in the form of explanations of the reasons a particular job candidate was not successful often also obliged the manager to provide coaching and counseling as to how the candidate might be successful in the future:

> We wanted people to have a positive experience of being interviewed—even if they weren't a serious candidate. We talked with all 15 unsuccessful candidates and told them where they needed to strengthen their presentation.

> I talked with all the candidates regarding their highs and lows in the interviews and explained the decision process to them.

Other candidates, perhaps because they were considered to have more potential value to the corporation, and perhaps because they exhibited greater resentment or disappointment at not being chosen, received more support and more extensive career counseling:

> _____ feels discarded because he didn't get the job. [Manager A] and [Manager B] both spoke to _____ and recommended he stay in his current job for another one or two years and to get a lot more experience in this role.

At other times, the counseling appeared to be more perfunctory:

> _____ was quite positive about not getting the job. I let him know where his shorts were and what he needed to develop.

For one manager, discussions with unsuccessful candidates served the purpose of ensuring that the recommended appointment would not be sabotaged by resentful co-workers. This particular manager also talked with his boss to make sure the prospective appointment was also supported at that level:

> I talked with all the rejects, and they all said they could work with [the selected candidate] with no problems. I also spoke with [another senior manager], and he supported the choice as well.

But discussions with unsuccessful candidates, either to smooth their feelings, to counsel them in how they might present themselves better in subsequent interviews, or to discuss potential career development plans, did not always occur. Explanations as to why these discussions did not happen were framed in terms of a reluctance to generate expectations that might not be met:

> We did have people identified as potential successors for the position, but we didn't share that information with the staff because there would have been lots of disappointment if the opportunity didn't happen.

Other managers were reluctant to repeat a message that could sustain potential feelings of disappointment and resentment:

> Many of the people who applied for this position had applied for the previous one we'd just filled. So we knew most of them quite well. Because I'd spoken to them only a short while

ago, I didn't want to go through the process of telling 'em that they didn't get this job for the same reasons they didn't the last time around.

Nevertheless, several managers went to considerable effort to maintain the motivation of employees who had just been unsuccessful in a competition for a vacant position:

> I personally called all the rejects and, if they asked, told them why they didn't make it. I also pumped them up so they wouldn't be discouraged from trying again. If you do that, you've got to be sincere in your encouragement of others.

> One of the guys who had applied was working on his grade 12 and seemed to be someone we should encourage. So we made him a relief supervisor.

Running through the many varieties of rationalizations provided by ForestCo's managers is the theme that many accepted either full or partial responsibility for the eventual outcomes of the staffing decisions they made. For some managers, this felt responsibility was linked directly to their belief that they would be held accountable as the prime causal agent for the staffing decision and its subsequent performance outcome. Other managers felt similar levels of responsibility, even if they did not believe they themselves would be held to account, as they had internalized organizational standards and codes of conduct that indicated that they should be responsible for such decisions. Whatever the origin of the forces that led managers to feel responsibility for the outcomes of staffing actions, most managers followed staffing actions beyond the selection decision. They continued to intervene in the staffing process, as they conceptualized their task as being more than simply assigning the selected candidate to the vacant position.

ForestCo's managers were not unappreciative of these risks, issues, and possible actions they might experience as a consequence of their staffing selections. Over time, this awareness led many of them to develop orientations toward staffing that were manifest in statements of their felt responsibility and accountability for the quality of their appointments. Many ForestCo managers interviewed exhibited different orientations toward their personal accountability for organizational staffing. No doubt, different experiences with staffing in combination with different personalities produced different orientations toward these feelings of accountability. In the discussion that follows, attention is concentrated on the cognitive constructions of managers who expressed little felt responsibility for staffing outcomes.

Rationales for Reduced Responsibility

Many of ForestCo's managers accepted the uncertainty associated with accomplishing successful staffing and viewed staffing and selection as merely one component of their much larger set of managerial responsibilities. These managers did not view staffing as unimportant, but rather as a task to be completed expeditiously. Once the task was completed, they could quickly turn their attention to other priorities. Moreover, risks associated with staffing decisions were not seen to be inherently large. Typically, these managers viewed their staffing experiences as additional managerial experiences from which they could learn:

> I try to make the best decision I can at the time, and if I make a mistake—well, that's life and it's not necessarily a monumental failure. You learn from your mistakes and move on.

A similar rationale was offered by another manager who appeared to have an implicit and tolerable benchmark of risk:

There weren't any risks associated with hiring _____, at least not any more than would be experienced in hiring anyone else.

Other managers were less willing to interpret a failed appointment as their mistake. Instead, they focused on factors outside their control that could influence staffing outcomes. To them, acceptance of the risks associated with staffing meant that they should learn from their experiences—but in doing so they should seek the reasons for failure among aspects of the context, and attributes of the candidate, as well as in the quality of managerial judgment that led to the staffing decision. This pragmatic and realistic posture enabled managers to lead less stressful lives—though at the risk of diminishing their sense of personal accountability for staffing outcomes:

You just can't provide for all eventualities that may happen around a succession.

There's always the risk of a bad hire. When that happens, we need to reflect and learn as to what went wrong. Often, politics and circumstances are most influential as to why people don't make it in their jobs. It's often not just the person.

Managers also moderated their feelings of personal accountability for less than successful staffing choices by placing some emphasis on the appropriateness of the procedures used to make the selection decision. In this view, outcomes were subject to many influences beyond those of the manager nominally responsible for the staffing action. All that a manager could reasonably do, therefore, was to make sure he exercised due diligence in the process leading to the choice of the successful candidate:

Mistakes are made even though we've done everything to make sure we hired the right person.

As far as I'm concerned there aren't too many consequences for bad hires. They're just seen as mistakes and that you did your best at the time. What is important is that you do as thorough a job as you can at the time of selection or hire.

Other managers saw very little risk associated with their staffing decisions, either because they were unaware of potential risks or because they did their best to cover all potential risks in the prior staffing process. These managers expressed little concern with the risk associated with their staffing actions because they were confident they had made the correct choice. While self-affirmation of choice is also a personal tactic for reassurance, affirmation through public proclamation of the candidate's suitability by the manager responsible for the appointment also reinforced the apparent legitimacy of the selection decision:

There was no risk in selecting _____ because of his prior experience in the different mills. He was absolutely the best we had.

_____ is a low-risk appointment. He's an exceptional fit to the job—and he's been checked out.

Other managers exhibited less confidence in their staffing choices. Rather than use their tentative discomfort as a spur to remedial actions, however, they tended to distance themselves from any personal accountability for the staffing decision. In the following illustration, the manager combined rationalization and affirmation to forestall potential doubts about the correctness of his past staffing action. Interestingly, this rationalization was framed in terms of multiple issues, none directly related to organizational performance. Instead, there were several implicit criteria associated with the rationalization of the selection decision. These criteria concerned the potential loss of organizational skills, the organization's obligations to the employee, the lack of competition from "fast-trackers," and the assertion that any other choice would have to have identified, by definition, an outstanding and therefore most unusual alternative candidate. In this rationalization, the self-evident superiority of the chosen candidate left the manager with little choice and therefore little responsibility:

> We didn't want to lose _____. He'd earned the right to be in this job. There were no fast-trackers left to be trained. Besides, anyone else would have had to be outstanding to be selected over _____ at this time.

In a second illustration, the supervisor who was nominally responsible for selecting and appointing of a direct subordinate distanced himself from any accountability for the appointment by adducing the intervention of his manager. In this supervisor's mind, responsibility for the appointment had been taken by his Divisional Manager, implying that he, the immediate supervisor, was not responsible for ensuring that the appointment was successful. This lack of responsibility implied little incentive for further actions should the appointment begin to work out poorly. This posture was reinforced by this manager's final comment indicating that the performance requirements were sufficiently trivial that all that was required was a "warm body." In terms of the norms of contemporary personnel management, this criterion certainly appears to be a less than satisfactory one:

> I'm not really accountable for this appointment, as the Divisional Manager chose his preferred candidate. He's free to make a change if the appointment doesn't work out. Besides, all we needed was a warm body.

Sentiments such as this were generalized by another manager who expressed his opinion regarding the relationship between accountability, responsibility, and motivation to ensure successful staffing:

> There was no pressure or influence from outside brought to bear on me in this selection. Arm-twisting isn't encouraged because managers have to be accountable for their choices. A manager can't be accountable for choice that's imposed on him from above.

The degree of responsibility for staffing outcomes that ForestCo's managers felt was also reduced when they emphasized the postselection behavior of the successful candidate. In their partially self-fulfilling prophecy, new appointees had to be "willing to make it happen" if the benefits of their selection were to be realized. Although there may be considerable truth to the ascription of success to personal talent and effort, limited ascriptions such as this omit the possibility that discrimination, bias, political tactics, other factors, and random luck may also influence outcomes:

> It's up to her if she wants to grow and if there'll be opportunities for her in the future. It's up to her as to where she wants to go.

> The only remaining issue regarding this appointment is that _____ must organize himself better. He's got lots to learn.

Finally, personal accountability and felt responsibility for the outcomes of staffing were minimized by choosing employment contracts between the manager and the employee, whereby an arm's-length relationship could be more easily maintained. The emotional distance characteristic of these relationships functioned to reduce postdecision dissonance should the time come for that relationship to be severed. ForestCo's managers still remembered the recession and had no wish to revisit the psychic pain of that experience:

> Hiring employees on contract makes sense because there are no benefits costs, pay rates
> are attractive, and when people leave it's not as painful. What we're doing is hedging the
> future in that we won't have to eliminate a ForestCo employee.

Interestingly, the choice of a contract employee reinforces the potential depth of feelings of felt responsibility for full-time, permanent appointments. While the hiring of contract employees could occasionally make economic sense, personal obligations of managers to their subordinates were very powerful influences on the sentiments and behaviors of ForestCo's managers, as evidenced in the managerial reactions to the cutbacks of the early 1980s.

Most staffing experiences were used as sources of information about likely consequences of that particular staffing action or even of related staffing actions. Occasionally, unusual experiences could lead a manager to reflect on wider organizational issues. For example, two different managers reflected on what they thought they learned from their involvement in staffing actions that were complicated by the development of intimate relationships among employees. Problem recognition was relatively clear—but the actions that should be taken were still problematic:

> It's an interesting question as to whether we should have a formal policy about the
> overlap of personal and corporate relationships. I've heard opinions on both sides of the
> argument. Old [Founder] balanced his repugnance for nepotism and his interest in seeing
> the sons of employees come to work for the family firm by ensuring that sons worked in areas
> outside those managed by their father. But these days, with there being so many more female
> professionals and an increased likelihood of extramarital affairs, it's real difficult to know
> what to do. We're still struggling with how to recognize, and perhaps respond to, close male–
> female relationships that overlap formal lines of authority.

A second manager had fewer reservations regarding what he would do if he found that coworkers had developed personal relationships that interfered with his view of organizational propriety:

> Co-mingling isn't a good thing and relationships between males and females shouldn't
> become too familiar. If relationships become intimate, I'll move people around to separate
> those who are too close.

There were many tensions between the various features of staffing choices and their outcomes. There were several overt, externalized constituencies to whom the responsible manager could potentially be accountable. In addition, many managers developed their own personal standards against which they compared actual outcomes from staffing assignments in which they had been involved. There were also multiple rationales, both real and perceived, for not accepting responsibility for high-quality staffing outcomes. Nevertheless, an active interplay among these considerations shaped the postselection appreciations, motivations, and actions of managers involved in staffing organizational positions. Further framing of postselection actions derived from individual and collective appreciations of ForestCo as an ILM containing career ladders and lines of progression. Internal mobility, implicitly along lines of progression, required an ongoing commitment to training resulting from assignments. This is the topic addressed next.

THE INTERDEPENDENCE OF TRAINING AND STAFFING

At its core, the collective view of training within ForestCo was that skilled and competent employees were critical for the firm's continuing adaptation to current and future performance requirements. Within the organization-wide perspective of ForestCo's salaried ILM, training focused on the development of supervisors, technical specialists, and managers. As new demands were placed on the firm, learning and adapting to new requirements was an accepted view of corporate survival. One illustrative pressure came with the recognition that increased quality was increasingly part of competitive strategy:

> Quality has become an extraordinarily important issue. It's pushing people to think differently as to how we do things and will require different training than we've done in the past.

Training and staffing were highly interdependent. It was generally accepted that the primary means to be used for supervisory and management development should be work itself—including the challenge and learning associated with the performance of a succession of varied and progressively more difficult jobs. Staffing was viewed as a critical component of staff development and training, since this process controlled the allocation and assignment of employees to jobs. The flip side of this perspective was that training issues had a significant effect on selection and staffing decisions, as described previously. As selection and allocation decisions could provide an initial opportunity for training, many managers maintained a close overview of new appointees to review how they adapted to their new positions, and to intervene should action be warranted. From a developmental perspective, good selection decisions were a bonus. While good selection decisions could screen out candidates judged unlikely to do well, if any one of several "reasonable" candidates was selected, the candidate's subsequent experience and learning associated with that experience would produce the critical and valued skills required in the future:

> We were willing to throw the right person into this job and then to invest two to four years in developing them into a Superintendent.

Continuity in appointments was also regarded as a critical objective in staffing organizational positions. Succession planning was not treated as a formal, lockstep exercise in which every position had a clearly identified successor. Even when succession plans had been made, subsequent staffing actions did not always follow those plans. Succession planning was a planning and organizing technique that was applied downward in the hierarchy from the vantage of the person doing the planning. Managers and supervisors consciously anticipated future moves and acted to facilitate the training and development of potential candidates for positions likely to become vacant. This process occasionally included a manager's identifying and training his own replacement:

> I feel I shouldn't be able to move unless I have someone ready to do my job. I have to groom people to take on additional responsibility. The company has to tackle and accept the cost of training.

These general orientations toward training were clearly evident in a number of specific cases. For example, the task of developing employees for the job of Superintendent was not seen simply as a naturally occurring consequence of the short-term market forces whereby a Superintendent's job was filled once it became vacant. There was value in anticipating and planning for future vacancies in key positions. Through career planning, developmental activities were not left to the relatively random consequences of competitive staffing. Someone somewhere had to take on responsibility both for the ongoing selection of suitable candidates and for several years of coaching and grooming. With completion of these responsibilities, there would be at least one employee, but preferably more than one, with the experience and training to be regarded as a well-qualified candidate for those positions when they became vacant. Thus, general concerns with development could lead to the selection, appointment, and subsequent training of a specific person:

> We decided he needed to spend some time in the woods and to get some hands-on experience. That's why he got the assignment as Assistant Forester in [Division A].

Although an implicit strategic orientation to training was occasionally evident in the comments of ForestCo's managers, they were nonetheless aware of the ongoing tension between consumption of and investment in human resources. By definition, training was future-oriented, whereas many managers saw themselves as being in short-term contests and challenges for personal and departmental survival. These features of the training context led many managers to develop a cautious and implicitly conditional approach to staffing as an ongoing commitment to training. In this view, training was not an unconditional right. Training was an expensive investment of personal and organizational resources and should be provided only to those candidates who either had "the base knowledge" or were considered to be "a worthwhile asset":

> If people have the base knowledge, then we can afford the time for them to learn to do their work.

> If people are a worthwhile asset, there's value in walking them through the ranks to develop them further.

When training was provided, both the employee who was to be the beneficiary of the training and the context in which the training was to take place had to favor investments in the development of skills and competencies. Employees who were to be afforded learning opportunities were required to have basic skills. Similarly, various features of the job situation, such as supervisory willingness to train, had to be in place to permit an initial assignment of someone who might not initially produce fully satisfactory levels of job performance:

> As long as they knew lumber, I was willing to run them through the ropes and give them further training.

> We could afford to train someone who was lacking in competence because this was a secondary role.

Despite a pervasive, strategic concern with future organizational adaptation and the general appreciation that training functioned to support organizational survival, personal responsibility and accountability for training were often not as exigent as the requirements for short-term departmental performance. Individual managers were often busy with their own crises—with the consequence that beneficial but longer-term outcomes were shunted aside in favor of more urgent concerns. Thus, there was a significant resistance to accepting candidates who required training:

> I'm real busy firefighting, and there's just not enough time to train someone in the subtleties of lumber grading and the nature of quality control in this mill.

Other rationalizations for a manager's not embracing a training philosophy, and for that reason being unwilling to invest further in the development of employees assigned to their departments, included an exclusive focus on immediate, bottom-line measures of departmental performance. Conflicts between immediate and future objectives favored short-term performance, as a manager's department could become vulnerable in the future should potential moves, favorable to a manager's subordinates, become actualities:

> We're desperately trying to improve our bottom line, and we don't want to invest in training that won't have an immediate payoff. I'm vulnerable if either _____ or _____ move on to new positions, but right now I just don't have the resources to double-up on a position so a new person can gradually learn these jobs.

The possibility of other future organizational moves was also a component of another manager's rationalization for his overt reluctance to appoint someone who needed training. Implicitly, this manager did not wish to invest the local resources of his department in the development of an employee who could leave shortly thereafter. Such departures would provide no payback to the manager's unit in the form of newly learned skills being applied to departmental performance. Such tensions are classic manifestations of conflicts between local, short-term interests and longer-term, organization-wide considerations:

> We just don't have a lot of training time available. We can't afford to train someone for a year and then lose them to somewhere else.

Despite the common sentiment voiced above, many managers were prepared to accept the reciprocity associated with working within a social and organizational network. They were appreciative and grateful when their departments were recipients of skilled human resources that had been developed elsewhere. They rarely objected when their prize protégés left to apply their locally developed talents in other departments. But custom and practice embodied in the day-to-day dynamics of the organization gave most managers a sense of how long someone would normally remain in a particular position. Local investments in training were, therefore, viewed as short-term exercises, in which payoffs from training should become apparent quickly before persons with skills moved elsewhere. From the perspective of local rationality, initial skills preferably should be developed elsewhere, either as part of a basic education or as part of a vestibule job in another part of the corporation:

> We're not prepared to teach initial skills. That would be a major cost in training time.

A final potential inhibitor to investments in the training and development of younger subordinates was the possibility that such investments were occasionally resented by managers. There is more than a hint of snippiness in the following remark, which presents a very limited view of the linkage between staffing and a responsibility for training and development:

> I'm not a trainer and this isn't a classroom. There's a job to be done and I'm not prepared to train them any more than is necessary.

Nevertheless, most managers paid more than lip service to training, and their actions following the initial appointment were intended to help ensure that the appointment worked out well. These actions varied in their focus. Some aimed at the immediate adjustments of new appointees to their new roles; others took a longer-term view and monitored the performance and behavior of appointees beyond their initial assignment.

MANAGERIAL ACTIONS TO FACILITATE EMPLOYEE DEVELOPMENT

Concerned for the overall welfare of the organization, their newly selected and appointed subordinates, and themselves, ForestCo's managers often followed through on initial staffing decisions to facilitate employee development. They did so in several ways. They helped new appointees become familiar with the task requirements and coworkers of their new positions and began what was often a long-term process of coaching, monitoring, and assessing subsequent performance. Supervisors actively worked to expose their subordinates to challenges that helped them develop skills and capacities that could be used either directly or in preparation for further assignments in the company. In ForestCo's "let the managers manage" philosophy, it was considered critical that aspiring managers become independent and develop the capacity to behave and manage autonomously without the need for direct support and supervision.

Familiarizing New Appointees in New Jobs

Once a staffing selection had been made, especially if the new assignment involved a move to a new department, the manager responsible for the appointment often helped the new appointee enter the new task and the organizational milieu (Ostroff & Kozlowski, 1992). Such easing functioned to reduce the new appointee's uncertainty regarding the new job. It also helped reduce the appointee's personal anxiety. In addition, introductions by the Regional Manager impressed on other departmental heads the Regional Manager's support and approval for the new appointee:

> _____ started him at [Division A] by introducing him to everyone there and having him spend some time with each department head in logging.

At times, overlaps in appointments would be arranged:

> I wanted some overlap between _____, who was leaving, and _____, who was coming in. I arranged to have them overlap for two to three weeks.

However, such overlaps, in which the outgoing person provided direction and counsel to the incoming appointee, rarely lasted much longer than a few days. For one thing, these overlaps were administratively awkward, as two persons were paid for occupying the same nominal position. Also, managers were often keen to use new appointees as a way of introducing change. For more senior and supervisory appointments, they were reluctant to have too many past practices continue without independent examination by the new appointee. Moreover, they wanted new supervisors and managers to learn the important managerial skill of taking charge and asserting their independent authority:

> I arranged for a few days of overlap between _____ [the new appointee] and the previous supervisor. In general, I judged it didn't make sense to have two supervisors there at the same time. _____ was taken around by [the previous supervisor] for a few days of familiarization, but after that he was on his own.

Once the new appointee had taken up his or her position and had been helped through the initial familiarization period, the immediate responsibilities of the manager to that appointee were dispersed into a longer time frame.

Development beyond Initial Familiarization

Felt obligations to provide support for appointees had much to do with the manager's general orientations toward training and development, the attributes of the individual appointees, and the situation in which new appointees found themselves. Though managers rarely regarded new appointees as being perfect, they also rarely used actual or potential imperfections in candidates as rationales for not following through on general obligations to train and develop skills and capacities. There was a general notion that "one danced with the gal you brung to the dance." Managers were expected to work with what they had. While they were not expected to make silk purses out of sows' ears, they were expected to do what they could with the human resources and talents available to them:

> We brought in _____ and are pleased with his choice. He fits in well and is what we expected—maybe even more than that. There's always concerns when you hire someone. _____ didn't have strong field operations experience, and we wondered if someone had seen a flaw we hadn't and had made him an administrator for that reason. But because he had other strengths, he needed the field experience if he was to fill in the hole in his rounding-out as a professional.

The effects of ForestCo's traumatic history of the early 1980s continued to be felt during the time of this study in the later 1980s, as personnel policies continued to emphasize promotion from within and limitations on hires from the ELM. One consequence of this hangover of past policies was that managers struggled to obtain a clear appreciation of the standards that they were to attempt to meet with internal appointees before they could search for candidates from outside the corporation. At times, this process resulted in what a number of managers described as selections that chose "the best of the worst." When they made such appointments, managers expressed a reluctant obligation to meet the appointees' development needs:

> _____ was the best there was at the time we searched for someone for that position. But he's going to have to get over his meek and mild manner if he's going to get his points across in a meeting. The mill manager feels that _____'s appointment is a mistake. Maybe, but beggars can't be choosers. _____ isn't perfect, but he was the best we had.

Similar concerns were expressed by another manager. In this instance, misgivings regarding the appointment and the effort required to bring the appointee up to acceptable standards were ameliorated by the complementary skill development of others in the same organizational unit. Past appointments that produced less than desirable results were often made for reasons of expediency. Even when the reasons implicated in expeditious moves became less compelling with the passage of time, obligations to maintain a subordinate's career continued to motivate development efforts:

> There weren't all that many candidates for the job—but I still don't feel I shortchanged myself as I did when we selected _____. In that case we hired the best of two candidates and ended up with someone who turned out not to be very competent. We're working with him to bring him up to the standards he has to accomplish in order to get promoted. However, his overall usefulness decreases daily as [two more junior members of the team] get stronger.

In contrast to the previous illustration, some managers were motivated to ensure that high-quality development occurred because they had a personal stake in the outcome of a previous appointment:

> There's some risk for _____ because she's being thrust into a male environment. Some people think she won't be able to function well because of that. I disagree. I think she's the best person for that job.

At times, such commitment to the development of additional skills and capacities was made for reluctant appointees who were unsure they wished to accept the demands associated with developmental opportunities:

> _____ initially had trouble with the move because he loved his previous job. But he accepted the new job because he had faith in his boss and understands he's got to move and get additional grooming if he's going to go anywhere in the organization.

Despite the myriad small rationalizations that could deflect managerial actions from felt responsibilities to oversee the training and career development of subordinates, managers nonetheless continued to monitor the performance of new appointees within their jurisdiction. Part of this ongoing surveillance was directed at managerial objectives, especially those related to the development and maintenance of appropriate standards. Such signaling of standards was important for both new and established appointees, and especially so when the manager was also recently appointed:

> It's important for the manager, especially if he's new, to ensure that his subordinates understand his standards.

As new appointees became established in their new roles and demonstrated that they could function adequately in their new jobs, the nature of supervisory oversight changed. Coaching and counseling new appointees to obtain desired levels of performance gradually evolved into more regular performance reviews. One manager had generalized his experience with the task of communicating supervisory standards into advice and prescriptions for others in the corporation:

> You should do an informal visit with your staff every few months and let them know what you think of their performance. That way, you avoid any big trauma at performance appraisal time. You have to be frank if you're not to pay the larger price associated with standards not being met.

But being frank and providing honest feedback could result in the communication of none but negative views to subordinates. At least one manager also had an additional prescription regarding the provision of performance feedback:

> We could improve employee relations if managers started giving more positive feedback and positive recognition to people. It's quick and easy to give lots of negative feedback. But the result is that when people see their boss coming, they expect bad news.

Regardless of how feedback was provided, managers needed to relate current performance to expectations at the time the appointment was made. Ongoing surveillance of new appointees was required in order to see whether previous appointments would yield a satisfactory outcome—in terms of both individual performance and the long-term fit of appointees with the group with which they were currently working:

> You have to do an ongoing assessment of whether the right person was picked, based on their successes and their fit with the group.

These general prescriptions often produced individual evaluations not dissimilar to the one reported below. Taking into account the context of the appointment, performance was considered to be acceptable, but could be improved:

> _____ is doing well, but he needs to get tougher. That's coming. He's had good results for the past six months after quality and efficiency had been so low for many, many years.

An appointee to a position was rarely chosen with the idea that this assignment would be the last the employee would ever receive. Staffing was viewed as a component of training, because employees were expected to continue developing the skills and capacities required to facilitate the ongoing adaptation of the firm to its changing environment. Potential future moves and the management of such moves were also part of the rationale that supported ongoing surveillance of subordinates' performance well beyond their initial appointment.

Managing Moves for On-the-Job-Development

The purpose of monitoring the performance of subordinates, especially that of subordinates who had been appointed to positions on the watch of the current supervisor, was to assess their development as potential candidates for other positions that became vacant. Responsibility for managing these future moves, however, was understood to be shared between supervisor and subordinate. Subordinates were expected to play an active role in interpreting job requirements. Their focus on selected job demands, and the manner in which they shaped their work experiences, were factors that supervisors considered in searching for candidates for vacant positions:

> Employees need to consider where they are and what they need to move forward so they can become candidates for the jobs that are posted. They have to look at what level they want to end up at and get training according to their goals. When you're doing hiring, it's not just a matter of filling a hole. You must always think about future needs up the ladder.

This shared responsibility did not imply, however, that favorable results would necessarily result from candidates' investments in their jobs and careers. There were clear limits as to what moves could be guaranteed in the future. Within their own units, managers could outline possibilities and make conditional promises regarding successions and could even prepare and groom candidates for likely positions. But they could not guarantee such moves because of unanticipated exigencies. Even larger qualifications applied to moves in the larger organizational context outside the current supervisor's sphere of influence:

> It's real important that people understand we can't guarantee their future career. What we can do is provide challenges in the present which will support them when future moves are being considered.

One additional exigency not within the control of either supervisor or subordinate was the move of the supervisor to another position in the organization. Once a supervisor left a particular organizational unit, his ability to influence appointments in the unit he left behind was severely restricted. Plans for the subsequent career development and placement of subordinates could be left with employee relations managers and passed on informally to a manager's successor. But implementation of these plans could not be guaranteed. Successors were not obliged to follow through on previous plans for career development and assignment, except in the occasional instance when the previous manager became the supervisor of the position just vacated:

> We decided to give _____ an interim move. He became a Divisional Accountant with the expectation that within the next two years he'll have to demonstrate his capacity to become a financial manager. While we were working this out, I felt quite vulnerable, as _____'s not ready yet to step into my job, and I couldn't find anyone to fill my position were I to leave.

Within these limitations, subordinates were given appointments that gave them a new vantage point from which to consider possible future moves. What they decided to aim for and how their plans were executed was partially up to them. They needed to inform others about the desired directions in which they wanted their careers to develop. However, actual outcomes also depended on opportunities becoming available and the candidates' demonstrating the capacity to pursue those career directions:

> This new position for _____ will be a training job where he'll both see and learn more about various avenues for future positions.

If the requirements for a particular line of advancement could be met, managers were willing to spend time and energy in developing their subordinates. When these plans worked out, managers were willing to talk, often with pride and satisfaction, about their role in developing managerial talent for the firm:

> _____ wanted a challenge, so he accepted the sideways move to [Division A]. He brought good skills with him and I'm grooming him for succession. He's now a top potential manager for Woodlands.

Consideration of future moves, many of which were likely to be closely interdependent with other moves, led ForestCo's managers to develop an appreciation of the continuing dynamics of staffing. Deciding on future moves was partially dependent on how long a manager thought a subordinate should stay in his current job. The desired length of stay, in turn, was dependent upon how quickly the potential candidate could learn the full complement of skills demanded in that position. One of the functions of ongoing surveillance, then, was to assess the manner, the content, and the speed of subordinate learning. In doing this, the baseline for assessing these performance attributes was often that established by previous occupants of that position:

> He'll do a better job than his predecessor. In fact, we expect to get more out of him because he's a fast learner. Within nine to ten months he's come from learning administration to handling administration and negotiating grievances. He's already expanded beyond the initial position because he had to work without the benefit of much day-to-day supervision. He's quick to learn from the experience of others and knew that if he got into a jam he could turn to [the unit supervisor] for help.

Less detailed but more straightforward views of time-in-position expectations were occasionally generalized into ideas regarding the length of time required for investments in training and development to pay off. Not surprisingly, managers who invested in subordinate training looked for subordinates to stay longer than did other departmental managers who were searching for experienced and trained supervisors:

> We hope _____ will stay at least four to five years in view of the investment we've made in training.

Despite the best of intentions and the comprehensiveness of career planning, the future, of course, was never certain. Managers had no guarantee that appointees would develop the additional skills and capacities required for moves from their most recent appointment:

> I have no immediate concerns about _____ being able to do the job. But I'm much less confident about how he'll develop from here.

The close relationship between staffing and the development of the critical skills and capacities required for organizational survival led managers to consider individual careers before, during, and after particular appointments. Career development of appointees from within departments was rarely regarded as a frequently interrupted experience, with discontinuous learning occurring from one appointment to another. Instead, learning was regarded as a continuous process, with learning opportunities and performance requirements of a prior appointment merging with those of the subsequent assignment. Even when appointees originated from outside a department, past performances of candidates were extrapolated through immediate expectations onto various future career options. Control of future development, however, was limited by high degrees of uncertainty. Managers therefore actively monitored, assessed, and occasionally intervened in the ongoing development of appointees.

The Desired Outcomes of Development

Although ForestCo's managers could not guarantee how a potential developmental move would turn out, they believed quite strongly in a personalized view of management. That is, managers held a collective view of the requirements of their own occupation in this organization. They might have to work in different organizational structures, with different technologies, and with different markets, but they themselves, and others like them, needed to rely on their personal capacities to meet the challenges of the future. This notion of self-sufficiency appeared as a significant subtheme in comments on the nature of the supervisory and managerial skills that needed to be developed. Initially, these ideas emerged as managers outlined their strategy of arranging only minimal degrees of overlap between the departing job occupant and the new appointee. In their view, it was important for new appointees to develop their own ideas of what was important, and to act on the basis of that independent judgement, rather than to rely on the customs and practices of their predecessors:

> I felt it was important not to indoctrinate _____ into the job by telling him all the details of the problems with the drivers. I wanted him to go into the job without any preconceived ideas of what is going on and what is possible. When I give a manager a job, I want him to have the tools and authority to do it.

Once new appointees were in place, a supervisor's short-term development goals would be oriented to specific technical objectives. In the longer term, managerial autonomy was a highly valued outcome:

> My short-term goal is directed at the technical aspects of this business. But in the longer term, I have to concentrate on the development of my staff. I want my people to be able to roll up their sleeves and work without a baby-sitter.

This theme was repeated with variations. Some managers believed that the sudden immersion into the complex and urgent realities of managerial life quickly sorted out those who would survive and those who would not:

> He'll be rotated through a number of supervised assignments. But he'll also be thrown into the deep end a few times, more of a trial-by-fire experience, to round out his supervisory training.

Other managers believed in a more gradual and protected approach, but the development of managerial autonomy remained a final objective:

> This new job is a learning process for him because he hasn't run a shift by himself before. If he gets into trouble, there's someone he can turn to, but he's got to learn for himself what works and what doesn't.

While the attainment of specific knowledge and skills was often mentioned as a potential outcome of developmental assignments, generic outcomes depended on the particular interactions between the appointee's personal capacities and the challenges emerging from the requirements of the position:

> You've got to give a guy a shot at showing what he can do.

Nevertheless, there were several paths by which managerial skills could be obtained. At times, these paths could consist of temporary or permanent assignments, could be located in an operating mill or in a regional office, or could be associated with one or another functional occupation:

> We needed a short-term Project Accountant and chose _____ to do that job. This was a temporary assignment because once the mill was up and running, we wanted him to be trained as the Sales Manager. We hoped he'd be a better overall manager as a result of the change in function and the new experience. If he's going to go anywhere in this organization in the future, it's important he gets some mill experience.

Some assignments were oriented to particular aspects of a person's portfolio of managerial capacities. Development of interpersonal skills, for example, was regarded as complementary to a person's location in the network of organizational interdependencies. Assignments to central positions often required appointees to refine their interpersonal skills. Jobs that required high levels of interaction provided greater learning opportunities for candidates who had the capacity to take advantage of a large number of organizational contacts:

> Development of _____'s people skills is going to be a big part of his job for the next couple of years. His technical skills are just fine. He'll also be more visible to people in the division, as he'll have to develop contacts with all the division's managers. He's going to be at the hub of the action.

For a number of professionals and managers, being at the hub of the action at ForestCo also meant that they were often required to deal with external agencies. Public relations skills were increasingly being demanded. Such demands for dealing with external relationships were increasingly critical as environmentalists challenged forestry practices:

> We need to formalize training and standards of performance for employees in the organization. For example, we've encouraged _____ to broaden his skills, and he's now going to Toastmasters.

Responsibility for liaising with external constituencies required technical knowledge, an even-tempered personal style, and knowledge of how to deal with representatives of the media. Because ForestCo had multiple plants and logged in different areas of the province, different managers were held to be responsible for the public's perception of ForestCo's stewardship of the public lands the company was licensed to manage. Their skills were of critical importance, as public awareness of and concern for the quality of the physical environment could conflict with corporate interests in the efficient harvesting and utilization of wood fiber:

> _____ needs to develop more now that he's back handling the whole spectrum of issues for the company. We've told him he needs to build his public relations skills and how to deal with the media.

But for many other jobs, development of skills required for internal operation of the firm was the primary concern. Further refinement of technical skills was one such illustration:

> We've invested a lot of money in training him to be a technical electrical specialist.

> We have to give _____ experience in process engineering.

Although the primary means used to develop managerial knowledge and skills was on-the-job training and development, off-the-job education occasionally complemented that process. In a few instances, the experience provided by a particular move was designed to complement and supplement other education and training occurring elsewhere:

One of the purposes of this position is to provide a broader base of experience for someone who's getting their degree. It's an opportunity for her to expand her knowledge and to develop some expertise before moving into the next position. She can build contacts so that in the future when we have a question we'll know where to go to get the answers. She's got one year left to do that.

Also, because a number of professions (e.g., accountants, engineers, lawyers, foresters) have both educational and work-related qualification requirements, some moves were made to satisfy the legal or quasi-legal requirements of the relevant regulatory body:

Being assigned to this job will save a year of formal training. _____ has two years in which to complete the six required courses and get his certificate. Once he's got that and with this experience, he'll have satisfied the legal requirements for the position.

Finally, some employees were targeted for specific off-the-job education courses that would complement on-the-job development:

As a requirement of his job, he'll have to attend the Silviculture Institute in Washington.

A brief summary of managerial actions to facilitate employee development suggests that the range of issues that can enter into a staffing decision is quite wide. Managers making staffing decisions often attempted to extrapolate the past experiences of candidates to estimate performance in both the immediate- and the longer-term future. Evaluations of performance also typically included estimates of each candidate's capacity to develop even more from future job demands. While on-the-job development was considered the primary means through which supervisors and managers could develop the skills and capacities to perform well as senior managers and executives, off-the-job education and training occasionally complemented internal development.

SUMMARY

In ForestCo, staffing was rarely viewed, or acted upon, as an isolated managerial activity. Staffing was most often seen as an integral component of the overall task of managing an organizational unit. Staffing moves were anticipated, planned for, executed, and followed up in an organizational context that shifted and changed both independently and as a consequence of the staffing actions being considered. In contrast to most textbook treatments of staffing, which consider staffing to be synonymous with the processes of selection and to terminate once the selection task has been accomplished, this chapter has focused on postselection activities of supervisors executing various managerial aspects of staffing.

From the perspective of ForestCo's overall ILM, staffing was regarded as the primary means through which critical managerial skills and capacities were developed. Selection of candidates with demonstrated capacities to learn and develop further, together with their assignment to demanding jobs, were key components of the processes of organizational maintenance and renewal. As ongoing training extended beyond the initial selection and assignment processes, desired but uncertain future outcomes of staffing decisions continued to shape managers' behaviors toward candidates and appointees once initial appointments had been completed. However, because unanticipated circumstances and consequences often had the potential to interfere with the attainment of intended objectives of a staffing action, managers were sensitive to a variety of risks associated with staffing. Individual assessments of these risks predisposed managers to engage in postselection actions.

Four classes of risk were identified. First, some managers, particularly those who were relatively new to their jobs, were unsure how to execute a staffing action and feared making a mistake. Other managers, even ones with considerable experience, were aware that having to put their reputations at risk was an ongoing part of their managerial lives. They were aware that when they made controversial decisions, their personal judgment would be examined and commented on more than if they did what was expected. Evaluations of risk to their personal or managerial reputations influenced each manager's propensity to intervene in postselection staffing activities. A second source of risk to the person responsible for an appointment was that the intended and expected performance of the appointee would not be realized. Such outcomes held negative repercussions for the organizational unit in which the staffing assignment occurred. A third aspect of risks associated with staffing concerned those that could affect the new appointee. New challenges were not always overcome. Although alternative assignments were sometimes possible, there was rarely a guarantee that an employee who accepted a new assignment would have an instance of failure ignored in future appreciations of his or her career history. Fourth, in any appointment, there were consequences for those candidates considered but not chosen. The largest risk in this instance was to the survival of the motivational dynamics that maintained the organization as a social system. In particular, managers were concerned about the future motivation of unselected candidates and the potential likelihood that they would question the legitimacy of the system that chose others over them.

Different managers expressed different degrees of felt accountability for their staffing decisions. Often, the outcomes of a staffing assignment were influenced by exigencies outside the responsible manager's personal control. Also, more senior management occasionally influenced the choice of appointee, thus diminishing the immediate supervisor's felt responsibility for the success of the staffing action. Approximately half the managerial and supervisory respondents indicated that they felt a substantial responsibility to follow through on previous selection and staffing decisions and to ensure that these decisions worked out well.

Depending on perceived risk, assessments of external accountability, and feelings of personal responsibility, managers were motivated to act so as to increase the likelihood that positive outcomes would emerge from their staffing actions. Generally, these actions were framed in terms of the training and development likely to occur from subsequent on-the-job experiences. Postselection staffing actions familiarized new appointees with their new jobs, ensured that development beyond the initial familiarization occurred, and ensured that candidates were evaluated for further on-the-job development through subsequent moves. In these ways, staffing was considered to be an integral if not a key mechanism for accomplishing managerial training and development.

Review of Part III

Staffing actions and decisions are instrumental behaviors. Managers engage in staffing activities to accomplish various personal and organizational goals pertinent to the complex social systems of which they are a part. Understanding managerial staffing actions and decisions therefore requires one to develop an appreciation of the larger social system within which each manager acts. But there is no single "truth" to our understanding of managerial behavior. As in the tales of *Rashomon*, Lawrence Durrell's *Alexandria Quartet*, or other similar stories, there are multiple truths to staffing, which depend on the particular perspective from which understanding is sought.

The argument in the preface to Part III was a conventional one that appreciations of staffing can be developed from three complementary perspectives on organizations: rational-, natural-, and open-system models (Scott, 1992). Each perspective requires a different set of assumptions regarding the key features of organizational functioning. Rational- or closed-system models are consistent with the abstract goal-attainment assumptions of bureaucratic rationality. Natural-system models view organizations more from the perspective of the personal and social motives of organizational participants. Finally, open-system models view organizations as being interdependent with the environments in which they are located.

In each of Chapters 8 through 12, descriptions of the staffing activities of ForestCo's managers have been examined to see to what extent managers' reports of their own staffing behaviors invoked ideas or assumptions from either of the three perspectives just described. Chapter 8 introduced key features of staffing in ForestCo's organization. Initially, it considered ForestCo's recent history and traced the consequences of the recession experienced in the early years of the 1980s for staffing decisions at the end of that decade. It also presented a contingent view of the tensions inherent in internal labor markets (ILMs), namely, the choice of either a competitive, market-based approach to the assignment of employees to positions or an administered process subject to substantial managerial discretion. Chapters 8 and 9 elaborated on these aspects of organizational staffing, providing additional detail on administered appointments and posting processes, respectively. Chapter 10 presented evidence on the cognitive frames used by Forestco's managers to assess candidates being considered for possible appointment to vacant positions. Finally, Chapter 12 extended the temporal context for staffing beyond the selection decision and reported on postselection considerations and behaviors of staffing. A summary of each of these general topic areas as interpreted through each organizational frame of reference is presented in Table R.2.

Table R.2. Review of Organizational Perspectives on Staffing

Staffing topic	Organizational model		
	Rational-system	Natural-system	Open-system
ILMs as contexts for staffing	Increased competition Increased speed Cross-fertilization of ideas Knowledge of candidates Subordinate training	Managerial control Managing lines of progression Maintain social system Participation–legitimacy Subordinate motivation/cooperation	Effects of history on managerial values and organizational demography Subordinate motivation and training
Administered staffing	Uncertainty reduction Supply of future skills Organizational adaptation Fine-tune original roles New jobs Reorganizations	Managerial control Managing lines of progression	Organizational adaptation
Posting systems	Overt intent } Implement competitive labor market Manifestly rational decisions Posting as learning process	Maintain social system Reinforce hierarchy Control rewards/promises Implicit intent } Maintain social system Legitimacy of appointments Rationalization/confirmation of appointments Interview panels	
Selection criteria	Bounded rationality Use of jobholder schemata Signals of performance Experience Age Time in rank	Management of lines of progression Mobility and stability Advancement potential Assignments as rewards Individual dispositions Team values/culture	Contextual effects Community and family Gender stereotypes Adaptation to unknown futures Development of generic skills
Postselection aspects of staffing	System survival Training and skills development Avoid disruptions to performance Conflicts between different rational perspectives	System survival Careers of subordinates Motivation of subordinates Manager as agent Responsibility and accountability Limits to felt responsibility	

As illustrated in the table, no single perspective dominates. Both rational- and natural-system models were strongly represented in all five topic areas dealing with staffing. Open-system models were most strongly represented and were key to bookend Chapters 8 and 12, which introduced the context for staffing decisions and extended staffing considerations beyond the traditional focus on employee selection. This positioning of open-system models reflects the sequence in which the issues in Part III have been presented. Open-system models are important and influential for understanding what might be characterized as the three middle topics of staffing—administered appointments, posting systems, and selection criteria—but are implicit rather than explicit features of the explanations provided. It would be better to examine the effects of open-system models on, and their consequences for, these three internal topics through a comparative study of ILMs rather than through the single case study of ForestCo. Nevertheless, all three perspectives on organizations are demonstrably requisite frames for presenting and understanding staffing practices.

Traditionally, staffing has been regarded as being synonymous with rational models of employee selection. Rational models were used either directly in selection decisions in which candidates competed for jobs that were well defined or indirectly as the preferred philosophical framework for managerial explanations of their reasons for acting as they did. Rational models supported managers' choices between two primary means of staffing: administered staffing decisions and use of the posting system. Increased competition, faster decisions, cross-fertilization of ideas within the company, managers' knowledge of candidates, and candidates' knowledge of possible jobs, as well as subordinate training in how to compete for jobs, were all invoked as rational criteria for choice among alternative mechanisms to accomplish staffing.

Rational philosophy and related criteria were also used in further descriptions and explanations of both administered and posting systems. Administered staffing procedures reduced the levels of uncertainty experienced by both managers and their subordinates and were judged to provide improved guarantees of the supply of skills required in the future. In addition, administered staffing also facilitated the microprocesses of organizational adaptation. Managers could fine-tune interdependent organizational roles to the capacities of available subordinates, assign well-known subordinates to perform new, not-well-known jobs, and accomplish complex reorganizations involving substantial changes in both persons and positions. Execution of these functions linked rational- and open-system models. In competitive environments, firms need to adjust and adapt to changing conditions if they are to survive. Rational assignments of candidates to a shifting array of duties, roles, and responsibilities overtly served the function of organizational adaptation to changing circumstances. If there is any conflict between perspectives here, it lies more between different versions (e.g., short-term vs. long-term) of organizational rationality than between rational and open systems. Rationality per se is quite compatible with open-system perspectives.

Systems of rational selection were manifested most overtly in implementation of posting systems. Jobs were typically well defined, as were associated candidate characteristics and the knowledge, skills, abilities, and other attributes required for superior job performance. Moreover, orderly, systematic, rational decision models were used within most selection processes that used the posting system. Posting also served to disseminate information about jobs to potential candidates and to provide information about potential candidates to managers who were almost always searching for suitable appointees. In assessments of economic rationality embedded in market behavior, more information is invariably regarded as better than less. The information function of posting contributes to

ILMs that are more economically efficient. Improved person–job matches come from situations in which there is more rather than less information. There is little question that ForestCo's managers used rational models extensively to choose one staffing system or another and to make sense of their staffing activities regardless of the staffing procedure used.

Rationality, however, is not the whole story. As much as rational models were used to make sense of staffing and the functioning of ForestCo's organization, there was an equivalent emphasis on natural features of ForestCo as a social system. Neither managers nor their subordinates conducted their roles "in the spirit of formalistic impersonality"— the manner prescribed for an ideal bureaucracy. Feelings of belonging, personal attractions, passion, affection, and enthusiasm were extraordinarily important supports to the stability, and lubricants to the adaptability, of ForestCo's organization. Personal motives and rewards, as well as networks of obligations and trust, were critical for the maintenance of various elements of ForestCo as a social system. These social systems were not nurtured and maintained just for the social satisfactions of ForestCo's employees. They were also key components required for the maintenance of ForestCo as a rational system of goal attainment. The management of employee mobility along lines of progression, in particular, served both rational and natural functions. Mobility along a line of progression of increasingly challenging and difficult jobs developed skills required for future organizational performance and, as well, provided opportunity for increases in both intrinsic and extrinsic individual satisfactions.

Management of mobility along lines of progression also replenished and reinforced existing social systems. The obligations owed to supervisors by subordinates chosen for positions of higher status and reward reinforced the organizational hierarchy. ForestCo's managers were rarely indifferent to such consequences. As their staffing actions maintained the social system of which they were a part, these actions also fulfilled important functions for ForestCo as a rational system. Management of lines of progression enabled supervisors to exercise increased control over the resources available to them to pursue organizational objectives and to enhance their roles as agents in those processes. The interdependence between natural and rational systems facilitated organizational adaptation and survival into the future.

Representatives of ForestCo's organization attempted to control exigencies so as to reduce risks to organizational survival and to increase organizational efficiencies. Managers learned from past experiences, and this learning modified both actual and perceived reality. For example, relative evaluations of either administered or posting staffing arrangements at any one time were strongly influenced by appreciations of ForestCo as an open system interdependent with its environment. The experience of the recession in 1981–1982, in particular, had a profound effect on the way ForestCo managed its ILM and staffing systems at that time and on managerial perceptions and orientations to those experiences some eight years later. This recession and ForestCo's reactions to the resultant economic conditions had both immediate and continuing effects on the demography of the organization as a consequence of changes in employee flows. A pronounced increase in numbers of layoffs, accelerated regular and early retirements, and a severe reduction of hires from the external labor market, disrupted career expectations and employee motivations and reduced the supply of skilled talent at the end of the decade. The experience of the recession also had a profound effect on the values of managers and their subordinates. In implementing survival policies, supervisors violated their social roles and their own expectations of themselves. Their actions also violated the trust that subordinates had in their supervisors' capacity to follow through on promises of job security in implicit employment contracts.

Under these circumstances, it is highly likely that the managerial values articulated at the time of this study were oriented more toward natural-system issues because of the experience of the recession. Such contextual effects, however, are "noticed" only through an open-system perspective. Thus, the degree of emphasis given to either rational or natural models as appropriate lenses through which to view organizational staffing is itself modified by the degree to which one selects closed- or open-system perspectives that ignore or give explicit attention to the historical context.

The relationship between rational and natural models of organizations for developing appreciations of organizational staffing was most acute in assessments of posting systems. In the discussion immediately following the introduction of Table R.2 above, posting systems were characterized as strongly manifesting aspects of a particular type of organizational and bureaucratic rationality. Both conceptually and temporally, well defined jobs preceded considerations of candidates whose characteristics were assessed on the basis of their contribution to job performance. Selection decisions typically followed formal rational decision procedures. Posting also increased the diffusion of information about jobs and candidates throughout the organization, increasing the prospect for economically efficient assignments of persons to jobs. The overt purpose of posting was to implement a competitive internal labor market. As presented in Chapter 10, however, a strong complement to this overt intent was the implicit objective of maintaining ForestCo's ILM as a social system. The primary function of posting was to increase the legitimacy attributed to appointments and the subsequent distribution of rewards, power, and influence in the organization. In posting, there was a mutual complementarity between rational- and natural-system appreciations of staffing.

The interdependence of rational- and natural-system models for understanding the staffing practices of ForestCo's managers was also evident in the criteria managers used to infer the likely performance attributes of candidates. Jobholder schemata that included notions of experience, age, and other attributes were used as signals of potential job–person matches. Such schemata served rational objectives such as cognitive parsimony, but not necessarily the interpretations of rationality built into contemporary models of employee selection. Many other candidate attributes or jobholder schemata derived from managerial concerns with their management of lines of progression. Other management issues often emerged from aspects of the local context to become intertwined with traditional selection criteria such as future job performance. For example, criteria such as the need for mobility or stability, advancement potential, and time in rank were also used to discriminate among candidates for positions. These criteria served both rational and natural models of organizations. In other circumstances, however, the two perspectives could lead to different prescriptions. Assignments used as rewards for past service or loyalty, and those that acknowledged individual and personal needs, typically served social-system requirements only. While it could be argued that managers who failed to look after their subordinates could incur unsatisfactory performance from resentful and unhappy employees, such arguments appear to be weak when viewed from rational-model perspectives. Assignments that have immediate job performance as their objective are strong alternatives to assignments made solely for the maintenance of the social system. Managerial preferences for either rational- or natural-model perspectives could lead to different substantive actions.

Even more interdependence between rational-, natural-, and open-system models was manifest in postselection, follow-up considerations of staffing. Ensuring the continued development of the generic skills of selected candidates met rational-system objectives, as such skills helped the firm develop capacities to respond to unforeseen future exigencies. Disruptions of future departmental performance could be avoided if there was sufficient bench-strength of skilled subordinates available to meet future demands. In developing subordinate knowledge and skill, however, managerial actions also reinforced employee motivation and supported patterns of career development. Thus, there is a mutual dependence between social and rational purposes. But there was even more evidence of natural-, social-system considerations evident in the expressed rationales of ForestCo's managers. Many managers were acutely aware of their dual roles as supervisor and subordinate and their collective interdependence as actors within a bureaucratic milieu. Agency effects were quite strong, as managers sought to pursue rational organizational objectives within their appreciations of their own self-interests, responsibilities, and systems of accountability.

The view of staffing presented in Part III is one that is far more complicated, uncertain, contingent, and paradoxical than traditional presentations of employee selection. Staffing activities are implicit in emerging, shifting, environmentally dependent social systems. Factors not normally considered in abstract, bureaucratic models of rational systems emerge from local situational and temporal contexts to qualify the implementation of standardized procedures for employee selection. Past and current situations, as well as the reactions of organizational representatives to previous and current circumstances, produce shifting contexts for the execution of staffing. Within these local contexts, actions often served both rational- and natural-system functions. At other times, the degree of emphasis given to either rational- or natural-system orientations could lead to competing prescriptions for action. The degree to which either system perspective could dominate or become subordinate in the cognitive frames of local managers depended on the larger temporal and contextual environment. In such a context, prescriptions for appropriate staffing decisions and actions cannot be readily obtained. Staffing requires substantial managerial judgment that is contingent on diagnoses of each situation and should not be reduced to formulaic prescriptions.

IV

Summary and Review

12

The Operation of Internal Labor Markets

Summary and Review

INTRODUCTION

Organizations are the dominant feature contemporary society. They are the primary vehicle for accomplishing collective purposes, whether the purpose be to engage in business or other economic activities, to put a man on the moon, or to govern ourselves. The internal activities of organizations also mediate processes of social and career mobility. Employees enter organizations, move to positions of increased reward and status within them, and eventually leave these employment systems. These mobility processes are shaped by a variety of forces, mechanisms, procedures, decisions, and actions that comprise the internal labor markets (ILMs) of organizations. This book has presented an examination of the operations of a specific ILM—the salaried employment system of ForestCo, a large, multiplant manufacturing firm in the forest products industry.

This examination of ForestCo's salaried employment system has been guided by previous theorizing from three nested perspectives and intertwined levels of analysis. First, ForestCo's ILM was examined from the points of view of two types of system-level perspective: (1) ForestCo's organization viewed as either rational-, a natural-, or an open-system models; (2) ForestCo's employment system viewed as the flows of employees that maintained, and occasionally modified, the dynamic equilibrium of the employee stocks that comprise the salaried workforce complement.

Second, ForestCo's ILM was examined from the perspective of two samples of vacancy chains discerned in patterns of employee mobility. Vacancy chains were conceptualized as linked sequences of staffing actions in which an internal move of an employee from one position to another led to subsequent staffing actions to fill the position just vacated.

Third, ForestCo's ILM was examined from the perspectives of managers who executed these staffing actions. Managers had considerable discretion as to how they engaged in staffing. They often had the freedom to choose between two primary procedures for staffing positions: administered appointments or the posting system. In addition, managers had further discretionary control over the details of the manner in which the chosen procedure was used. Their choice of procedure strongly influenced who was chosen, and, as well, produced related effects such as social and legitimacy consequences.

There are strong mutual interdependencies among these perspectives on ILMs. Macro-, system-wide considerations of both organizations and employment systems provide alternative and at times competing appreciations of the context within which vacancy chains and staffing actions occur. For example, actions developed to serve natural-system objectives could be judged irrational or illegitimate from the perspective of bureaucratic rationality. Similarly, observed variabilities in procedures and judgments could occur because of different contextual conditions that reinforced open-system perspectives. For example, the demography of an organization's workforce was shown to influence both objective antecedents of staffing, such as uncontrollable exits due to retirements, and subjective assessments, such as the energy, creativity, and innovativeness of those remaining. Moreover, both quantitative and qualitative assessments of overall organizational objectives influence the nature of issues considered in subsequent staffing decisions. As a consequence, understanding why staffing occurs as it does often requires an appreciation of the wider organizational context. Microbehaviors were also shown to influence macroconditions. For example, linked patterns of staffing actions that comprised vacancy chains aggregated to produce the employee flows observed at the macrolevel of the employment system. In turn, these employee flows maintained or modified the size, composition, and overall demography of an organization's workforce: a contextual condition that framed subsequent staffing decisions. There is substantial reflexivity among these interconnected perspectives on ILMs.

The examination of ForestCo's ILM from system-level perspectives illustrated several relatively idiosyncratic attributes of this particular firm in its particular industry at this particular stage of its life cycle. Most notably, its production operations, such as sawmills or paper mills, were grouped so as to realize various economic advantages to be gained by providing it access to geographically dispersed supplies of wood fiber, and these groupings influenced the form of the interdependent systems of skill, knowledge, and jobs that constituted the firm's employment system.

Moreover, the recent history of this firm was also shown to have had a profound effect on both macro- and microaspects of its ILM. The recession experienced in the early 1980s led to regional groupings of departments and production operations. These groupings in turn influenced the formation of certain functions (e.g., to meet the need for consolidated income statements from Regional Offices) and their geographic placement (e.g., Regional Offices located in towns geographically distant from Head Office). The recession also strongly influenced immediate flows of employees, as many persons were "invited" to take early retirement, others were laid off, and hirings were severely curtailed. Repercussions from these immediate reactions to the recession were felt several years later. The firm underwent an initial and enduring demographic change that seven or eight years later produced an imbalance between the demand for skilled employees for vacant positions and the supply of candidates to fill them. Moreover, managerial reactions to the behaviors required of them during the manage-for-survival conditions of the recession continued to influence the attitudes, values, and actions that determined staffing decisions.

System-level perspectives of ForestCo's ILM also focused attention on the dynamic properties of this firm's employment system. There were continuing flows of employees into, through, and out of this ILM that had appreciable consequences for the stability of the resultant job–person matches. Considering only hires and promotions, and excluding consideration of lateral transfers and job evolution in which jobs change without formal recognition, at least one in five employees experienced mobility in some form in any one year. The ForestCo employment system was in a state of dynamic equilibrium such that small changes in employee flows could produce, even over a relatively short time, substantial changes in the organization's demography and the demand/supply characteristics of staffing actions.

The dynamic nature of ForestCo's ILM permitted flexible internal responses to external pressures for organizational adaptation and change. Managers responsible for local staffing actions could modify job requirements and adjust the performance dimensions associated with jobs to be filled. In this way, issues associated with the strategic management of the corporation could be readily introduced into the set of criteria used to select persons who would support implementation of emerging corporate strategies.

The underlying dynamism of ForestCo's ILM did not arise solely from the greater magnitude of employee flow rates in comparison to the size of employee stocks. The set of jobs into, through, and out of which different groups of employees flowed also changed flexibly in response to both external and internal conditions. The strongest evidence of this mutability was in the data obtained on vacancy chains in ForestCo's ILM. Both the statistical distribution of vacancy chains by their length and the more detailed analyses of managerial decisions associated with specific vacancy chains yielded substantial evidence that jobs changed frequently. Most vacancy chains were relatively short, comprising two or three person-moves. Because of the shifting demands placed on individual organizational units and the relatively stable attributes of employee resources available to meet those demands, longer vacancy chains were encountered less frequently. Stable sequences of job vacancies could not be sustained in these flexible, dynamic organizational systems.

Examination of ForestCo's ILM from staffing decision and action perspectives reinforced the appreciation of this dynamic, adaptive employment system as a flexible learning organization. Staffing decisions were often suffused with concerns regarding the training and development that could be expected to occur as a consequence of the selection and assignment of an employee. Employees were regarded as adaptive learners who were considered responsible for developing new skills and knowledge from the opportunities available in challenging assignments. Learning was very much considered to be an on-the-job phenomenon. As a consequence, selection processes very often focused more on persons than on jobs.

Selection and management of subordinates was also viewed as a personal process involving subordinates' personal loyalty and fealty to their supervisor. The normative and procedural requirements articulated in the personnel literature to meet the demands for nondiscriminatory selection were challenged by managerial interpretations of their roles and responsibilities. This finding represents a substantial collision between normative theory and actual practice. It is an issue to which we return later in this chapter after a more complete examination of staffing practices in ForestCo's ILM.

The preceding discussion has been presented as a post hoc justification for the conceptual and methodological means by which this examination of ForestCo's ILM was conducted. With this study as illustration, we argue that more complete appreciations of ILMs can be obtained by examining them from the three interdependent perspectives of the study: employment systems, vacancy chains, and staffing decisions and actions. That argument aside, the overall purpose of this summary and review is to describe the actual staffing operations of a large company and to contrast this description with accepted conceptual perspectives of ILM operation and the supporting normative treatments of employee selection. The model of ILM operation developed in Chapter 1 is presented first as the paradigm to which practice is compared.

A MODEL OF INTERNAL LABOR MARKET OPERATION

The model of ILM operation presented in Chapter 1 proposed that ILMs could be viewed as a system of five antecedent elements that, through the intervening process of staffing, produced four outcomes that maintained and reinforced the operation of the ILM. Those five antecedent elements were limited ports of entry, job ladders, the criteria used for promotions and cutbacks, the stringency of rules governing managerial discretion, and the reward or compensation system associated with the assignment of employees to different jobs. The four outcomes of ILM operation were the intra- and interfirm patterns of employee mobility; the training of generic, occupational, and job-specific skills; employee motivation; and job security. The following sections present revised appreciations of each of these elements and outcomes as a function of its role in shaping, and being influenced by, the staffing activities of the organization. Although this discussion necessarily follows the linear sequence of conventional writing in seeking to make sense of what was found, this linearity should not be allowed to mask the profoundly interdependent nature of all elements and outcomes of this specialized social system.

INTERNAL LABOR MARKET ANTECEDENTS

Managerial Discretion

In ideal-type conceptions of ILMs, dominated by administrative rules, managers have little discretion regarding the form of job ladders and the criteria they may used to select employees for promotion and layoff. Consequently, in these systems, which have been labeled "simple structures," managers have little influence over the assignment of different employees to different jobs (Spilerman, 1986). This conceptualization was derived largely from descriptions of blue-collar employment systems, in which a formal contract between unionized employees and representatives of the employing organization left little opportunity for managerial discretion.

Typical salaried employment systems, however, which have been labeled "unitary structures," are usually not dominated by such formal contracts (Spilerman, 1986). The fundamental conditions of risk and reward for salaried employees are different from those for unionized hourly employees. In salaried employment systems, managers typically have considerable discretion as to how jobs should be defined and which employee qualities would be most suited to performance of those jobs. ForestCo's salaried employment system is no exception to this general rule. Managers in this organization are able to exercise considerable local autonomy in how they manage the organizational units for which they are responsible.

In terms of staffing, ForestCo's managers could, and often did, define jobs according to their appreciation of the complex array of tasks, responsibilities, obligations, habits, customs, and personnel resources generally available. Managers invariably had some overall judgment of various aspects of the total performance required of their organizational units, and often used staffing opportunities to adjust and modify the set of individual job definitions to which available personnel resources would be assigned. Most interestingly, managers faced least resistance and had increased opportunity to change and modify job definitions when jobs were vacant. Occurrences of vacant positions typically required staffing activities and at the same time presented brief windows of opportunity to modify job requirements. Thus, processes of organizational adaptation and change were closely associated with staffing activities.

While these phenomena generally obtained, they were not the same everywhere. Some managers had greater opportunity and need to change the jobs in their departments than did others. Lower-level managers had less power and authority to reorganize their departments than did managers in the higher levels of the organizational hierarchy. In addition, some managers experienced great pressure to change—because of cost and market factors, changes in available technology, changes in the business environment, or even changes in the mix of internal resources available to them. Although not all jobs changed at each staffing opportunity, many did so as a function of the pressures and opportunities available to each manager in each situation.

In addition to their discretion as to how they defined jobs, ForestCo's managers also had substantial opportunity to select the staffing procedure to be used to search for and identify candidates for positions. In executing these staffing procedures and personnel selections, managers were able to influence the scope of the search for candidates as well as the selection of the criteria to be used in making those staffing decisions. In ForestCo, two primary methods of staffing were observed: posting procedures and the administered appointments. In the posting procedures, notices of a vacant position were posted throughout various locations in the firm and interested and qualified persons were invited to apply for consideration for appointment to the advertised position. In an administered appointment, the supervisor or manager responsible for the selection and assignment of an employee to a vacant position made that judgment without recourse to posting.

Posting procedures allowed employees a measure of influence over their organizational destiny, as they could apply for vacant positions. Their applications were known at least to themselves and to the persons making the selection, with the consequence that judgments that selected one candidate over another were potentially open, albeit only after the fact, to the scrutiny of others in the organization. The public nature of posted appointments also tended to be reinforced by the relatively common practice of using a panel of interviewers to review applications of candidates applying for posted positions.

In contrast, administered appointments were usually made at the discretion of the immediate supervisor responsible for the person appointed to the vacant position. Candidates were not always aware of vacancies in other departments, nor were they sure that they had been considered as candidates for any given vacancy for which they might be qualified. Only rarely did they have any information regarding the relative status of their possible candidacy. Managers making administrative appointments could keep their own counsel and could avoid detailed scrutiny of their decision processes, though the final outcomes of their staffing decisions could be discussed and commented upon once they became public.

Posting procedures were implicitly required by ForestCo's formal policies for all appointments for positions and employees below the senior manager and executive ranks. However, the opportunity for managerial discretion was written into ForestCo's formal policies by means of a releasing condition that posting was not required in those situations in which "a fully qualified successor had been clearly identified." It was clear that this conditional clause permitted the exercise of considerable discretion on the part of ForestCo's managers regarding their selection staffing procedures. Approximately two thirds of all internal appointments were made using administrative appointments rather than the nominally preferred posting procedures. That is, the general organizational rule regarding posting was honored twice as often in the breach as in the observance.

There is a paradox in this feature of organizational staffing at ForestCo. In ideal-type models of ILM operation (i.e., simple structures based on unionized, hourly employment systems), administrative rules frequently dominate over market mechanisms for the assignment of employees to organizational positions. Certainly, in managerial circles, there is a preponderance of arguments that promotions based on uniform rules such as seniority often lead to misallocations of less skilled human resources to the best-paid and most critical jobs. From this perspective, therefore, managerial discretion is often regarded as permitting the introduction of market-based influences of price and performance into the allocation of employees to jobs. In this view, managerial discretion is desirable because it permits, subject to the quality of managerial judgment, increased allocative effectiveness of job–person assignments. In contrast, the formally endorsed policy for selection and assignment of employees at ForestCo was that of posting—a procedure that generally facilitated the application of market comparisons, at least internal ones, to the allocation of employees to jobs. Thus, the nominally preferred method of staffing, namely, posting, was one that ostensibly met the criterion of economic effectiveness. Why, then, would managerial discretion be used so extensively in a salaried employment system to sidestep procedures that were supposed to produce results argued for so adamantly in ideal-type, hourly employment systems?

The provisional answer to this apparent paradox embodies several overlapping parts. As discussed in Chapter 9, which reviewed the implicit background logic associated with the use of the posting system, the overt intent in the use of such competitive market mechanisms is to identify and appoint the person best suited to a well-defined vacant job. Such motivations derive from models of bureaucratic rationality in which stable jobs are well defined and candidates can be effectively assessed in terms of likely future job performance. But the conditions necessary to manifestly rational staffing decisions are not always present. Jobs, especially new jobs, are frequently not well known and cannot be defined independently of the talents and capacities of other employees assigned to interdependent jobs. In addition, there is often substantial uncertainty and risk associated with assessments of candidates that are meant to indicate whether they will perform at high levels in the future. Moreover, the administrative procedures used to implement posting possess their own efficiencies and requirements. Posting took time and was ineffective when positions needed to be filled with some urgency. Posting yielded decreasing returns when it was used repeatedly for similar positions. Once a given position had been posted, managers usually had a good knowledge of all potential candidates, especially if a similar position was posted shortly thereafter. Posting also had the potential to disrupt established patterns of employee development. Investments in the training of subordinates could yield little return to a supervisor if trained subordinates were attracted to positions elsewhere before they had paid off their obligations to their supervisor in terms of current performance.

As argued previously, however, the primary purpose for posting positions was not that of rational goal attainment. Posting served primarily to maintain local departments and the whole organization as natural social systems. The dominant ideology within ForestCo's employment system was that of a competitive labor market. Appointments and assignments were legitimated by the competitive processes through which they were obtained. With the grounding of a small proportion of appointments in a competitive process, all appointments gained in legitimacy. This legitimacy also reinforced the existing hierarchy, increased acceptance of the existing social system, and strengthened the authority of senior managers in the organization.

But the administrative arrangements of the posting system also undercut the operation of ForestCo's ILM as a natural social system. ForestCo's managers were not robots programmed to fulfill organizational goals and objectives. They were persons with their own interests who were nevertheless also acting as agents within the ForestCo system. As such, they were most interested in developing, extending, and maintaining the social system of which they were a part. They often wished to exercise personal control over the employment subsystems in the units for which they were responsible. With such control, managers could follow through on prior promises of rewards for jobs well done. Moreover, increased flexibility came when managers could invest in training and experiment with temporary assignments. Managers' jobs were more powerful, more fun, and personally more satisfying when they could exercise control over the human resources in their organizational units. The net effect of these factors led managers to use their discretion to *not* follow formal organizational policies, a practice that in turn allowed them increased administrative control over staffing assignments.

Administrative appointments were generally preferred and used most frequently because they permitted managers to exert increased control over the rewards, motivations, and training of employees for whom they were responsible. Most managers exercised a direct, hands-on approach to the management of the human resources under their direction. They believed that they needed to reduce the uncertainty associated with their management of the flows of employees into, through, and out of their units. Therefore, they often took a long-term, comprehensive perspective on their management of lines of progression. Employees were frequently chosen as much for their potential to move two levels beyond the current assignment as for their suitability for the current vacancy. Managers were reluctant to disrupt planned-for successions with moves from outside their organization. As posting offered greater potential for interunit moves that could disrupt orderly progressions along career ladders, this staffing procedure was used much less frequently than administrative appointments.

Preferences such as those noted above could become routinized in sequential and nested decision protocols. ForestCo's managers looked first to use administrative appointments unless there were strong reasons for doing otherwise. If a local, within-unit appointment could be arranged, managers would do so. Only when local successions were unsuitable would they consider employees from outside their local unit. And only when internal candidates were found to be unacceptable, or anticipated to be so, would staffing searches shift to solicit applications and consider candidates from the external labor market (ELM).

The opportunity to hire from the ELM, then, was the second primary source of managerial discretion in the use of administrative rules to staff vacant positions. In these situations, managers used their discretionary choice not to search among, or select from, the set of internal candidates already employed by ForestCo. A constant background issue for all staffing decisions was the set of qualifications, capacities, and potential performances that outside recruits could possibly bring into the organization. The ELM provided an implicit set of standards against which the best of those from within would be compared. However, there was no cheap or efficient way to establish these standards independently for each vacant position. Therefore, the occasional sourcing of appointments from the ELM benchmarked the qualities and levels of pay required to obtain these capacities. These judgments necessarily had to be delegated to the independent assessment of the responsible manager, as he was the person most familiar with the candidate requirements. Thus, the requirement for ForestCo's ILM to be grounded in the general social and ELM context provided further opportunity for the exercise of managerial discretion in the operation of ForestCo's ILM.

The philosophy of "let the managers manage" that characterized the discretionary nature of staffing at ForestCo was a necessary element in the linkage between the ILM and the ELM. Staffing was a highly complex, social process that defied standardization. If these processes were reduced solely to the administration of bureaucratic rules, the latitude of adaptive change and adjustment of this organizational system to shifting external and internal demands would be severely abridged. The great degree of managerial discretion permitted in this system was critical to the *potential* for each and every staffing action to compare candidates from the ILM and the ELM. That this comparison was manifestly not made at each staffing opportunity is judged to be of little consequence. That there was an opportunity for each manager to search widely within the firm, or to search the ELM helped affirm the imagery that widely dispersed internal standards differed little from those in the ELM.

While the exercise of managerial discretion could be extraordinarily useful to the operation of ForestCo's ILM, it also held the potential for misuse and abuse. Hypothetically, for example, local managers could use their authority and discretion to appoint cronies, to establish fiefdoms, and to abuse wider social standards regarding equality of opportunity. Indeed, as noted in Chapter 11, individual supervisors occasionally expressed personal opinions that were not only politically incorrect, but also counter to the expressed and legally required policies of the corporation. Reports of these comments have not been censored. Indeed, they have been reported fully to meet the normal disclosure requirements of social science research. Nevertheless, these expressions of personal prejudice and the effects of such expressions should be evaluated within the context of the larger social system in which they occurred. There were substantial opportunities for the exercise of individual discretion in staffing, but no manager could exercise complete independence in his choice of either the staffing process or the person to be appointed.

All supervisors and managers were held responsible for certain levels of performance. Appointments that threatened unit performance also threatened the career prospects of the person responsible for the appointment. Self-interest and the need to maintain reputational capital undoubtedly limited the frequency of appointments that failed to meet normal standards of performance. Also, all appointments were nominally subject to oversight by each supervisor's supervisor and a representative of the employee relations function. While subversion of corporate-wide policies and standards had the potential to occur here as they could in any large social system, it was judged that no one could persist in such transgressions without the risk that someone would blow the whistle on their activities. Moreover, as both line management and the functional specialty of employee relations had oversight on all staffing activities, and were often involved in planning for staffing, the exercise of managerial discretion was often done publicly under the scrutiny of multiple points of view. Within the context of an adaptive, self-maintaining system, actions with the potential to damage the collective reputations of all others in the corporation could be censured and thwarted.

Other restrictions on managerial autonomy and discretion came from the complex network of task and social interdependencies between organizational units and their managers. Some of these restrictions, such as budgetary and complement controls, had the functional role of ensuring that the actions of individual managers and their departments were closely integrated into the objectives of the firm as a whole. Discretion was permitted and encouraged, but managers were held responsible and accountable for their actions. Discretionary actions often had to be justified in terms of their contribution to accomplishment of normative organizational goals.

Though limited and subject to oversight, considerable opportunity was nevertheless afforded ForestCo's managers to exercise discretion in how they operated the staffing system of their organization. This discretion qualified the influence of the four remaining elements of the ILM model—limited ports of entry, job ladders, criteria for promotion and cutbacks, and the compensation system—on the outcomes from the operation of the salaried ILM in this firm.

Limited Ports of Entry

In stereotypical *simple-structure* models of ILMs, ports of entry from the ELM into an ILM are few and located at the bottommost levels of the organizational hierarchy (Spilerman, 1986). Once entry has been gained in such structures, encompassing rules such as company seniority, possibly modified by education and merit, control advancement to positions of increased reward and status. Alternative models of ILMs such as the *unitary structure* of Spilerman (1986) are silent regarding the prevalence and location of ports of entry, but depict advancement as dependent on managerial control and judgment.

ForestCo's ILM may be regarded as a variant of a unitary structure. Entry into Forest-Co's ILM was limited, as ForestCo's managers expressed a preference for persons already employed in the organization when filling all but the lowest-level positions. Ports of entry were both prevalent and widespread. Vacancies at *all* levels of the organizational hierarchy could potentially be considered as ports of entry from the ELM into ForestCo's ILM, though this tendency diminished as a function of increased hierarchical level. For example, as noted in Chapter 2, more than 80% of the Secretarial and Clerical occupational group (salary grades 2–5) vacancies were filled by hires from the ELM, whereas the approximate proportions were 55% for salary grades 6–10, 41% for salary grades 11–15, and 25% for the highest grades. The discretion available to ForestCo's managers to manage each staffing action as they saw fit, together with their preference for administrative appointments, meant that current subordinates and known employees were often advantaged in their consideration for vacant positions. Because of the influences operating in each local situation, however, jobs that had previously served as ports of entry would not necessarily be used for that purpose the next time they became vacant. Very few jobs, other than those in the lowest levels of the organizational hierarchy, were almost always designated as permanent ports of entry, and very few jobs were ineligible to serve as ports of entry for particular candidates, depending on the local conditions affecting a vacancy situation.

Within this job system, several factors shaped ForestCo's managers' preference for current employees. First, current employees were considered to be already familiar with various aspects of the internal operating procedures of the firm. They were often familiar with their coworkers and in many instances had already developed cooperative relationships with others. Current employees were therefore preferred over recruits from the ELM because, other factors being equal, they would take less time to learn how to perform at acceptable levels.

Second, current employees were regarded as being better known than recruits from the ELM. Evaluations of their performance could be made with greater confidence because supervisors often had samples of their job performance in a related job. Predictions of future performance in a new job necessarily entailed some degree of uncertainty. Other factors being equal, the appointments of inside candidates were judged to have lower associated risks than those of external candidates.

Third, most managers were concerned with maintaining the motivation of their subordinates. For the most part, then, managers offered incentives and inducements to current employees to work diligently and to learn new skills. In particular, managers wanted subordinates who performed beyond minimally acceptable levels. A critical component of this motivational system was the implicit reward associated with promotion to new and more challenging jobs that offered higher levels of compensation. Each time a manager chose an external recruit over an internal candidate, that move could dislocate, depending on where in the hierarchy it occurred, one, two, or several promotions of internal candidates up a line of progression. Thus, choices of external candidates posed potential risks to the maintenance of the social viability of the internal organizational system.

For these reasons, ForestCo's managers generally preferred internal candidates over those from the ELM. Nevertheless, ForestCo's managers were still free to search outside labor markets for candidates for almost any position that became vacant. Deciding whether and how to search was often a complex and contingent judgment.

Job Ladders

In stereotypical ILMs, job ladders are conceptualized as specific sequences of jobs through which employees move. As employees obtain mastery of lower-level jobs, they develop the organization-specific skills and experience required to perform well in higher-level jobs. In *simple-structure* ILMs, job ladders typically follow a fixed hierarchy in which the job at the next higher level pays marginally more than the one below it.

The most striking feature of conceptions of job ladders in ForestCo's organization was that they were rarely if ever defined in terms of an ascendance through a series of specific jobs. Instead, ideas of progression were generally understood in terms of sets of similar jobs to which a particular person might be assigned. The particular job progression a candidate would experience depended on the confluence of both personal characteristics and organizational demands at the time staffing choice opportunities became available. Evaluations of organizational demands were influenced by perceptions of shifting external and internal contexts as manifest in job vacancies and the availabilities of other candidates. Candidates' capacities and availabilities were similarly changing through time and indicated by their stage of development in a prior job, local exigencies, and the personal development requirements and interests of each employee considered. Job ladders were most often conceptualized as generic constructs used instrumentally to understand how additional skills and capacities could be developed in particular employees. Often, a specific job progression, as represented by the assignment of an employee from one job to another, was thought of only as a component of a potential job ladder when someone was being considered for that move. The potential became the real when the move was actually made.

Much of the reason for this view of job ladders was that jobs were seen to be less stable than the persons performing those jobs. Even in this traditional firm, which operated in a mature industry, jobs were continually being created, modified, and phased out. Although unit performance often depended on the performance of certain tasks, there was rarely a single, fixed way in which a complex, shifting set of tasks could be distributed across a set of jobs. Further, there was rarely a single, fixed way in which any particular job could be done. Organizational units were often reorganized into different configurations of persons in jobs as a function of demands placed on unit performance and the availability of persons with their person-specific skills and capacities. Jobs were rarely defined precisely. Broad, generalized notions of jobs were developed from appreciations and analyses that derived from formal, rational theories of bureaucracy. However, the requirements of each job, especially its interdependence with other jobs, and its contributions to unit performance were most often viewed in light of the potential contributions from a specific person in that job.

Because of this dynamism, managers faced considerable difficulty in managing the temporal features of lines of progression. Specific jobs that may have been anticipated as parts of a potential line of progression and succession were often nonexistent or unavailable when the time came for an individual employee to move on. Similarly, job opportunities often became available when preferred candidates were actively involved in other projects. In this dynamic job environment, formally established job ladders, as reinforced by repetitive employee moves between jobs, made little sense.

Evaluations of mobility along lines of career development included beliefs that it was necessary for individual employees to remain in certain jobs for more or less specific lengths of time. Brief stays in jobs were discouraged because short assignments provided insufficient time for in-depth training to occur. Brief stays were also discouraged by managers who wanted returns in unit performance for their investments in employee training and development. All these factors led managers to focus more on persons than on jobs. Issues of mobility in the organizational system favored concepts of individual training and development rather than progression through a fixed succession of jobs. Job ladders and lines of progression were therefore seen more as vehicles for personal development than as organizational attributes alone.

Reinforcing this personalistic perspective on job ladders was the pervasive emphasis, in staffing decisions, on training and development of employees. Job moves were seen as the primary means of providing the challenge and opportunity for employees to develop new skills and capacities. Even employees who were not obviously moving from one job to another had jobs that continued to evolve and change as they confronted different demands from changes in products, markets, technologies, and the general economic and social environment. In addition, individual job requirements changed because different employees were assigned to other jobs that might be interdependent with a job requiring more stable occupancy. Training and the development of skills and capacities were therefore seen as a natural outgrowth of extended job experiences. Job moves, and implicitly job ladders, were most often seen as the means to develop further skills and capacities, which were attributes of employees, not of jobs. Finally, the learning that a particular employee could derive from his or her experience of a particular sequence of job moves appeared to depend partially on his or her personal qualities.

Thus, for the many reasons discussed above, job ladders were most often viewed as generic, personal progressions rather than as specific steps through which an employee moved one after the other.

Criteria for Promotion and Cutbacks

In ideal-type, rational models of personnel selection, the only criterion used to select from among several candidates is that of anticipated future performance in the job for which the candidates are immediately being considered. There is little question that this criterion was indeed also a necessary element in all the staffing decisions examined at ForestCo. There were few if any instances, however, in which anticipated future performance was the *only* consideration that led to the selection of the chosen candidate. In all staffing decisions, a large array of other criteria were also considered in the selection process. These other criteria may be grouped into three sets of factors: attributes of candidates themselves, issues associated with maintenance of the organization as a social system, and secondary, contextual factors derived from both individual candidates and features of this particular organization.

In ForestCo, as in any organization, selection from among several candidates for a particular job was an uncertain, judgmental process. No selection was guaranteed to work out perfectly. There was never a clear or firm answer to the question of how much better, or worse, the organization would have fared had another person been chosen. A variety of selection situations could be encountered. In a proportion of the selection situations in which posting procedures were used, the primary criterion for selection could be that of anticipated future performance in a specific job. However, even when job specifications were a central part of the selection process, as in posting, selection criteria could also include the anticipated performance of the candidate in several potential jobs to which he or she might eventually be assigned. In some posting situations and even more so when administrative staffing processes were followed, candidate development could become a more important selection criterion. An important part of the candidate evaluation process, then, involved judgments about the capacity of each candidate to benefit from the immediate assignment, to contribute immediately and in the future to organizational performance, and to benefit in terms of increased capacity from the development opportunities arising from these assignments.

In making selection judgments, managers qualified their estimates of anticipated candidate performance with one or another degree of confidence in the accuracy and stability of these assessments. Thus, they might pass over a candidate of considerable but untested promise in favor of a reliable appointee who offered significantly less upside potential but also less downside risk. Because of this confidence factor, a candidate's past experience and performance in a similar, related job were used most frequently as the best guides to future performance. Thus, candidates were often screened and ranked according to attributes of their past experience—including the length of time with the organization and their tenure in previous positions. Assessments of these attributes were often made within the group of candidates being considered as well as against implicit age–rank norms assumed by the persons making these selection judgments.

Not all criteria used for promotions derived directly from issues of job or organizational performance. In seeking to fine-tune matches between persons and jobs, managers occasionally considered other attributes of candidates, such as their personality, gender, and family situation. Similar attention was also given to secondary attributes of the organizational unit in which the vacancy was located. For example, when testing to see whether a potential assignment "made sense," managers would consider the nature of the group and "team" requirements for new appointees. These secondary attributes, and inferences regarding the person–job–organization "fit," derived from the immediate, local context of the position to be filled.

While the preliminary screening phases of the selection process involved judgments about the work output and organizationally related attributes of candidates, later concerns focused on issues of organizational maintenance. These issues assumed greater importance when the assignment of short-listed candidates to a particular organizational position was being considered. Managers responsible for the continued operation of a particular organizational unit reported that they spent much time considering how potential assignments would fit with the management of various segments of the lines of progression under their jurisdiction. Depending on the location of the vacant position and local circumstances, candidates could be chosen for stability or mobility. If assignments were made with subsequent mobility in mind, keen assessments of advancement potential were attempted.

In natural-system models that emphasized the social nature of organizations, a substantial number of staffing actions were also made to meet the personal needs of subordinates. For example, appointments were occasionally arranged to assist preretirement transitions, to help employees move to locations more suitable to their family needs, or to provide assignments that could facilitate educational objectives. In making appointments such as these, managers visibly helped maintain collaborative relationships between themselves and their subordinates. These relationships, and the trust they helped sustain, were essential ingredients for maintenance of the organization's social system. As demanding and difficult assignments often had to be made with only the promise of future reward, managers demonstrated their trustworthiness by subsequently following through on implicit promises to look after the personal needs of subordinates. By promising but delaying rewards to subordinates for their current efforts to learn jobs and new skills, managers gained much valued flexibility in staffing assignments. They also regarded these social exchanges to be important for the maintenance of a suitable motivational climate for the accomplishment of organizational purposes. Of course, managers were not without their own personal interests in making staffing assignments. Managers were not insensitive to the political and personal power concomitants of staffing assignments.

In no staffing situation was a predetermined suite of criteria used to select employees for positions. Instead, each staffing opportunity generated its own set of job-derived demands and candidate-derived discriminations. For some jobs, advancement potential was regarded as a critical requirement because of fast-paced technological change. In other jobs, stability was preferred because long-term, stable relationships were required for the maintenance of cooperation within an organizational unit. In terms of candidate-derived discriminations, candidate energy could become a selection criterion if only one candidate was found to display extraordinary energy and enthusiasm.

From a perspective on organizational decision making, selection decisions can be regarded as a "garbage can" full of opportunities for choice (March & Olsen, 1976) from which related problems and possible solutions can be plucked and matched. A job vacancy was rarely viewed simply as an opportunity to engage standard operating procedures to select a clonelike replacement for the person who just left that job. Because people became attached to their definitions of their jobs, and often resisted the imposition of job definitions supplied by others, the vacation of a position was often a trigger for organizational change. The vacating of positions reduced the constraints on possible change within an organizational unit. Therefore, choice opportunities associated with staffing vacant positions often became associated with other organizational issues, problems, and proposed solutions. Political issues were rarely absent from staffing, as various aspects of organizational change became intertwined with questions of staffing.

An organizational change associated with staffing could be minor or substantial. For example, managers frequently used the occurrence of a vacancy to redefine the job to be filled or to redefine the interdependencies between the focal job and other jobs in the organizational unit. At other times, the retirement of one or more senior persons could occasion a substantial reorganization of most of the jobs in the department(s) that contained those positions. Vacant positions and subsequent staffing actions presented managers with opportunities to realign, both materially and symbolically, the activities of their organizational unit with the demands of their immediate and emerging organizational situation. Therefore, multiple issues, many only partially related to the immediate performance of a vacant position, were often invoked in each local context as being pertinent to the definition of jobs and the selection and assignment of persons to those jobs. Managers who focused their attention exclusively on a continuation of previous job performance, through attempted replications of the prior person-in-job, lost their chance to use important and visible choice opportunities to close with other related problems and solutions.

Compensation System

The simple-structure model of ILM operation presented previously assumed a relatively close association of jobs, job level, and amount of compensation received. In this view, the ILM is seen as a logical and tightly organized rational system of organization. In fact, there were several significant tensions in the operation of ForestCo's ILM, in which different values, processes, and outcomes produced conflicting signals as to which actions should be taken. As summarized so far, the most significant challenge to the tight, rational administration of the firm's ILM came from the considerable opportunity managers had to exercise discretion in how they defined jobs and whom they chose for those jobs. This discretion and the subsequent emphasis on persons rather than positions, as well as the consideration of training and development from assignments for medium- and longer-term futures, meant that current, immediate compensation did not appear to be a significant factor in staffing.

The structure of ForestCo's salary schedule is very similar to the structures used by other human resource systems of large bureaucratic organizations exhibiting a unitary structure [cf. the salary system of an insurance company described in Spilerman, (1986, p. 75)]. A single salary structure covers all jobs, which are assigned to grades as a function of their "equivalence" measured in some way. A salary range is associated with each pay grade—though there is substantial overlap in the ranges of proximate pay grades. Thus, the same salary could be paid to employees who were paid at, say, the top of grade n, somewhere in the middle of the ranges associated with pay grades $n+1$ and $n+2$, and at the bottom of pay grade $n+4$. Short-term salary increases could occur because of upward movement within a salary grade, or when an employee moved from one salary grade to a higher one. The largest salary increases occurred, however, when an employee's salary placement moved both upward through salary grades and upward within each higher salary grade. The latter type of salary increase could occur without a formal move or promotion. It was used to reward ongoing performance for those employees who were either temporarily or permanently plateaued in their mobility through the organizational hierarchy as indexed by salary grade.

In a few instances, the posting of a position at a lower salary grade inhibited applications from persons who were already working at jobs assigned to the same salary grade. But for the most part, managers often gave quite vague answers when asked to report the salary grade of the position in their unit that had recently been filled. Managers were even more vague about the salary grade of the position that the successful applicant vacated to take his or her current assignment. Though it was an original assumption that the operation of ForestCo's ILM could be assessed through an analysis of salary grade changes associated with moves in vacancy chains, this analysis could not in fact be implemented.

Despite the lack of a strong association between current compensation and salary grade, the organization's compensation system was an important background against which the career development of employees occurred. The promise of a relatively secure, well-paid future with the organization was often given greater consideration than the particular salary increase associated with an immediate move from one job to another. This phenomenon occurred partly because of the longer-term outlook on future positions encouraged by the mobility ethos of the ILM. It also occurred, however, because the initial period of an assignment, especially one anticipated to last several months or even years, was often viewed as probationary. While a modest, initial salary increase was usually assigned to persons being "promoted," further salary increases were usually held in reserve and awarded at later periods contingent on assessments of development and performance. It was therefore not uncommon for the actual salary as well as the salary grade of a job to fall in a pay range commensurate with the skills, capacities, and experience of the person in that job. For these reasons, an important part of the adjustment system of this organization was the opportunity for managers to increase the salary rewards flowing to subordinates by "promoting" them through regrading their jobs. In many of these "promote on development" situations, the job itself might have changed little, but presumably the person's performance in the job had changed substantially.

The loose coupling of the compensation system with job assignments permitted considerable flexibility in assigning and rewarding employees in the organizational system. The discretion available to local managers to play with the salary grades of jobs in their departments (though the permissible salary adjustments were limited to a small range) gave them considerable opportunity to use the reward system to serve their personal and managerial goals. They could control the allocation of rewards that had great symbolic significance by making small changes in salary and salary grade. While the general features of the compensation system were important for the overall management of the ForestCo organization, detailed aspects of changes in compensation associated with changes in jobs were not measurable in this study of ForestCo's ILM.

INTERNAL LABOR MARKET OUTCOMES

The model of ILM operation advanced in Chapter 1 proposed that the five structural antecedents just described, in conjunction with organizational staffing, contributed to four outcomes that served the interests of both employers and employees. These outcomes were the patterns of mobility into, through, and out of the organization; the training of generic, occupational, and job-specific skills; employee motivation; and various guarantees of job security. In the following sections of this review, the initial conceptualizations of these outcomes are reevaluated in light of a comprehensive appreciation of ForestCo's ILM that resulted from this study.

Training of Generic, Occupational, and Job-Specific Skills

Training of generic, occupational, and job-specific skills was a significant issue in a majority of the staffing decisions studied. A few staffing appointments were considered to be terminal ones in that candidates were chosen for their stability rather than their mobility. These candidates were not expected to advance beyond the immediate positions to which they were being appointed. With the exception of these less frequent appointments, however, most other staffing decisions gave explicit consideration to the development capacity of candidates being considered. Successful candidates were chosen with the explicit understanding that they had the potential to advance at least two levels beyond the position for which they were being considered. In making staffing choices, managers looked to past demonstrations of learning to indicate how well candidates would learn in future jobs. Their assessment of candidates' potential to learn from previously unforeseen challenges was ongoing, but became more focused and competitive when candidates were being considered for appointment to a specific vacant position.

While the general philosophy behind ForestCo's approach to staffing implicitly included notions of unrestricted personal development and unlimited potential to learn, there were in fact limits to the amount of training and development that took place. These limitations occurred as a consequence of staffing preferences that were built into established routines for selecting candidates for jobs and that circumscribed the actual career paths found within the organization. First, job candidates often needed certain base skills and qualifications to be considered for various entry-level jobs in the firm. For example, educational and professional certifications were required for access to entry-level jobs associated with professional occupations such as engineering, accounting, forestry, and chemistry. Candidates who did not have these professional qualifications were rarely, if ever, considered for these jobs.

Second, even for those who were able to satisfy these initial occupational qualifications and certifications, further development of their skills, and opportunities to demonstrate their mastery of these skills, depended on the organizational and geographic location of the jobs to which they were assigned. Full development of organizationally relevant skills and capacities depended on the mobility outcomes of the staffing system. Employees assigned to jobs that were geographically removed from mainstream operations were less known than those who became visible through daily interactions with more senior managers. Employees assigned to departments and regions that underwent contraction rather than expansion had fewer opportunities for advancement. Also, employees who were assigned to the most challenging jobs, and who demonstrated that they could meet and master those challenges, were advantaged in subsequent competitions for higher-level positions. It was noted, however, that although expectations of organizational advancement and career development were not necessarily unrealistic, there were nonetheless no guarantees that such advancement would take place.

Because of the dynamism of ForestCo's organizational system, the size and scope of job challenges that provided opportunities to learn new skills and capacities and provided exposure to senior management could not always be determined in advance. Accelerated development could occur because employees had to learn to cope with unforeseen difficulties associated with environmental exigencies. These difficulties could include phenomena such as accidents, public protests, and product and market dislocations. In other circumstances, additional challenges could occur because a more senior employee in a key job became sick and incapacitated and a junior employee would be required to take on additional responsibilities. Junior employees could also develop mentor–protégé relationships with one or more of their supervisors and receive support, coaching, and challenging assignments. Other junior employees could have bosses who exploited their talents and did little to invest in their training and development. Thus, although the staffing philosophy of this firm explicitly provided for the possibility of unlimited training and development, its capacity to deliver was often restricted. Such restrictions were not necessarily intended, but emerged from the practical realities of developing and using specialist, occupational knowledge in the context of a large, complex, dynamic organizational system.

In addition to restrictions associated with the organizational system itself were those that derived from individual talent. Talent alone did not determine developmental opportunity. Employees with extraordinary talents might be limited by the vagaries associated with development opportunities. Conversely, employees with more prosaic talents might be advantaged by fortuitous conjunctions of their skills and the developmental challenges to which they were assigned. Some employees thrived on pressure; others found it debilitating. Some employees were expert at the technical details of their jobs, but had little insight into or talent for general management. Other employees found that assignments to locations that could accelerate their development were socially unacceptable to their spouses. Some employees found their health and energy levels to be barely sufficient to meet the challenges associated with increased responsibility. Talent, energy, health, family circumstances, local fit, and other factors interacted to produce career and organizational mobility outcomes that could not be predicted in advance. Staffing assignments presented opportunities for development and in fact often had training and development as their intended consequences, but appointment of a candidate to a vacant position did not guarantee that development would occur. The exact nature of any development that did occur depended on the emerging and often unanticipated challenges associated with that job, the managerial style of the employee's supervisor, and the employee's inherent capacities.

Employee Motivation

In stereotypical treatments of ILMs, employee motivation to perform work is not presented as a major issue. Motivation to meet job requirements is presumed to accrue from the exchange relationships built into the different levels of compensation associated with assignments to jobs at different pay grades. The primary motivational concern is that of the willingness of senior employees to train those junior to themselves. Thus, the core motivational issue in stereotypical models concerns the motivation to deliver a commoditized view of employee training.

Motivation to deliver job performance and motivation to train others are not substantive issues associated with staffing in ForestCo's organization. Motivation to perform beyond minimal job requirements was an accepted part of ForestCo's employment culture. Such values were supported by the "progressive" competitive ethos of ForestCo's organization, as most, but not all, salaried employees were assumed to want positions of increased responsibility, challenge, and pay. Rewards, and motivation to receive these rewards, had both present and future temporal attributes. In the present, it was unhelpful to interpret motivation to perform as a direct consequence of the rewards associated with current performance. First, the contribution of current job performance to organizational objectives could rarely be measured. Second, even if organizational contributions were indicated by the salary grades of positions, the actual level of current compensation was related only loosely to the job grade of the position to which an employee was appointed. Third, rationalizations for striving and performance beyond minimal requirements were internalized by employees as accepted social and organizational norms. Further, these norms were reinforced by the competitive ethos of staffing.

Because of the aforedescribed loose associations between pay and indicators of potential contributions, cognitive and social constructions of rewards became more important determinants of motivation and behavior than immediate compensation. Rationalizations for expenditures of current effort on job performance were maintained by the assumptions of the generally accepted interpretive frame for ForestCo's ILM that future rewards had the potential to be greater than current ones. Career progression was a core construct through which managers and employees made sense of ForestCo's ILM. Motivation was directed toward training and development as instrumentalities for future job performance and future rewards. Motivation to perform well beyond minimally accept-

able levels was also a strongly maintained social and organizational norm. These interpretations were supported by managers "talking the talk" and proclaiming organizational
values as well as by occasional evidence of unusual appointments. For instance, while
promotion prospects were quite rosy for younger employees, and declined with increasing age, average promotion prospects did not decline to zero as employees approached the
usual retirement ages of 60 years or more. The relatively few, but highly visible, promotions of older supervisors and managers reinforced the view that even if individual
rewards had not increased recently, the future could potentially produce increased rewards for most employees.

The social norms and values that maintained levels of employee motivation were
vulnerable to external forces. It was quite clear that the recession in the early years of the
1980s disrupted the previously stable flows of employees into, through, and out of the
organization. Expectations of continued and implicitly guaranteed employment for loyal
employees, as well as anticipated advancements for those who performed well, were
severely impaired by the cutbacks in 1981–1982. For those who remained with the firm,
supervisors and subordinates alike, the baseline belief in the capacity of the organizational
system to meet everyone's motivational requirements was severely threatened. Because
they had internalized the legitimacy of the organizational system and had acted in accor-
dance with those beliefs, many managers had great difficulty dealing with the layoffs they
were required to impose for organizational survival during the years of the recession.
Supervisors and managers who personally survived layoffs, but who were instrumental in
engineering the exit of others from the firm, expressed as their greatest concern that they
had violated their personal values. To continue to be credible to themselves, as well as to
their subordinates, managers needed to believe in the appropriateness of the rewards and
incentives associated with the motivational outcomes of ForestCo's ILM. The policies
implemented to survive the recession threatened the motivational assumptions necessary
for the maintenance of the socially constructed order of the organizational system.

Far more specific issues of motivation also lay behind the continued overall preference of most of ForestCo's managers for internal candidates over those from the ELM. This
preference provided existing employees with increased opportunities to increase their
status and reward. As noted previously, however, there were no guarantees of continuing
rewards for internal candidates, especially for those who failed to demonstrate either the
motivation or the capacity to learn new skills and capacities. Both internal competition and
the ever-present possibility that a job would be awarded to an external candidate reinforced acknowledgment and awareness of the personal risk associated with diminishing
motivation to perform.

Other instances of specific motivational issues in the maintenance of ForestCo's ILM
were encountered in the managers' concerns for and behaviors toward employees who
were unsuccessful candidates in public job competitions. Aware of the potentially debilitating consequences to employees of not being successful, many managers made a
particular point of working with these candidates to maintain their morale and to guide
them to the training that would help their job applications in the future. In this, managers
worked to maintain collective assumptions that supported the continued operation of the
organizational as a natural, social system.

Finally, motivational issues also influenced those managers who made staffing appointments in order to meet their subordinates' personal needs. Employees who were
regarded as either valuable or deserving could occasionally persuade their supervisors to
consider their personal needs in selection decisions. A few staffing appointments were
made to arrange the physical relocation of such employees—either to ease a transition into

retirement from a remote and isolated assignment or to ease family stress when an employee's spouse was incompatible with the local community.

This particular study of ForestCo's ILM was not designed to seek direct information on the motivational attributes of the firm's employment system. Employees were not directly questioned or surveyed regarding their aspirations and motives. Insights into the motivational outcomes of experiences in ForestCo's ILM were derived from the expressed concerns of managers who included considerations of subordinate motivation in their staffing decisions. Other studies, perhaps ones more focused on motivational issues, would no doubt provide additional insight into the ideas presented here.

Job Security

In stereotypical simple-structure models of ILMs, job security was noted as a concern of experienced employees who were called upon to train those junior to them. In this, there is potential conflict between employers and employees, and both employers and employees wish to develop organizational arrangements that serve and protect their interests. Senior employees can protect themselves from unscrupulous employers who would replace them with the lower-paid workers whom they have trained if it is a condition of training that the trainers have greater job security than recent entrants. Again, this view implies a commoditization of employee skills and training that can be passed from one person to another.

At ForestCo, training and development were viewed as being dependent more on interactions between challenging job assignments and individual capacity to learn from experience than on packages of skills being passed from one employee to another. The motivation to undertake training and to demonstrably learn from experience was more strongly associated with future status and rewards. Nevertheless, issues of job security were partially related to those associated with employee motivation to learn from experience. In the belief systems of ForestCo's salaried employees, threats to job security upset their established assumptions that given acceptable performance, they would remain employed until they decided to retire or to leave for opportunities elsewhere. While there may have been a small number of occasions when a supervisor advised a subordinate to "shape up or ship out," maintenance of a motivational climate within the organization was rarely dependent on immediate and direct threats to job security. Decrements in employability could emerge gradually, as employees realized that they were stuck in positions in which more was being demanded of them than they could produce. For the most part, however, job security became an issue when products and plants became uneconomic and obsolete. For salaried employees, terminations and layoffs were socially constructed as unavoidable consequences of the destructive adaptation associated with a capitalistic, competitive economy.

When plants closed, more senior salaried employees could be transferred to ongoing jobs in other divisions. These transfers acknowledged the value of these employees to the organization and the obligation of the employer to look after their interests. Obligations to existing employees were discharged as long as there was little discernible cost associated with discharging them. However, when implicit obligations were judged to be counter to the overall welfare of the organization, organizationally determined imperatives dominated. Nevertheless, terminations and layoffs that occurred because of adherence to organizational rather than individual objectives violated core organizational values, inducing anxiety in ForestCo's managers and upsetting the motivational climate for their subordinates. Issues of job security did not feature prominently in explanations for staffing provided by ForestCo's managers. By minimizing the visibility of threats to job security, ForestCo's managers were better able to maintain the ideological climate that nourished the socially constructed, mutually supportive employment system of the firm. Job security was an important background feature of the operation of this ILM only insofar as the threat of its loss threatened the legitimacy of the arrangements that supported the continued operation of ForestCo's ILM as a natural, social system.

Patterns of Intra- and Interfirm Mobility

While patterns of intra- and interfirm mobility are definite outcomes of stereotypical ILMs, they are considered more as secondary consequences of arrangements designed primarily to serve and protect the interests of employers and employees. One consequence of simple-structure ILMs, that is, ILMs having few ports of entry and well-established lines of progression, is that levels of labor turnover would be small and, consequently, ceteris paribus, levels of hires would also be comparatively small. Employees would be disadvantaged by interfirm mobility, as they would lose their comparative advantage of firm-specific knowledge and its associated company seniority. In these circumstances, patterns of intrafirm mobility would be stable and there would be a general progression of all employees as a group (with continuous renewal) from lower to higher levels of jobs.

From both staffing and vacancy chain perspectives, this study of ForestCo's ILM yielded little definitive information about patterns of intra- and interfirm mobility. However, the view of this ILM from the perspective of the organization as a whole reinforced insights gained from investigations of staffing actions and vacancy chains. The primary feature of ForestCo's ILM is its dynamism. Different flow rates of employees into, through, and or out of the firm had great potential to change the internal composition of this employment system. As has already been noted, ports of entry into ForestCo's ILM from the ELM occurred at almost all levels of the organizational hierarchy. Similarly, employees also exited from the corporation at all levels. There was not a one-for-one correspondence between these flows, however. While aggregate flows generally balanced, there was a tendency for the distribution of entries to be slightly lower in the grade hierarchy than that of organizational exits. As expected, there was a tendency for there to be general patterns of upward mobility within the corporation, but this overall effect was muted by the large flows of employees both into and out of ForestCo's ILM at almost all levels of the grade hierarchy.

Past changes in flow rates also became constituents of future conditions. Patterns of mobility in this corporation were strongly influenced by its past history as well as by its current policies and practices. In particular, the recession of the early 1980s threatened the survival of the organization as an economic entity. Senior management introduced personnel policies such as massive layoffs and severe limitations on hiring that changed employee flows in a major way in 1981–1982, and in lesser cumulative ways for the ensuing five or six years. For example, the layoffs had an immediate effect on the organizational demography that continued to evolve through to the end of the decade as a consequence of past actions, continuing effects of limitations on hiring, and aging of employees. These phenomena so affected employee flows as to produce demographic effects that were still being felt some eight and ten years later. In addition, the personnel policies developed previously as tactics for economic survival continued to influence how managers thought about, and acted, when confronted with a vacant position. While these changes undoubtedly helped the organization survive, the changes in flows resulting from changed personnel policies reduced both then and subsequently the ILM outcomes of job security and employee motivation.

Traditionally, and especially when reinforced by current policies, ForestCo's managers continued to display a qualified preference for internal candidates. Vacant positions were filled with internal candidates, rather than by hires from the ELM, in a ratio of approximately 3 or 4 to 1. There was also a significantly stronger propensity to fill vacant positions at the upper levels of the organizational hierarchy with internal candidates. That is, there was a stronger propensity to make rather than to buy the skills and capacities required for senior-level positions. Even so, there was a potential for candidates from the ELM to be hired into almost any level of the organizational hierarchy.

Appreciations of ILMs as systems of employee flows have heretofore not been well developed. While organizational demography had been identified as a significant antecedent condition of internal organizational phenomena, there has been relatively little work done on the antecedents of demography. There appears to be considerable opportunity for further research on this topic.

STAFFING ACTIONS

Staffing actions are both component processes of the ILM model used as background and implicit standards for this description of ForestCo's ILM, as well as the third "nested" perspective used as an overall frame for this study. The previous discussions of ILM antecedents and outcomes have included some considerations of staffing decisions and actions, but have not subjected them to a critical examination.

Most contemporary treatments of staffing consider this organizational function to be synonymous with employee selection. Employee selection has received significant attention in the past 30 years, as past patterns of social inequality have been attributed to widespread instances of employment discrimination. Processes of employee selection that were already grounded in rational, scientific models of organizations have been even more tightly woven into such models as a consequence of social legislation designed to reduce employment discrimination on the basis of race, religion, gender, age, and disability. At present, normative models of employee selection embrace a rational, quantitative scientism that permits examination of selection processes for evidence of improper discrimination, in which selection is based on criteria that do not demonstrably serve the criterion of future work performance.

In models of bureaucratic rationality, jobs are the primary components of organizations. Jobs are seen to derive from rational/analytical deconstructions of organizational objectives into groups of tasks, duties, and responsibilities considered to be units of work assignable and performable by appropriately qualified persons. As noted by Miner (1987) in her characterization of the pervasiveness of the strong vacancy assumption, jobs precede, both conceptually and temporally, considerations of persons assigned to those jobs. This assumption "is so fundamental that it is often tacit" (Miner, 1987, p. 329) and is an often unacknowledged feature of the extensive psychological and personnel literature on employee selection. These two features of employee selection—a built-in emphasis on jobs derived from traditional models of bureaucratic rationality and larger social pressures to demonstrate that selection manifestly serves job performance—have reinforced a job-based approach to staffing that is rarely questioned in applied psychological and personnel literature.

Yet this emphasis on jobs qua jobs was not what was found in ForestCo's employment system. To a considerable extent, ForestCo's managers thought about the performance of work in terms of the human resources available to perform that work. Persons, rather than jobs, were the primary units of analysis used to explore and articulate staffing choices. Although ForestCo's managers used constructs of jobs to develop criteria against which to assess individual capacities when posting processes were used in staffing, posting procedures were actually used in only a minority of the staffing situations encountered.

Several explanations can be adduced for this finding. The primary view, based on managerial explanations and social constructions of why they acted as they did in making selection decisions, was that jobs were considered more transitory and variable than the enduring attributes of candidates considered for those jobs. Jobs were not regarded as enduring, stable attributes of organizations. Even though ForestCo was a large, well-established firm in a mature industry, it was experiencing pervasive organizational change originating both outside and inside the corporation. From outside, new social values, public scrutiny, and emerging legislation were challenging existing ways of doing business. New coalitions and mergers among competitors, as well as developments in new products, markets, and technology, were also requiring ForestCo's managers to adapt to new circumstances. Within ForestCo, there was an underlying dynamic of employee flows as current employees either retired, quit, or were laid off. New employees were hired, and selected current employees were promoted or transferred. Management of these flows was often problematic, as the qualities and quantities of the supply of candidates were rarely synchronous with emerging demands. There was therefore considerable job change within organizational units. Departments were reorganized, old jobs were dissolved, existing jobs were modified, and new jobs were created.

These microprocesses of organizational change and adaptation were intimately associated with staffing. Staffing was the primary means by which ForestCo's managers adjusted their units to both exogenous and endogenous change. Selection and assignment of employees to modified or new jobs was an ongoing concomitant of organizational adaptation. Staffing was intimately associated with organizational change generally, and job change in particular, for other reasons as well. Managers interested in implementing organizational change experienced the least resistance to change by jobholders when vacancies occurred. Managers had increased degrees of freedom to move employees from one position to another when one or more positions were unoccupied. More important, however, the demand characteristics or job requirements could be modified most readily when there was no job occupant to resist changes to established procedures and practices. Because of these background factors, jobs were not regarded as fixed and enduring. Most jobs were not expected necessarily to retain their previous specific demand characteristics when they became vacant and targeted for selection decisions. Jobs were often regarded as less stable and more ephemeral attributes of job–person matches that lay at the core of the selection process. Therefore, ForestCo's managers focused their attention on what they regarded as the more enduring and attributes of their subordinates in making selection decisions.

A second set of factors that led ForestCo's managers to emphasize attributes of persons rather than jobs in employee selection derived from their interests in training and development. The organizational functions of training and development were regarded as being intertwined with employee selection and staffing. There was considerable mobility in ForestCo's salaried ILM. Excluding the incidence of lateral transfers and of job evolution, more than one fifth of all ForestCo's salaried personnel changed jobs in any given year. This mobility represented a substantial challenge to the maintenance of ForestCo's organization as both a goal-oriented rational system and an enduring natural social system. Subordinates were expected to develop new skills and competencies, both to maintain the organization and to permit adaptation to new challenges and demands that had not yet been experienced.

Thus, the focus on employees rather than jobs in employee selection did not assume that employee dispositions and capacities to perform were set and unchanging. The development of new skills and the demonstrable capacity of subordinates to learn from experience came from staffing assignments that challenged existing levels of knowledge and skill. Staffing selections were therefore rarely made for the sole purpose of assuring adequate performance of the immediate job for which a candidate was being considered. Managers noted that they frequently looked for a candidate's capacity to move two or three levels above the immediate position for which the candidate was being considered. The concern with training and the subsequent emphasis on individual capacities for development that would enable the candidate to benefit from such training, including propensity to remain loyal to the firm, reinforced a person- rather than a job-based approach to employee selection and staffing.

This general finding presents a potential puzzle for students of ILMs. On one hand, job-based models of employee selection are presented as normative practice in the psychological and personnel literature. In addition, such models have been strongly reinforced by legal interpretations of pervasive social legislation designed to limit discrimination only on the basis of immediate job performance. On the other hand, there is strong evidence that such models made little sense in the interpretive frames of ForestCo's managers. This collision of normative and actual practice deserves further exploration.

In stereotypical models of employee selection based on models of bureaucratic rationality, jobs and persons are regarded as independent entities. Jobs are considered to derive from reductionist analyses of unit goals and objectives, which in turn are derived from functionalist reductions of overall organizational goals. Jobs are regarded as relatively stable attributes of organizations in that they will likely outlive their incumbents. Persons can come and go in a particular position or job, but the performance of that job is expected to vary little as a consequence of which persons, assuming technical competence, are assigned to that job. Indeed, one of the ascribed strengths of the bureaucratic form is that systems of abstract rules improve the uniformity and predictability of performance. Moreover, a bureaucratic style characterized by formalistic impersonality is regarded as a prerequisite for impartiality and administrative efficiency. Personal relationships, which can include hatred and passion as well as affection and enthusiasm, have little or no place in these administrative systems. In contemporary manifestations of the bureaucratic form, persons are viewed as partial reflections of the jobs to which they are assigned. Attention is paid to persons only to the extent that their technical qualifications could impinge on job performance.

The independence of jobs and persons just asserted, however, does not appear to be an accurate reflection of how managers actually think about jobs. There is preliminary evidence from the psychological literature on social cognition that managers use *jobholder schemata* (Perry et al., 1994) to organize their knowledge about people who perform jobs and about people who are assigned to particular occupations (Cohen, 1981). In this literature, there is preliminary speculation that the jobholder schemas formulated by managers emerge from their having repeatedly observed persons performing jobs. Jobs and the attributes of persons who perform those jobs therefore become closely associated. Jobs are social constructions that are maintained through managerial talk and interactions with persons assigned to particular jobs. The common concerns of managers, together with pressures for shared beliefs and assumptions in a single organizational setting, reinforce cognitive linkages between attributes of persons and the nature of jobs. Such associations would occur as a consequence of everyday managerial behavior. Thus, the cognitive and conceptual independence of jobs and persons assumed by rational models of selection may reflect a convenient legal schemata that has little basis in light of recent developments in social cognition.

The assumed independence of persons and jobs, and the assumed dominance of jobs over persons in employee selection, can also be challenged from within the field of personnel practice. Consider, for example, standard treatments of job analysis used to elicit understandings of the performance dimensions of jobs that are then used to prepare interview questions or behaviorally anchored rating scales for performance appraisal. These procedures often involve the collection of samples of critical incidents that illustrate either superior or inferior performance (Janz, et al., 1986). Once collected, these samples are then sorted into "similar" subcategories of job performance. Once labeled, these subcategories are then used as the basis for specific questions used subsequently in selection interviews. Thus, in an essentially circular process, selection methods that nominally emphasize the importance and independence of the dimensions of job performance as the criteria used to discriminate among candidates are derived from descriptions of the behavior of jobholders. In these procedures, the implicit separation of the concepts of jobs from those of jobholders appears as an artifact of the need to fit such schemes into a model of bureaucratic rationality, rather than as a reflection of underlying cognitive processes.

As has been noted, jobs and jobholders were not considered to be independent entities in ForestCo's organization. Moreover, personal attributes of employees were often regarded as being the primary considerations in making staffing assignments. Inferences regarding past behaviors were attributed much more to enduring personal dispositions than to the demand features of jobs to which candidates had previously been assigned. In observing this phenomenon, one is led to ask whether ForestCo's managers are merely engaging in the "fundamental attribution error" (Nisbett & Ross, 1980) in emphasizing enduring dispositions as the basis for predictions of future behaviors. Is their search for enduring dispositions as a basis for employee selection a misguided pursuit of a mirage? Dispositional explanations of individual behavior in organizations have been characterized as being flawed in both concept and method as well as incurring substantial costs and risks (Davis-Blake & Pfeffer, 1989). The primary arguments for emphasizing situational rather than dispositional explanations for individual behavior are that dispositional researchers have ignored the stable, nondispositional attributes of employees and jobs (e.g., race, gender, real earnings), attributes of the work itself (e.g., autonomy, complexity), and attributes of the social network of which the employee is a part (Davis-Blake & Pfeffer, 1989, p. 396).

These arguments are not considered to represent strong support for an interpretation of ForestCo behavior as consisting primarily of attribution error. First, in selection decisions in which relatively similar persons are being considered for a single job, nondispositional attributes such as group identity are unlikely to generalize, or be generalized, to specific individual dispositions. Second, the attributes of the work itself are likely to be well known and to have been similar across candidate histories. Third, all candidates have been and are at present embedded in similar, if not identical, social and organizational matrices. Moreover, because most candidates considered for vacant positions had occupied several previous positions and experienced several job situations, differences in past behaviors could not unrealistically be attributed to enduring dispositions. Finally, even if there was some discounting of situational influences, ForestCo's managers were concerned not with the primary determinants of individual behavior in organizations, but instead with assessments of the relative merits of candidates for future assignments. Thus, one should not ignore or discount managerial behaviors that emphasized persons rather than positions. Their approach, even if potentially flawed, is sufficiently different from that presumed to hold in rational models of employee selection that normative presentations of such models should be viewed with a healthy skepticism.

A further complication that arises from this review of staffing as practiced in ForestCo's ILM concerns the methods currently used to pursue equal employment opportunity. As has been noted, the procedural rules to assess employment practices assume ILMs to have simple structures that are consistent with models of bureaucratic rationality. As illustrated extensively in Part III, however, ForestCo's staffing practices, which are regarded here as illustrative of those of many other large corporations, also include behaviors that make sense primarily from the perspectives of natural- and open-system models of organizations. Proponents of employment equity have not confronted the potential conflict between their prescriptions for organizational change and the prescriptions of those who acknowledge the legitimacy of alternative perspectives. There is a distinct possibility that practices, behaviors, and perspectives that legitimate the social aspects of organizational maintenance could be considered illegal from institutionalized perspectives of bureaucratic, rational models.

Complicating these issues even more is the use of the term "natural" as an alternative basis for employment decisions. From the perspective of social cognition, namely, the processes through which persons assess other persons, a built-in bias may exist for managers to cognitively construct jobholder schemata in which their concepts of jobs are not independent of their experience with persons previously associated with those jobs. Natural models of both organization theory and social cognition present ideas that are inconsistent with legal procedures used to implement employment equity. Failure to recognize these conflicting schemata could limit both the legitimacy and the accomplishments of employment equity initiatives.

FUTURE DIRECTIONS

Because this chapter is primarily a summary and review of what we think we now know as a result of this study, it is important to understand the extent to which these results can be generalized to other organizations and to discussions of ILMs. There are two distinct features of the study described in this book: an emphasis on a single firm and a descriptive/inductive approach to the phenomena under investigation.

This is a study of a particular firm, in a particular industry, in a particular place, at a particular time. There is no question that many of the detailed findings, including illustrations of staffing issues and dilemmas, are unique to this particular firm at this particular time in its history. Indeed, considerable effort has been expended to document the effects of specific contextual factors on the operation of this firm's ILM. It should be clear that these specific factors are not expected to be those that influence the operation of other ILMs in other circumstances. It is expected, however, that the ILMs of other firms would be influenced similarly by contextual factors pertinent to their situations. Identified herein were a number of different contextual factors that were influential for ForestCo. These factors should provide a useful guide to contextual factors that may influence the operation of ILMs elsewhere.

The second methodological attribute of this study to qualify the findings reported herein is the descriptive/inductive nature of this investigation. To a considerable extent, this study presents a description of organizational staffing as seen and interpreted by the supervisors and managers who were responsible for the staffing activities. When possible, we have presented the managers' own words and interpretations to describe what they did and to account for why they did what they did. The investigation presented in this book is therefore both a case study and an ethnography. The elicitation of information from ForestCo's managers, however, has been strongly guided by both theoretical and methodological concerns. First, this study of staffing derived from an interest in the practices, theories, and concepts of ILMs. Because of this interest, the investigative methodology was not one of examining staffing practices in general, but staffing in the context of vacancy chains, which were judged to correspond to the job ladders or lines of progression so critical to ILM theory. Second, the data used to describe staffing activities, and to interpret their meaning for the operation of ForestCo's ILM, are selections from the interviews conducted with ForestCo's managers. Other researchers could cull different quotations from the interview transcripts and perhaps organize and interpret those quotations differently. The descriptions of staffing obtained from ForestCo's managers have been reported in considerable detail to permit the possibility of alternative interpretations.

Although the focus of this investigation has been to understand the influence of staffing on the operation of ForestCo's ILM, we have not been unaware that our reports of the manner in which managers and supervisors thought about related issues could initiate inquiry along other avenues. Thus, a second reason for letting ForestCo's managers speak for themselves in this book is that there remain several underexplored, and perhaps even unexplored, aspects of managerial behavior and thought relating to the maintenance of the human resource system in this organization. Other researchers are invited to use these detailed descriptions of ForestCo's operations to discern and explore these issues.

For this author, at least, one consequence of the conflict between theoretical models of ILMs and actual managerial practice presented previously is the realization of extensive job change in ForestCo's organization. Although no specific measure was made of the extent of job change, subjective estimates based on aggregate vacancy chain statistics and analyses of specific vacancy chains suggest that the phenomenon is widespread. Certainly, the proportion of jobs dissolved, created, redefined, and relocated as a proportion of all vacancies within ForestCo is expected to be greater than the 22–27% found by Stewman (1986) in his study over a two-decade period of a more stable state police organization. In addition to job dissolution, creation, redefinition, and relocation in ForestCo's organization, there was also evidence of jobs being shaped to fit the capacities of incumbents and also of "job molding" (Miller, 1988), in which jobs are shaped by the activities and abilities of persons assigned to positions. The pervasiveness of job change is an unacknowledged aspect of ILM theory and an underexamined aspect of organizational life in general. As noted by Miller (1986, p. 329) "...jobs *per se* are a strangely neglected topic of research.... Sociological knowledge of how jobs come to be defined and work arrangements organized is disparate and incomplete." Indeed, we can argue that we have no coherent theory of jobs. Development of such a theory is essential if we are to appreciate and understand this central feature of contemporary society. A theory of jobs could help us better understand contemporary manifestations of bureaucracy, the functioning of ILMs, and the effects of jobs and job schemata on employment discrimination.

A further aspect of the extensiveness of job change in ForestCo's organization is the contribution this flexibility makes to organizational adaptation and change. The bureaucratically grounded interests of managers are expressed in multiple local adjustments of persons and positions to create a bureaucratically moderated marketplace for labor. In this process, the interdependent and often concurrent creation of jobs and selection of candidates to perform those jobs places great discretion in the hands of local managers. Thus, in this employment system at least, it appears that the highly sought-after adaptive flexibility of employment systems is obtained with the qualification that local managers represent the "buyers" in the firm's ILM. This places substantial discretionary authority and power with managers who may choose not to pursue larger social interests.

The consequences of letting the managers manage can be explored further by examining a recent report on high-performance workplace models of human resource management (Betcherman, McMullen, Leckie, & Caron, 1994). This report proposes six elements required of all variants of high-performance employment systems (Betcherman et al., 1994, p. 96):

- A *flexible work organization* in which work rules and job descriptions are fluid, employees are able to use discretion to get the job done, and formal and informal hierarchies are minimized.
- A commitment to *training* to deepen and broaden employees' skills.
- Increased *employee involvement and participation* in the operation of the organization.
- Policies to promote *sharing*, most obviously of the financial rewards from good performance, but also of information and privilege.
- A *work process designed to improve health and reduce stress.*
- *Family-friendly policies* that support employees in balancing their work and domestic responsibilities.

ForestCo's salaried employment system is not a perfect match with these proposed requirements, but most elements do appear to be present in ForestCo's organization in one form or another. Flexible work arrangements lie at the heart of the operation of ForestCo's ILM. There is continuous and extensive job change, in which wide but ultimately circumscribed managerial discretion permits the exercise of managerial self-interest to drive marginal, incremental change in organizational practices. Formal hierarchies, at least as represented by rigid grade hierarchies, are not present, as the relationship between monetary salary and salary grade is a flexible one.

Intertwined with the background ideas of flexible organizational arrangements are fundamental assumptions of the adaptability of employees who are compatible within such systems. Employees are expected to accept high degrees of responsibility for their own learning. Training is not regarded as a commodity to be passed from one skilled person to another, but rather as the consequence of employees responding to the challenges of difficult assignments that stretch and develop their skills and capacities for further work. When viewed this way, training was also a fundamental feature of ForestCo's ILM embodied in the decisions and assignments of managerial staffing actions.

It is difficult to know exactly what Betcherman and colleagues mean by their proposed requirement for increased employee involvement and participation in the operation of the organization. Certainly, within ForestCo's salaried employment system, almost all supervisors and managers were also regarded as subordinates and employees. They held dual citizenship in two complementary and conflicting roles. While there might be occasions when their self-interests as employees were orthogonal or counter to their self-interests as supervisors and managers, this was generally not so. Most members of this employment system had an active interest in, and could participate directly in, decisions and actions that advanced the interests of the organization. Reciprocal values of trust and loyalty were implicit in most employment relationships. Once revealed, actions that served individual self-interests but failed the test of collective, managerial interests could place an employee's career in jeopardy. Thus, the general system of role relationships, which encouraged all members of the employment system to become involved and participate in the operation of the organization, was implicitly embedded in assumptions of organizational stewardship.

A somewhat similar set of arrangements held for the sharing of financial rewards for good performance. As moderated through the perceptions of one's supervisor, good performance was expected to result initially in salary progression through the salary range associated with a salary grade, and eventually in either a regrading of the position or a move to a different position at a higher salary grade. While such moves were not guaranteed, there was sufficient evidence from promotions observed throughout the system as a whole that personal advancement was a possibility. In many departments, managers who were planning for succession actively supported and developed a number of their subordinates so the subordinates could potentially be appointed to their position if they themselves were promoted or transferred elsewhere. Again, the reciprocal dependence between supervisor and subordinate meant that each had interests in the other's welfare. A lack of sharing of information would be expected to occur only on those relatively infrequent occasions when there was a large asymmetry between the interests of supervisor and subordinate.

The final two requirements noted by Betcherman and colleagues are those of work processes designed to improve health and reduce stress and to have family-friendly policies in place. There was small and modest evidence for these elements in ForestCo's ILM, but their presence may be regarded as a second-order consequence of the personal discretion available to managers and the personal interdependencies between supervisors and their subordinates. While trust and loyalty were important features of personal interrelationships in this collective system, they had to be demonstrated, earned, and reinforced over intense and often lengthy work interactions. Managerial behavior that was seen collectively by a majority of interested peers and subordinates to contribute to additional stress would limit managerial capacity to earn loyalty and trust. Similarly, managers who failed to demonstrate loyalty to key employees in providing arrangements that could ease family difficulties could expect to be treated in the same way.

These "requirements," however, were not guaranteed. Employees had few "rights" other than those defined by legislation and the collective interests of those caught up in the firm's ILM. Managerial discretion could therefore become a double-edged sword. What collectively might be regarded as too much accommodation to an employee's family and health requirements could jeopardize collective trust and faith in the legitimacy of a manager's judgment. On the other hand, too much attention to the bottom line, to the exclusion of any responsibility for the welfare of deserving subordinates, would also limit a manager's reputation and capacity to elicit cooperation in the future.

For the most part, ForestCo's salaried ILM is judged to be a high-performance workplace employment system. To a considerable extent, it meets the requirements of Betcherman and colleagues' model, but reveals an underlying complexity that could qualify assessments of its "success." As argued here, the attainment of flexibility requires that individual rights be subordinated to the collective interests of those in the employment system. Moreover, these collective interests are interpreted and moderated by managers who are permitted much discretion. Such discretion also permits the possibility of bias and local subversions of parts of the system as a whole. As described here, the employment system is responsive to its external environment as interpreted by the members of the system itself. When larger social objectives reflect interests of those not already included in the employment system, those objectives are unlikely to be acknowledged.

Thus, within this detailed working out of ForestCo's high-performance workplace model, managerial discretion could limit attainment of other social purposes. Nevertheless, within these restrictions, this detailed description of ForestCo's ILM represents a working model of organizational flexibility and adaptability. Others who are also interested in finding and elaborating high-performance organizational systems are encouraged to adapt and extend this model.

CEOs and senior managers interested in gaining competitive advantage by implementing high-performance organizational systems could learn from, and possibly refine, several of the features found in Forestco's ILM. We have argued that staffing activities are one of the key processes of organizational adaptation and change. If staffing is key, then it should be managed, monitored, and executed as a critical process. Staffing should not happen by default, but should be subject to the care and attention due any critical performance activity. To accomplish this objective, staffing should be framed, that is, identified and reinforced in corporate language, as a key performance process. Managers should review the staffing performance of their subordinates who are themselves supervisors of other salaried personnel. In addition, these managers should also expect to have their staffing functions subjected to examination and review by their supervisors. In each case, assessments of overall managerial performance should be based on how well staffing has contributed to organizational performance.

In doing this, however, extraordinary care needs to be exercised not to limit considerations of performance solely to rational output measures. The review of staffing perspectives on ILMs discussed in Part III illustrated the depth of interconnections among rational-, natural-, and open-system models used to explain organizational activities. In particular, extensive natural, system-maintenance activities were shown to provide very important support functions for the attainment of rational objectives. The balancing of opposites familiar to most senior managers is here manifest in the opposition and tension between decisions that may appear to be irrational within short-run rational-model perspectives but support natural-system requirements. The underlying paradox is that the short-run support of natural-system functions can contribute positively to longer-term rational perspectives!

Complicating this confusion even more is the appreciation that local adaptations to these strategies are often required because organizations are evolving adaptive systems dependent on their environments. Contextual dependence and constantly shifting environments require management not to treat staffing as a standardized, rule-bound procedure. What might appear to be local rationality at one time in one situation may not necessarily generalize to different contexts. If staffing is one of the primary means used to obtain organizational adaptation, staffing objectives and local criteria at the departmental level need to be linked conceptually to medium-term organizational goals. Both the procedures used to accomplish staffing and the criteria used to select among competing candidates should not be assumed to be invariant. They need to be examined and tested frequently. Persistent care and attention dedicated to the staffing function is one requirement of a high performance organization.

Within the frame of this general caveat, senior managers are urged to consider the multiple functions of staffing. Staffing is an ongoing means through which organizational evolution and adaptation occur. Staffing also needs to be articulated as the primary means through which employee development is obtained. Staffing is not synonymous with formal academic models of employee selection. For example, the stereotypical treatment of employee selection is that performance in the immediate job for which candidates are being considered is the primary criterion to be used in selecting among competing candidates. This is a myopic and limited view of staffing. Staffing decisions and actions are an integral component of managerial work. Staffing decisions should link individual job performance to role interdependencies within units and departments to longer-term perspectives that consider the long-run survival of the employment system. Staffing decisions should seek to develop the talents and capacities of employees within the frame of administrative efficiencies and effectiveness associated with staffing procedures.

A further means through which senior managers can seek high performance through the staffing procedures of their organizations is to sample and audit the staffing flows and vacancy chain processes in their organizations. Flows of employees into, through, and out of employment systems are the key mobility processes that maintain and modify employee stocks. This is an under-recognized feature of employment systems. Many corporations expend considerable effort to collect data on the composition and demography of their organizations. Far fewer corporations, however, collect data on employee movements into the organization such as hires, movements within the organization such as promotions and lateral transfers, and movements out of the organization such as voluntary quits, layoffs, and regular and early retirements. While some appreciation of these characteristics of the overall employment system can be obtained from accumulated experience, such knowledge can be deepened and exposed to further inquiry if the base data are available for analysis. For example, data on the rates of entry and the hierarchical locations of these entry flows provide important information on the sources of supply used to replenish the human resources of the organization. Similarly, data on internal flows and samples of illustrative vacancy chains could be important benchmarks and indicators of the cross-fertilization of ideas and the spread of interdepartmental knowledge in the firm. Relating data on entry and exit flows also permits investigation of the implicit reward systems incorporated in the formal compensation system of the organization. Moreover, when individual records are matched, career structures can be appreciated in light of the overall dynamics of the employment system that is being managed. Without informed understanding of the interdependencies among various human resource functions, the separate parts are unlikely to produce a coherent whole. Understanding of the dynamic stability of employment systems and the multiple ways in which these systems can be changed by relatively small changes in employee flows remains an elusive, but nonetheless attainable, objective.

There are no perfect organizations and no perfect employment systems. Each may be viewed from multiple and at times competing perspectives. Attachment to only one of these, in turn, could lead a manager to pursue objectives and engage in actions different from those which would remit from attachment to different perspectives. Organizational history, industry characteristics, workforce composition, local situations, and temporal context all influence how employment systems and ILMs are likely to operate. There is no precise model, therefore, to guide future explorations of these key aspects of contemporary society. Nevertheless, further exploration of the issues identified here is encouraged and eagerly anticipated.

References

Albright, L. E. (1979). Staffing policies and strategies. In D. Yoder & H. Heneman (Eds.), *ASPA handbook of personnel and industrial relations*, Vol. 4 (pp. 1–34). Washington, DC: Bureau of National Affairs.

Althauser, R. P. (1989). Internal labor markets. *Annual Review of Sociology, 15*, 143–161.

Althauser, R. P., & Kalleberg, A. L. (1981). Firms, occupations and the structure of labor markets: A conceptual analysis. In I. Berg (Ed.), *Sociological perspectives on labor markets* (pp. 119–149). New York: Academic Press.

Barnett, W. P., & Miner, A. S. (1992). Standing on the shoulders of others: Institutional interdependence in job mobility. In *Proceedings of the Academy of Management* (pp. 159–162). Las Vegas:

Baron, J. N., Davis-Blake, A., & Bielby, W. T. (1986). The structure of opportunity: How promotion ladders vary within and among organizations. *Administrative Science Quarterly, 31*, 248–273.

Baron, J. N., Dobbin, F., & Jennings, P. D. (1986). War and peace: The evolution of modern personnel administration in U.S. industry. *American Journal of Sociology, 92*(2), 350–383.

Baron, J. N., Jennings, P.D., & Dobbin, F. (1988). Mission control? The development of personnel systems in U.S. industry. *American Sociological Review, 53*, 497–514.

Barrick, M. R., & Mount, M. K. (1991). The big five personality dimensions and job performance. *Personnel Psychology, 44*, 1–26.

Beer, M., Spector, B., Lawrence, P. R., Mills, D. Q., & Walton, R. E. (1985). *Human resource management: A general manager's perspective*. New York: Free Press.

Bennison, M., & Casson, J. (1984). *The manpower planning handbook*. London: McGraw-Hill.

Betcherman, G., McMullen, K., Leckie, N., & Caron, C. (1994). *The Canadian workplace in transition*. Queens University, Kingston, Canada: IRC Press.

Bill, D. B. (1987). Costs, commitment, and rewards: Factors influencing the design and implementation of internal labor markets. *Administrative Science Quarterly, 32*, 202–221.

Bridges, W. P., Villemez, W. J. (1991). Employment relations and the labor market: Integrating institutional and market perspectives. *American Sociological Review, 56*, 748–764.

Burawoy, M. (1979). *Manufacturing consent*. Chicago: University of Chicago Press.

Capelli, P., & Sherer, P. D. (1991). The missing role of context in OB: The need for a meso-level approach. *Research in Organizational Behavior, 13*, 55–110.

Chase, I. D. (1991). Vacancy chains. *Annual Review of Sociology, 17*, 133–154.

Chatman, J. A. (1989). Improving interactional organizational research: A model of person–organization fit. *Academy of Management Review, 14*, 333–349.

Cohen, C. E. (1981). Person categories and social perception: Testing some boundaries of the processing effects of prior knowledge. *Journal of Personality and Social Psychology 40*(3), 441–452.

Conner, R. D., & Fjerstad, R. L. (1979). Internal personnel maintenance. In D. Yoder & H. Heneman (Eds.), *ASPA handbook of personnel and industrial relations*, Vol. 4 (pp. 203–244). Washington, DC: Bureau of National Affairs.

Czarniawska-Joerges, B. (1992). *Exploring complex organizations*. Newbury Park, CA: Sage Publications.

Daniel, C. (1986). Science, system, or hunch: Alternative approaches to improving employee selection. *Public Personnel Management, 15*, 1–10.

Davis-Blake, A., & Pfeffer, J. (1989). Just a mirage: The search for dispositional effects in organizational research. *Academy of Management Review, 14*, 385–400.

Dick, A. D. (1974). Job evaluation's role in employee relations. *Personnel Journal, 53*(3), 176–179.

DiPrete, T. A. (1989). *The bureaucratic labor market.* New York: Plenum Press.

Doeringer, P. B., & Piore, M. J. (1971). *Internal labor markets and manpower analysis.* Lexington, MA: Heath, Lexington Books.

Eder, R. W. (1989). Contextual effects on interview decisions. In R. W. Eder & G. R. Farris (Eds.), *The employment interview: Theory, research and practice* (pp. 115–126). Newbury Park, CA: Sage Publications.

Edwards, R. (1979). *Contested terrain: The transformation of the workplace in the twentieth century.* New York: Free Press.

Elbaum, B. (1984). The making and shaping of job and pay structures in the iron and steel industry. In P. Osterman (Ed.), *Internal labor markets* (pp. 71–107). Cambridge: MIT Press.

Forbes, J. B. (1987). Early intraorganizational mobility: Patterns and influences. *Academy of Management Journal, 30*(1), 110–125.

Gatewood, R. D., & Feild, H. S. (1994). *Human resources selection,* 3rd Ed. Fort Worth: Dryden Press.

Gitlow, A. L. (1992). Chief executives and the corporate culture. *National Productivity Review, 11*(4), 479.

Goldstein, I. L. (1986). *Training in organizations: Needs assessment, development, and evaluation,* 2nd ed. Monterey, CA: Books/Cole Publishing.

Granovetter, M. (1986). Labor mobility, internal markets, and job matching: A comparison of the sociological and economic approaches. *Research in Social Stratification and Mobility, 5*, 3–39.

Guion, R. M. (1993). The need for change: Six persistent themes. In N. Schmitt & W. C. Borman (Eds.), *Personnel selection in organizations* (pp. 481–496). San Francisco: Jossey-Bass.

Guion, R. M., & Gibson, W. M. (1988). Personnel selection and placement. *Annual Review of Psychology, 39*, 349–374.

Gunz, H. (1989). *Careers and corporate cultures: Managerial mobility in large corporations.* New York: Blackwell.

Heilman, M. E. (1983). Sex bias in work settings: The lack of model fit. *Research in Organizational Behavior, 5*, 269–298.

Heilman, M. E., Block, C. J., Martel, R. F., & Simon, M. C. (1989). Has anything changed? Current characterizations of men, women, and managers. *Journal of Applied Psychology, 74*, 935–942.

Heneman, G., & Heneman, R. L. (1994). *Staffing organizations.* Middleton, WI: Mendota Press.

Homans, G. C. (1950). *The human group.* New York: Harcourt.

Jackall, R. (1988). *Moral mazes: The world of corporate managers.* New York: Oxford University Press.

Jacobs, D. (1981). Toward a theory of mobility and behavior in organizations: An inquiry into the consequences of some relationships between individual performance and organizational success. *American Journal of Sociology, 87*(3), 684–707.

Jacoby, S. M. (1985). *Employing bureaucracy: Managers, unions, and the transformation of work in American industry, 1900–1945.* New York: Columbia University Press.

Jacques, E. (1990). In praise of hierarchy. *Harvard University Review,* Jan.–Feb., 127–133.

Janz, J. T., Hellervik, L., & Gilmore, D. C. (1986). *Behavior description interviewing: New, accurate, cost effective.* Newton, MA: Allyn & Bacon.

Judge, T. A., & Bretz, R. D. (1992). Political influence behavior and career success. Paper presented at the Annual Meeting of the Academy of Management, Las Vegas.

Kalleberg, A. L., & Sorenson, A. B. (1979). The sociology of labor markets. *Annual Review of Sociology, 5*, 351–379.

Kanter, R. M. (1984). Variations in managerial career structures in high-technology firms: The impact of organization characteristics on internal labor market patterns. In P. Osterman (Ed.), *Internal labor markets* (pp. 109–131). Cambridge: MIT Press.

Kanter, R. M. (1989). *When giants learn to dance.* New York: Simon & Schuster.

Keenay, G. A., Morgan, R., & Ray, K. H. (1977). A model for recruitment planning in a company. *Personnel Review, 6*, 43–50.

Keyfitz, N. (1973). Individual mobility in a stationary population. *Population Studies, 27*, 335–352.

Kepner, C. H., & Tregoe, B. B. (1965). *The rational manager: A systematic approach to problem solving and decision making.* New York: McGraw-Hill.

Kerr, C. (1954). The balkanizations of labor markets. In E. W. Bakke, P. M. Hauser, G. L. Salwer, C. A. Myers, D. Yolker, & C. Kerr (Eds.), *Labor mobility and economic opportunity* (pp. 92–110). Cambridge MA: MIT Press.

Kleiner, M. M., McLean, R. A., & Dreher, G. F. (1988). *Labor markets and human resource management.* Glenview, IL: Scott Foresman.

Kochan, R. A., Katz, H., & McKersie, R. B. (1986). *The transformation of American industrial relations.* New York: Basic Books.

Lansing, J. B., Clifton, C. W., & Morgan, J. N. (1969). *New homes and poor people.* Ann Arbor: Michigan Institute for Social Research.

Lawrence, B. S. (1987). An organizational theory of age effects. *Research in the Sociology of Organizations, 5,* 37–71.

Lazear, E. P. (1991). Labor economics and the psychology of organizations. *Journal of Economic Perspectives, 5*(2), 89–110.

Lazear, E. P. (1992). The job as a concept. In W. J. Bruns (Ed.), *Performance measurement, evaluation and incentives* (pp. 183–215). Boston: Harvard Business School Press.

Levine, E. L. (1983). *Everything you always wanted to know about job analysis but were afraid to ask.* Tampa: Mariner.

Levinson, H., & Rosenthal, A. (1984). *CEO: Corporate leadership in action.* New York: Basic Books.

Mahoney, R. A., Milkovich, G. T., & Weiner, N. (1977). A stock and flow model for improved human resources measurement. *Personnel, May–June,* 437–444.

March, J. G., & Olsen, J. P. (1976). *Ambiguity and choice in organizations.* Bergen, Norway: Universitetsforlaget.

March, J. G., & Simon, H. A. (1958). *Organizations.* New York: John Wiley.

Martin, N. H., & Strauss, A. L. (1959). Patterns of mobility within industrial organizations. In W. L. Warner & N. H. Martin (Eds.), *Industrial man* (pp. 85–110). New York: Harper & Row.

Marullo, S. (1985). Housing opportunities and vacancy chains. *Urban Affairs Quarterly, 20,* 364–388.

MacKay, D. (1982). *Empire of wood.* Vancouver: Douglas & McIntyre.

Milkovich, G. T., Glueck, W. F., Barth, R. T., & McShane, S. L. (1988). *Canadian personnel/human resource management: A diagnostic approach.* Plano, TX: Business Publications.

Miller, J. (1988). Jobs and work. In N. Smelser (Ed.), *The handbook of sociology* (pp. 327–359). Newbury Park, CA: Sage.

Miner, A. S. (1987). Idiosyncratic jobs in formalized organizations. *Administrative Science Quarterly, 32,* 327–351.

Mintzberg, H. D. (1979). *The structuring of organizations.* Englewood Cliffs, NJ: Prentice-Hall.

Mintzberg, H., Raisinghani, D., & Theoret, A. (1976). The structure of unstructured decision processes. *Administrative Science Quarterly, 21,* 246–275.

Moravec, M. (1990). Effective job posting fills dual needs. *HR Magazine, Sept.,* 76–80.

Nisbet, R. E., & Ross, L. (1980). *Human inference: Strategies and shortcomings of social judgment.* Englewood Cliffs, NJ: Prentice-Hall.

O'Reilly, C. A., Chatman, J. A., & Caldwell, D. F. (1991). People and organizational culture: Profile comparison approach to assessing person–organization fit. *Academy of Management Journal, 34,* 487–516.

Osterman, P. (Ed.) (1984a). *Internal labor markets.* Cambridge: MIT Press.

Osterman, P. (1984b). White-collar internal labor markets. In P. Osterman (Ed.), *Internal labor markets* (pp. 163–189). Cambridge: MIT Press.

Osterman, P. (1987). Choice of employment systems in internal labor markets. *Industrial Relations, 26*(1), 48–63.

Ostroff, D., & Kozlowski, W. J. (1992). Organizational socialization as a learning process: The role of information acquisition. *Personnel Psychology, 45,* 849–874.

Patton, J., & Smith, R. S. (1949). *Job evaluation.* Chicago: Rand-McNally.

Perry, E. L., Davis-Blake, A., & Kulik, C. T. (1994). Explaining gender-based selection decisions: A synthesis of contextual and cognitive approaches. *Academy of Management Review, 19,* 786–820.

Peter, L. J., & Hull, R. (1969). *The Peter principle.* New York: William Morrow.

Pfeffer, J. (1993). Barriers to the advance of organizational science: Paradigm development as a dependent variable. *Academy of Management Review, 18*(4), 599–620.

Pfeffer, J., & Cohen, Y. (1984). Determinants of internal labor markets in organizations. *Administrative Science Quarterly, 29,* 550–572.

Pinfield, L. T., & Berner, M. F. (1992). The greening of the press: A case study of stakeholder accountability and the corporate management of environmentalist publics. *Business Strategy and the Environment, 1*(3), 23–33.

Pinfield, L. T., & Berner, M. F. (1994). Employment systems: Toward a coherent conceptualization of internal labor markets. *Research in Personnel and Human Resources Management, 12*, 41–78.

Presthus, R. (1962). *The organizational society: An analysis and a theory.* New York: Knopf.

Quaid, M. (1993). *Job evaluation: The myth of equitable assessment.* Toronto: University of Toronto Press.

Robson, G., Wholey, D. R., & Barefield, R. M. (1992). Institutional determinants of individual mobility: Bringing the professions back in. Paper presented at the Annual Meeting of the Academy of Management, Las Vegas.

Rosen, B., & Jerdee, T. H. (1976). The influence of age stereotypes on managerial decisions. *Journal of Applied Psychology, 61*, 428–432.

Rosenbaum, J. E. (1984). *Career mobility in a corporate hierarchy.* Orlando, FL: Academic Press.

Schein, E. (1978). *Career dynamics: Matching individual and organizational needs.* Reading, MA: Addison Wesley.

Schein, E. (1990). Organizational culture. *American Psychologist, 45*(2), 109–119.

Schein, E. (1993). The role of the founder in creating organizational culture. *Organizational Dynamics, Summer*, 13–28.

Schmitt, N., & Borman, W. C. (1993). *Personnel selection in organizations.* San Francisco: Jossey-Bass.

Schneider, B., & Schmitt, N. (1986). *Staffing organizations,* 2nd Ed. Glenview, IL: Scott, Foresman

Scott, W. R. (1992). *Organizations: Rational, natural and open-systems,* 3rd Ed. Englewood Cliffs, NJ: Prentice Hall.

Silverman, D., & Jones, J. (1976). *Organizational work: The language of grading, the grading of language.* London: Collier Macmillan.

Smith, T. H. (1941). *The marketing of used automobiles.* Columbus: Bureau of Business Research, Ohio State University.

Snow, C. C., & Snell, S. A. (1993). Staffing as strategy. In N. Schmitt & W. C. Borman (Eds.), *Personnel selection in organizations* (pp. 448–478). San Francisco: Jossey-Bass.

Spilerman, S. (1986). Organizational rules and the features of work careers. *Research in Social Stratification and Mobility, 5*, 41–102.

Staw, B. M., & Ross, J. (1985). Stability in the midst of change: A dispositional approach to job attitudes. *Journal of Applied Psychology, 70*, 469–480.

Stettner, N. (1969). *Productivity bargaining and industrial change.* Oxford: Pergamon Press.

Stewman, S. (1975). Two Markov models of system occupational mobility: Underlying conceptualizations and empirical tests. *American Sociological Review, 40*, 298–321.

Stewman, S. (1981). The aging of work organizations: Impact on organization and employment practice. In S. B. Kiesler, J. N. Morgan, & V. K. Oppenhiemer (Eds.), *Aging: Social change* (pp.). New York: Academic Press.

Stewman, S. (1986). Demographic models of internal labor markets. *Administrative Science Quarterly, 31*, 212–247.

Stewman, S. (1988). Organizational demography. *Annual Review of Sociology, 14*, 173–202.

Stewman, S., & Konda, S. L. (1983). Careers and organizational labor markets: Demographic models of organizational behavior. *American Journal of Sociology, 88*(4), 637–685.

Stiglitz, J. E. (1991). Symposium on organizations and economics. *Journal of Economic Perspectives, 5*(2), 15–24.

Stinchcombe, A. L. (1965). Social structure and organizations. In J. G. March (Ed.), *Handbook of organizations* (pp. 142–193). Chicago: Rand McNally.

Stinchcombe, A. L. (1990). *Information and organizations.* Berkeley: University of California Press.

Tetlock, P. E. (1985). Accountability: The neglected social context of judgment and choice. *Research in Organizational Behavior, 7*, 297–332.

Turner, R. (Ed.) (1974). *Ethnomethodology.* Harmondsworth, U.K.: Penguin.

Wachter, M. L., & Wright, R. D. (1990). The economics of internal labor markets. *Industrial Relations, 29*(2), 240–262.

Weber, M. (1946). *From Max Weber: Essays in sociology* (translated by H. Gerth & C. W. Mills). New York: Oxford University Press.

Weissburg, M., Roseman, C., & Chase, I. D. (1991). Chains of opportunity: A Markov model for the acquisition of reusable resources. *Evolutionary Ecology, 5*, 105–117.

White, H. (1970). *Chains of opportunity: System models of mobility in organizations.* Cambridge: Harvard University Press.

Wholey, D. R. (1985). Determinants of firm internal labor markets in large law firms. *Administrative Science Quarterly, 30,* 318–335.

Williamson, O. E. (1975). *Markets and hierarchies.* New York: Free Press.

Williamson, O. E., Wachter, M. L., & Harris, J. E. (1975). Understanding the employment relation: The analysis of idiosyncratic exchange. *Bell Journal of Economics, 6,* 250–278.

Index

PLENUM STUDIES IN WORK AND INDUSTRY
COMPLETE CHRONOLOGICAL LISTING

Series Editors:
Ivar Berg, *University of Pennsylvania, Philadelphia, Pennsylvania*
and Arne L. Kalleberg, *University of North Carolina, Chapel Hill, North Carolina*

PLENUM STUDIES IN WORK AND INDUSTRY
COMPLETE CHRONOLOGICAL LISTING